MASSACRE ON THE MERRIMACK

Hannah Duston's Captivity and
Revenge in Colonial America

JAY ATKINSON

Guilford, Connecticut

An imprint of Rowman & Littlefield

Distributed by NATIONAL BOOK NETWORK

British Library Cataloguing in Publication Information Available

Library of Congress Cataloging-in-Publication Data

Atkinson, Jay, 1957-
  Massacre on the Merrimack : Hannah Duston's captivity and revenge in colonial America / Jay Atkinson.
      pages cm
  Includes bibliographical references and index.
  ISBN 978-1-4930-0322-8 (hardcopy) — ISBN 978-1-4930-1817-8 (ebook) 1. Duston, Hannah Emerson, 1657—Captivity, 1697. 2. Indian captivities—New England. 3. Indian captivities—Merrimack River Valley (N.H. and Mass.) 4. Women murderers—Merrimack River Valley (N.H. and Mass.)—Biography. 5. Abenaki Indians—Wars. 6. United States—History—King William's War, 1689-1697. 7. Indians of North America—Northeastern States—History—17th century. 8. Merrimack River Valley (N.H. and Mass.) —History—17th century. 9. Haverhill (Mass.)—Biography. I. Title. II. Title: Hannah Duston's captivity and revenge in colonial America.
  E87.D97 2015
  973.2'5092—dc23
  [B]

                                                                2015013265

In memory of Maureen Burns Tulley,
because every writer needs a good librarian

I remember in the night season, how the other day I was in the midst of thousands of enemies, & nothing but death before me.

—MARY ROWLANDSON, 1682

Contents

Prologue

Near City Hall in Haverhill, Massachusetts, on the old two-lane road to Salisbury Beach, is the green, oxidized figure of a stern-looking frontier woman with a hatchet in her right hand, her head angled downward and slightly to the left. She is pointing at something with her left hand, and stands ready to wield the hatchet. As a young boy, I was intrigued by this life-sized statue, which is encircled by a low, wrought iron fence and shaded by giant oak trees. On our way to the beach on a thick, humid summer afternoon, we'd cross the Merrimack River on the singing bridge and ascend toward G. A. R. Park, where the statue is located. Sitting in the backseat, I'd get my father's attention and point out the window, asking who was depicted there.

"That's Hannah Duston," my father would say. "She killed the Indians."

Prior to 1726 the town of Methuen, where I grew up, was part of Haverhill, and as a teenager I spent a great deal of time camping out, fishing, and roaming the same parcel of woods that contained the Duston homestead and where Hannah's story began. That story persisted in my imagination for many years, and continues to stir debate in local schools, barrooms, and coffee shops. A short time ago, the Duston saga finally worked its way onto my desk and I began spending long afternoons on the third floor of the Haverhill Public Library, in a quiet, seldom-visited room packed to the ceiling with a mostly uncataloged array of rare Hannah Duston materials: local maps and surveys from the early colonial period; yellowed broadsides and historical pamphlets; long-out-of-print local histories; obscure scholarly articles; and other ephemera. A short distance from the library in the storeroom of the Haverhill Historical

Society is an assembly of Duston artifacts, including the purported scrap of woven cloth torn from Hannah's loom during the raid; household objects; tools and farming implements; and other items from the late seventeenth century. And, in the company of an energetic local historian, I made several forays into the woods on the northwestern edge of Haverhill, which is still a patchwork of conservation land, dormant farms, ragged brown meadows, and dense stands of fir, oak, and birch trees. It is a stark and thrilling corner of northeastern Massachusetts, a place that looks much as it did three hundred years ago. The Puritans who originally settled this area believed that Satan resided in nature, and that the Indians they had relegated to this dense forest and who sporadically raided their homesteads and farms were emissaries of the devil.

Three years ago, in the predawn hour of March 15, on the 315th anniversary of Hannah's abduction by the Indians, I stood in these woods a mile or so northwest of downtown Haverhill, not far from the banks of Little River. I was in a low-lying, weedy dell close to where the original Duston homestead was located, and where the raiders seized their captives and burned the house to the ground. As a sourceless light came up on the tangled vines and underbrush, shaping out the trees overhanging Little River and revealing the contour of the land as it rose toward what was then called Pecker's Hill, I realized this was the place I'd been heading all along, in the back of the family station wagon in the 1970s and across my career as a writer. This was the story I had been looking for.

But how to tell it? Once a staple of eighteenth- and nineteenth-century versions of American colonial history, a tale compelling enough to be retold by such literary figures as Cotton Mather, Samuel Sewall, John Greenleaf Whittier, Nathaniel Hawthorne, and Henry David Thoreau, the saga of Hannah's captivity and revenge has been neglected by more contemporary writers and scholars (though it continues to inspire artists). In his introduction to a 1987 illustrated reprint of Mather, Whittier, Hawthorne, and Thoreau's accounts of Hannah's story, the editor Glenn Todd framed in scholarly terms the same questions I had grown up hearing: "Is it right for Hannah to kill children because one of her own had been killed? Are Indians less human than the English? What is the meaning of murder perpetrated upon not one, but ten victims who are asleep? Did Hannah kill the children because she thought that if she spared them, they would immediately rouse the Indians at a neighboring camp to pursue her? And is there a more important question: Is this genocide? Is this the ruthless extermination of the Native American race at its root, the killing of Indian children before they can reproduce? . . . Are Hannah's acts only another instance of the barbarity that underlies all human history, the heart of darkness that cannot be escaped by paddling a canoe back to civilization?"

Lingering in the woods, with the cry of seagulls echoing from the river, it occurred to me that Todd's questions could not be answered through scholarly inquiry: at least, not that alone and entirely of itself. Only through a carefully researched narrative rendering of the events of March 15–30, 1697, would today's readers be able to get at the moral truth of what happened to Hannah Duston, and what she had caused to occur. Besides that, it was a ripping good yarn, the kind that can captivate a broad audience. A writer might come across such a story once in his or her lifetime. My investigations also made clear that Haverhill's early settlers were engaged in an ongoing appraisal (and not, in the modern sense, an appreciation) of the landscape and its natural condition, mostly because of the drudgery and danger of their everyday lives. Therefore, Hannah was likely to focus on the threats and obstacles presented by her environment, as well as what she perceived as the overriding savagery of the region's native inhabitants. No doubt Duston surmised that her only response to these hazards was her own savage persistence. To further my understanding of that reality, over the past couple of years I have hiked, biked, and snowshoed large portions of the route that Duston's captors took after the raid; I've also undertaken overnight canoe trips on the Merrimack River in late March, enduring some of the harsh conditions Duston and her companions encountered during their escape (we didn't fear being overtaken by the Abenaki, but the river was vast, bone chilling, and clogged with floating ice and debris). I based the chapters that depict Hannah's raw experience on my firsthand knowledge of that terrain, as well as the accounts Duston herself provided to Reverend John Pike, Samuel Sewall, and, most notably, Cotton Mather. In these sections of the book, I made no attempt to re-create dialogue, or to imagine the thoughts and motivations of the participants, beyond the obvious. But my own journeys indicated that the best way to tell Hannah Duston's story was through the landscape and through the lens of the prejudices, preconceptions, and preoccupations of the seventeenth-century colonial settlers and the Indians.

That first morning in the woods, with snow scattered about and the air wintry and raw for March, I traced a course outward, parallel to Little River, coming quite near to the place where Thomas Duston, on horseback, would have first discovered that the Indians were attacking his farm and family. By that time, I had a spent more than a year poring over maps, studying the accounts of Mather and Sewall, conducting extensive research into colonial weaponry and farming techniques and militia tactics, and had come to know the layout of the original Haverhill settlement well enough to make a drawing of it in the dark. But climbing Pecker's Hill at the pace that the youngest Duston children would have traveled, through the brambles and sedge and over fallen trees, I began to see and hear the tale I'd studied on the page for so long. Thomas Duston was a brick maker and farmer and owned a draft horse, which would have been sturdy and formidable. Since he was urging his seven children uphill to the garrison house, it was the imposing size of horse and rider, not the speed of his mount, which was a deterrent to the Indian advance. After their zigzag ascent of Pecker's Hill, Duston's bulky plow horse would have been lathered up and spent. The Marsh garrison house, in the practice of the day, included a stable of swifter horses for the purpose of distributing messages to the other watch houses, or in the case of a large-scale attack, to Salem or Boston, and it was upon one of these horses that Thomas Duston, once his children were safe, galloped back down Pecker's Hill to find his wife and infant gone and their home engulfed in flames.

Perhaps twelve-year-old Nathaniel Duston was faster running uphill than his seventeen-year-old sister Elizabeth, and it's possible that Hannah's right shoe was left behind in the burning house and not the left one. But my careful consideration of the historical record has led me to logical conclusions about these and other facts present in the story. Although no one can prove for certain these minute details, I have made good use of the enormously valuable archive at my disposal to ensure a historically accurate and engaging narrative. There is no disputing that Hannah's story is the story of the frontier, in microcosm: an incursion by European settlers onto native lands, the savage response of the original inhabitants, and a solution perpetrated by the newcomers that led to the eradication of the Indians. Bring Hannah's particular ordeal to life, and American history becomes something palpable and real.

A frieze that depicts the four main events of Hannah Duston's story girdles her statue in G. A. R. Park: her capture by the Indians; her husband's defense of the children; her slaying of the Indians on Sugar Ball Island; and her return down the Merrimack River. The narrative rendering of these four events is the spine of this book. It's also interesting to note that the venerated nineteenth-century author and historian, Francis Parkman, included an account of Hannah's exploits in Volume II of his monumental *France and England in North America*, published in Boston in 1877. In the preface to that book, Parkman wrote, "The conclusions drawn from the facts may be matter of opinion, but it will be remembered that the facts themselves can be overthrown only by overthrowing the evidence on which they rest, or bringing forward counter-evidence of equal or greater strength; and neither task will be found an easy one."

Jay Atkinson
Methuen, Massachusetts

Chapter I

The Raid

March 15, 1697
Haverhill, Massachusetts

At first, Thomas Duston thought it was a chorus of seagulls. Although the settlement of Haverhill, Massachusetts, was a dozen or so miles from the coast, and Duston was surrounded by a thick forest of birch, elm, oak, scrub pine, and underbrush, gulls often foraged inland along what the Pentucket Indians called the Monomock, or "River of Sturgens," especially now in early spring, when the blanket of snow had begun receding into the woods. Half a dozen rods from where he stood was a tributary called Little River, which ran north to south, draining its torrent into the Merrimack, as the English called it. The cries Duston heard were no farther away than that.

Goodman Duston made a *tch-tch* sound under his breath, calling to his horse, which was a few feet away. The sun was not yet above the horizon, but Duston had already been at work for nearly two hours. Upon stoking up the hearth and emptying their nightjars, he and his eldest son, also named Thomas, had milked the cows beneath the lean-to in the darkness, afterward loosening them to graze downhill toward his clay pits and Little River. Then fourteen-year-old Thomas went back inside to rouse the other children, and to see his mother Hannah, who had given birth to a daughter, Martha, her twelfth child and ninth surviving one, just a week earlier.

In the pre-dawn gloom, Duston had saddled his horse and taken down his flintlock rifle, riding out behind the meandering cows to visit the clay pits and examine the buds of his apple trees. Some years past, the Merrimack had cut a swath fifteen rods wide through the forest, leaving behind a grassy depression after the river changed course to its present location. Along this corridor of bottomland, Duston had planted enough apple trees for a modest orchard the year his son, Thomas Jr., was born. A tempest overnight now drew him to the orchard, to measure what the night winds had done to his trees.

A former constable, Duston was a skilled brick maker, soldier, and orchard-keeper, with a twenty-acre spread at the northwesterly edge of the settlement, where several years earlier he had constructed a wooden dwelling-house, barn, brick kiln, feed lots, lean-to, and privy. His land sloped downward across tilled fields and a well-cropped winter pasture until it reached a dense hedgerow, then leveled out for a hundred rods or so, past the clay pits and kiln to the orchard. The pits had only just begun to thaw, and after worrying at the uppermost edge of the clay with a spade, Duston had remounted his horse and passed through the scrub to inspect his fruit trees, jogging along one of the many Indian paths meandering through the woods.

The screeching he heard drifted over from the east, where the sun was ascendant, the cries echoing among the nascent apple trees and carrying to Duston and his horse. His orchard ran east-west on a ribbon of open ground, an irregular passage through the forest that was devoid of trees except for the ones he had planted. This glade demarcated the northern edge of his property, eventually running into Little River to the east, and losing itself in the trackless wilderness to the north and west.

Duston's horse, its ears pricked up, shuddered through its nostrils and came over, stamping and snorting and tossing its head. Duston stepped on the reins where they traveled over the ground, soothing the horse while unslinging his musket from its scabbard. The *whoop-whoop-whoop* and *eeeng-eeeng-eeeng* that he originally mistook for sea birds had grown louder now, rising up from various places along the northwestern perimeter of the settlement, giving three-dimensionality to a landscape that was still mostly unseen, cloaked in the early morning fog. Goodman Duston, at forty-five, was a short, thick-wristed, broad-shouldered fellow, attired in mud-encrusted boots, dirty leggings, a rough brownish tweed coat, and a flat-brimmed hat. Understanding that it was not seagulls he heard, but a war party of Indians coming toward him, and toward his outlying neighbors—by now, the main body of Indians had broken into smaller bands and were raiding several points along the edge of the village, which was their preferred tactic—his movements were no less deliberate than if he had been out hunting squirrels or rabbits. He hefted his musket, running his hand along the barrel, and then spat upon the ground.

Quieting the horse with a low, murmuring tone, Duston brought the rifle up perpendicular to his midpoint, cocked back the tumbler mechanism, and examined the flint. Good for approximately fifty shots, the flint's stability in the cock was a precarious matter, and something as harmless as his light jog down from the house and barn may have dislodged it. The cries of the war party drew closer, echoing across the meadow; Duston estimated that a band of eight to twelve savages, equipped with torches, were crossing his line ten or twelve rods to the east, doubtlessly making for his house, the only dwelling place within a mile of his current location. He saw the shifting globes of light from the torches thrust upward against the screen of fir trees as the Indians hurried past. Obscured each from the other by tendrils of fog and the darkened trees, he never saw the Indians, nor they him.

When Duston was satisfied that the edge of the flint was directed at the frizzen, which would strike a spark across the whole surface, he opened the pan, first drawing a cartridge from the shot pouch on his hip. Biting off the paper top while gripping it between his thumb and forefinger, he shook some of the gunpowder into the frizzen pan and spread it carefully. The devilish noise of the savages passed him by, louder now, moving toward the hedgerow that bordered his lower pasture. Still, Duston didn't hurry. If he rushed things, he wouldn't have a loaded gun, and the gun and the fact of being on horseback were the only marks on his side of the ledger, and the only chance he had of saving the life of one or more of his family.

With the last three fingers of his right hand, Duston closed the frizzen pan and lowered the butt of his musket to the ground. If one remained intent on what he was doing, and cool-headed in the face of the enemy, a musket could be prepared to fire in less than a minute. A skilled marksman could load his rifle in just about thirty seconds. But some men were dead before they had loaded a single shot. Their gaze darted wildly about and their hands shook; they dropped the cartridge in the weeds or scattered their powder over the ground. Duston had seen that happen in the late war. Because it took time and you had to load your musket from a standing position, it was best to angle yourself behind a tree or other natural obstacle, limiting your silhouette. And it was best to keep your nerve, even if musket balls were flying all around and it appeared you were about to be overwhelmed.

Shaking his powder horn, Duston squared his right elbow to that shoulder and tapped some powder into the barrel. He took the bitten-off cartridge from his mouth, and seizing the ramrod at its midpoint, detached it from the underside of the musket and used the rod to push the cartridge down inside the barrel of the gun. He struck two quick hard strokes to position the shot flush against the powder, then withdrew the rod, again securing it to the musket barrel. Duston cranked the tumbler back to half cock, and holding the gun away from him in his right hand, he used his left to sweep up the reins, then left-footed himself into the stirrup, and mounted the horse.

By the recession of their cries, Duston knew that the Indians had entered the lower fields beyond the hedgerow and were gaining on his house. Probably not more than fifty rods separated the raiders from his front door and the children, including the infant, Martha, and his next youngest, Timothy, just three years old, still in his nightshirt. But the speed at which the Indians and their bloody screams of "*Woach! Woach! Ha-ha-ha-woach!*" traveled away from him indicated the raiders were on foot, however; choosing a parallel course through the trees, Duston went around the far side of his kiln, found the mouth of the clay road, and dug in his heels, sending up clods from the horse's hooves. A short way along, he veered into the undergrowth, branches and thorns scratching at him, until he broke clear, vaulted the outermost fence, and went dashing uphill through the meadow.

Now on open ground, Duston could see black pillars of smoke rising from gaps in the woodland where some of his neighbors' homes were located. The goal of these raids, which were planned by the French, modeled on Iroquois tactics, and carried out by hired Indians from Maine, was first and foremost to spread terror along the frontier. Over a grassy hillock to the east, Duston heard the yelling of a separate band of raiders—then more distant shouts, a single musket blast, what sounded like someone pleading, and finally the mortal agony of a settler as the Indians fell upon him, screaming in a chorus. It all happened swiftly, and much too far away for Duston to intervene.

Even now, nearly sixty years after its settlement, Haverhill was the edge of the frontier, with a vast wilderness stretching from a mile beyond Duston's orchard across great distances to the Saint Lawrence River and the stronghold of Count Frontenac, the provincial French governor. For eight years, Frontenac had been inciting the Abenaki, Huron, Ottawa, and other bands to attack the English settlements, sheltering them in Quebec and paying them hard cash for scalps. By nature, the Indians were a heartless lot and would burn down everything the settlers had built, slaughter their livestock, and bludgeon their women and children—*his children*, Duston knew. Often, a small number of English settlers deemed fit or useful were carried away as captives, and sold to the French as slaves. Just two years earlier, a pair of Haverhill boys, fifteen-year-old Isaac Bradley, and Joseph Whittaker, age eleven, had been abducted by the Indians while working in the Bradleys' cornfield.

Riding out of the saddle, his musket at arm's length, Goodman Duston traversed the lower field and, cramming the horse at a low place in the hedge, passed over in a graceful arc. The landscape changed again, inclining toward the dark frowning shape of Pecker's Hill, with Duston's own homestead, barn, and lean-to silhouetted in the foreground. The hedge divided a pasture from a plowed field, and as the horse's hooves struck the hard pan of the road, Duston glanced at the acre of earth he and young Thomas and twelve-year-old Nathaniel had turned over the day before. After a difficult winter, he had made the cornfield ready for planting by the sweat of his brow, and now he cursed what he saw there, twisting the horse's mane with his left hand and kicking at its flank.

Nine or ten raiders were crossing the field and converging on his home. There were two Indians out front—a large man with a shaven head wielding an axe, and the other savage, who was lighter and faster, running ahead with a French rifle in one hand and a knife in the other—with at least a half dozen more scattered across the field behind them. They were all young warriors, not one of them past thirty years of age, naked or halfway so, painted for war, and laden with the instruments of death: clubs, hatchets, knives, lances, and steel-tipped pikes, along with one or two muskets. As Duston rode parallel to the Indians and then beyond, going pell-mell along the road, he was fortunate in one regard: By taking the most direct route from the tree line to the house, the raiders, despite the ferocity of their war-whoops, had begun to slow down, and were laboring over the deep furrows. The Indian closest to him, staggering in the mud, his shaven head purple with berry dye, screeched as Duston thundered past, rearing up with a large axe in his hand. He was naked but for the war paint and screaming like the devil. But horse and rider easily outdistanced him, approaching the house at a gallop.

On Duston went, nearing his front door, with several of his children frozen in tableau at the base of the hill, mouths agape as they stared downslope at the whooping raiders coming toward them. One child carried a pitchfork and another a wooden pail, as the younger ones had just started on their chores.

"Indians!" shouted Duston, pounding over the hard-packed earth in front of his barn. After a brief delay necessary to their comprehension, the children threw down their tools and hurried back toward the house.

"Thomas! Elizabeth!" said Duston. "The Marsh house."

Young Thomas was already running in that direction with three-year-old Timothy slung over his shoulder, and Nathaniel and eleven-year-old Sarah close behind. Onesiphorus Marsh and his son, Onesiphorus Jr., who were detailed to the local militia and well armed, occupied the Marsh house, which constituted the nearest garrison and was nearly a mile away upon Pecker's Hill. Immediately Duston reckoned that if the Indians broke into separate parties, as he expected they would, the slowest of them would overtake young Tom, the swiftest of his children, before he got even halfway to the garrison.

"Indians!" Duston yelled again, throwing himself down from the horse, and rushing into the house. At the same instant, the first Indian stumbled out of the furrows and began running across the meadow with a French rifle in his hand.

The Duston house was a squat, plank-sided, one-and-a-half-story building, nearly three rods lengthwise and two deep to accommodate all eleven inhabitants, with a half-gable on the back end that provided a loft where the children slept. Inside the great room was a stone hearth running along the entire left-hand wall, two rough windows on each of the remaining walls, and a half-door to the right where they could retrieve logs from the nearby woodshed and deposit the nightjars. Coming inside,

Duston glanced about the open space of the room and then retreated to the doorway to gauge the Indians' progress.

"Raiders," he said.

A red-coaled fire was burning in the hearth. Beside it, lying in a rope bed, was his wife Hannah, with her nurse, Mary Neff, a widow who lived a half-mile distant and was assisting the family, standing near the window. Mary was holding onto the week-old infant, Martha, staring out the window with a horror-struck look on her face.

Hannah Duston was a large-bosomed woman, thirty-nine years old, tall and sturdy with a carriage that delivered the same day's work as a man. Under normal circumstances, she would have been outdoors by now, digging the new privy hole, hauling firewood and water, and supervising the children. But the arrival of Martha, her twelfth child and the ninth to survive, had been especially difficult for her. Hannah had lain in her sickbed a week, which had never before kept her confined even for a day.

In the whirl of an instant, Goodman Duston's glance took in the burning hearth, the littered sideboard and hank of bread, his wife's loom, and the heavy piece of broadcloth protruding from it, as well as the odds and ends of furniture and tools littering the room. From their twenty years together, Duston knew that he and Hannah were possessed by the same notion: to save one or two of the children. Hannah was a frontier woman, born in Haverhill on December 23, 1657, the eldest of Michael and Hannah (Webster) Emerson's fifteen children. In the course of her life, she had known privation, hardship, and death, having already buried three of her own children due to illness: four-year-old John, thirteen-year-old Mary, and three-month-old Mehitable, twin sister to Timothy. In fact, Hannah and Thomas both understood that her present weakness made it unlikely she would survive the raid.

Like the other settlements in Massachusetts, Haverhill was a Puritan community, and a lot of time in the Duston household was spent in prayer. Certainly, one of the most significant tenets of the Puritan faith was self-sacrifice, which also meant charity toward others. Goodman Duston believed that by quitting the premises at the right moment, he could take up the middle ground between his wife and infant here in the house, and his fleeing children, drawing the Indians to the base of Pecker's Hill, where he would make his fight. By so doing, he might be able to save one or more members of his family, if not himself.

Close at hand, Duston heard the bloody screams of the approaching raiders. He and Hannah looked at one another and with silent assent he backed away from the sickbed, indicating with a glance toward the half-door that Hannah and Mary Neff and the infant should sneak out that way after he exited the front. All of this transpired in a matter of a few seconds.

Duston pivoted toward the front door, leveling the gun as he emerged into the yard. The Indians, nearly a dozen of them now, were converging from all sides. The nearest raider, the powerful, naked Indian with the shaved head, was almost close enough to throw his axe. Duston's horse, wild-eyed at the prospect of the Indians, had skittered toward the corner of the house, and Duston walked quickly to the animal, pausing alongside its flank. Raising the musket to his shoulder, he took dead aim at the closest Indian, who hesitated for just an instant. Yet there were many of them, all moving toward the front door of the house.

Duston scowled at the axe-wielding Indian and leaped onto his horse. Going around the left side of the house, past the stone hearth, he was startled by a raider who was much closer than he expected. He crowded the horse's bulk directly at the Indian, who leaped sideways and flung his lance at the same instant. It flew past Duston's head in a rising blur, and clanged against the stonework. He urged the horse onward, striking out for Pecker's Hill, which rose from a dense ring of trees nearly a mile ahead. Behind him, Duston heard the first two raiders screaming as they burst into the house.

Approaching the tree line, Duston kicked the horse up the slope and loosened a yell of his own, shaking his musket in the air. Glancing over his shoulder, he saw a line of savages pouring into the house like bees into a hive, the mud-packed walls quaking in the tumult. Seconds later, one of the warriors popped through the half-door, as two more Indians rounded the front of the house, and then another right behind them. Immediately the four warriors began running in the direction the children had gone. Thomas had no way of knowing if Hannah and the others had gotten away, but he had not seen them leave the house.

Just forty rods from his front door, Duston overtook the first of his children: eleven-year-old Sarah, stumbling over tree roots and falling into the brambles. Ahead of her, but not very far, were her younger sister Abigail and twelve-year-old Nathaniel, who looked back so frequently they

8

were making little progress, bumping into each other, and into rocks and fallen timbers that littered the way. The other children, led by the oldest, nineteen-year-old Hannah, were scattered over the terrain only a short distance ahead; Duston had hoped he would meet them by the steepest pitch of the hill, with the garrison house close at hand.

With the Indians yelping and screeching as they charged through the undergrowth behind him, Duston was faced with an impossible decision. It had already occurred to him that the best chance for any member of the family to survive along with him was to grab one of the children and ride for the garrison house. But which one? Should he take up one of his sons, perhaps Thomas or Nathaniel? A strong boy would be most helpful in rebuilding whatever the Indians left behind after the raid. And having at least one male child would improve the chances of the Duston name continuing on. But his two oldest sons had experienced some of what this life had to offer, however scant in amount, and the youngest children had seen very little of it. How not to pity his girls, especially Abigail and Elizabeth, who staggered along wild-eyed with terror at the prospect of what the Indians would do to them. Or on Timothy, just a short ways ahead, practically being dragged uphill by young Tom, who no longer had the strength to carry him. If Duston rode off with one of the others, all of these would be murdered shortly thereafter. It was a painful choice, no matter how he looked at it.

The placement of the garrison house reduced their chances of ever reaching it. Although it stood on the highest feature of the surrounding land, the approach was a series of low ridges and hillocks, uneven ground at best, drained by little creeks and rivulets choked with snowmelt. As the children struggled over these obstacles, past felled trees and rocky outcroppings and messy packets of snow, Duston glanced up Pecker's Hill, which seemed near at hand yet never drew closer.

He knew that, even in Haverhill, others had been forced to choose from among their children—it was a hard life, after all—and were not thought lesser of. You preserved what you could of this life and made way for the next. But he found he could not do it.

So, making himself rigid in the saddle, Duston whistled ahead for Thomas, and jerking the horse around by the bridle, faced downhill with the barrel of his rifle aimed at the uppermost opening in the brush. He told his oldest son to gather everyone in the shadow of horse and rider, then to turn about and make way for the apex of Pecker's Hill in the straightest possible line. He was determined to save them all, or none would be saved.

Duston reached into his shot pouch, withdrew another cartridge, and gripped the paper end of it between his teeth. When it came time to fire his gun, Duston wanted to reload as quickly as possible. Looking down, he checked the position of the flint for the second time, cocked the tumbler of his musket all the way back, and tensing his shoulders and abdomen, let out a great cry and rode straight downhill through the underbrush. It wasn't long before the first Indian presented himself, the agile raider with the French rifle, a bare-chested, copper-skinned youth with a scalp lock and diagonal charcoal markings on his face. Running uphill, he had the musket down by his hip, his knife in the other hand. Duston rode straight for him, surprising the raider, who dropped his musket while raising his knife toward the horse's breast. With the weight and heft of the animal bearing down on him, the warrior attempted to leap off the trail but Duston rode close, and struck the Indian a hard blow with his boot as man and horse rushed past.

Two more Indians, nearly shoulder to shoulder, were a few rods lower on the hill, carrying an axe and a pike, respectively. Duston pulled his horse up short by the head, jerking the reins, and then dismounted. It was always better to shoot with one's feet planted on the ground. He leveled the gun and drew a bead on the larger of the two men: a gigantic warrior who was perspiring freely, steam rising from his shaven head. Immediately the Indians hollered at Duston and split apart, one shaking his axe and circling to the right, the other hefting his stone-tipped pike and branching off the other way. But Duston's blood was up and he presented a formidable obstacle. Still at a distance of three or four rods, the raiders became more wary, angling off through the trees. In all his dealings with Indians, Duston had known them to favor ambushes and stealth, not frontal attacks. This hesitation allowed Duston to remount the horse and swing around to his left, ready to fire his gun or use it as a club. He was intent on putting the raiders off their pursuit, giving the children more time to clamber out of the tree line onto the upper slope of the hill, where they might come under the protection of the militiamen's guns.

Goodman Duston knew that the Indians, some without rifles, unmounted, and already divided by the terrain and the plentitude of raiding targets, would break off their pursuit before they got too close to the Marsh garrison. They were at a significant disadvantage on foot, trudging uphill over cleared ground. From behind fortifications, and unloading heavy shot at a propitious angle, Onesiphorus Marsh, his son, and perhaps Sergeant Haseltine and a handful of other militia, would present the raiders with a daunting obstacle.

But getting to that dividing point where the Indians might falter was still at issue. The garrison was situated beneath the crest of Pecker's Hill, a bald edifice rising out of the surrounding woodlands that had been shorn of trees from the peak downward more than two dozen rods. The slope there was littered with stumps, and now, with the coming of spring, Marsh and his son had scorched the ground cover and brambles with a series of controlled fires, providing a clear view all around. The Marsh house was the only fortification on the northwesterly edge of the settlement (though Duston had recently dug a cellar hole on an adjoining hill, where he planned to construct a sturdy garrison made from his own bricks.) It was a dark, gaunt, two-and-a-half-story house, built from a chamfered beam sixteen inches wide, hand-split lath, and a massive central chimney made of fieldstone set on a ten-foot-square granite base. The chimney was functional for cooking, trade work, and heating the lower rooms; it also served as castle keep, a stone wall two rods long and twenty-five feet high with firing positions chinked out of the rock.

Each corner of the house featured an adjoining sentinel post, which was an eight-foot-square box made from logs with a sally port on each side. Additionally, the top floor of the building was studded with gun stock posts and featured an armory containing at least twenty muskets, ample powder and shot, and hatchets, knives, lances, and pikes. In the root cellar was an iron grate that concealed a tunnel entrance; the passageway burrowed downward several feet and then beneath three rods of open ground to the tree line behind the house—an escape route of last resort.

Trampling through the brush, Duston circled the terminus of Pecker's Hill, menacing first one Indian and then the other with his gun barrel, hoping to surprise the remainder of their pursuers with his aggressiveness. Though mostly unseen, the shrill cries of the raiders continued to announce their location, and Duston, who had ridden a considerable distance from the garrison house, now swung the horse around to a more advantageous position, bringing him uphill on a diagonal that maintained a barrier between his children and the Indians, until, emerging from a clump of bushes, he returned to the spot where he had started his maneuver.

When Duston broke from the tree line and began ascending the flank of the hill, he saw all eight of his children stumbling and crawling toward the Marsh house. But the steepest pitch remained ahead of them and the two youngest children, Timothy and six-year-old Jonathan, were so frightened and exhausted their older siblings had resorted to dragging them by the arms. Duston kicked his flagging mount up the incline, and just as he glanced behind him, three Indians emerged from the brush, gripping their weapons and moving cautiously in sight of the garrison. This was the closest they had gotten to him and the children.

Nearly in sight of the guns arrayed against them, the Indians were at risk of losing their advantage in numbers and terrain, conditions under which they were more likely to flee than fight. Still, his older children, Hannah, Elizabeth, and Tom, were attractive as captives, who could be exchanged for silver or other compensation after the raiders marched them to New France. And the Indians were also motivated by scalps, which were as valuable as beaver pelts on the Saint Lawrence River. During the eight-year course of King William's War, a three-year-old child's scalp sold for the same price as a thirty-year-old soldier's, though Governor William Phips of Massachusetts had discontinued the paying of bounty several months earlier. In New France, the crafty old territorial authority, Count Frontenac, was still offering money for English scalps, an inequity that was producing lamentations all across Haverhill that morning. Duston could hear the mortal screams of his neighbors and detected several large fires scattered in an uneven line to the east. The closest of these, with its plume of black smoke, rose from the tree line in the vicinity of his own house.

Two of the Indians were making a dash for the closest of the Duston children, Jonathan, who was sobbing and screaming as he was dragged along by his older brothers—even more loudly when the raiders began to draw closer and his siblings dropped his stretched out limbs and began running for their own lives. Duston came up short with the reins just above the patch of ground where his son lay cowering in the snow behind one of the stumps. The Indians were very near young Jonathan, and Duston had but one shot and his knife to defend his son with. Dismounting, he lumbered downhill toward the raiders, unsteady on his feet after the frantic ride that had brought him there.

There was hallooing from up above. The sun had angled itself above the low, dark ridge to the east, illuminating the upper portion of the garrison house, which glowed against a deepening blue sky. Onesiphorus Marsh, his son, and two other armed men had exited the rear door of the house and were advancing over the stubbled apex of the hill. Two more rifles appeared in the gunstocks atop the structure, and John Haseltine, on horseback and brandishing a pike, had also arrived. Duston scrambled downslope and grabbed Jonathan by the collar, pointing his musket at the Indians, who were less than two rods away, their scalping knives out.

The Indians saw the militia rushing down the hill and, yelping and screeching, shook their weapons in the direction of the English, and then bounded back toward the forest. As the children reached the door of the garrison, one by one they were yanked inside by its occupants. Thomas Duston, his gun still loaded and cocked with the first shot, jogged over to his horse and began leading it uphill by the bridle. His horse was suited for field and farm, not for carrying messages or leaping over fences. Horseflesh being somewhat rare in the settlement, Duston, now guaranteed that his children were safe, hailed Sergeant Haseltine and with a gesture, inquired whether he might trade his exhausted mount for the other man's horse. With soldiers' pay for himself and his son, in addition to what he could put by from farming, fishing the weirs, and hunting game, Onesiphorus Marsh always had at least two steeplechasers in the loose-box attached to the garrison house. In the case of alarm, he was prepared to send outriders to the village, and if need be, to other nearby towns who might be able to send assistance.

All the men atop the hill could see the black smoke rising from the gap in the forest below, and it was decided that Thomas would ride back down on a fresh horse along with the Marsh boy, while two of the militia followed on foot to see what could be done about Hannah and the Indians. Sergeant Haseltine ran over to take Duston's exhausted horse, and as Thomas crossed the open ground to change mounts, he could see dense woodlands stretching to the horizon, and the billowing pyres of smoke rising into a deep blue sky. He hadn't stood upon a cleared hill in quite some time and could survey all of Haverhill from this vantage point.

Chapter II

Dispossessed

It had been almost sixty years since an Indian had lingered on that same hilltop and claimed dominion over the vast timberland below. But prior to the landing of the Pilgrims in 1620, and the removal of a group of Puritans from Newbury and Salem to Haverhill several years later, the wilderness that met Thomas Duston's eye was the territory of the Pennacooks, a confederacy of more than a dozen Algonquin tribes and their subsidiary bands. (These bands included the Pentuckets, whose fishing villages and hunting grounds had previously occupied a large parcel of land near the mouth of Little River in Haverhill.) From the latter part of the 1500s well into the next century, the Pennacooks were led by the great chief, or sachem, known as Passaconaway, who settled his people alongside a broad twisting river known as the Monomock.

One of the first historical mentions of the river comes in 1603, from Pierre du Guast, Sieur de Monts, who received a patent to claim Acadia—described as all the land from the 40th to the 46th parallel—in the name of France. That year or the next, De Monts, who was acting as the lieutenant-general of Acadia, visited the Abenaki on the St. Lawrence River in Quebec, and wrote: "The Indians tell us of a beautiful river, far to the south, which they call the Merrimack." In June 1604 the explorer Samuel de Champlain, assisting De Monts, sailed along the coast of Maine, journeying as far south as Cape Cod. Encountering some friendly Indians near the mouth of the Piscataqua River, he gave them some bread and iron tools and in the midst of their goodwill asked them to describe the coast. Using a piece of charcoal to mark its position on a board, by gestures and exclamations the Indians convinced the explorer that the Merrimack River was an important feature of the regional landscape. The next day, Champlain tacked along the coast southward until he found it, temporarily naming it Riviere du Gaust, or Gas, depending on the translation.

The origin of the name "Merrimack" is not entirely clear, though there are several intriguing possibilities. Generally, all the Indian tribes of the eastern seaboard from the Carolinas to the Great Lakes region of Canada were Algonquin, named for the language they spoke. (Although there were many dialects, in most cases Indians of different tribes could make themselves understood.) One interpretation is that Merrimack is the Algonquin word for "sturgeon," the large, migratory fish that were so plentiful in that section of the river. The Algonquin language is known for its proclivity toward word-pictures, marking the landscape with names that could literally be recognized when the actual places they stood for were encountered. Thus, Indians who lived in that territory may have wished to memorialize the river's powerful current, naming it "merroh" (strong), and "auke" (a place). Another viable interpretation is that the Pennacooks conflated the words for island ("mena") and place ("auke") to create "Mena-auke", or island place, which the English settlers took to be Merrimack. More than a half-mile wide in several locations, the Merrimack is dotted by wooded islands along much of its length, including a small, triangular-shaped isle north of present-day Concord, New Hampshire. The Indians called it Sugar Ball Island, and it was believed to have been the summer residence of Passaconaway.

Although the great leader of the Pennacooks had been dead for thirty years by the time of the 1697 raid on the settlement at Haverhill, the peculiar combination of time, place, and condition that led to the attack cannot really be understood without first reckoning the story of Passaconaway, his allies, and his enemies.

It is noteworthy that the Indians who were occupying the New World when explorers and then settlers arrived had not, and generally would not, write the story of their own history. For centuries prior to contact with outsiders, and during the occupation and eventual co-opting of their ancestral lands, the Indians did not busy themselves with transcribing a counter-narrative to the ones created by the English, French, and Dutch settlers who transplanted them. As history goes, the narratives of conquered peoples are always written by the conquerors. Furthermore, the Indians did not possess the skill of writing in their own tongue, as written language did not exist in their culture. Nearly all the accounts of Passaconaway, who was arguably the most significant Indian leader of the contact period and for decades thereafter, were provided by well-educated settlers, particularly members of the clergy and other early historians, and therefore contain a significant cultural bias. But even these prejudiced renderings agree that Passaconaway was an intelligent, physically imposing, and charismatic figure, a man who did not suffer fools yet often exuded personal warmth, and who commanded the respect of his fellow Indians and white settlers alike. Several early commentators were quite aware of the massive injustice being heaped upon the Indians of what became known as New England, thereby mitigating their biases, at least to a degree. So by examining and comparing their accounts of the great chief, a reliable portrait of Passaconaway emerges—one that gives us a better understanding of who the Indians were and why they acted, and reacted, as they did.

Born sometime between 1555 and 1573, Passaconaway, like the rest of his people, was not given a lasting name until he reached his maturity. An Indian's proper name, often a word-picture in itself, was meant to identify an individual through his or her most prominent characteristics. In the colonial period, the great chief's name was often spelled Papisseconawa, from "papoeis," a child, and "kunnaway," meaning bear. From this it is inferred that, even in his youth, Passaconaway, or "Son of the Bear," was a large, intimidating man whose feats of strength and prowess as a warrior made him a formidable opponent. To be elevated, however, beyond merely sachem or chief (also called sagamore), to the title of Bashaba, which is roughly equivalent to emperor, the so-named must be more than just handy in a fight. By uniting the Pennacooks, Agawams, Wachusetts, Wamesits, Winnipesaukees, Pequawkets, Pawtuckets, Pentuckets, Sacos, and several other tribes that occupied a great swath of wild country stretching from the lakes region of central New Hampshire to Cape Ann and the mouth of the Merrimack River in Massachusetts, Passaconaway was for several decades able to defend this territory—via debate and diplomacy, inter-tribal marriage, feats of what appeared to be magic, and by outright warfare—against the Penobscots and Tarrantines to the northeast, and the cruel and ferocious Mohawks to the west.

The endurance of the Pennacook confederacy is impressive when considering that a vast number of Indians occupying the easternmost portion of the region between Rhode Island and central Maine were decimated by a plague that struck the area sometime between 1615 and 1620, when the Pilgrims arrived. By 1640, when Haverhill was settled, the estimated total population among the New England Indians was fifty thousand, with more than half of these residing in Connecticut and Rhode Island, and more than a quarter in Maine. Severely diminishing the Massachusetts tribes (much of southern and central New Hampshire was considered part of Massachusetts until state lines were redrawn to their current position in 1741), this pestilence, most likely influenza or smallpox accidentally passed to the Indians by white explorers or fishermen, left the warlike Narragansetts, Tarrantines, and the Five Nations of the Iroquois, including the Mohawks, largely untouched. An English explorer named Richard Hawkins, stopping along the Massachusetts coastline in 1615, reported that so many Indians had succumbed to this plague there were not enough survivors to bury the dead, with piles of sun-bleached bones occupying the tattered remains of the wigwams. Ninety percent of the Massachusetts Indians were believed to have died from illness not long before the English settlers arrived, which no doubt simplified the task of taking over their land. During Passaconaway's lengthy tenure, he ruled over approximately three thousand people, including at least five hundred seasoned, skillful warriors. But these numbers were most likely reduced by the pestilence and did not rise to anything close to their original fighting strength until the reign of Passaconaway's volatile grandson, Kancamagus, many years later.

Already well into middle age when the Pilgrims arrived, Passaconaway was invited to meet the English, and along with other powwows, or medicine-men, was soon dispatched into a dark swamp for three days, whereupon, according to Cotton Mather, the Bashaba and his retinue attempted to conjure against the invaders, asking the Great Spirit to strike them with a plague or capsize their ships. Although many tales of Passaconaway's necromancy are unsubstantiated and certainly seem apocryphal, there are enough similarities among various recollections to consider a few of them. In a feat of aquatic prowess, Passaconaway gathered several witnesses, including at least one Englishman, and promised to swim underwater across the Merrimack River at a place so wide it seemed impossible. Passaconaway began his swim on the far bank, and his English guest reported that a mist obscured his vision until the Bashaba emerged from deep water in front of the spectators, apparently having drawn only one great breath. (With the experience and skill of a professional magician, the chief of the Pennacooks may have waited for a foggy day to attempt this gambit, and with the assistance of his considerable athleticism deceived the assembly.) In winter, when the trees were hung with clumps of dead leaves that resembled shrouds, Passaconaway would pluck one and burn it to ashes, then submerge these in water and produce a new green leaf, which he would allow a spectator to examine and take away with him. He was known to handle venomous snakes without fear or harm and to exhibit the sloughed-off skin of a snake from which he could produce a live serpent that witnesses then took into their own hands.

Despite what one thinks of these reports, Passaconaway was clearly a remarkable man, the sort of personality who comes along once in an age, with abilities and resources that were unknown and unfathomable among both the new settlers and his own countrymen. And it is also likely that by the time he departed Plymouth and returned to his stronghold at Pennacook, the Bashaba had determined that the English could not be defeated, either by conjuring or through force of arms. Though he had, in 1620, enough warriors at his disposal to push these few settlers back into the sea, Passaconaway realized that soon enough the English would be arriving in great numbers, and there was no sense fighting an enemy that could not be defeated. The great Bashaba had a further motive for making peace with the white man. With the strength of the Pennacooks diminished by recent wars as well as by sickness, an alliance with the English would protect Passaconaway's people from their local enemies, particularly the Mohawks to the west and the Maine Indians to the north. Although an acclaimed warrior who had taken Mohawk scalps and personally hefted a bow so large that other men were unable to draw it back, Passaconaway decided almost right away never to take up the hatchet against the English.

In fact, just a few years after emerging from that Plymouth swamp, Passaconaway transferred an enormous tract of land to the English in what amounted to a wholesale forfeiture known as the Wheelwright Deed. On May 17, 1629, the Bashaba of the Pennacooks, and other noted sachems and sagamores, were said to have affixed their marks to a document alongside that of the Reverend John Wheelwright, lately of Boston, and "some of the respectable planters of Saco and Piscataqua," that ceded ownership of a parcel extending thirty miles from the existing Massachusetts line northward into New Hampshire, and from the Merrimack River to the Piscataqua, which at that time formed the border between Massachusetts and Maine. Although some early historians have validated the deed and others consider it a forgery, it is true that Passaconaway gave up exclusive use of that region without a fight. His later actions make it clear that by allowing the English to settle the territory from Exeter to Concord, New Hampshire, he hoped to create both an ally of the settlers, and a barrier between his people and the Mohawks.

Whatever the authenticity of the Wheelwright Deed and other land transactions between the Indians and the whites during that period, the nature of these contracts reflected a fundamental difference between what the Indians believed themselves to be giving up and what the English thought they were acquiring through force of law. Indians often marked the boundaries of their land with natural objects like rocks and trees, moving from one region to another as it suited them, without entertaining the notion that they somehow possessed the land beneath their feet. (In a real sense, the Indians believed that the land possessed them and all the other creatures that resided upon, above, and beneath it, as their equals.) When the Indians ceded their exclusive land rights in exchange for some token consideration, it was with the understanding that they would continue to hunt and fish there, living alongside the English. Thus the sachems often responded angrily when their fishing weirs were confiscated, their hunting grounds cleared for farming, dams built upon their rivers and streams, and their people told to go live elsewhere.

For their part, the English were soon thrust into a battle for control of the New World and its abundant resources with the French, whose stronghold was far to the north, on the St. Lawrence River in Quebec. Within a relatively short time, the French, whose economy was based on fur trading, would prove adept at engaging, recruiting, and through the agency of their ruthless Jesuit missionaries, indoctrinating the Indians of Quebec and the Great Lakes into a certain bloody-minded version of Catholicism, with the goal of hiring, bribing, or conscripting their warriors to act as French trading partners and mercenaries. That meant trapping beaver, otter, marten, and other fur-bearing animals, as well as raiding English settlements in New England, New York, and Acadia, which at the time included parts of Maine and nearly all of the Canadian Maritimes.

From the English perspective, forming alliances with the Pennacook would prove to be a marriage of convenience, at least for the time being. Despite the enormous ocean that separated them from Europe, the English and French powers in the New World could not escape the influence of their sovereigns abroad, try as they might. Within just a few years these bitter enemies would be engaged in a protracted series of wars that reflected the sometimes conflicting interests of those who had to do the actual fighting and the colonial designs of the absentee monarchs that the settlers represented, though often grudgingly.

It would be a holy war—between the Protestants who fled England so they could worship as they saw fit and the French Catholics and their Jesuit fathers who traveled to this verdant continent to expand an empire. The fact that two religions could not have worshipped a more similar God is an ironic footnote to the carnage that would ensue. Like every other holy war before or since, it was a war of terror: of betrayal and slaughter; of burning settlements, murdered children, captives, dismemberment, and slavery; not a war fought by professionals on open ground, imbued with a sense of military honor and chivalry, but a seemingly interminable series of skirmishes, sieges, ambuscades, feints, and failures, engaged in by a rogue's gallery of campaigners who often shifted from one side to the other and back again with little notice. Through a quirk of geography and an accident of fate, the tiny settlement of Haverhill, Massachusetts, remained part of the English frontier for several decades, a speck on the edge of the wilderness that separated two world powers. And scattered throughout this trackless woodland was its original proprietor, who became known as the Indian.

According to an early seventeenth century account, the Indians of New England were "between five or six feet high, straight-bodied, strongly composed, smooth-skinned, merry countenanced, of complexion something more swarthy than Spaniards, black-haired, high foreheaded, black eyed, out-nosed, broad shouldered, brawny armed, long and slender handed, out breasted, small waisted, lank bellied, well thighed, flat kneed, handsome grown legs, and small feet." As a people, they enjoyed such rude good health that "most of them being fifty before a wrinkled brow or gray hair betray their age" and were known for strong white teeth, low infant mortality rates, a constitutional resistance to cold temperatures, and the general absence of sedentary afflictions and congenital deformities. Partly as a result of their strenuous way of life, and a diet consisting of small amounts of fish and meat and an abundance of wild and cultivated plants, the colonial era Indians were often long lived, with some exceeding one hundred years of age.

As several historians of the period have observed, the life of the Indian wasn't all that bad. He spent most of his time outdoors, cared little for the world beyond his daily survival, earned no wages, paid no taxes, and had a voice in local councils that were usually presided over by a sachem whom he was acquainted with personally. He lived in a patriarchal society (though the opinions of women were typically respected by the community), leaving much of the arduous household work to his squaw, and spent a lot of his ample free time hunting and fishing, or engaged in sport, including ball and stick games, wrestling, shooting contests, and wagering. For those under the yoke of an austere Puritan leadership, relegated to the same social position they had occupied in England with regard to land ownership and freedom of trade, and required to answer the whims of a king and country they had fled, the collective lot of the Indian did not lack a certain appeal.

The Indian tribes that lived in the vicinity of the Merrimack River, like the other tribes of New England, would often move their villages a few miles to take advantage of better hunting or fishing grounds, or for seasonal activities like planting corn, squash, pumpkins, and beans. The band would sometimes change their name to reflect their new surroundings. For example, if a few families migrated to Amoskeag Falls on the Merrimack to construct a fishing weir, they were Amoskeags, and if the same people traveled that winter to fish through the ice at Lake Winnipesaukee, they became Winnipesaukees. This habit provides insight into how the New England Indians in general, and the Pennacooks in particular, reacted to the appearance of the English settlers on the banks of the Merrimack. Indians were inclined to welcome visitors, to treat them with hospitality, and to believe their stated intentions—until something occurred that changed their minds. They enjoyed trading what they had for what their visitors possessed and took delight in getting the best of the bargain. And since the Indians were guided by customs, and not a set of written laws, they prized oratory and eloquence, and were known, under the right circumstances, as good listeners.

Some early writers had a contrary opinion, including George Wingate Chase of Haverhill, Massachusetts, writing in 1861, with the Indian wars long over in New England, although still raging in the western territories. These commentators, smarting from what they considered the brutality of Indian tactics, exhibited their prejudices openly, refusing to acknowledge even the smallest positive quality in their former enemies. Denouncing all Indians as "slothful, improvident, deceitful, cruel and revengeful," Chase writes, "They have been called eloquent. Never was a reputation more cheaply earned. Take away the commonplaces of the mountain and the thunder, the sunset and the water-fall, the eagle and the buffalo, the burying of the hatchet, the smoking of the calumet, the lighting of the council-fire, and the material for their pomp of words is reduced within contemptible dimensions. . . . Occasions were not wanting, but the gift of impressive speech was not his."

The fact is, Indians were able to express their opinions during tribal gatherings, which is more than many settlers, especially those who did not own land, could say of their own town meetings. Often, at village councils, Indian neighbors in dispute were allowed to speak at length about their grievances, and when they were finished the assembly would remain silent for several minutes while considering what had been said. There is a story, reported by early historians, about a Swedish missionary who was invited to preach to the assembled chiefs of the Susquehanna on the origins of Christianity, including Adam and Eve's banishment from the Garden of Eden. When the sermon concluded, one of the chiefs responded by saying, "What you have told us is all very good. It is indeed bad to eat apples. It is better to make them all into cider. We are much obliged by your kindness in coming so far to tell us these things, which you have heard from your mothers."

The Indian orator continued by regaling their guest with one of the tribal legends, explaining how the Great Spirit had bestowed corn, beans, and tobacco upon the Susquehanna. The missionary reacted with scorn, dismissing the story as a mere fable, while he had journeyed across an ocean to deliver the sacred truth of Christ. In turn, the Indian orator pointed out that their visitor had obviously not been schooled in common courtesy and expressed indignation that the Indians had believed the minister's story, but he had not reciprocated by believing theirs.

In the early years, Passaconaway had taken the settlers at their word. He agreed to share his territory, to trade with them, and to fight alongside them against the Mohawks and other common enemies. Over the ensuing decades, the Bashaba kept faith with the English, and by doing so was able to keep the peace, though his pride was often wounded by the injustices he and his people were made to suffer. Though Indians were regularly mistreated, imprisoned, uprooted, and put to death without consulting the tribal leadership, several early historians have noted that Passaconaway delivered one of his warriors to Massachusetts authorities so he could stand trial for murder. A man named Jenkins, who had been trading with the Pennacooks, was found murdered in a Pennacook wigwam in 1631. It's a distinct possibility that the wise old sachem made the gesture as a way of underscoring the disparity between the Pennacook's sense of justice and fair play, and that of the English.

Eleven years later, a rumor abounded that Passaconaway was massing for an insurrection, and a platoon of forty soldiers was sent to Rowley and Ipswich, where the Bashaba often resided in springtime, to arrest him. Violent thunderstorms prevented the troops' speedy departure, and news of the patrol reached Passaconaway, allowing him to retreat into the wilderness ahead of the soldiers' arrival. Unfortunately, his second son, Wonalancet, was not likewise forewarned. Despite there being no evidence that warriors were gathering for an attack on the English, Passaconaway's son and his wife were taken prisoner by the soldiers, Wonalancet was bound with rope, and the captives were forced to march toward the white settlements.

Seeing his chance, Wonalancet slipped the rope and fled into the underbrush, but the soldiers fired, wounding him, and he was recaptured. Realizing that Passaconaway would perceive this unwarranted abduction of a family member as a great insult, the Massachusetts authorities sent a warrior named Cutshamekin, who had been captured with Wonalancet, to find Passaconaway and invite him to Boston to hear their apologies. Passaconaway sent back a terse reply: "Tell the English, when they restore my son and his squaw, then I will come and talk with them."

But Passaconaway was an old man by this time. That same year, Wonalancet and his squaw were returned to him, and in exchange,

Passaconaway delivered up "the required artillery" to the English, probably a cache of firearms and other weapons. In 1642, Passaconaway and Wonalancet signed articles of agreement formally submitting to the authority of the Massachusetts government. (By 1644, all the tribes in proximity to the Massachusetts Bay colony had signed a treaty that established English authority, made the Indians subject to colonial laws, and agreed to protect these tribes from outside attacks.) This marked the end of Pennacook sovereignty. Settlers became more numerous, closing out more of the Indians' hunting and fishing grounds, and Passaconaway was relegated to an ever-diminishing parcel of land, leaving him and his people destitute.

In the spring of 1660, when Passaconaway was believed to be in excess of one hundred years old, he delivered a final oration to his people at their ancient fishing ground, Pawtucket Falls on the Merrimack River. (An Englishman named Daniel Gookin was said to be in attendance, though his account is not altogether reliable. Perhaps this is due, in part, to difficulties with transcribing and translating such a speech from memory. By his own report, clergyman and historian William Hubbard was also there. Variations on Passaconaway's speech, though similar in many ways, appear in several accounts by early historians.) In all these reports, there is a valedictory air, at once wistful and defiant, with a final admonition to the assembly that must have saddened them as much as the sight of their withered champion. In the historian Chandler E. Potter's version, the great Bashaba struggled to his feet before a vast crowd of Indians, many of whom had journeyed a great distance to bid their sachem farewell.

Hearken to the words of your father. I am an old oak that has withstood the storms of more than an hundred winters. Leaves and branches have been stripped from me by the winds and frosts—my eyes are dim—my limbs totter—I must soon fall! But when young and sturdy, when my bow—no young man of the Pennacooks could bend it—when my arrow would pierce a deer at an hundred yards—and I could bury my hatchet in a sapling to the eye—no wigwam had so many furs—no pole so many scalps as Passaconaway's! Then I delighted in war. The whoop of the Pennacooks was heard upon the Mohawk—and no voice so loud as Passaconaway's. The scalps upon the pole of my wigwam told the story of Mohawk suffering.

*The English came, they seized our lands; I sat me down at Penna-
cook. They followed upon my footsteps; I made war upon them, but they
fought with fire and thunder; my young men were swept down before
me, when no one was near them. I tried sorcery against them, but they
still increased and prevailed over me and mine, and I gave place to
them and retired to my beautiful island of Natticook. I that can make
the dry leaf turn green and live again—I that take the rattlesnake in
my palm as I would a worm, without harm—I who have had com-
munion with the Great Spirit dreaming and awake—I am powerless
before the Pale Faces.*

*The oak will soon break before the whirlwind—it shivers and
shakes even now; soon its trunk will be prostrate—the ant and worm
will sport upon it! Then think, my children, of what I say; I commune
with the Great Spirit. He whispers me now "Tell your people, Peace,
Peace, is the only hope of your race. I have given fire and thunder to
the pale faces for weapons—I have made them plentier than the leaves
of the forest, and still shall they increase! These meadows they shall
turn with the plow—these forests shall fall by the axe—the pale faces
shall live upon your hunting grounds, and make their villages upon
your fishing places!" The Great Spirit says this, and it must be so! We
are few and powerless before them! We must bend before the storm!
The wind blows hard! The old oak trembles! Its branches are gone! Its
sap is frozen! It bends! It falls! Peace, Peace, with the white men—is
the command of the Great Spirit—and the wish—the last wish—of
Passaconaway.*

When the old Bashaba sat down, an encompassing silence fell over
the multitude.

Against his own expectations, Passaconaway lived at least three more
years, or several more, depending on the account, though the governing
of the Pennacooks ceded to Wonalancet by 1669 or thereabouts. Upon
the death of Passaconaway, runners were sent in all directions and a huge
number of mourners appeared for what became the largest Indian funeral
on record. When an Indian died, his corpse was wrapped in skins and
placed in a seated position in the grave, knees bent to his chest and facing east, toward the rising sun. It was also customary to bury the dead
man with his bow, arrows, and shield; tribal ornaments; his birch bark

cup and wooden bowl, and perhaps a sack of maize, dried fish, and other sustenance—items he would need on his journey to the land of the dead. Such was Passaconaway's reputation that 6,711 animals were brought to his gravesite as offerings. According to an early historian, these included "99 black bears, 66 moose, 25 bucks, 67 does, 240 wolves, 82 wild-cats, 3 catamounts, 482 foxes, 32 buffaloes, 400 otter, 620 beaver, 1500 mink, 110 ferrets, 520 raccoons, 900 musquashes, 501 fishers, 3 ermines, 58 porcupines, 832 martens, 59 woodchucks, and 112 rattlesnakes." He was reportedly buried in a cave near the summit of Mount Agamenticus in York, Maine.

If Passaconaway and then Wonalancet had pursued a strategy of cooperation with the settlers—one that had kept the Massachusetts settlements mostly untouched by war—there were other sachems who would persuade their followers to take up the rifle and the tomahawk against the English. The most prominent of these was Metacom, known to the English as King Philip, the son of the great chief Massasoit, ruler of the Wampanoag. Massasoit had for several decades lived peacefully alongside his neighbors in the Plymouth Colony. But by the late 1660s, colonial authorities had developed the infuriating habit of compelling Indian sachems to appear in front of a tribunal over rumors they were planning an insurrection or had formed alliances with other tribes the English authorities considered unfriendly. (The reason for this systematic decentralization of Indian power was simple: The rapid expansion of the colony required more land.) Most of these rumors were unfounded, although that didn't spare the Indians called before the authorities, including King Philip in 1667, from the additional indignity of receiving what amounted to a legal bill for their troubles. A few years later, when colonial authorities demanded that the Indians turn over their weapons, forfeit what remained of their lands, and submit to English law, they got the Indian uprising they seemed to be asking for.

In 1675, King Philip helped engineer a bloody campaign against the settlers, drawing Indians from several tribes in a concerted attempt to drive away the English once and for all. (However, Philip's entreaties to Wonalancet and the Pennacooks were unsuccessful, with the Bashaba retreating into the wilderness with the remaining one hundred or so of his followers.) Between 1675 and 1676, King Philip's War leveled at least a dozen frontier towns and killed an estimated twenty-five hundred

English settlers, or 5 percent of the colonial population. On the Indian side, approximately five thousand lives were lost, a staggering 40 percent of their population. Pitting neighbor against neighbor, it was the first American civil war, where those on each side felt betrayed by the other.

The uprising ended in August 1676, when the English finally cornered King Philip and his warriors in a Rhode Island swamp. Attempting to slip the cordon of soldiers and "praying Indians"—Christian converts in service to the English—that surrounded him, King Philip was spotted by Captain Benjamin Church, who led the expedition. Said to be so corpulent that he always had a soldier nearby to assist him in walking, Church leveled his rifle in Metacom's direction but it misfired, whereupon Alderman Seaconet, himself a Wampanoag acting as guide to the English, took aim and shot his own chief through the heart. The soldiers drew and quartered King Philip's corpse, and his head was carried to Boston and put on display. It would be the New England Indians' most significant insurrection and their most ignominious defeat. Like the South would be nearly two hundred years later, the Algonquin people were ruined.

If an Indian felt he had been insulted, his rights trodden upon, or betrayed by someone whom he trusted as a friend, he would seek revenge and was often quite patient in waiting to extract it. At the conclusion of King Philip's War, a large number of warriors who had escaped the final siege made their way north to Pennacook territory on the Merrimack River. During the war, Wonalancet had kept peace with the English but refused to fight against other Indians for reasons of loyalty. Given the flexibility of tribal affiliations and the custom of adopting Indians from other tribes into one's own, the Pennacooks eventually became hosts to a large cohort of "strange" Indians who had fought against the settlers. The General Court of Massachusetts became aware of this and sent a party of militia to the Pennacook stronghold, with orders to seize the fort and disperse the Indians who had gathered there.

Before the English arrived, Wonalancet and his followers retreated to the adjoining marshland where they watched the soldiers burn the village and trample their winter food supply. Most of the young warriors had not had the opportunity to engage in battle during Passaconaway's reign and were itching for a fight. But Wonalancet did not allow his men to give their position away, and the Pennacooks retreated deeper into the forest.

In September 1676, the defeated and disconsolate Indians fled Rhode Island for the hinterlands. Wonalancet and other sachems, including Squando, were compelled to sign a peace treaty in Dover, then located in Massachusetts and known as Cocheco, at a trading post operated by Major Richard Waldron. Shortly thereafter, probably in the spirit of celebration that attended these events, four hundred Indians were lured to Cocheco, under a promise of safe conduct from Major Waldron, for a festival of contests and games. At the same time, a large contingent of soldiers under Captains Syll and Hawthorne arrived at the settlement. Although Major Waldron was known to cheat Indians at his trading post, equating his fist with a pound when weighing beaver and other furs, in this instance he was said to oppose lying in wait for the Indians and ambushing them en masse. After all, Waldron had given his word. Instead, he helped the other officers devise a strategy that would save some lives, particularly among the white soldiers and settlers.

On the morning after their arrival, the Indians were invited to take part in war games, including a kind of "sham fight" between them and the militia that would employ a great deal of martial pomp and ceremony, and include the firing of cannon. On a field surrounded by dense woods the militia appeared with drums beating and pennants flying, caparisoned for parade in their heavy field coats, shot pouches, boots, and haversacks. The English were on one side of the green, and the Indians on the other, who were delighted when they were given a cannon mounted on wheels. Since they were unfamiliar with its operation, the artillery piece was delivered to them with a squadron of English gunners. Manning the drag ropes, the Indians were ordered to bring the cannon about, temporarily ranging it along one of their own columns. At a prearranged signal, the English gunners fired the artillery piece, knocking down a number of Indians, some of whom were killed.

Though claiming the discharge had been an accident, additional troops emerged from the woods and enclosed the Indians on all sides, disarming them without firing another shot. Wonalancet and approximately one hundred Pennacooks, including Pequauquakes and Ossippees, were allowed to leave the settlement, while the so-called strange Indians, more than two hundred of whom were believed to have fought against the English, were marched to Boston. As many as eight of these were hanged, and the majority forced into slavery in Barbados. Early historians noted that it is highly probable that a number of these Indians were sold, not because they had taken part in King Philip's rebellion, but for motives of profit. Passaconaway's son-in-law, Winnepurkitt, was believed to be among them.

The sham fight marked the nadir of the relationship between the Pennacooks and their former allies, the English, and underscored the inability of the settlers to grasp Indian values of loyalty and respect. The actions of the Puritan leadership in the early years of the settlements, and certainly late in the seventeenth century during the Salem witch trials, demonstrate that the New World was less a venue for the pursuit of religious freedom than a forum for their particular brand of paternalistic oppression, the enforcement of superstition as God's law, and a warped sense of Manifest Destiny that would eventually choke out the existence of the Indians. In this case, the Indians were particularly incensed that Waldron and his confederates had duped them into bringing other Indians as their guests, betraying both groups. As wars and rumors of wars percolated across the frontier, the Pennacooks seethed, biding their time until an opportunity arose to even their account with Major Waldron.

Wonalancet and his family were in dire straits. With no real friends among the English, the Mohawks occasionally venturing into his territory, and many of his tribesmen fleeing to the sanctuary of St. Francis in Canada, the Bashaba of the Pennacooks was reduced to living "under supervision of Mr. Jonathan Ting," who had purchased most of the Pennacook land, near the settlement of Dunstable. In September 1677, Wonalancet and what was left of his band were captured by St. Francis Indians and brought to Canada. It's likely that this maneuver was undertaken to convince the English he had gone over to the French against his will, alleviating any suspicion of betrayal. In his place rose a new sachem of the Pennacooks, Wonalancet's nephew, Kancamagus, a fiery, somewhat unpredictable warrior who was called John Hawkins by the English.

Kancamagus's father, Nanamocomuck, the eldest son of Passaconaway, despised the English after they unlawfully condemned him to a Boston jailhouse. Later he removed his family to Maine, where Kancamagus was raised among the Androscoggins, a more restless and warlike tribe than the Pennacooks. By 1684, Kancamagus had returned to his ancestral lands and assumed the title of sachem, bringing with him a respected warrior named Mesandowit and a band of hot-tempered

Androscoggins. Kancamagus resembled his grandfather in physique and athletic prowess, and by his uncanny ability to draw other Indians toward him, though his upbringing among the Maine tribes and his impetuous demeanor made him a much more dangerous figure than Passaconaway, especially where the English were concerned.

The number of strange Indians rallying to Kancamagus at Pennacook alarmed the Massachusetts authorities. Among these Indians were some of the warriors taken at the raid on Cocheco, who had been sold into slavery but had made their way back to New England. (It seemed likely to colonial historians that Kancamagus and several of his hand-picked warriors had also been present at the sham fight but were allowed to go free.) While simultaneously pursuing Kancamagus as an ally, Massachusetts officials made a pact with his mortal enemy, the Mohawks, paying them to raid Indian villages across New England.

Kancamagus received word that the Mohawks, who were of superior fighting strength, intended to raid his territory and "kill all the Indians from Mount Hope to Pegypscott." Kancamagus, having been elevated to Bashaba, traveled to New Castle at the mouth of the Piscataqua River to ask New Hampshire's provincial lieutenant governor, Edward Cranfield, to protect his people from their ancient enemies. Kancamagus introduced himself and the Indians' concerns by way of a letter, dated May 15, 1685:

Honur Governor, my friend.

You my friend, I desire your worship and your power, because I hope you can do some great matters this one. I am poor and naked and I have no men, at my place, because I afriad allwayes Mohogs he will kill me every day and night. If your worship when please pray help me you no let Mohogs kill me at my place at Malamake rever called Panukkog and Natukkog. I will submit your worship and your power. And now I want powder and such alminishon, shott and guns because I have forth at my hom and I plant theare.

This all Indian hand, but pray you do consider your humble Servant,

John Hogkins.

Beneath Kancamagus's Anglicized signature appeared the marks of fourteen other prominent Indians. It's clear from this showing that

Kancamagus, when confronted with the threat of a Mohawk invasion, saw the English as the devil he knew, and like his grandfather, was willing to enter into a bargain with the colonial forces. When his message to Cranfield did not a prompt an immediate response, he wrote another letter that same day and had it delivered to the governor, along with a few beaver skins.

> *May 15th, 1685*
> *Honour Mr. Governor. now this day I com your house, I want se you and I bring my hand at before you I want shake hand to you if worship when please, then you Receive my hand, then shake your hand and my hand. You my friend because I Remember at old time when live my grant father and grant mother then Englishmen com this country, then my grant father and Englishmen, they make a good gouenant, they friend allwayes, my grant father leuing at place called malamake Rever, other name Natukkog and Panukkog, that one Rever great many names and I bring you this few skins at this first time I will give you my friend. this all Indian hand*
> *John X Hawkins, Sagamon*

The second note—and the beaver skins—drew Cranfield's attention, and the Bashaba was invited to the governor's residence that evening. But the message to the Indians further stated that Governor Cranfield had been called away on other business, leaving a member of the Council in his stead. Kancamagus was therefore instructed to plead his case to a Mr. Mason. The Bashaba subsequently wrote to Mason hinting that one of his concerns, besides the imminent descent of the Mohawks, was that colonial officials refrain from punishing any Indians suspected of drunkenness in and around the settlements. To Kancamagus's mind, such transgressions were an internal matter, not subject to English law. Cranfield and Mason ignored this letter, probably because they were aware of Kancamagus's requests before he made them. This prompted a final message from the Bashaba.

> *mr mason pray I want Speake you a few a words if your worship when please because I come parpos I will speake this Gouernor but he go away So he Say at last night and so far I understand this Gouernor*

his power that your power now, so he speake his own mouth, pray if
you take what I want, pray com to me because I want go hom this day
  your humble servant
  John Hogkins, Indian Sogamon.
  may 16th, 1685

Apparently, the meeting never took place. Insulted by this treatment, the Bashaba gathered his motley followers and retreated into the wilderness, with Kancamagus probably returning to the Androscoggins in Maine. Concerned by this development, the English sent a messenger to Pennacook, asking the great chief why he had departed the region. Knowing the English feared an attack by the mixed band of Pennacook and strange Indians, Kancamagus sent back a diplomatic reply, insisting it was hatred of the Mohawks, not the English, which had led to his departure.

Eventually, Kancamagus was convinced to return to Pennacook, and on September 19, 1685, he and Mesandowit signed a treaty between the Provinces of New Hampshire and Massachusetts and the Indians of said provinces, putting the Indians under the protection of the colonies. As a result, there were no significant hostilities between the New England Indians and the English settlements for the length of the agreement, which expired in 1689.

A few years earlier, in 1684, King Charles II of England had vacated the Massachusetts Bay colony's charter, forcing its government back under his control. Despite all the dangers and travails the colonists had suffered by claiming the wilderness, they soon found themselves once again beholden to the crown's authority, though with their ancestral enemies the French, hostile Indians, and the Atlantic Ocean between them.

Shortly thereafter, King Charles II died and was succeeded by his brother, James II. In the majority, England was a Protestant nation and bristled under James's forced return to Catholicism. In November 1684, William of Orange, who had married King James II's daughter Mary, landed in England and seized the throne, in what became known as the English Revolution. (Chase calls the establishment of the Church of England and the abrogation of the Pope's authority "only a transfer of the tiara from the Tiber to the Thames," bringing with it more forfeitures of property and goods, and more burnings at the stake.) James II fled to France and asked King Louis XIV for assistance. France was predominantly Catholic and thus, Louis XIV supported James, leading to King William's War, which began in 1689. This conflict soon spread to their respective colonies and became a border war, leaving the Pennacooks and their assemblage of strange Indians occupying the middle ground. (One in eight New Hampshire settlers were killed or captured in the war, which lasted until 1697.) Louis de Baude, or Count Frontenac, the French governor in Quebec, favored the tactic of hiring or otherwise inducing bands of Indians to attack settlements on the English frontier. One of the most barbaric of these massacres took place at Cocheco, the location of the sham fight thirteen years earlier.

Unfortunately for the residents of Cocheco, the onset of King William's War coincided with the expiration of the treaty between the English and the New England Indians. That left what the historian Francis Parkman called an "unstable mob of warriors, guided by the impulse of the hour" occupying the wilderness between the French stronghold at Quebec and the English frontier settlements. Referred to by the French as *Les Hommes des Bois*, or Men-Brutes of the Forest, the Indians were often as unreliable as allies as they were unpredictable as antagonists. Perhaps the English had committed the original sin of the New World when, in 1605, a trader named George Weymouth landed near Cape Cod and then sailed approximately 150 miles north, where he remained for several weeks trading with the Indians. Before departing, he kidnapped five of the Abenakis, later selling them as slaves. Nine years later, during one of the expeditions undertaken by Captain John Smith, his shipmate, a man named Hunt, took twenty Indians captive and sailed for Malaga, where they passed into bondage. These betrayals, as well as other moral insults heaped upon the Indians by both the English and the French, no doubt affected their view of the intruders and led to an almost interminable series of crosses and double-crosses. Parkman wrote that the Indians "were of a race unsteady as aspens and fierce as wild-cats, full of mutual jealousies, without rulers, and without laws; for each was a law to himself. It was difficult to persuade them, and, when persuaded, scarcely possible to keep them so." Perhaps that's true, but anyone familiar with the later imperial activities of those who took over the North American continent might visit the lines written in 1968 by journalist Michael Herr. While covering the war in Vietnam, Herr encountered a "demi-enlightened, Annamese aborigine" called the Montagnard: "Many Americans considered them to be nomadic, but the war had more to do with that than anything in their temperament. We napalmed off their crops and flattened their villages, and then admired the restlessness in their spirit."

How the colonial authorities handled Passaconaway, Wonalancet, and Kancamagus and the eventual dismantling of the Pennacook confederacy forms a sort of miniature, a working prototype, of the long-game strategy that would play out over the next two centuries, resulting in the complete takeover and settlement of the New World by its European invaders. The seeds of the Indians' obsolescence had already been planted by the colonists: the initial appeals for assistance; a wolf's brand of friendliness; the encouragement of trade and trade partnerships; a rushing tide of immigrants, and the gradual but steady encroachment on Indian land; the increase in the number and size of frontier settlements; large-scale timber removal and agricultural co-opting; exertions of military force; the purchase of Indian mercenary forces to stir up internecine warfare; dubious treaties, tribal relocations, and, finally, a ruthless, unapologetic genocide. With the advantage of three hundred years of hindsight, the entire affair was *a fait accompli* by the time Passaconaway emerged from that Plymouth swamp.

In the spring of 1689, with their strategy not fully formed, the colonial authorities became worried about the angry restlessness their tactics had created among the Pennacook. Kancamagus and his warriors, including Mesandowit, Paugus, and Wahowah, known as Hope-Hood, the "Indian-rubber devil," a skillful, resilient, and bloody antagonist, had long been stewing over the insults hurled at them by Governor Cranfield and other representatives of the colonies. There were several additional grievances that had kept their anger at a low boil, the most prominent the English habit of negotiating with the Mohawks, offering them bounty to attack the Pennacooks. Also, Passaconaway's son-in-law Winnepurkitt had been sold as a slave, and though several Indians captured during the sham fight had managed to escape and return to New England, burning in their desire for revenge, Winnepurkitt remained in bondage.

By June 1689, Kancamagus was the leader of a confederacy that included members of his own tribe, as well as Pequauquakes, Sacos,

Androscoggins, and other Maine Indians who gathered at the Basha-ba's fortress at Pennacook. Two friendly Pennacook Indians, hearing of a planned attack upon the English, informed the militia captain at the settlement in Chelmsford that Kancamagus and his band were going to assault the Cocheco garrison. Their bloodiest intentions were focused on Major Richard Waldron and Captain Peter Coffin, who they believed were most responsible for the treachery wreaked upon the Indians thir-teen years earlier.

On June 22nd, the militia captain wrote a letter to a member of the governor's council stating Kancamagus's intentions, and the councilor enclosed the original letter with his own note stating that "John Hawkins," i.e., Kancamagus, was the "principal enemy" and sent the packet to Gov-ernor Simon Bradstreet in Boston. Bradstreet's apparent indifference to the warning, the pace of colonial mail, and a delay at the Newbury ferry prevented a subsequent letter from the council secretary informing Wal-dron and Coffin of the situation from arriving at the settlement until June 28th, the day after the attack occurred.

On the evening of June 27th, Mesandowit, who was known to Major Waldron, visited the old man at his trading post. While they were having supper, Mesandowit noted the large number of Indians he had encoun-tered about the settlement and asked Waldron what he would do if strange Indians should appear. Without the least bit of concern, Waldron replied that he could summon one hundred trained soldiers merely by lifting a finger. Having fulfilled his sense of loyalty toward Waldron for their past acquaintance, Mesandowit said nothing more about the matter and soon went on his way. Sometime after, Waldron retired for the evening without posting a guard.

Cocheco was a fortified settlement—the main thoroughfare enclosed by a stockade and the village itself containing five garrison houses, includ-ing Waldron's on the north side, with Peter Coffin's, and another main-tained by Coffin's grown son, to the south. Each of these structures was encircled by a timber wall that featured a barred gate, as well as the narrow entrance to the house itself, which was also barred and bolted. Because of the trading post, there were always a number of Indians in and about the settlement and after darkness fell, a pair of squaws approached each of the garrison houses and asked for a night's lodging by the fire, which was a common occurrence.

The squaws were admitted to all the garrison houses, except for the one owned by Coffin's son. The lodgers settled by the hearth, and the gates and doors were again bolted shut. At midnight in each of the houses, after the settlers had gone to bed, the squaws quietly rose up, unlocked and unbarred the entrances and went out, disappearing into the shadows. Simultaneously, five or six warriors appeared at each garrison and crept inside. At Waldron's house, an Indian was posted at the inner door and the other warriors, with Kancamagus himself possibly among them, crowded into the ground floor and rushed up the stairs toward the major's sleeping chamber.

Waldron was by then eighty years old, a vigorous, ornery man who had lived a rustic outdoor life. Hearing the Indians' tread upon the stairs, the major sprang out of bed, grabbed his sword, and rushed at the intruders in the narrow upper hall, his furious counterattack driving them backwards, toward the head of the stairs. For an instant, the momentum was in the old soldier's favor. But when he attempted to dash back and retrieve his pistols, one of the Indians darted after him and struck Waldron with the flat side of his hatchet, knocking him off his feet.

Screaming and jeering, the Indians dragged Waldron down the stairs, tore off his clothing, bound him to a chair, and hoisted their captive onto the largest table they could find. They taunted Waldron about his habit of lording over the Indians, equating his fist with a pound when he weighed their beaver skins, and asked who would judge them now as they hacked off his fingers. Forcing the other whites in the house to prepare a meal, the Indians stood around the table feasting and shouting at their naked captive. When they were through eating, the warriors began circling the table, shouting and poking at Waldron with their rifle butts and pikes.

Drawing their knives, the Indians slashed Waldron's chest as they went around the table, each thereby "crossing out his account" with the old trader. At the sight of Waldron's blood, their frenzy increased; they cut off his ears and nose and stuffed them into his mouth. Waldron passed out from shock and when he began to topple forward, taking the chair with him, one of the Indians held the major's sword beneath the lip of the table and another shoved him off the edge, impaling Waldron with his own blade.

Many other Cocheco residents met a similar fate. Waldron's son-in-law Abraham Lee was killed; also, his neighbor Otis and several others in his house were murdered, including Otis's son and two-year-old daughter, Hannah, whose head was dashed against the stairs. One episode seemed to capture both the powers of discrimination and the capriciousness of the Indians, all at once. That night, a woman named Elizabeth Heard happened to be returning from Portsmouth by boat with her children. Hearing the commotion, she urged her charges along and fled toward Major Waldron's house, which was illuminated in the darkness. They banged on the outer gate for some time, though no one came, and finally one of the boys heaved himself over the palisade into the yard. In a matter of seconds he climbed back over, reporting that an Indian with a rifle was guarding the door to the house. Uncertain of what to do, Elizabeth Heard told her children to run away, though she was too overcome with fright to go with them.

After gathering herself, Heard crawled into some nearby bushes. Near daylight, she saw a warrior coming toward her hiding place, armed with a hatchet and a pistol. Throughout the night, Heard had been tormented by the bloody screams and pleadings of her neighbors and now she was about to be discovered. But when the Indian drew close and saw who was concealed there, he looked straight at her, appeared to smile faintly, and passed by. Apparently, Heard, or a member of her family, had sheltered an Indian during the chaos of the sham fight years earlier and was spared on that account.

In all, twenty-three settlers were killed at Cocheco, and twenty-five taken as captives. Six houses, including Waldron's, and the mill upon the Piscataqua River, were burned to the ground. After decades of insult and abuse, after being dispossessed of their land, preyed upon by corrupt traders and swindlers, demeaned by colonial authorities, and sold out to the Mohawks, the Indians' blood was up. There would be more brutal attacks in the coming years, and in 1697, shortly before King William's War ended with a peace treaty between the English and French, the tiny settlement of Haverhill, Massachusetts, would be the site of the most remarkable Indian raid in colonial history.

CHAPTER III

The Settlement

Haverhill was first settled in 1640, twelve years before Thomas Duston was born, when a dozen Englishmen and their party consisting of sixty persons, migrated closer to the Merrimack River from the nearby towns of Newbury and Ipswich. The land was chosen, at least in part, because it was situated at the head of tidewater in the Merrimack, with roughly thirteen navigable miles between the village and the river's mouth in Newbury. The original settlement, as well as contemporary Haverhill, is located at 42 degrees 47' north latitude and 71 degrees 4' west longitude, which lies within the Atlantic seaboard lowland, a smooth coastal strip of land containing several low-lying hills. The highest elevation in Haverhill is only 325 feet.

In colonial times, Haverhill was nothing but dense woodland, with only a few cleared spaces believed to be old Indian fields. The area was inhabited by remnants of the Pawtucket band, which populated the coast from the northern portion of Massachusetts Bay, including the town of Salem, to York Village in Maine. The local Indians were known as the Pentuckets, and at the time of Haverhill's settlement the band numbered somewhere between one and two hundred individuals. Just prior to European contact at the beginning of the seventeenth century, a series of Indian wars lowered that number, and it was further reduced by the illnesses brought to North America from the continent between 1615 and 1616, as aforementioned. By the spring of 1697, the native population in the Haverhill area was probably no more than thirty Indians.

When the settlers first arrived, a small number of Pentuckets lived along the river in the area, where they had constructed their wigwams and built fishing weirs. Their work was seasonal: hunting, netting and trapping fish, the gathering of wild plants and shellfish, and a little horticulture. The use and method of construction of the fishing weir made Haverhill a very attractive place for new settlers, given the abundance of fish in that part of the Merrimack River. The Indians drove thousands of wooden stakes into the sandy bed of the Merrimack just below the first set of natural falls, creating a sort of densely arranged fence that stretched three-quarters of the way across the river. When the ocean tide swelled a dozen miles downstream, increasing the river flow, massive schools of fish would swim up past the weir looking for food. A short distance along they would meet the obstacle of the falls, massing there, and then get trapped among the stakes when the tide went out. This created the sort of reliable food source that the settlers coveted.

Early relations between the Pentuckets and the English were peaceful. The Merrimack in this vicinity was teeming with sturgeon, bass, salmon, shad, and alewife, the harvest of which the English at first shared and then appropriated for their own use—perhaps causing the first bout of ill will between the parties. Nevertheless, in 1642 the settlers negotiated a deal with the Indians, providing for the transfer of a large triangular parcel of land extending from the mouth of Little River, eight miles along the westerly bank of the Merrimack, then six miles east and an equal distance to the north. The land was sold for three pounds, ten shillings. An aged Passaconaway signed the deed, alongside the marks of the lesser sachems, Passaquo and Saggahew, each of whose insignia was a crudely drawn bow and arrow.

The first settlers, especially the six men who signed the deed, considered themselves the sole owners of the aforesaid land, dividing and parceling it out however they pleased. This led to many vigorous disputes between these men and those who came after them. At the first town meeting in 1643, it was agreed that three hundred acres would be surveyed and marked out for house lots. Although many of those who arrived in Haverhill in the early years were hopeful of an opportunity to own land, there must have been some disappointment when the men who signed the original deed set strict limits on how much land could be claimed. The intractability of these founding landowners combined with the threat of Indian attacks left the settlement sparsely populated for many years.

The original tract, known as Pawtucket Plantation, was incorporated as the town of Haverhill in 1645, and contained land that would eventually be divided into the Massachusetts towns of Lawrence and Methuen, as well as Hampstead, Salem, Atkinson, and Plaistow that were later situated in New Hampshire, when the state boundaries were redrawn in 1740 and 1741. Haverhill became the twenty-third town admitted to the English colony of Massachusetts and was originally inhabited entirely by Congregationalists, who were Puritans. Quakers arrived in Haverhill around 1655, but they were considered inferior and discouraged from taking part in community life. This sort of mistreatment, which sometimes rose to levels of brutality, was common when the Puritans were confronted with other Christian denominations that had fled the continent in pursuit of religious freedom. By all accounts, the Puritans were a testy lot, who often ruled through intimidation and violence.

Haverhill and its people were far from the established Puritan towns of Ipswich, Newbury, and Salem, and though the first few decades after its settlement were relatively uneventful, after King Philip's War, the town was vulnerable to Indian assaults. Several early historians have mentioned that settlers attending church services in Haverhill and surrounding towns traveled to their fortified places of worship with a prayer book in one hand and a rifle in the other. After the start of King William's War in 1689, prompted by overseas tension between the world powers of England and France, attacks on Haverhill and other English settlements became frequent and increasingly violent. In 1675, Haverhill's population stood at approximately three hundred English settlers and twenty-five "Negro slaves," according to nineteenth-century historians. On May 3rd of that year, Ephraim Kingsbury became the first Haverhill casualty in the Indian war, with Thomas Kimball of nearby Bradford killed the very next day and his wife, five children, and a neighbor, Thomas Eastman, taken into captivity. Due to the number and ferocity of local Indian attacks, over the next thirty years, Haverhill's population did not change very much.

The wealthiest Haverhill settlers, those with a net worth of two hundred pounds sterling or more, were granted the largest house lots, which measured twenty acres. Individuals of lesser wealth were granted lots that decreased in size proportionally to a settler's net worth. In the first division of Haverhill's land, the house lots were laid out in mostly perpendicular strips with common acreage left in reserve. That shared acreage, known as "accommodation grounds," was also parceled out according to wealth, with those granted the largest house lots also receiving greater access to the village meadow and planting grounds. In 1645, settlers agreed that individual landowners could keep a horse, ox, cow, or calf on each acre of common land. By this time, approximately thirty houses were contained within the village, with several more scattered outward from the banks of the Merrimack for a mile or two. Marking the village's permanence, the first meetinghouse and enclosed stockade were built in 1648. The majority of the houses were situated near to one another in the village center, facing what later became known as Mill Street, a common road that lay between them and the Merrimack. This was done to provide greater security in the event of Indian attacks. Even as late as 1697, Thomas Duston's homestead, which he had built several years earlier, was still one of the most remote, on the northwesterly edge of town.

Thomas Duston's father, also named Thomas, arrived in Maine in 1633, as part of a commercial expedition led by John Winter, where the elder Duston was probably employed as a barrel maker, or cooper, or perhaps as a fisherman. It seems likely that when his four-year term of service, which he had agreed upon as a term of his passage, had ended, Duston moved from Richmond's Island in Maine to Cocheco, New Hampshire, or Dover as it was later called. Court records indicate that the elder Duston had some scrapes with the law, over minor debts and "necklecting the ordinance of God upon the sabath day," or non-attendance at church, for which he and his wife, the former Elizabeth Wheeler, were fined ten shillings. In 1652, Duston was "admitted as a freeman" in Kittery, Maine, and sworn in as a town constable. His son Thomas Jr. was born the same year, most likely in Kittery.

It's clear that Thomas Duston Jr., a brick maker and carpenter, was a resident of Haverhill by 1675, since registered deeds show that he built a house there by or before that year, probably on land given to him by his mother. (Haverhill records also indicate that Thomas Duston Jr. was one of twenty-eight local men who served as militia in King Philip's War, also placing him in the settlement by 1675.) He built a second house, described as a "cottage," in January 1675 and finished a third homestead by January 13, 1679, according to land records. Thomas Duston Jr. is the only

Haverhill resident listed on those early deeds who is credited with building more than one house during this period, indicating that other local families hired him to do so. Then, on November 4, 1679, Duston bought "about 18 acres of upland in Haverhill" for twenty pounds from Theodore Atkinson of Boston. There are no other land purchases in Duston's name, except for an additional one-and-a-half-acre strip he bought for twelve pounds in 1863. According to the deed, that piece of land was contiguous with the larger parcel once belonging to Theodore Atkinson "upon which Thomas Duston now hath built his house and now dwells." With no evidence to the contrary, it's fair to surmise that Duston and his wife and family were living here when the Indians attacked Haverhill on March 15, 1697.

Thomas Duston Jr. and Hannah (Emerson) Duston were married in Haverhill on December 3, 1677. The groom was twenty-five years old and his bride was twenty days shy of her twentieth birthday. Hannah gave birth to their first child, a daughter, also named Hannah, eight months and nineteen days later. In the next twenty years, she would have twelve more children, nine of whom lived to adulthood and were married. Eventually, Thomas and Hannah would have seventy-nine grandchildren.

On March 15, 1697, Haverhill was protected by two watch houses, four houses of refuge, and six garrison houses occupied by as many as eight English militia apiece. Upon first alarm, townspeople whose homes were not directly connected to any of these structures immediately removed themselves there, along with any belongings or livestock that was at hand. If there was sufficient warning, settlers would leave their homes devoid of furniture, resigning themselves to building another homestead after the raiders had burned it down. When Goodman Duston was confronted with the approaching savages and needed to decide quickly in which direction he and the children were best disposed to flee, the Marsh garrison was the obvious choice. Although the watch house near the corner of Main and Pond Streets, a location east of the Duston home, was somewhat nearer as the crow flies, getting there meant transporting the children across Little River, in the midst of the spring thaw. According to period maps, the Emerson and Webster garrisons were next in proximity, but reaching them would also require fording the river. The White, Ayer, and Bradley houses were too far east, on the other side of Main Street.

The Marsh garrison, like most of the safe houses along the frontier, was built from massive logs flattened on either side and notched to fit securely into thick-set poles erected at each of the house's four corners. Mud brick was plastered between the logs and on the interior walls, which enclosed an open space of several square rods, containing a larder, ample storage of powder and shot, a central armory where the guns, swords, and pikes were kept, and several fighting positions and sally ports. In most cases, a tower projected from the roof of the garrison, providing an unobstructed view in all directions, and the soldiers dug a tunnel from the house's root cellar beneath the open ground to a position just inside the tree line. The tunnel exit was usually hidden by a large flat stone, dirt, and brush, providing a means of escape should the garrison be overrun.

Although Haverhill had never before suffered an attack in force, it did not come as a total surprise to Goodman Duston that Indians had raided the settlement. In the autumn of 1695, an Indian raiding party had surprised two Haverhill youths working in the fields and taken them captive. In 1695 and 1696, Indians killed settlers in Exeter, twenty miles to the northeast, and on June 26, 1696, Indians attacked Portsmouth, roughly thirty miles north of Haverhill at the mouth of the Piscataqua River. The savages crossed over the Piscataqua from York Nubble, paddling to the beach in canoes just after first light. Upon entering the town, they killed fourteen settlers, ransacked five homesteads, and captured four of the English. They scalped one man and left him bleeding on the ground, but he managed to get up and run away.

The enterprising captain of the Portsmouth militia, a fellow named Shackford, organized a reaction force and set out in pursuit of the Indians and their captives. With a flanking maneuver, Shackford and his men were able to reach the summit of Breakfast Hill before the retreating Indians could gain the tree line. Concealing themselves, the militia formed a skirmish line and rushed downhill amidst a fusillade of musket fire. The Portsmouth men were able to free the captives and recover much of what the Indians had stolen from the settlers' homes and outbuildings. But the raiders, seeing they had lost the advantage, adroitly began to tumble and roll down Breakfast Hill into a swamp, where they disappeared among the rotting trees and eventually made their way back to the canoes and escaped.

Arranging for his children to be cared for, Goodman Duston ran to the shed containing Marsh's livestock. Quickly he emerged leading a horse by the reins. And then Duston, having clambered into the saddle, turned the horse around swiftly and, jamming his hat on his head, rode back downhill toward his farm. Atop a fresh, spirited horse, with Marsh's son on a capable mount just behind him, Duston beat it pell-mell down the footpath toward his homestead, which was marked by twisting billows of smoke. The Indians would show no quarter among women and children, and Duston never expected them to. He had been all his life among the Indians, first at Dover, and then here in the settlement of Haverhill. As a boy, Duston learned by his own observation that the Indian was possessed of treachery, and could appear at any moment with the intent to do grievous harm, a lesson that was reinforced by his experience in the late war.

Some among the English took advantage of the Indians' simple nature, kindling resentment and leading to violence, but the French Jesuits went far beyond that, plying the tribes with whiskey, creating a market for white captives and slaves, and arranging bounties for scalps. The Indian was always at leisure, with no rents coming due, or any troublesome debts. In Duston's experience, the Indians resembled the wild Irish in dreading labor more than poverty. The Reverend Cotton Mather often said that the Indians' abundant free time left room for the devil to do his work. But, as a general rule, the Indians also possessed great power of the will, to the point of sullenness, allowing them to suffer torture or even death without any appearance of fear. This implacability made the Indian a formidable enemy, as he was likely to inflict the same sort of horrible punishment on others that he himself endured, without concern or empathy. According to what Duston heard from those neighbors who had business in Salem or Boston, even the French, who had loosed the northern tribes upon the English in the first place, had begun to contemplate the Indian with apprehension and dread.

The Indian was cunning, and he was swift; he could spring forth from a dozen secret hiding places, and if he felt himself wronged, he could be tireless in seeking revenge—even if it meant the loss of his own life. Indian boys, proving their manhood, were known to stand in a group where they would insert burning embers into their armpits, holding them there as a sort of contest. Anyone who cried out or ran away was deemed unfit to become a warrior. So it was that Indians were known to exact their most vicious payments from the weak, whom they despised most of all, and would often inflict their bloodiest savagery on women and children, even upon infants and the aged, who could not possibly do them any harm.

In the distance, Thomas Duston could hear the alarm-guns ring out from the watch houses and garrisons, distinct in their regularity as opposed to the sporadic banging of riflery in a fight. Recovering from their initial surprise, the townspeople were bringing themselves to bear against the raiders. Duston and his horse rammed their way through the brush into the upper pasture.

From there Duston had a clear view of the house. Thick black ruffles of smoke poured from all the windows and the flames had eaten a large hole in the roof and were pouring down the rear walls. The wind shifted, bending the column of smoke toward the ground, and the riders ducked their heads and plunged into it. Choking and gagging, Duston and the Marsh lad arrived at the front door, muskets bristling, and Duston flung himself down from the horse. Holding a rag to his face with one hand and clutching his flintlock in the other, he ran toward the front of the house. The door was open, broken at the hinges after being rammed. He tried to enter, but the invisible broils of heat emanating from the interior of the house drove him back. He ran along the front wall of the structure and up the west side toward the half-door. Kicking it open, Duston paused for the outrushing heat, dust, and tongues of flame that ensued, then poked his head inside.

Plumes of living fire climbed up the interior walls and devoured most of the furnishings. The place had been thoroughly ransacked. Crockery and other household items lay shattered everywhere, and pieces of clothing were strewn from a chest of drawers—which was disappearing beneath ringlets of flame—to the front door, as if someone or something had been dragged along the floor. All the windows had been busted out, and a lone shoe occupied the cleared space in the middle of the room.

Duston half-expected to find the hatcheted, bloody corpses of his wife and child but there was nothing except the fire. All their work had been destroyed. From this vantage point, he could angle his head to peer out the front door of the house at the deepening blue sky and the pasture-fields and the impenetrable line of trees beyond. Nothing stirred but for the flames licking and devouring the walls. Hannah, the baby, and their neighbor, Mary Neff, were gone.

When Thomas warned her of the raid and then set out after the children, Hannah rose from her sickbed but was not strong enough to flee. Handing her infant over to Mary Neff, she instructed her friend to bundle Martha up and go out the side door, making their way for the upper fields and Pecker's Hill. But no sooner had Mary and the child gone outdoors when Hannah, sitting on the edge of her bed, saw Mary backing into the room with Martha clutched against her breast. Two Indians came through the half-door in the same instant, nearly doubled over, their faces painted a vivid crimson with berry dye. One of them wore a breechclout suspended around his waist by a thong, and the other was naked. Coming into the house they straightened up, brandishing their lances, and began their devilish yelling while knocking over and smashing every household object within reach. The front door, which had been secured with a wooden bolt after Thomas had gone, was battered open at the same instant and three more Indians rushed in, carrying lit torches and screaming. Presently, Mary Neff and the infant Martha joined with their cries.

Though Hannah was expecting it, the sudden appearance of the raiders and the violence of their actions stunned her. The berry dye, their rank odor, and the grime that rose to their knees from crossing the river lent the Indians an almost otherworldly appearance. In her nightdress and bare feet, Hannah remained immobile, gaping at them. But she did not cry out.

Hannah Duston knew from past experience with the Indians that the only way for a prisoner to save her own life was to demonstrate that she was not afraid to lose it. So when one of the raiders grabbed her infant from the arms of a terrified Mary Neff, Hannah rose to her feet and seized Martha back from the Indian and returned her to the nurse. For an instant, the warrior turned his fierce gaze upon Hannah, but she stared right back. Other Indians had entered the house and were ransacking it, taking up as many useful items as they could carry and setting fires about the room with their torches.

Menaced by another Indian who wanted her bedclothes, Hannah moved over to the fireplace, standing between the raiders and Mary Neff and the child. Nearly as tall as the raiders capering about, and sturdy on her feet, Hannah refused to sit down until one of the Indians put the flat of his hands on her shoulders, forcing her onto the hearth stone. Taking out a knife, the Indian whirled around to cut away the piece of broadcloth

Hannah had been weaving, and then battered the loom into pieces with his axe. More raiders came pouring into the house, emptying the larder of cured pork and maize and bacon, and speeding the fires with torn up bedding and other refuse. Figuring the three of them would have been killed by now if that was the Indians' intention, Hannah tried to grab up a few items of clothing for her and the infant. She had managed to put on Thomas's heavy coat and one of her shoes when two of the Indians grabbed her under the arms and dragged her out the front door.

Through the smoke and dust she saw the Indians crowding out the doors and leaping from windows as the individual fires inside the house merged into one gigantic pyre and the flames crackled in loud reports. Behind her through the gaping doorway came Mary and the baby, stumbling and choking in the haze of the yard, as the Indians prodded them and jeered, thrusting their lances at the sky. More Indians were loitering at the edge of the plowed field, waiting for them.

Soon they were marching away from the house, downslope across the field, through the gap in the hedgerow, and hurried at pike and knifepoint across the pasture toward the darkened woodlands. Another band of raiders was coming across open ground to join them, with several more captives in tow. Hannah stumped along in one shoe, her gaze darting about for an opportunity to escape. But there was none.

The sun burned cold on the horizon, becoming smaller as it rose. The frozen ground crunched under their tread, and here and there the bogs and sloughs were glazed over with ice. As the morning grew brighter, the Indians stopped whooping and yelling, and now threatened their captives with pikes and wooden clubs to make haste in silence. There were nine or ten Indians in their party, and when they reached the ribbon of land that contained the orchard they were met by several more Indians. They rose up from the underbrush along the western bank of Little River and without a word joined them on the path that fed into the woods going north. Low trees, their crowns flattened by the wind, crowded together along the embankment. Glancing back, Hannah recognized most of the other captives, including her neighbor Hannah Bradley, but there was at least one, an adolescent boy, who was a stranger to her.

The Indians no doubt had plans to march their prisoners—those who could endure the journey—hundreds of miles through the wilderness to Quebec, there to be sold in bond to Count Frontenac, the French royal governor. The captives were forced to move swiftly, their breath escaping in little white plumes. There were now more than twenty Indians in the party, and by Hannah's count, twelve or thirteen captives, though she was near the front of the column and wasn't certain of the number. She was discouraged from looking back through a combination of sharp grunts and the occasional jab in the spine with a club, as she limped along, her legs weakened by several days of inactivity. The snow grew deep in places, hardened into a crust on top, and with each step, Hannah punched a hole in the drifts, her bare foot aching from the cold.

Mary Neff had managed to bring up Martha and they had fallen in behind her. Hannah Duston exchanged glances with Mrs. Bradley, and was also comforted by having her friend Mrs. Neff alongside her. Fifty-one-year-old Mary Corliss Neff was a person of great fortitude and character. She had been born in the old Samuel Corliss house on Broadway, September 16, 1646, a member of the only Haverhill family said to receive their grant of land directly from the King of England. Her husband, William Neff, had been killed by Indians at Pemaquid, Maine, in 1681. She possessed a calm, deliberate manner and had survived a number of hardships prior to these events.

As the sun angled in, portions of the undergrowth were sharply illuminated, revealing every detail of the scabby tree trunks and dead leaves. Gray vines snaked down from the trees, entangling themselves with the dried grasses and sedge. From somewhere behind her, Hannah heard voices and turned to see one of the raiders push a gray-haired settler out of the line. The man tripped on a clump of grass and the Indians hurled himself atop the man, inflicting several swift blows with a tomahawk. Then the Indian climbed off his victim, his deerskin mantle splattered with blood, and rejoined the column. Hannah glanced at Mary Neff and the women shuddered; they had to keep up the pace, or the same would happen to them.

The young male captive, who was a stranger to Hannah Duston and Mary Neff, doubled back along the path and approached the Haverhill man lying on the ground. Apparently this boy had been with the Indians long enough to gain a measure of trust, since he was allowed to depart the column, however momentarily. Reaching down, he grasped the man's right foot and lower leg, and pulled off his shoe. Jogging back to rejoin the column, the boy slipped into line and handed the shoe to Hannah

Duston. In a low voice, he said his name was Sam Lenorson and that he had been taken from Worcester, Massachusetts. Then he turned back and spoke to his master, an Indian named Bampico.

Just as the path entered a stand of birch trees, the ground padded with snow all around, a young white girl, no more than ten or eleven years old and dressed only in a shift, broke away from the captives and ran off between the trees. Just as quickly, a young raider bounded after her, overtaking the girl near a swollen brook that wound through the grove. While she was still running, the Indian took the girl off her feet with a swinging blow from his pike. She collapsed into the water with a splash, and keeping her submerged with his foot, the Indian bludgeoned the girl with the butt of the pike. A pool of crimson rose to the surface and began to swirl in the current.

At this Mary Neff started, a loud "huh" escaping from her throat. This increased the infant Martha's cries, which had been reduced to fitful sobs by the nurse's soothing tone. Urged along the path once more, Mary was soon flanked by an Indian on each side, who threatened her with gestures and guttural sounds, insisting that she hush the infant. One of the Indians thrust his arm across Mary's chest, stopping her abruptly, and just as Hannah turned to assist her, the Indian grabbed the baby from Mary's arms. At the edge of the glade was a single apple tree, and striding to its base, the Indian swung the howling infant by the ankles, smashing her head against the tree. There was a pathetic sound. The Indian dropped the bloody, mangled child in the snow and continued on his march.

Hannah and Mary Neff ran over to the apple tree and stared down at the tiny corpse, horror-struck. The other captives were herded along, clutching at each other as they passed in a dumb-show, their faces blanched and constricted, and then a trio of young raiders approached the mourners. They grinned and mocked the women, pointing down at the dead infant, and beating their chests in exultation. Hannah stared back at them with hollow, lifeless eyes, and one by one they left off and rejoined the column.

Another Indian came up, prodding the two captives with his axe. He grunted at them, pointing up the trail. Grasping each other by the forearms and wrists, Hannah Duston and Mary Neff continued northward, heading into a dark wall of trees.

Chapter IV

A Forced March

As they departed the last bit of cultivated land, the mood of the savages changed from threatening and boastful to stealthy and cautious. They were strange Indians, inhabitants of another territory, and they hurried the captives along at the point of their lances, maintaining silence through angry gestures and glances. Three of the captives had been murdered since they lost sight of their farms, all of whom were either helpless, like the infant Martha, unwilling to go with the Indians, or unable to keep up with them. While the rest of the settlers moved along beneath the snowy pines, Goodwife Duston noticed that the handful who remained—not all of them young, but hardy—were capable of matching the Indians' grueling pace and hadn't offered any resistance or voiced a single complaint. Those were the only reasons they were still alive.

The party had traveled a short way into the forest when, after a brief conference among the savages, a quartet of warriors, some of the youngest and largest who had taken part in the raid, broke off from the others. Choosing a narrow deer trace that ran along the river, they made great haste back toward the village. Two of these warriors had muskets and the others were armed with lances and hatchets. Watching them race away, Duston and Goodwife Neff were startled back into motion by a sharp prodding in their lower backs. Without so much as a word, the Indians forced their captives onward, moving farther away from the settlement— and any possibility of rescue—at an alarming speed.

Duston and Neff leaned on each other for support, their gowns encrusted with mud as they rushed along in the pine-scented gloom.

Hannah wore her husband's field coat, and since it had been very cold in the house that morning, each of the women had donned her skirt, bodice, two pair of linen sleeves, and an apron over the shift, underskirt, chemise, and double stockings she had worn to bed the previous evening. In addition to these items, their heads were covered by the kerchiefs and caps they always wore, even indoors, because of the ash and soot. The penetrating chill, had they taken any notice, stung their faces and hands, and crept down the back of their necks. Beneath the trees their footing was uncertain, a dim latticework of icy rocks, exposed roots, and blotches of snow, and they knew that a stumble or grunt of surprise could mean their skulls being crushed by the blow of a hatchet.

Having seen her week-old infant and two of her neighbors murdered without warning, Duston went where she was directed without feeling her limbs, or the sharpness of the air against her skin, trotting along on instinct, like a herded animal. Intermittently, it was like she had ceased to exist and was aware of only a numbing series of disconnected moments, her entire being emptied of any thoughts, recollections, or desires—even for freedom from this persecution. With her husband, and several of her children, most likely dead or dying from their wounds, all she knew was terror.

In this trancelike state, Duston failed to mark the captives in front of her diverting from the path until she felt Mary Neff clutch at her arm and draw up short. There on the half-frozen ground was a dead Englishman, stripped naked and disemboweled, lying right where she was about to tread. Steam was rising from the mass of bloody entrails piled up beside the corpse, which emitted the overpowering stench of blood even in the cold air, like a newly slaughtered pig or oxen. The front part of the man's skull, including his face, had been nearly shorn off by the force of the blow. Apparently he had been overtaken while making his way toward the settlement earlier that morning, perhaps on his return from hunting. It did not matter now. Because of his wounds, Duston would not have recognized the man even if he had been their closest neighbor.

They had not paused before the corpse longer than a few seconds when the women drew the ire of one of their captors. The Indian, a chieftain or sachem, was attired in nothing but a breechclout, with a string of bear teeth around his neck. His hair, which had been plucked or shaved back from his forehead, was long and thick with bear grease, worn in a braid that was strung with bits of metal and seashells. He had a pole-ax in his hand and raised it to shoulder height, gesturing up the trail. Quickly, Goodwives Duston and Neff, and the English boy, who had just come up, veered around the dead man, the three captives rushing ahead in silence.

Several captives and a few warriors had already rounded a bend in the trail, heading northwest, away from the ice-clogged span of Little River. But the chieftain kept pace alongside the two women and the boy, occasionally hefting his ax and taking it up with both hands. He was half-starved and gaunt, his eyes deep in the hollows of his skull, with sinews running downward from his neck to the point of his shoulders, working in minute detail in his arms and across his chest when he repositioned the ax. The Indian was smeared all over with a grainy, oxidized paint the color of iron; he appeared neither young nor old, his bony face streaked with red and black markings radiating outward from his hooded eyes and upward, over his brow, giving him a frightening visage. His clan sign—a fish—was emblazoned across his torso in bright yellow and vermilion against a black background. A long scar gouged his ribcage from a previous battle, and one of his ears was mangled.

Duston had known so-called praying Indians—those who had converted to Christianity and either lived among whites in the settlements or in nearby encampments known as "praying towns." Although there were very few, if any, Pentuckets residing in the vicinity of Haverhill during Goodwife Duston's lifetime, there's little doubt she had seen Indians during her infrequent trips to Rowley and Salem, as well as the occasional Christian Indian who paddled downriver to do some trading. But she had never seen a strange Indian—accoutered for war, his blood up, and in a killing mood—before that day.

The sachem was an Abenaki, from one of the fierce river tribes in Maine, known collectively as the Tarrantines. These Indians, most likely the Androscoggins and the Sacos, who not long before had offered sanctuary to the warlike Kancamagus of the Pennacooks, had descended on Haverhill two years earlier and taken young Isaac Bradley and Joseph Whittaker captive. Boys of twelve or thirteen were suitable for adoption into the tribe: too small to fight back, but strong enough to work, and young enough to eventually forget the settlements and farms they were taken from.

The English lad who was with the Tarrantines on this particular raid looked about the same age as Hannah's own son Nathaniel, who was twelve. At first glance, Duston and the other captives probably took the boy for one of the Indians. His hair, falling to his shoulders, was lank and ragged; grime covered his face and neck, and he was dressed in a pair of foul-looking trousers and a torn deerskin mantle. He also walked freely among the Indians, without the stooped furtiveness of the other captives. But when Goodwife Duston had put on the dead man's shoe that the lad had brought to her, their eyes met, and it was plain he was English.

The boy spoke at least a few words of the Tarrantines' language, enough that the young chieftain lowered his ax, replied in an offhand manner, and with a last baleful glare at the two English women, continued up the trail. It took Duston another moment before she realized that he was the savage who had grabbed baby Martha away from them a half hour earlier. So it was here that a new emotion—something besides fear—must have been planted in Hannah's breast, lodging itself there like a knot in a tree. She felt the knurl of it, hard and rough. But more Indians came up and dogged their heels, gesturing the captives onward.

The boy remained beside the two women, going on in silence. Up and down they went, over hillocks and into snow-filled gullies and washes, and across frozen brooks. Their breathing was labored. Presently another Indian, the boy's master, came up and spoke to him and then passed onward, with several other Indians and another cluster of whites still behind them. Dwarf pines, jacketed with snow, were clustered thickly beneath the tall, skeletal birch trees. Together the party climbed a larger series of hills, descending into snowy ravines each time. Off to their right, the sun was little more than an hour in the sky, obscured by a large gray mass of clouds. The captives staggered along, not knowing or caring about their destination, living moment to moment. The last dwelling house of the settlement was far behind and growing more distant as they mastered each obstacle before them.

At length, the war party and their captives emerged from some fir trees, crossing a field of thigh-high sedge and skirting a small pond, which was skimmed over with ice. The boy captive indicated they should drink, and each of them knelt quickly, punched a hole in the thin ice, and drank several handfuls of the cold, sweet water before the Indians roused them to their feet. They were steered across an oval plain covered in a brittle layer of snow that crunched underfoot. Ahead was a knoll that rose from the patchwork of dried marshes, old Indian fields, and bands of tall gray trees that ran back over the ridge the way they had come. At the top of this hill, with a stand of fir trees backgrounding them, the Indians stopped, flinging down their stolen bounty. By an ancient oak tree that had been toppled by lightning, the Indians pointed with their hatchets and lances, forcing the captives to sit on the ground.

From a blackened split in the tree, the savages removed a few bundles wrapped in moose hide. Working quickly, the Indians, steam rising from their bare heads and torsos, unrolled the bundles and began pulling out ragged items of clothing, almost all of them made from animal hide. The mantles, simple deerskin or raccoon capes worn with the fur against the skin, were tied in a knot at the peak of the left shoulder, leaving the right arm exposed. Fit snugly about the waist with a hollow belt made of woven fibers and reeds, the mantle fell to mid-thigh with a tail, or flag as it was called, hanging in the back. Next, the warriors donned their leggings: well-worn deerskin punched with an awl and sewn into a tube. These hung from the belt by lateral thongs and were fastened beneath the foot, many of them fringed or imprinted down the outer length with clan images of the fish or bear. The captives, shivering on the ground, soon realized that the savages were preparing themselves for a much longer march, through cold, hard country.

From this vantage point, Goodwife Duston and the other captives gazed back over their route, traced easily through the beaten-down rushes and trammeled snow along the edge of the pond. Anyone following the war party would be visible for nearly half a mile, with nothing but a few shallow ravines that veined the lowlands to offer cover. But no one pursued them. The militia was not coming, and Duston's heart must have sunk.

While the Indians wrapped the iron tools, household items, bolts of cloth, and food they had stolen in the deerskin bundles, from across the vale a few tiny figures gradually enlarged to reveal four Indians running fast and steadily over the open ground. They dropped from the ridgeline opposite where the captives looked on, plunged into the first ravine, and, heads bobbing, their strides tossing up clods of snow, made their way swiftly past the frozen pond, through the gray tangle of the meadow, and up the near slope.

The Indians who had guarded the retreat from Haverhill now rejoined their brethren, steaming and snorting from the effort; one of them, doubled over with his hands upon his knees, began retching. He had a gash on his upper arm, the blood having spattered his hand, and with the agitation of that bloody hand he had made prints upon his breechclout. No Indian offered him any word or gesture of solace, and in less than a minute he had straightened up and began to exhibit the same impassive expression as the others.

So, having finished retying their moccasins and thongs, the other Indians rose from the ground, and chucking a deerskin bundle to the scouts who had just returned, they arranged their bobcat skins and tightened their belts and gaiters. The raid had been successful to this point, and now they were determined to move their captives north to an Abenaki village, probably the French mission at Chaudière, 250 miles distant. Here they could sell their captives to the French, who would trade them to the English for French prisoners, or sell them back to their families. One or two, including the English lad who traveled with them, might be adopted into the tribe to replace a warrior who had been killed on the journey. Just as beaver furs were an important commodity in this New World, human lives were frequently bought, sold, and traded between enemies, or abroad through the slave markets.

Standing by the blasted tree, the Indians spoke to one another in a language unfamiliar to the whites. Then one of the savages retrieved his papist beads, and a group of them knelt together and prayed in the manner they had learned from the Jesuit priests. Following this, a warrior took an earthenware bowl from the pile of stolen goods and ran downhill to fill it with water from the pond. Upon his return, each of the Indians removed a palm full of Nokehick, or "no-cake"—Indian corn that had been parched and pounded into meal—from the hollow of his belt or from a narrow skin bag, washing it down with the cold water. The settlers looked on, but were given nothing to eat or drink.

Wrenched from their homes at daybreak and two hours beyond their customary first meal, the surviving captives were exhausted from their rapid flight into the wilderness. All about them, with tomahawks and knives at the ready, the savages were moving about in a confident manner. They were outfitted for the weather, knew their way through the country, and seemed to have suffered few injuries, or even any significant discomfort. Huddled together on the ground, the settlers were cold, wet, hungry, and miserable. Now that some of them, at least, realized that their present situation offered no more than a prelude to the grueling journey that awaited them, they stood and began milling about. To soothe themselves, and to demonstrate to the Indians that they were not planning to escape, the settlers gathered by the crooked tree and began to pray. Someone recommended the Gospel of Matthew, and in a quavering voice one of the men recited Chapter 11, a passage that Goodwife Duston had always found comforting:

"Come to me, all you who are weary and burdened, and I will give you rest. Take my yoke upon you and learn from me, for I am gentle and humble in heart, and you will find rest for your souls. For my yoke is easy and my burden is light."

Though the savages had said their own prayers without interruption, they drew near to the captives and began mocking and deriding them. Among them was Hannah Duston's master, who had killed baby Martha and threatened her and Goodwife Neff with his ax. The sachem, who spoke a little English, barged into the prayer circle, laughing and taunting them. Jeering at the two women in particular, the Indian strutted up and down, in effect daring them to continue. But Goodwife Duston raised her eyes to his and held the warrior's gaze. With the savage just inches away, the war paint swirled over his face in a nightmarish vision, she was bolstered by a psalm she had been taught as a girl.

Give sentence with me, O God, and defend my cause against the ungodly people; O deliver me from the deceitful and wicked man. For thou art the God of my strength; why hast thou put me from thee? and why go I so heavily, while the enemy oppresseth me?

Gamboling about, the Indian seemed more in a playful mood than a bloody-minded one, though the savages were known to change their minds rapidly. For her part, Goodwife Duston was not inclined to turn her gaze downward, or otherwise act submissive. After all, she probably believed that her entire family was now dead. And Duston had seen the most innocent of the captives, her newborn infant, slaughtered against a tree, and two other neighbors slain without remorse.

Staring across the open vale, in a small but audible voice, she recited from Psalm 43:

"O send out thy light and thy truth, that they may lead me, and bring me unto the holy hill, and to thy dwelling; And that I may go unto the altar of God, even unto the God of my joy and gladness; and unto the harp will I give thanks unto thee, O God, my God."

Although this insolence may have angered her master, the other Indians continued to laugh and jibe with one another, and through some kind of social restraint, the sachem did not raise his ax or his hatchet against her. Then the captive boy spoke to the Indian in his own language and led Goodwife Duston away.

Meanwhile, the savages, dressed in their hides and bristling with weapons, made ready to depart. The whites, forced to carry the bundles of stolen food and other goods, were herded together and started along the trail. From height of land, Duston, a little apart from the rest, gazed back at the horizon, and the distant plumes of smoke that appeared above the village. At the bottom of the ravine a soft white rind drifted in tendrils over the ground and was whipped away by the breeze. As the Indians began padding away, the only sound was the wind cresting the knoll and rattling the uppermost branches of the trees.

Nothing but hazy vistas greeted Goodwife Duston in every direction, the forest ridged like a dark blue sea: vast, uncharted, and lost to history. As she looked on, Duston understood the temptation suffered by Lot's wife, gazing back upon Sodom, and the wages thus demanded of her. Only one thing was now certain: God had brought them to this desolate place for His own reasons, and only God could deliver them.

Suddenly a voice barked at her, and Duston was jabbed in the ribs. Without looking back, she hoisted up her bundle and continued on.

During the period in King William's War when Haverhill was attacked, the French colonial government was engaged on a number of fronts simultaneously. Even before the explorer Rene Robert Cavelier de La Salle had claimed all the territory drained by the Mississippi River for King Louis XIV in 1682, the French had been fighting for dominance in the west, while coveting the enormous fur trapping and fishing grounds from the eastern seaboard to the Great Lakes. They maintained a running war with the five tribes of the Iroquois for control of Hudson Bay; declared their sovereignty over Newfoundland; and were fighting the English, specifically the "Bostonnais," for Acadia, a huge, mostly unsettled wilderness that included Nova Scotia, New Brunswick, and nearly all of Maine. The bloody competition over the fur trade, which for several decades also involved the Dutch and the Swedes, eventually settled into a prolonged frontier struggle between France and England. Though the Haverhill captives could scarcely have been aware of this, their farms and homesteads represented the southernmost boundary that the French had thus far attempted to establish.

The fact that colonial authorities on both the English and French sides, including government, military, and religious leaders, were a remarkably vain, conniving, greedy, and thin-skinned lot, further complicated what was a thorny situation to begin with. During an era when their respective monarchs were frequently embroiled in armed conflict with one another, the difficult passage of ships across the North Atlantic ceased during the long, tumultuous New England winters, interrupting the exchange of official correspondence and leaving the colonial governments to their own infernal devices. The appointed royal governors and their religious counterparts—particularly the Jesuits in French Canada, and an array of Puritan clergymen to the south—often acted like ill-tempered children, constantly running afoul of one another in the darkest months of the year. Then, in springtime, they began pleading their cases in a barrage of obsequious letters to the royal court, insisting on more guns, ammunition, money, troops, and frequent confirmations of their presiding authority. Preoccupied with other, domestic intrigues within Versailles or the Court of St. James, the French and English monarchs would be called upon to sort out the problems of their subjects thousands of miles away, in a mist-shrouded wilderness they had never visited, populated by bands of cruel savages that did not recognize their authority or comply with their edicts.

At least on the surface, the French colonial government seemed to have two distinct advantages over the English, and one significant disadvantage: Their economy was based more on the fur trade than agriculture, which meant that a good number of their most adventurous settlers ranged far afield, dealing with a myriad of hardships while exploring new territory. (In

1535, the French explorer Jacques Cartier sailed up the St. Lawrence. Five years later, Cartier ordered the construction of a fort—not a farm—on the hill at Quebec.) French trappers and bushrangers were more intrepid and mobile than their agrarian opposites: accustomed to traveling in extreme weather, making their living by the gun and the hatchet, and routinely trading with the Indians. Also, French missionaries, especially the proud, learned Jesuits, who possessed, among other significant attributes, a keen sense of divine entitlement, seemed more willing than the English clergy to endure harsh conditions in their effort to win Indian converts. They also were more likely to advocate for cruelty and terror as useful elements in what they considered a holy war against the infidels.

Beyond the machinations of the Jesuits, French military officers were generally more competent, professional, and bold than the English militia commanders. The French were also willing to take the fight to the southern frontier, far from their stronghold in Quebec, and were adept at making allies among the warlike Indian tribes. But their most formidable enemy, lurking to the west, hampered this expansionist philosophy. The "fivefold league" of the Iroquois—Mohawks, Oneidas, Onondagas, Cayugas, and Senecas—were skilled fighters, hardened by decades of incessant warfare with other tribes, inured to the cold, skillful in their tactics, and wild and bloodthirsty in the field. The Iroquois also controlled the vast territory west of the lake tribes, including the Huron and Ottawa (who were terrified of them), hindering their adversary's ability to trap and trade there. At critical junctures, this dynamic strangled the French colonial economy, allowing the English to add or fortify settlements in Maine and Massachusetts.

By 1690, English military victories in Acadia and the desirability of their trade had several Abenaki tribes on the verge of making peace with the Bostonnais. These developments compelled King Louis XIV of France to urge his colony to stir up the Abenaki to attack the English, before any lasting truce could take hold. Certainly, these tribes were well situated to damage English expansion in the territory. From Chedabucto (later called Halifax), on the eastern coast of Nova Scotia, where the French occupied a fishing station and rude fortifications, far southward along the coast to the English settlements of Piscataqua, York, Wells, Oyster River, and Haverhill, there were few inhabitants besides scattered bands of the Abenaki—"a race as wild as their haunts."

They were river Indians, quartered on the Saco, Penobscot, Androscoggin, St. John, St. Croix, and the Kennebec. They planted their crops upriver in springtime, traveling by canoe to the rugged coastal inlets to fish, gather clams and oysters, and shoot water-fowl and seals; in autumn, they returned to the river valleys to harvest their beans, corn, and pumpkins, then spent the winter hunting for caribou, moose, bears, beavers, and deer. In the war of persuasion and conversion waged by the colonial powers, the French Jesuit and seminary priests got to these remote tribes first, baptizing them into the Catholic faith, celebrating mass in crude wooden chapels, and sending them to plunder the English frontier.

Second only to the Iroquois in war craft, cruelty, and physical endurance, the Abenaki shared untold square miles of dense wilderness with just a tiny, scattered contingent of French traders, fishermen, clergy, and *coureurs de bois*, or bushrangers. In fair weather and foul, these Indians traveled over well beaten paths to visit their brethren at the mission villages on the St. Lawrence and to trade for arms, ammunition, and liquor with their French masters, an arrangement overseen by the provincial governor, Count Frontenac. By providing the Abenaki with bounty for their captives (while also stirring them up with tales of the English incursion on their fishing and hunting grounds), Frontenac cultivated this agile, aggressive, and unpredictable Indian force, which stood between the French settlements in Quebec and the English strongholds at Boston and Albany, New York.

This arrangement had its difficulties. Due to the vast distances that separated the Acadian villages—at Chedabucto, and along the Bay of Fundy—from the government in Quebec, French settlers often found it more convenient to trade by sea with the Bostonnais, enraging French officials and exposing those rustic colonials to the danger of "parliamentary ideas" and the heresy of Puritan beliefs. The fact that many French officials and military officers in the region also carried out illegal trade with the Bostonnais—including the curé at Port Royal, a French priest named Father Petit—did not simplify Frontenac's problems. Beyond that, the English conducted a few successful raids by sea, capturing the French fort at Chedabucto, along with two French naval vessels.

Barring new peace negotiations, the Abenaki blocked English access to the settlements in Quebec by commanding the trails and passes through the northern woods in New Hampshire and Maine. Therefore, the entire

French diplomatic and military strategy in the territory, according to Villebon, sent by King Louis XIV to govern Acadia, was to "prevent the Abenakis from occupying themselves in anything but war." Eventually, Governor Villebon ordered the militia to construct a fort on high ground overlooking the St. John River, near the present-day location of Fredericton, New Brunswick. Far from the Atlantic Ocean, and separated from New England by miles of trackless forest, Villebon's command was unassailable, allowing him to summon Tarrantines to the post and entice them to form war parties.

Governor Villebon and his compatriots, including a missionary priest named Thury, who was shepherd to the Penobscots, soon began inciting the river tribes to mount assaults against the English frontier. In January 1691, 150 Penobscot warriors, joined by a band of Kennebecs and a few Canadian militia, made an arduous journey southward to York, Maine, traveling over the frozen rivers and streams on their snowshoes. By February 4th, they had ascended Mount Agamenticus, where they maintained a cold camp, not wanting to alert the English settlement below with the smoke from their fires.

At dawn, using tactics nearly identical to those employed six years later at Haverhill, the Indians fired a shot to begin the attack, and with war whoops and screams, fell upon the village in the midst of a snowstorm. Various French accounts insist that eighty residents were taken captive and approximately one hundred English settlers, many of whom were women and children, were killed, often in gruesome ways. Reverend John Pike, of Newbury, Massachusetts, who would later record Hannah Duston's ordeal in his journal, listed the English casualties at York as forty-eight killed and twenty-three taken captive. Most of the village was burned to the ground, as well as dozens of neighboring homesteads and farms. Livestock was slaughtered in large numbers, and the invaders carried away nearly everything of value, both real and perceived.

In a final indignity, an elderly local minister, a graduate of Harvard College and figure of respect in the community, was shot dead as he attempted to mount his horse. After the carnage had ended, one of the Abenaki warriors donned the slain clergyman's robes and delivered an insulting lecture to a group of frightened prisoners. When the Abenaki returned to Villebon's stronghold on the St. John River, they were feted with elaborate speeches and gifts, war songs, and barrels of French wine.

Now that the Abenaki had been bloodied, the French rallied them to strike an even heavier blow against the English. Joined by seasoned Canadian militia, as well as bands of Micmac and Malacite warriors from Atlantic Canada, a large war party of Kennebecs and Penobscots amounting to more than four hundred combatants paddled across Penobscot Bay in 1692, intent on the English town at Wells, Maine. Luckily for the settlement, which had been attacked the year before, the remaining English were a tough lot, most of them handy with a rifle and already barricaded in the five garrison houses when the raiders arrived on June 9th.

Commanded by the resourceful Captain Convers, a detachment of fifteen militia occupied the largest of these structures, which was surrounded by a tall palisade of sharpened logs. As the combined French and Abenaki force drew closer, the English were reinforced by three small vessels that sailed up a neighboring stream, containing fourteen additional men and valuable supplies. All of this good luck would be required in the furious defense of Wells that ensued.

The Indians, spurred on by French officers in full regalia, attacked the sloops that were now tide-bound in the estuary, while another force ran full tilt, whooping and screeching, toward Convers and his men in the garrison house. But the sailors aboard the vessels and the militia inside the house were veteran campaigners, picking their targets and returning fire with deadly accuracy. Eventually, the tidewaters rose, giving the boats some maneuverability, while the defense of the garrison house continued. After a period of sniping from their loopholes, there was a brief lull, whereupon Convers and his militia steeled themselves for the direct assault they feared was imminent.

The Indians, naked or nearly so, painted for war and spattered by the blood of settlers they had murdered on their farms, emitted a horrible din of screaming and yelping. One of the English soldiers, perhaps unnerved by this display, mentioned the possibility of surrendering to the French officers. Hearing this, Captain Convers growled, "If you say that again, you are a dead man."

Indian tactics, so often successful when they caught an enemy unawares, precluded the sort of mass attack that would have overwhelmed the tiny garrison. Even the spirited harangue of a French officer couldn't convince the raiders to abandon their practice. Instead, the Abenaki continued to scream, caper about, and fire intermittently on Convers and his men. One warrior, who spoke a little English, dared the militia to fight them on open ground. In response, the settlers laughed and hooted. Supported by their women, who supplied ammunition and loaded the extra muskets, Convers and his detachment kept up a steady rate of fire.

Again the warrior called out, "If you are so bold, why do you stay in a garrison house like a squaw? Come out and fight like a man."

But Convers would not be provoked. "Do you think I am fool enough to come out with thirty men to fight five hundred?" he asked. Another Indian shouted that the raiders would cut the English "small as tobacco before morning," to which Convers responded with an oath.

Losing interest, the Abenaki turned their attention to burning and looting the village, slaughtering cattle and horses, and attempting to set fire to the sloops by sending a burning raft floating down the creek. This gambit was unsuccessful, and the war party soon gave up, turning northward for home.

Captain Convers wasn't through fighting. In the following year, 1693, he and a large party of militia ranged into Abenaki territory, building a stone fort on the Saco River. Soon afterward, there was a peace conference, where representatives from thirteen Maine tribes signed a treaty with Massachusetts authorities. This development, in turn, led to new machinations by Villebon, the French governor of Acadia; more feasting and flattery; sumptuous gifts, including twenty-five hundred pounds of gunpowder and six thousand pounds of lead conveyed to the Abenakis; and a trip to Versailles for two of their sagamores.

Villebon, as adept at convincing the Indians to break treaties as the English were at brokering them, with Father Thury and an enterprising French officer named Villieu as his agents, persuaded the most contentious of the Abenaki chiefs, a firebrand named Taxous, that peace had been struck without consulting him. Taxous perceived this as a grave insult, as the French had hoped. Soon he and his volatile band of warriors, accompanied by Villieu, Thury, and other malcontent Indians, began the long wilderness trek to Oyster River, later renamed Durham, an English settlement twelve miles upriver from Portsmouth.

Traveling by canoe to the frontier, 105 warriors, the priest, and Villieu were joined by mission Indians from the St. Lawrence and a band of Kennebecs, which more than doubled their number. The town, situated along the river and consisting of a dozen garrison houses, a church, mill, and scattered farmhouses, was sleepy and unguarded when the Indians approached. Day had not quite broken when Taxous's warriors, positioned at strategic points overlooking the village, responded to the single gunshot that marked the attack by descending in a fury.

A settler named Thomas Bickford maintained a fortified house close to the river. Alerted by the first crackle of gunfire, and with no militia garrisoned there to assist him, Bickford hurried his family into a small boat and pointed it downriver. Immediately he withdrew to the house, barred his gate and narrow door, and cleared several firing positions. Using the sort of ingenuity that was key to survival on the frontier, Bickford moved from window to loophole and back again when the raiders advanced, discharging his musket and issuing orders in a loud voice, as if half a dozen men were occupying the house.

Bickford added a touch of dramaturgy to his ruse by changing in and out of various coats, hats, and caps as he charged about the house. Stymied by this *mise en scene*, and what they thought was significant opposition, the Indians quit the area.

Those in the other, unprotected houses were not so fortunate. More than a hundred residents, many of them women and children torn from their beds, were killed: tomahawked, bludgeoned, lanced, or shot down as they tried to flee. The Indians also rampaged through the surrounding countryside for six or seven miles, burning down more than twenty houses and making off with a total of twenty-seven captives while committing several atrocities along the way. (Taxous and fifty warriors, eager for more scalps, journeyed onward, and a few days later assaulted the town of Groton, Massachusetts, slaughtering an additional forty English settlers.)

During the carnage at Oyster River, Father Thury went into the local church, which had been left untouched by the Indians. Taking up a piece of chalk, the haughty cleric wrote a message of some sort on the pulpit. (Since it was most likely in Latin, or perhaps in French, the specifics of his parting missive are unknown.) Amidst the burning wreckage of the town, Father Thury proceeded to celebrate mass for the jubilant savages; then he, Villieu, and the Indians withdrew to the rallying point where they had stashed their canoes.

Bloody events like the raids on York, Wells, Oyster River, and, a few years later, Haverhill, were caused by the tectonic shifts of two continents—the inexorable movement of the New World and the old one toward each other. But powerful, stubborn individuals also nudged things along. Nearly all of these were white males interested in gaining riches, prominence, prestige, or all three. Often possessing a rough-hewn, frontier charisma, these men included Governor Villebon, Father Thury, and Count Frontenac himself, an intriguing figure, who struck the perfect balance between flattering the Indians with his eloquence and bonhomie, and casting himself as the Great White Father, who would be disobeyed at the Indians' peril.

But not even Frontenac could control the Machiavellian plotting of the Acadian priests. Although the Indians were properly baptized into the Catholic Church, taught to pray the rosary and venerate the Host, they were also told that Jesus was a Frenchman born in Bethlehem, a town in France. (This dubious catechism included the assertion that the Virgin Mary was a French lady, and that it was the English who murdered Christ.) By the winter of 1697, the Maine priests and those of the mission villages in Canada had used this peculiar brand of theological chicanery to litter the frontier with corpses. But even after their devastating attacks on York and Oyster River, the French clerics learned that the English would not be easily pushed off their marks. Certainly, wilderness fighters like Captain Convers and Thomas Bickford lacked the outsize personalities and expansive social vision of Frontenac, Villebon, and Thury. But they were capable, resolute men, obstinate in their beliefs and dogged in their efforts to resist the French incursion into their territory.

Perhaps no individual embodied these qualities more than a thirty-nine-year-old English woman, who, in the waning light of March 15, 1697, was several miles northwest of Haverhill, Massachusetts, trudging through snowdrifts with the other captives, in possession of little else but her will to survive.

All that terrible day, Goodwives Duston and Neff were hurried northward without more than a few minutes of rest, and nothing to eat or drink. By mid afternoon, warmer air had descended through the crabbed branches of the trees, bringing up a thick ground fog that swirled around the Indians and their captives as they walked.

After departing the ridge that allowed their final glimpse of the settlement, the party crossed a series of whaleback hills, or drumlins, long gradual rises that were grouped in pairs throughout the locale. From the tallest of these, the captives gazed at a vista that promised nothing more than a succession of these hills, and the reaches of what appeared to be an endless forest.

The trace followed Little River again, then veered northwest past a series of icy kettle ponds, over some rocky ground, and then onward to more hills. Along the way, shifting banks of fog, some of them enormous, obliterated segments of the landscape. This effect gave the captives the impression they had left Haverhill entirely and were traveling through a spirit world—perhaps even the land of the dead. In low-lying areas between the hills, trees grew so thickly that many of them were nothing but tall black spires, devoid of their branches and gleaming in the half-light. They appeared so suddenly in the mist that more than once Duston believed an ominous figure had materialized before her, though whether it was a specter or a forewarning of what was to come, she did not reckon. Often enough, Duston walked straight into one of these gnarled trees, banging her shoulder or cutting open a shin.

Up one hill and down another, loomed over by the ghostly trees, the band of captives plodded along in snow that often rose to their thighs. The Indians, emptying two or three of their remaining bundles, withdrew several pair of snowshoes made from rounded boughs of white oak and strips of hide, allowing them to pass over the crusted snow. But the captives often plunged through the brittle top layer, digging a posthole with every step.

At the end of her strength, Duston was forced to climb an enormous, double peaked hill, nearly toppling into a ravine when the fog prevented her from seeing she had reached the summit. A cold rain fell steadily now, like a million needles against the skin, and her left foot, covered with the dead man's shoe, burned with a kind of fever. The rain, dimpling the snowy hillside below, drew up such a copious measure of fog that the embankment appeared to smolder, as if, moving just ahead of them, a wildfire had ravaged the countryside.

The sun, which had been obscured by clouds and fog all day, had slipped behind the bulwark of hills to the west. Descending the slope, Hannah and Mary Neff picked their way among a thicket of young trees, the air and sky enveloping them in dense gray vapors. Occasionally they spotted the young Worcester boy off to their left or right, though never far away, flitting between the trees.

Just as Hannah decided she couldn't go on, a decision that would surely result in her getting knocked in the head with a pole-ax, the Indians threw down the light burdens they were carrying and began to exult. The place they had chosen was little more than a swamp, a thickly forested bog consisting of little patches of dry ground and tufted weeds still crested with snow. Nearby was a tiny creek that had overflowed, which supplied the Indians with fresh water, and the mossy trees and low ground provided good cover, as well as protection from the wind. A mass of charred sticks on the ground indicated that the Indians had camped here before, and several of them now rummaged through the undergrowth for dry branches and tinder.

Digging into recesses of feathery brush, bracken, and lopsided piles of deadwood that the rain, drumming against the snow, had not penetrated, the Indians brought this material to a crescent of dry land—a kind of shoal in the midst of the bog—and erected a canopy of pine branches and boughs. Here they made preparations for a fire, amassing a great mound of duff and twigs and moss beneath the canopy, adding long strips of bark from the underside of a fallen birch that they shredded into what looked like horsehair.

Sitting against a tree, Duston watched these movements carefully, since neither she, nor any of the other prisoners, including the boy, knew what the Indians intended to do next. All day each of the captives had fretted privately about where they were heading and what would occur when—if—they got there. Goodwife Duston looked on as the boy's master, whom he called Bampico, crouched by the pile of shredded bark and twigs. He wasn't carrying the steel and flint that the English used to start a fire. Instead, from a little bag made from a woodchuck's skin, Bampico took out a faceted mineral stone and, tied fast to the end of a little stick, another small, flat stone, a contraption that looked like a miniature wand, or pole-ax.

With just a few light strokes of the awl, the Indian dropped first one, then a second glowing spark into the gray fluff of the touchwood. A ribbon of smoke rose up, wavered and thickened, and the light in Bampico's hands intensified, grew larger, and then burst upward in a reddish yellow plume, igniting the punk. The Indian added a few slender twigs he had put aside, and fire was established.

Hannah didn't dare move any closer to the fire. The hem of her skirt was soaking wet, heavy with mud, and she couldn't halt the tremor in her limbs or the clattering of her jaw. Cold, dry air would have been preferable to the chill that enveloped her, with the dampness intensifying as the day receded. When it grew dark, the silvery water that filled the depression where the Indians had made their camp seemed to rise higher, leaving only tiny hillocks of dry ground, humped up tufts of bulrushes, or the exposed roots of trees, often just enough for a single person to draw up his or her knees, and wait out the night.

Soon the Indians had a ragged blaze going and were stamping around on the little shoal and yelling, their warped shadows thrown up against the overhanging trees. No one was guarding the captives, nor had they been bound to one another or restrained in any fashion. There was no reason to. The wilderness was their jailer; water nearly surrounded them, thousands of trees less than a yard apart grew in every direction, and the gloaming hung overhead like a shroud.

At first it may have seemed imprudent for the savages to light a fire, and interrupt the stillness with their yelps and cries, for fear that militia from Haverhill or nearby Rowley had followed their tracks. But without seeming to do so, they had taken several precautions that limited the possibility of their detection. Two hours earlier, a pair of runners had broken off from the party and headed back toward the settlement, as another group of warriors had done in the immediate aftermath of the raid that morning. Now they returned, bare-chested and bare-legged, panting like animals that had been driven to exhaustion, streaming with perspiration and, by turns, gagging, clearing their throats, and expectorating in the direction of the fire. Judging by the frenzied reaction of the other savages, the Abenaki were confident that no one was pursuing them and grew even more raucous. From their various locations on the periphery, the captives no doubt felt the last of their hopes plummeting into despair.

But Hannah refused to drop her head or make bargains with herself. The situation was so desperate, and her various pains and discomforts, some physical and others emotional and spiritual, so insurmountable that she probably began to think of herself as already dead—as having joined her kinsmen in a netherworld as dim and insubstantial as the place she now found herself in.

Still, Goodwife Duston, who had spent two-thirds of her life out of doors, couldn't help but admire the Abenaki's skill in woodcraft. Perhaps foremost, the Indians had built their fire in the lee of the hill, which shielded the glow of the flames from anyone that wasn't close on their heels. Smoke from the blaze mingled with the fog drifting over the lowland where they had encamped, and the snow-padded brow of the hill no doubt muffled their howls and screams. As night fell, they would be even harder to locate. Even if the camp was discovered, musket balls fired from a distance would have little chance of breeching the natural palisade formed by the trees all around them. And the fact they inhabited a swamp packed with so many trees and saplings made it impossible for an enemy to approach quickly or attack them in force.

The ground was saturated but for the tiny piece of land where the Indians had built their fire, which made for very slow going afoot. When the bonfire had fully caught, the savages began extracting a number of items from the loads they had forced onto the captives. Roaring and yipping while they danced about, the Indians produced chunks of bloody meat they had looted from the settlement: venison and bear haunch and quarters of roasting beef, which they impaled on sticks, rotated on a spit, or threw into a stolen kettle with some of the dirty water from the swamp.

Also yanked from the bundles were silver candlesticks; women's dresses and kerchiefs; bolts of cloth; embroidered linens and other finery; household tools, wooden bowls, and copper kettles; and several long knives and hatchets. There was also a brace of pistols and two long guns. Sitting nearby, each perched on an exposed root or tussock of dried grass, the captives looked on with dejection, or buried their faces in their hands. Goodwife Duston noticed the cloth that had been torn from her loom—nearly three weeks' labor—was draped over her master's shoulder as a mantle, while he thrust his lance at the sky and yelped like a demon.

Huddled there, unprotected from the wires of cold rain falling between the trees, Hannah must have seen in her mind's eye the burning farmhouse; her children scattered and crying; her husband, Thomas, his hair askew, with a glancing look of terror and hatred on his face as he stood in the doorway yelling about the raid. Then, still trying to focus her mind elsewhere, Duston was visited by the image she could least resist:

week-old Martha, her tiny red face pinched and suffering, as the triumphant savage raised the infant by the heels and shattered her skull against the tree.

That event, along with the other hardships of the day, weighed upon Goodwife Duston. They had traveled a long way at a furious pace, with nothing to eat and very little rest. Duston had walked that far at least once before, to Newbury, with her husband and two of the eldest children, Elizabeth and young Thomas. They had gone there on the sabbath, after their minister, the Reverend Benjamin Rolfe of Haverhill, had taken ill and was not able to conduct services.

Since the settlers were compelled by law to attend worship, and with Thomas having some matters before the town assembly, on that Saturday afternoon, which was considered part of the Sabbath, they departed Haverhill for the arduous trip. Bringing along the horse made the travel a little easier, as each was allowed to ride for a mile or so, in his turn.

Following the well-worn cart path that ran along the Merrimack River, the Dustons arrived in Newbury well after midnight. Public services began at nine in the morning on Sunday and occupied the next six hours, whereupon the family went back by the same route, finally arriving at their homestead long after darkness had fallen.

That darkness gathered about her now. And with the savages leaping and cavorting around the fire, Duston estimated they had so far journeyed about a dozen miles into the wilderness, which was also the distance to Newbury. Only this time, they had not encountered another living person all day, or witnessed so much as a flutter of smoke from a chimney. Perhaps it was true what Goodwife Duston had heard: not a single white person resided between here and Quebec, which was still a vast distance away.

Resting on a clump of bulrushes, her skirts held up to keep them out of the swamp, Hannah sat with her elbows on her knees and her chin resting on her clenched fists. Her left foot ached and her limbs felt heavy, while a keen hunger possessed her. The other captives were spread about the bog, watching the Indians in silence, nearly lost in the shadows. In her misery, Goodwife Duston recited a passage from Luke 17: "At the time of the banquet he sent his servant to tell those who had been invited: 'Come, for everything is now ready.'"

A few settlers glanced about in fear, but Mary Neff, standing close to Hannah, also bowed her head to pray. No sooner had Duston finished speaking when the Indian who had menaced them earlier broke off from the shivaree and waded across the bog, splashing knee-deep in the frigid water. The sachem was bare-chested, wearing only his breechclout and the cord strung with bear teeth around his neck. His eyes were bright, and the stones and seashells braided into his scalp lock made a jangling noise as he approached. Duston saw the Indian, but continued praying.

Halting a few feet away, the Indian regarded the captives with an amused expression. Over by the fire, he had speared a piece of venison with a stick, and now he tore off some meat and began chewing on it. In passing English, the sachem asked Duston why she was so dejected. When Hannah did not reply, the Indian told the captives there was no reason to concern themselves with praying.

"What need you trouble yourself?" he asked, in a mocking tone. "If your God will have you delivered, you shall be so."

Saying this, the Indian spat out a piece of gristle, sneered at them, and proceeded to stamp back through the water toward the fire.

The English boy was a short distance away. In fact, he always seemed to be nearby, watching. Though there were other female captives, he was determined, it seemed, to make himself useful to Hannah and Mary Neff. Before Goodwife Duston had even twitched a muscle in response to the Indian, the boy waded across the slough and knelt down beside her. Gesturing with his hand, he took Duston by the left ankle and eased off the dead man's shoe. Even in the poor light, her foot was visibly swollen and had a waxy, grayish-yellow sheen to it, mottled with a few white patches. Wincing, Hannah felt a deep pain within the bones of her foot, along with a terrific itching that ran up to her ankle. Her toes, pushed to one side and bleached to the shade of parchment, were altogether senseless.

The boy took a rag from his pocket and dried Hannah's foot and ankle by dabbing all around. Then he lifted up her foot and rubbed it gently for a minute or two, examining it as well as he could in the uneven light. Motioning for Duston to keep her foot out of the water, he sloshed over to a cluster of balsam firs, the tallest of which couldn't have exceeded ten feet. After some consideration, the boy selected the most robust of the fir trees and broke off several limbs where they attached to the trunk.

Upon his return, he paused further to strip a clump of dried oak leaves from another tree. The boy proceeded to stuff a fistful of these into Hannah's wet shoes, which he hung from a nearby sapling. Then he swaddled

Duston's afflicted foot in the rag, covering it the best he could, and started breaking the limbs of the fir tree into smaller pieces.

Finding a place to squat, the boy draped the largest oak leaves over his knee and began squeezing the pitch from the balsam onto the leaves. It was slow, tedious work, his hands growing filthy with the stuff, but eventually he had amassed a palmful of the sweet-smelling resin, which he mashed together with crumbled up oak leaves to form a poultice. Setting this aside, he untied the rag from Goodwife Duston's foot and once more dried her skin as thoroughly as possible.

Using the oak leaf to daub this salve onto Duston's foot, he spread it between her toes and over the bony promontories of her foot and ankle, then shook out the rag, compressed it around the wounded foot and tied it off again. A good portion of her flesh was still exposed, and when she realized this, Hannah groped beneath her skirts and produced the edge of her chemise. The boy foraged around in the muddy dell for an edged stone, and Hannah used it to tear a piece of dry cloth from her garment. The boy took the strip of material and wound it around the ankle and down over the rag, completing Duston's bandage.

Speaking for only the second time all day, the boy again told Hannah that his name was Sam Lenorson and that he had been taken from the settlement in Worcester some months before. Then he turned, plunging shin-deep into the swamp again.

The boy was industrious. He paced back and forth along a rim of snow-dusted ground that bordered the creek, where the earth was damp and matted with oak leaves and flattened clumps of sedge. After choosing a dead tree, he snapped off a branch and threw it on the ground. Sam tipped up the branch with his foot, resting one end of it on a rock; using this as a fulcrum, he stamped on the limb, breaking off a piece as long as his arm, and then prowled about with this simple digging stick, halting occasionally to probe at the ground. In the thicket were several vine-like plants that had entwined themselves on the tree trunks, rising to a height of three or four feet. Selecting the hardiest of these, which was of a thickness equal to the boy's finger, he began burrowing with his stick near the plant's root.

Having made several holes in proximity to each other, Sam grabbed the exposed root of the plant and began tugging on it. The root system, which ran to the other vines in a tangled network, writhed along beneath the surface of the ground like a serpent. Leaning back on his heels, the boy yanked so hard the root broke somewhere along its length, sending him onto his backside. Nevertheless, he succeeded in pulling a string of tubers from the muddy earth. There were five or six of them clinging to the thread-like root, each the size of a hen's egg and russet-colored like a potato. Digging and pulling and snapping at the root with his stick, the boy harvested enough of these groundnuts to fill his shirtfront, bringing them over to Hannah's location, where he dropped them in the milky water.

Next, Sam ranged around the periphery of the swamp, never quite beyond the limit of the firelight, digging up several more groundnuts and collecting as many acorns as he could find. Apparently, snow had covered them up until the rain fell, otherwise rodents would have scavenged them all.

The Indians did not object to the captives foraging for something to eat—they just refused to help. After Sam had finished gathering this repast, he uncovered a long, flat rock and placed it on the hot coals of the fire. After rinsing the groundnuts and acorns in the creek while allowing enough time to heat the rock, the boy arranged the tubers over the fire. Occasionally turning and pushing them about with his stick, within a short time Sam had roasted the groundnuts, then skimmed them off the rock onto a large scroll of birch bark that was lying nearby. Passing amongst the howling savages, he carried this meal to where Goodwives Duston and Neff sat watching him, and they ate.

As they split the fibrous tubers, the women burned their fingers and mouths, but this failed to deter them. Ravenous to the point of fainting, they devoured the smoking groundnuts, which had a potato-like flavor, and picked out the smooth white meats of the acorns, discarding their shells in the muddy water. When they had finished eating, the boy and the two women situated themselves as best they could with their backs against a large tree. The Indians continued their feasting and dancing and caterwauling long into the night, and the captives, no longer quite as hungry but chilled to the quick, nodded and started and jerked their limbs, in a state that approached and approximated sleep but never quite arrived there.

A half-hour before sunrise, Duston stirred at the first sign of motion in the camp. Amidst the circle of ashes left by the fire, several of the

Indians donned their deerskin mantles and moccasins and then prodded their fellows, who were still lying on the ground. Urinating into the
smoky fire pit and spitting, they ate handfuls of Nokehick washed down
by creek water, or else gnawed on the blackened joints of the previous
evening's feast, then tossed these bones into their ossuary. Soon the party
would be on the move.

Sore-limbed and stiff, Hannah roused Mary and then tied back her
skirt with vines to make gartered pantaloons that she secured around each
of her legs. The boy, rooting around by the smoky piles of the fire, came
back with a few stray groundnuts and, moving northward before they even
realized it, the captives gnawed at these roasted tubers as they walked.

On the second day, and even more so on the third and fourth, the
hills grew longer and steeper and white, covered with more snow than
the Haverhill captives had seen in over a month. Early on that fourth
day, while descending into a snowy ravine, Goodwife Duston's right leg
plunged through the crust to her hip, with her left foot, wrapped in ban-
dages and crammed into the shoe, remaining on top of the snow. It happened in an instant, throwing her awkwardly on her side, which made her
cry out.

Duston's master and two other Indians crowded around her, not from
any tender concern, but to see if she was able to keep going. Hannah possessed little doubt that her master, in particular, would take delight in killing her. But with Mary Neff and Sam Lenorson's assistance, she managed
to roll up on her left side, pull out her right foot, and stand up. A little
bit unsteady, Duston resumed walking under her own power, causing the
Indians to shrug and continue on at their usual rapid pace. Goodwife Neff
clutched at her mistress's elbow, no doubt realizing that if Duston had
been slow to get up, the Indians might have knocked both women in the
head and left them to the wolves.

The war party, now clearly on the retreat, did not travel as far between
the third and fourth removes as they had that first, horrific day. The terrain was more difficult, as winter lingered over the country, and the Indians appeared to be certain that they weren't being followed. Soon enough,
Goodwives Duston and Neff, guided by Sam Lenorson, began to follow close behind the Indians, who made a clear path through the drifts
with their snowshoes. Perhaps, in one of their moments alone, Goodwives Duston and Neff gazed back over their track and wondered why the

militia had not been called out from Newbury or Salem to pursue them. But they had probably determined, by the morning of the fourth day, that the task of locating the Indians at such a distance from the settlements would have been a difficult undertaking even for professional soldiers, and that the garrisons of Newbury and Haverhill were probably most concerned about their own vulnerability to attack.

By noon on that day, after enduring another short cold night and a long march, the party settled beside a small river. After meandering through a pine grove, the stream entered a wide, partially sunken marsh that was covered in snow. Scattered about were rust-colored cat o' nine tails and little tufts of saw grass and reeds that had broken through the snow. A scrim of ice edged outward from both banks of the river, but the middle of the channel was exposed. Carving an S across this plot of open ground, the black, almost metallic band of water eventually snaked around a bend to the west. In a swampy area near the tree line, there was a large, snow-covered pile of logs, gnawed at both ends, which indicated a beaver lodge had been constructed there. Pikes in hand, two Indians waded across the river to inspect it, while others in the party attempted to rig a seine across the river to catch fish. Three other warriors, armed only with their long bows, quivers of arrows, and skinning knives, pushed northward to hunt. Game was scarce in this country, and fast becoming a larger priority than moving the captives along, as it had been at the start of the journey.

While the Indians busied themselves, the captives sat down in the snow-covered field beside the river, wondering what they should do. For the first time in four days, there wasn't a single Abenaki warrior in sight, and they gazed around at the landscape, dumbfounded by their circumstances. Little talk passed among the captives during this interval, and what was said had nothing to do with trying to run away. There was no place to go, and the fact that they were prisoners of the open air must have stymied them.

Singly and in pairs, the captives began foraging in the vicinity where the Indians had left them, following Sam Lenorson's example in digging for groundnuts with a stick. Of the thirteen captives taken in Haverhill, which included baby Martha, eight remained alive. The Worcester boy, on the other hand, existed in a state of in-between, conferring with the Abenaki in their own dialect and moving about freely.

Over the next hour, the English settlers fanned out across the marshy ground, searching high and low for anything that looked edible. Taking Goodwives Duston and Neff with him, the boy walked along the riverbank heading downstream. In one area protected by fir trees where the snow had not fallen so thickly, Sam roamed along the embankment, peering at the river. Finally, he hopped off the bank, wading in knee-deep water till he reached some floating vegetation. Rooting around, he pulled up handfuls of marsh marigold shoots, also known as cowslip; fiddlehead ferns; and several young cattails. These he yanked out by the root, broke off the stalks, and then rinsed and wrung out the root ends. Working swiftly, he gave these to Duston, who followed alongside on the riverbank while the boy stripped the silky down from some milkweed pods, adding that to the collection of soggy plants.

Coming up from the river, Sam Lenorson indicated that the women should pile up these shoots and weeds, and fashion themselves a pair of digging sticks. Working alongside one another like sowers at planting time, they prodded and probed at the earth, turning up strings of groundnuts and another root called the Jerusalem artichoke, which grew slightly larger than the groundnut and was clumped together in twos and threes. The boy wound these studded roots together in a kind of horsetail that he draped around his neck. Then he gathered up the loose marigold shoots and cattails, fashioning a bundle that was easy to carry by wrapping a length of vine tightly around these damp grasses and ferns. Mary Neff slung this dripping packet over her shoulder, and the captives proceeded along the riverbank to the next clearing.

Jerusalem artichokes, which were sturdy and sweet, could be eaten raw, according to Sam, and he handed these around so they could fortify themselves as they walked. After all, there was no way of knowing how long the Indians would tarry in this location, or whether they planned to stop at all the following day. Thus it was paramount that the captives gather as much food as possible, as quickly as they could.

Around the next bend in the river, Sam motioned for them to slow down and then to halt altogether, since there were two Indians just ahead, digging with their pikes at the underside of the riverbank. Apparently, they had located a muskrat or otter's den and were busy hacking at and widening the entrance, and pulling out great batches of yellow water lily roots with the sharp end of their pikes. The boy made sure that the Indians saw them, and working out in the open, he and the two captive women occupied themselves by scratching at the ground with their digging sticks. Ignoring the Indians was a sign they posed no threat, nor did they hurry in the other direction or attempt to hide among the trees.

Upon first sighting the Indians, Sam had thrown off his yoke of groundnuts and artichokes, gesturing to the women to drop their bundles. If the Abenaki noticed how much food they had collected, there was a good chance they would confiscate it, forcing the work party to start over.

Within a few minutes, the Indians had extracted a large number of the sweet, gelatinous, pond lily roots. They stuffed them into a deerskin bundle, one of the warriors hoisted it to his shoulder, and the two Indians continued prowling downstream, their pikes at the ready. Once they were out of sight, the boy picked up the strings of groundnuts and artichokes and passed them to Duston, hurrying over to the place on the riverbank where the Indians had been digging.

Clambering into the shallow water, Sam plunged his head and shoulders into the gaping hole of the burrow. His upper body was completely swallowed up by the fetid earth, and his legs wriggled in the air.

Emerging moments later, his torso covered in mud, Sam held aloft two huge fistfuls of the water lily roots, which he explained were toothsome when roasted, with a flavor like mutton. Goodwives Duston and Neff expressed surprise that the Indians, who were also near starvation, had left such an abundance of the roots behind. But Sam explained that the Abenaki thought of themselves as kindred with the animals of the forest. If they deprived the muskrat of the entire food supply it had gathered before the snows had fallen, the Indians would be considered guilty of wronging a brother creature. The settlers, on the other hand, were more likely to take what they could get, whenever they could get it. Even so, the boy revealed, though he had confiscated most of the remaining lily roots, he had left enough behind to last the muskrat until warmer days arrived.

The captive women and the boy had no means of lighting a fire, which was required to make most of what they had gathered palatable. Two hours after the party had set out to look for food, the afternoon shadows were lengthening and the air had grown colder. Here and there, a damp chill emanated from places where snow filled the hollows and lay scattered over the ground in patches. In a copse of fir trees, the foragers divided up their bounty, making it appear as scanty as possible. They concealed the smaller items, like the groundnuts and artichokes, beneath their clothing, and made three small parcels from the roots, ferns, and milkweed down. All things being ready for a start, inedible rinds and nutshells and roots were cast aside, the small flat bundles were taken up, and the captives began to make their way upriver.

As they drew near the camp, they heard a ruckus up ahead, coming through the dense grove of trees in bits and pieces with some of it being carried off by the wind. Sam Lenorson gestured to his companions and, treading quietly, he decided to ford the stream, causing them to arrive on the bank opposite the encampment. If they didn't like what they saw, having the river between them and the Indians would increase their chances, however slightly, for an escape into the forest.

Sam chose the same ford where the trio of warriors had crossed earlier; Indians somehow always knowing the shallowest place in a river, the fastest route between two villages, the lowest pass through the mountains, and the best fishing and hunting grounds. And the boy's confidence in their masters was repaid when they splashed through water that was little more than ankle deep.

Gliding among the trees, the captive boy and the two women soon discovered that the cause of the row was a spontaneous celebration among the Indians over their hunting expedition. The three warriors had returned from the forest with a half-grown doe they had killed and partially dressed, slinging it by the hooves on a pole that two of the Indians carried between them.

Seeing this, the boy grinned, motioning to Goodwives Duston and Neff as he waded back over the stream into the camp. The Indians' success was good news for the English—not that they could be expected to share the meat with their captives, but it put them in a jovial mood. This made it unlikely the savages would harm any of the captives—they were worth more in trade than they were dead—or appropriate what little they had scavenged for their own meal.

The Indians had also raised a modest catch with their gill nets and spears; a mess of fingerlings was already roasting over the cook fire they had prepared. Maneuvering themselves as close to the fire as they dared, Sam Lenorson and the two women arranged their food in a space they had cleared in the snow, and began preparing it for cooking. Having duly organized these supplies, the boy, as he had done on the evening of their first remove, picked over the ground until he found a suitable flat stone, lodging it in the coals of the fire. His master, the warrior called Bampico, who had taken part in the hunt, was in such high spirits that he loaned the boy a copper pot he had plundered from the settlement.

Coming back to the women, the boy made a soup from river water, a few groundnuts he had pulverized with a rock, and some water lily roots, with a handful of meal he had scraped from the inner bark of a tree. In a quick, surreptitious movement, the boy snatched up a piece of offal from the butchered doe that had fallen to the ground, adding it to the pot.

While Sam was busy tending to their supper, Duston and Neff stood up to pray, thanking God in His mercy for what they had been given. But when they were pouring out their souls before the Lord, their Indian master, who had disrupted the women's prayers on two other occasions, circled the fire and stomped into their midst, scowling at them and making ugly sounds.

The sachem was a lean, battle-hardened man, who strutted about and tried to seem carefree, though a gleam of hatefulness shone in his eye. Continuing their prayers as best they could, the two women grasped each other's hands and stared at the ground between their feet. But the Indian, looming quite close to them, trampled on some of the ferns and cattail roots piled nearby, shouting in their ears when they attempted to recite the scripture. Drawing himself up between them, in his halting English the Indian said that when he lived with the Reverend Joseph Rowlandson in Lancaster, he prayed the English way, and believed it was good. But the French way, taught to him by the Jesuits, was much better, he said.

Huddling closer together, the women persisted in their supplications to the Lord. In a loud voice, the sachem told Duston and Neff that he was taking them to an Indian town, far beyond Pennacook, which was still many days' journey. If they made it to this place, beside the great river in Quebec, all the tribes of the Abenaki would be there. Then the captives, men and women alike, would be stripped naked and scourged with branches and deer hide thongs. The Abenaki would arrange themselves into two columns, armed with clubs and sticks and pikes, and the English would be forced to run the gauntlet between them. Along the way, the captives would be struck, kicked, bloodied, spat upon, and ridiculed; they would be derided for their heathen beliefs and mocked if they fainted or swooned. Those who survived this ordeal would be sold to the French as slaves.

Upon the conclusion of his speech, the Indian spat upon the ground and laughed, passing Sam Lenorson coming the other way as he returned to the bonfire. Knowing by now that the boy was on familiar terms with his own Indian master, Goodwife Duston, while continuing to follow the sachem with her gaze, caught the boy by the elbow as he reached them. Briefly, Duston instructed Sam to approach Bampico when the right moment presented itself, since there was a specific question she wanted the boy to ask him.

At length the surrounding hills faded into a thick gray mist, the darkened woods illuminated only by occasional flares of light from the bonfire. Against a screen of trees, the elongated figures of the Indians, projected as shadows, leaped and cavorted about while their butchered meat roasted on the spit. Scattered across the meadow, the English huddled together in twos and threes, squatting on bare spots they had cleared in the snow. Only Sam Lenorson moved between the Indians and their captives. When the soup was boiling hot, he retrieved the pot from the fire using two of the digging sticks and carried it back to the women.

The meal warmed and cheered them. After they got to the bottom of the soup pot, Sam Lenorson cooked a pile of water lily roots, fiddlehead ferns, and a few more groundnuts by placing hot stones on top of them. Then, at a time deemed appropriate by Hannah Duston, she conferred with Sam once more and the boy got to his feet. As the Indians loitered by the spit, picking at the broiled carcass of the doe and smoking pipes of tobacco, Sam took up the copper pot again and crossed over to the fire. Soon he was engaged in animated conversation with his master.

Amused by the question, Bampico roused the boy by the shoulders and answered him in a jovial tone. Taking up a pole-ax from the ground, the Indian swung it in a roundhouse manner, taking aim at an invisible enemy. The boy said something else, and the Indian nodded. Bending down to Sam with his hands on his knees, Bampico made some additional remarks, laughed with delight, and tapped the boy on the left temple with the fingers of his right hand. Sam nodded, lingering beside the fire for another minute or two. After warming himself for as long as he dared, Sam placed the copper pot on the ground and returned to the shadows.

The boy settled himself again between the two women, and since they were far beyond the warmth of the fire, they huddled together, shivering and trembling. When the three captives were eating, and also during the time when Sam had been conversing with Bampico, Goodwife Duston had kept her attention fixed on her own master. And while the Indians continued laughing and smoking over by the fire, Duston asked Sam Lenorson what the Indian had said in reply to his question.

The three captives sat with their limbs thrown over one another, dappled in the firelight that was cast over the meadow. Imitating Bampico's gesture, the boy freed his right hand and tapped at the bony ridge of his temple. *To kill a man*, the Indian had said, *you only had to rear back and strike him here.*

CHAPTER V

Count Frontenac and the Reign of Terror

As Goodwife Duston and her comrades stumbled through the rutted snow, their movement northward was no less predetermined than if they'd been tied to a rope hundreds of miles long, a phantom tether being drawn inexorably toward the chateau in Quebec that housed the French colonial governor. For it was through the continuous exertions of his office that the latest series of bloody raids were being mounted against the English settlements, and that surviving victims of these attacks were being carried off by savages who'd been goaded, bullied, fawned over, bartered with, or otherwise persuaded to undertake them.

The principal architect of this policy—indeed, the vital impetus that had littered the frontier with corpses and driven groups of frightened and dejected captives toward Quebec like some infernal engine—was none other than Louis de Baude, also known as Count Frontenac, the son of an influential French official, as well as the godson and namesake of King Louis XIII. Frontenac was, arguably, the most beguiling and charismatic figure in the saga of the New World during its first century. He was a person of diverse talents who expressed in his life and work both a confounding indifference to the suffering of other human beings and a warm-hearted kinship with the most primitive, naked savages that roamed the forests. Count Frontenac was also one of the key originators of a cruel strategy that would be embraced, often eagerly and sometimes with reluctance, by other prominent statesmen and leaders in the nearly three hundred years it would take to conquer North America. In his own time, and examined now from ours, Count Frontenac seemed, at once, to represent the endless possibilities, as much as the enduring horror, of the continent: a man who killed scores of innocent people, not from any perverse motivation, but with the firm and sincere intention of civilizing the world they lived in.

Of Basque origin, Louis de Baude was a professional soldier and adventurer of noble birth, a bold, reckless, often intemperate man who might have leaped from the pages of a novel by Alexandre Dumas. Eager to make a name for himself, Count Frontenac, who was born in 1620, ran off at age fifteen to enlist in the French army. Only nineteen years old, he was a volunteer at the siege of Hesdin, which was recaptured for France in 1639; by the age of twenty-one, Frontenac was a veteran of military campaigns in northern France, England, and Holland and at twenty-three, he was elevated to the rank of colonel while leading the Normandy regiment into several battles in Italy. At twenty-six, after being wounded several times and breaking his arm during the siege of Orbitello in Tuscany, Frontenac was promoted to *marechal du camp*, or brigadier general.

Within two years, Frontenac returned to his father's estate in France, bedecked with campaign ribbons and crisscrossed with scars, but still as proud, vain, and headstrong as when he set out—a reluctant courtier more suited to the parade ground and battlefield than the intricate maneuvering of the palace. But Frontenac was determined to benefit from his access to the royal court. Hanging in one of the nooks at Versailles is the oil painting of a lovely young French girl accoutered as Minerva, the Roman goddess of invention, wisdom, the arts, and military prowess, with a plumed helmet upon her head and a golden shield on her arm. Inscribed in the lower corner of the portrait is the model's name and title: *Anne de La Grange-Trianon, Comtesse de Frontenac*. She was just sixteen years old, the only child of the fifty-year-old widower La Grange-Trianon, Sieur de Neuville, when she caught the eye of the dashing Count Frontenac. Each as stubborn as the other, Frontenac and Mme. La Grange-Trianon married despite her father's objections, and soon Madame de Frontenac had given birth to a son, Francois Louis.

The couple was not suited for one another. They argued frequently, Madame de Frontenac's temper outstripping even that of her husband, which was considerable. Devoid of maternal impulses, Madame sent Francois Louis to the village of Clion to be raised by a nurse, and then joined the entourage of her court sponsor, the lively and influential

Mademoiselle de Montpensier, daughter of Gaston, the Duke of Orleans, and granddaughter of King Henry IV. For his part, Count Frontenac established his household at Saint Fargeau in north central France, where he entertained lavishly and was quick to provide visitors with a tour of his stables.

Although Frontenac was not particularly high born, he managed to win the favor of the queen and was often her guest at court. But he seems to have bristled at the quotidian details of being a gentleman, and at forty-nine, an age when most noblemen of that era, particularly those of legitimate accomplishments, were angling for a sinecure or other comfortable arrangement, Frontenac was appointed to a prestigious military post on the isle of Crete. During the fifth Ottoman-Venetian war, the Knights of Malta and the papal states, with naval assistance from France, held off invaders from the Ottoman Empire for more than two decades. During the bloodiest years of the conflict, from 1668 to 1669, a massive Turkish force besieged Candia, a Greek seaport on Crete's northern coast. And when Venetian emissaries visited France to plead for more aid, they offered to place their own troops under whoever Henri de la Tour d'Auvergne, the Vicomte de Turenne, chose to lead them. Turenne, as he was called, was a Marshal of France, one of the greatest field generals of all time and a man of impeccable military judgment. When he asked Frontenac to sail for Crete, the restless old soldier accepted both the honor and the unenviable task of Candia's defense. Although Candia fell to the Turks after a struggle that cost an estimated 180,000 lives, Frontenac's reputation as a leader possessed of significant tactical ability, fortitude, and courage grew as a result of his efforts on Crete.

This experience whetted Frontenac's appetite for an even greater challenge—particularly one where he would have a better opportunity to prevail and to prosper. In the meantime, his wife, Madame de Frontenac, had suffered a falling out with her sponsor, Mademoiselle de Montpensier, and their prospects at court had dimmed. (Their son, Francois Louis, died quite young, killed either in battle or a duel.) Despite these travails, Frontenac, never lacking in confidence, had won the attention of a certain Madame de Montespan, who was also the object of the king's affections. So Louis XIV removed a potential obstacle to his own desire and resuscitated his faithful servant's career, when, in 1672, he appointed Count Frontenac the governor and lieutenant-general for the king in all of New

France. In so doing, Louis XIV had granted Frontenac dominion-by-proxy over Canada in particular, and the great expanse of the New World in general. The task ahead was what he could make of it, and perhaps in his own secret thoughts, Frontenac believed he would finally transform himself into something that matched his ambition. In the far off wilds of Canada, he could become a sort of king.

Madame de Frontenac had no desire to visit New France and promptly announced her intention to remain behind. Neither she nor her husband had much in the way of property. But through the agency of the Duc de Lude, grand master of the king's artillery, Madame de Frontenac managed to obtain a suite of rooms within a massive building known as the Arsenal. From here, she was able to assist her peripatetic husband, sometimes directly, and other times in oblique fashion, on many occasions in the years that followed. Though the ardor of their romance and marriage burned very briefly, their relations were, in the modern sense, a kind of political alliance, a stroke of unexpected good fortune that buoyed Frontenac in the difficult times to come.

Accustomed as he was to the company of soldiers, the order of military campaigns, and the rooms of a country estate, Frontenac, now fifty-two years old, must have been taken aback when he sailed up the St. Lawrence River and caught his first glimpse of the rocky precipice that marked Quebec. A cohort of French settlers and the clergy, made up of Jesuit and seminary priests, had occupied this rock and the surrounding wilderness for several years, but what Frontenac saw resembled a primitive work camp more than a city, and for just a moment he must have regretted his lost wine cellar and tack room at St. Fargeau. A man of considerable intellect and enterprise, Frontenac was not prone to regret, and whatever initial disappointment he might have felt was soon replaced by admiration for the strategic advantages of the rocky precipice and its fortress, which provided a commanding view of the Quebec basin.

"I never saw anything more superb than the position of this town," Frontenac later wrote. "It could not be better situated as the future capital of a great empire."

For Louis XIV had not sent Frontenac to merely supervise a colony, but rather to expand France's influence in the New World, perhaps even by tripling or quadrupling the empire in geographical size, natural resources, exports, and military strength. Therefore, Frontenac wasted no time inspecting his new domain and engaging in lengthy conversations with the *coureurs de bois*, or bushrangers, as well as the French officers, soldiers, scouts, priests, converted Indians, and ordinary settlers and tradesmen. Already beginning to thrive with iron mining, shipbuilding, breweries, fishing stations, and seignories—the budding estates of French noblemen who had relocated to the New World—the enterprise that greeted Frontenac delighted him in its breadth and energy. Immediately he set out to improve what he saw as the colony's major weaknesses, particularly the primacy of the Jesuits in trading with the Indians, and the centralization of power through the monarchy, an influence that seemed very distant when viewed from the promontory of Quebec.

On October 23, 1672, Frontenac convened a general assembly of the three estates of the colony—the clergy, the nobles, and the commoners—in Quebec's largest church. Beyond his flair for military spectacle, Count Frontenac was a gifted, forceful writer and a convincing orator. No doubt Frontenac aimed his speech at those sitting beneath the church roof, and at King Louis XIV and his court, half a world away. In his remarks, the governor sought to flatter and cajole, while at the same time hectoring his audience and offering them a narrow range of options disguised as instruction. Over time, this admixture of obsequiousness, bonhomie, and condescension would become the hallmark of Frontenac's treatment of both the clergy and the Indians, eventually leading to his diminished reputation when his enemies began complaining to the king.

After he had exhorted each of these contingents to labor on behalf of Canada, Frontenac hinted that every man present had a lot to gain by following his advice: "It is needless, then, to urge you to act as I have counseled, since it is for your own interest to do so."

Right from the beginning, Frontenac admonished the clergy for profiting from their trade with the Indians, instead of turning their attention more fully to the clergy's principal mandate, the saving of souls. Believing the Jesuits, especially, to be far too concerned with accumulating wealth, Frontenac insisted they limit themselves to making the Indians subjects of Jesus Christ—and of Louis XIV. Certainly, the new governor had the best interests of the colony in mind when he set forth these prescriptions, but he didn't foresee that his affinity for the ancient privileges of his class would later alienate his sponsor, the king. And he underestimated the greed and jealousy of the clergy, as well as the central task he had outlined for them: converting the Indians to Catholicism, which he believed would pacify them.

Count Frontenac was not alone in misunderstanding the Indians' disposition toward spiritual matters; the French Jesuits and seminary priests were as ignorant in this regard as their Puritan counterparts in the English settlements. They failed to grasp that the Indians already possessed a defined, complex set of beliefs, and that the invaders were not attempting to implant a cosmology, but to *transplant* one for another, which is a different and more problematic task. Long before the first Europeans arrived, the Indians were immersed in a spirit world that drove the heavens, animated every living thing, and dwelled profoundly in each object on earth. Replacing this set of beliefs with another, especially one that included the deification of a bearded wanderer who'd lived centuries earlier in a desert land no Indian had ever seen was, at the very least, a daunting proposition.

But the central difficulty that plagued Frontenac was that he found it necessary to employ his most implacable enemy, the Catholic hierarchy, in an attempt to harness and control an equally dangerous one, the five-nation league of the Iroquois. Proud, cunning, and often ruthless, the French clergy, particularly the Jesuits, exerted a prior claim on the New World and its native inhabitants, having scattered themselves among the Indian villages at great personal risk while other settlers built fortifications to keep the Indians out. These clerics also felt immune to Frontenac's imprecations and orders, and perhaps, even beyond those mandates issued by the king himself, since they answered, ultimately, to the pope, not Louis XIV.

Shortly after Frontenac arrived in Quebec, a Jesuit bishop managed to intercept letters that Frontenac sent to one of the king's ministers, as well as the minister's written replies, thereby staying ahead of the royal governor's plans for remedying his situation. In a letter to another cleric sharing what he had discovered, the bishop advised his colleague to keep the details of this epistolary spy craft to himself, "Since, while it is well to acquire all necessary information, and to act upon it, it is of the greatest importance to keep secret our possession of such knowledge."

Frontenac often asserted, with good reason, that the Jesuit missionaries were more intent on piling up beaver pelts than enlightening the Indians spiritually, and that the priests and their bishops wished to keep the Abenaki and Algonquin tribes under their exclusive dominion. What both Frontenac and the clergy didn't comprehend was that the fur trade, more than any other incursion of the old world upon the new—including military might, the introduction of disease, and the co-opting of massive parcels of land—was the single most destructive force visited upon the Indians. Pursuing animal hides in order to exchange them for European goods, many of them useless in day-to-day living, would irrevocably upset a thousand years' worth of the Indians' seasonal activities, the alternating emphasis on hunting, fishing, and a rude sort of horticulture that sustained the tribes year-round. This disruption of their traditional way of life would set neighbor against neighbor and friend against friend; position former allies at each others' throats; drive New France into decades of conflict with New England; and place several tribes and the European settlers at the mercy of the most treacherous, bloody-minded, and unpredictable armed force in the New World, the Iroquois.

At the close of the previous century, the five tribes of the Finger Lakes region in western New York—the Cayuga, Mohawk, Oneida, Onondaga, and Seneca—agreed to a nonaggression pact and formed the Iroquois League. This politically astute union immediately vaulted the Iroquois over the other, more fractious tribes in their vicinity, with the ten major Iroquois villages and other, scattered hamlets encompassing nearly thirty thousand Indians across the Mohawk Valley. The league would later become a model for New World governments, including the formation of the United States; Iroquois leaders were selected for their eloquence and persuasiveness, and within tribal councils, women had a significant role in choosing these sachems, prosecuting wars, and determining the fate of captives.

The size and political strength of the Iroquois League was matched by the ferocity and brutality of its warriors; their reputation created such fear among other tribes that the sight of a lone Iroquois in enemy territory could ignite widespread panic. When Passaconaway, the great Bashaba of the Pennacooks, was a young warrior, the Iroquois would occasionally send raiding parties as far as New Hampshire. On one occasion, as the cry of "A Mohawk! A Mohawk!" went up from the neighboring hills, it sent the Pennacook running for their fortified complex on Sugar Ball Hill. After several attempts, an Iroquois ruse finally lured some of the warriors outside the palisade walls. In the terrible fighting that ensued,

Passaconaway added to his burgeoning legend by killing several Mohawks at close quarters.

A clash between the fur-hungry French and the warlike Iroquois was inevitable, since each nation was equally dependent on access to ever increasing swaths of territory. The French *coureurs de bois* were pushing westward in their insatiable quest for beaver skins, while the survival of a lone Iroquois village often required hunting grounds as large as 272 square miles. Under Count Frontenac, the French were intent on establishing a string of trading stations and forts stretching from Quebec to the eastern Great Lakes. However, when bushrangers entered the Mohawk Valley, they were surprised to find large, well-fortified Iroquois settlements, resembling city-states, which were in great contrast to the modest villages and flimsy palisades of their usual trading partners, the Huron and Oswego.

Unlike many other tribes, the Iroquois did not erect their most important villages along the banks of a river, or beside a swamp. Instead, they built their major settlements on hilltops that had been shorn of trees and provided clear views in every direction. These contained parallel rows of longhouses protected by earthen barriers and a network of ditches; elevated granaries that doubled as lookout towers; strategically placed weapons platforms; and other interior obstacles. The settlement was encircled by concentric rings of palisades built with large, pointed logs set close together, often with only a single, low entrance cut into the outer wall. The largest of these towns might encompass several acres within the palisades and numbered two thousand residents. Outside the fortifications were acres of fertile land where the women and children cultivated beans, squash, and corn. Startled by what they saw, trappers and explorers who came in proximity to these hamlets would refer to them as castles.

If the Iroquois League was respected and feared as a collective, the individual warrior was looked upon, even by other hostile Indians, as an almost supernatural deliverer of pain, terror, and savagery. Foreign even to other Indians, the Iroquois spoke a different language from that of the Algonquin and were of different blood. Molded for war from the early days of his youth, an Iroquois's temperament was forged in adversity, through daunting feats of hardship and courage, and perpetual warfare. The warrior shaved his hair on one side of his head, revealing the bony working of his skull, and wore it long on the other side, twisted into several topknots. His recklessness in battle and his capacity for cruelty and torture shocked both the French and the English, who were continually trying to enlist the Iroquois as allies. When the Seneca, the most populous of the five tribes and situated the farthest to the west, raided the Illinois, they reduced their villages to smoldering ruins and returned with several hundred captives. The fittest and strongest were adopted into the Seneca, and the rest were burned alive.

European chroniclers also remarked upon the stoicism of Iroquois captives under torture. An eighty-year-old half-blind Onondaga warrior, taken prisoner by mission Indians under French command, was trussed to a pole and then branded with red-hot irons. He neither cried out, nor begged for mercy. After several more trials by fire, the Iroquois began to jeer his captors. Finally, they stabbed the old man with a lance. As he died, the Onondaga said, "Learn from me, you dogs of Frenchmen, how to endure pain."

The hatred other tribes had for the Iroquois cannot be overstated. In Abenaki villages, when a pestilence took hold and began dispatching its inhabitants, the sachems conducted an elaborate ritual that included throwing five ceremonial bundles of tobacco into a roaring fire. The Abenaki considered tobacco the breath of life and believed their gods to favor it as a sacrifice. With clouds of aromatic smoke rising from the bonfire, the sachem prayed to the sun, to other spirits, and to the contagion itself to quit their village and travel to the country of their enemies, the Iroquois.

At various times, both the French and the English were able to transform the specter of the Iroquois into a political advantage. The Mohawks, in particular, were not content to menace only the lake tribes, but occasionally attacked the Nipmuc in Massachusetts, the Pennacook in New Hampshire, and the Abenaki tribes of provincial Maine. These raids and the threat of further incursions led a Connecticut sachem to visit Boston and Plymouth to seek the protection of the English, inviting them to build settlements in his territory. By the middle of the seventeenth century, the Iroquois, long the enemy of the Huron, were also terrorizing the Algonquin, Erie, Neutral, Ottawa, and Petun, commandeering their hunting grounds and interdicting the northern fur trading routes. As a French Jesuit wrote in 1653, "Never were there more beavers in our lakes and rivers, but never have there been fewer seen in the warehouses of the country. . . . (The Iroquois) are preventing all the trade in beaver skins, which have always been the chief wealth of this country."

In less than a single generation, the quest for beaver pelts overthrew every other New World commodity, shifting the emphasis from fishing, farming, logging, and mining almost exclusively to the hunting and trapping of beavers. For thousands of years, Indian tribes had fought wars and skirmishes over territory, but with the rise of the fur trade the competition for huge parcels of land became more pervasive, recalcitrant, and deadly. Coastal tribes, seeking to become indispensable as middlemen in the shipping of hides, fought devastating wars with inland tribes that had direct access to the beaver supply. The losses from these conflicts led to "mourning wars," where tribes that had been reduced in strength undertook further raids against their enemies, looking to replace their dead with captive warriors. Unspeakable acts of violence became commonplace, and, particularly among the Iroquois, torture and cannibalism became effective weapons of retribution in the so-called Beaver Wars.

The North American beaver, or *Castor canadensis*, is both a rodent and a "gnawer," thus a relative of squirrels, porcupines, and rats. The beaver, though averaging forty-five pounds or so, can weigh twice that and reach four feet in length. Indians had been hunting beaver at least since the Early Archaic period, from 8,000 to 6,000 BC. Unlike European settlers, who viewed beaver pelts as a mere product to be sold or traded for other goods, the Indians maximized their kill—eating, preserving, wearing, or otherwise utilizing just about every part of the beaver. They roasted whole beavers, often cutting thin strips of the meat, drying them over a smoldering fire, and then mashing them together with animal fat and berries into pemmican cakes, which, like Nokehick, was a handy, portable food that would keep on long hunting trips or other journeys.

Beaver pelts, so thick and luxurious they contained as many as twenty-three thousand individual hairs per square centimeter, could be stitched together to make water-resistant winter mantles and capes, mittens, and soft, long-lasting moccasins. By curing and tanning the skin, the Indians created a thin, durable hide from which they made warm-weather shirts, quivers, and bags. Castoreum, a pungent, yellowish liquid found in a beaver's castor sacs, which are glands located in the animal's groin, contains salicylic acid, the primary ingredient in aspirin. (Beavers are known to eat willow bark, which also contains salicylic acid.) The Indians used this substance as a curative for a multitude of ailments, including abscesses, colic, toothache, sciatica, and malignant fever. Beaver teeth were prized as ornaments, and the beaver's thick, powerful tail served the animal as a fat reserve; a built-in alarm that was used to alert other beavers by slapping the water; a body-temperature regulator; and a rudder while swimming. Also prized by the Indians as an aphrodisiac, the beaver's tail was often reserved for the tribe's sachem, to commemorate the hunt.

A beaver has four curved and beveled incisors, two upper and two lower, that act like chisels and generate enough force to grind through logs three feet in diameter. Embedded alongside the incisors in a beaver's large, flat skull are sixteen heavy molars, the jaws equipped with the power to masticate the bark, roots, twigs, berries, and leaves that comprise the mammal's vegetarian diet. Industrious, efficient in his efforts, and driven to prodigious feats of construction, the work habits of the beaver came to be looked upon with admiration and envy.

In the New World, beavers were found wherever there was water, but most often alongside ponds, either naturally occurring ones or meres they had created by building sophisticated dams. Capable of engineering marvels, beavers also leave their environment better than they find it, since their work increases the depth of ponds, reduces turbidity, enables sediment to drift to the bottom, and results in clearer water and a stable habitat for other plant and animal life. A family of beavers working together can build a forty-foot dam in a week. A thousand-foot dam, canted slightly upstream to reduce the force of the water on the middle section, would take the same beavers about two years to finish.

Indians revered the beaver. The northern Algonquin tribes believed the entire world was once covered in water, and only through the labor of massive beavers, otters, and muskrats, which swam to the bottom and piled up great islands of mud, were the landforms created that allowed the Indians to thrive. The Amikona, whose name means "People of the Beaver," believed their tribe originally sprang from the remains of the first beaver. The Cheyenne and the Paiute also held the beaver in high esteem, making this resourceful animal an integral part of mankind's origin story.

For their part, Europeans looked upon the exalted beaver and saw only a hat. Once considered ordinary among the more coveted pelts of the ermine, marten, and sable, this durable, smooth, water-resistant fur would rise to prominence because of a single item that men of purpose and industry simply couldn't be without.

Through a peculiar combination of utility and chance, the beaver hat became an indispensable fashion accessory and status symbol that held sway in England and on the European continent for close to three hundred years. This enduring boom market exhausted the supply of European and Eurasian beavers, or *castor fiber*, engendering a ceaseless demand that left the gentry nattily attired while scattering the corpses of settlers, traders, trappers, clergy, and Indians across North America.

One of the first references to the ascension of the beaver hat appeared in Geoffrey Chaucer's *Canterbury Tales* in the late fourteenth century. Chaucer's prosperous merchant in his "Flanderish beaver hat" is a kind of prototype for the English, Dutch, and French barons, burghers, and noblemen whose desire for this one item drove the trade in beaver pelts back and forth across the Atlantic Ocean for generations. It grew to the point where the height, the shape, and the workmanship of one's "castor" indicated the wearer's place in the social firmament, both in the New World and abroad. The distance the beaver pelt had to travel, the ardors of such a journey, and the laborious, multifaceted process the fur was subjected to on its way to becoming a felt hat were critical factors in making it such an expensive, sought after object. Felt hats were made from two sorts of beaver pelts: coat and parchment. "Coat" pelts had already been used as winter mantles or cloaks by Indians and were supple and broken in, shorn of the long, coarse "guard" hairs that affected the fur's softness and sheen. In many ways, these furs were preferable to the raw, freshly skinned "parchment" type, which had to pass through an extra step in preparation for their desired use. However, coat furs that had been worn through several rough seasons were often inferior, so once the technique for curing the raw fur was improved and streamlined, the parchment beaver became the hatter's favorite material.

It usually took an entire adult beaver to produce the eight to ten ounces of beaver wool, or "fluff," that composed a single top hat. First, the wool was shaved from the pelt with a razor sharp, semicircular knife. After mixing the sun-dried fluff of a beaver pelt with the greasy wool of a coat fur, the two sorts of fiber were "carded" together. This material was then weighed, bowed, and managed into a triangular shape known as a *capade*, or *gore*; ballooned into a large cone; dipped several times in a scalding hot mixture of sulfuric acid, beer-grounds, and wine sediments; then trundled over repeatedly with a rolling pin; and, finally, through an exacting combination of heat, moisture, and pressure, shrunk to half its former size.

Hat making was not without its dangers. During the early stages, a nitrate of mercury solution that was brushed on the pelt changed the fur tips into a desirable yellowish-red color (a process known as "carroting"), which often produced a wave of toxic vapors. Hatters exposed to these fumes over long periods usually developed the confused thinking, impaired speech, and staggering gait later attributed to mercury poisoning, leading to the phrase "mad as a hatter."

The shrunken, conical hats were stretched over wooden molds, which was known as blocking, whereupon the craftsman trimmed the excess hide from the edges, creating a narrow, curved brim, then rubbed the pelt to a sheen using pumice or a piece of seal skin. Once the hat was dry, it was stretched over a new block then placed into a large copper pot, where it was immersed in dye made from logwood, verdigris, copperas, and alder-bark. The pot was left to boil for an hour, and then cooled, with this process repeated several times. To stiffen the hat, it was brushed with gum Arabic and "Flaunder's glue," having already been rubbed on the inside with rosin, bee's wax, and mutton suet to enhance its waterproof qualities. The hat would also be lined with an inferior fur such as rabbit, and a leather band with the company's trademark stamped on it would encircle the lower inside edge.

At the conclusion of this exacting process, the item was placed in the window of an exclusive shop in London, Amsterdam, or Paris, and before long an immaculately dressed gentleman would emerge wearing a beaver felt top hat, unaware that upon his well-coiffed noggin he bore the entire skin of a much-revered animal; long, perilous hours of workmanship; and the innocent blood of trappers, Indians, settlers, and slaves.

Though the European purchaser of such a hat was able to pay with crowns, guilders, or francs, the Iroquois, Ottawa, Huron, Illinois, and other eastern Indian tribes of the late seventeenth century, who were known to descend from northern lakes and rivers to deliver as many as fifty thousand beaver pelts to a single trading post in a season, were not typically paid with cash money. Nor was it always practical for Indians to carry off the European clothing, firearms, household goods, and liquor they preferred to exchange for the hides they brought to market. In light of the burgeoning fur trade, the Indians and their European partners eventually decided upon shell beads as their shared commodity.

Originally used by the Indians for ornamentation and to commemorate treaties and the like, wampumpeague, or "wampum" as it became known, was made from hand drilling and shaping cylindrical bits of seashell into thin, hollow tubes—the more coveted black or purple shell, and the less valued white periwinkle shell. The best of these were collected on Block Island, and the Rhode Island and Connecticut shorelines, during the summer, after which Indian craftsmen spent the winter rounding, smoothing, and piercing them lengthwise. Eventually, three black or purple beads, or six whites, became equal to an English penny. These were arranged in patterns, strung sixty to a foot, and woven into attractive belts, bags, sashes, caps, necklaces, and other decorative items. One of King Philip's wampum belts was nine inches wide and, when hung around his neck, reached almost to the ground. When the sachem of the Wampanoag visited Boston in 1671, the wampum that decorated Philip's buskins, belt, and coat was worth twenty English pounds—a king's ransom in that era.

Cylindrical purple beads averaged five to the inch when strung, which came to three hundred and sixty beads for six feet—or one fathom—with English merchants willing to pay twenty shillings per fathom. The scarcity of the raw material, the skill and tedious labor associated with the drilling out and smoothing of the beads, and the beauty of the finished product combined to keep the value of wampum steady, even in times of chaos and war. For a long period wampum remained the primary currency in the New World, samples of it appearing as far from coastal New England as Wisconsin and the Dakotas. In fact, the so-called "diamonds of the country" remained in wide use as a commodity for trade until the American Revolution.

By the latter half of the seventeenth century, the English had driven the Dutch from the fur trade, but the Iroquois campaign of intimidation and terror, after several decades, had succeeded in paralyzing the further development of the New World's most important area of commerce. During the time that New England tribes were asking the English to shield them from their enemies, the lake tribe Indians aligned with New France faced a crisis of their own. After the Seneca had raided Illinois territory, decimated their villages, killed or captured many of their warriors, and were returning home, the Winnebagoes chanced upon a small party of these Iroquois and took one of their chiefs as a prisoner. While in the lodge of the Ottawa, where the Winnebagoes planned to detain the Seneca chief, a fight broke out among the Winnebagoes, their hostage, and several Illinois who were married to local Indian women and had learned of the massacre. The Seneca chief was killed in the melee.

The Ottawa and Huron, petrified that the murder of the Iroquois chief would lead to the utter destruction of the lake tribes by the Iroquois, pleaded with Count Frontenac to engineer a peace treaty. Frontenac, known as "Onontio" among the Indians, convened a meeting in Montreal attended by the Huron and Ottawa, who were united mainly by their fear of the Iroquois. Kondiaronk, a Huron chief known as the Rat, declared that Onontio was "master of the whole earth" and begged him for protection.

Count Frontenac resembled nearly all of the colonial leaders prior to and following his tenure, in that the lieutenant-general of New France believed Indians were inferior to Europeans in every way. But Frontenac also managed to distinguish himself from the majority of statesmen and peers who would govern the New World for three hundred years, since he had a genuine affection for the Indians; a paternal forbearance for many of their indiscretions; and an uncanny ability to connect with the most arrogant chiefs and sachems in a deep, personal way. When the Rat, speaking for the Huron, implored Onontio to assist them while denigrating the Ottawa for their role in the death of the Seneca chief, Frontenac reminded his visitor that the members of both tribes were his "children," and that he expected them to co-exist as brothers. Then he advised all the lake tribes to unite under a single treaty to secure protection from the French government. Moreover, Frontenac encouraged them to send gifts to the Iroquois, making it clear they wished to atone for the murdered chief. He also warned them against committing any new offenses that would raise the ire of the Seneca, or any other member of the Iroquois League.

Even before the Huron and Ottawa called upon him in Montreal, Frontenac had sent a royal emissary to the Iroquois, requesting a council where they could discuss trade arrangements and peace. The Iroquois replied by messenger, stating that they were the offended party, and that the royal governor must come to them. Frontenac brusquely declined their invitation, though the Iroquois persisted. Not long after the Rat and his delegation left Montreal, a French military officer paid a call on Count Frontenac. The officer's name was La Foret, the commander of Fort Frontenac, which the royal governor had ordered built on the shore of Lake Ontario, the gateway to Iroquois territory. La Foret was accompanied by a respected Iroquois chief named Decanisora and a retinue of fierce-looking warriors. Incensed by the murder of his countryman and flush with confidence in the might of the Iroquois League, Decanisora insisted that Count Frontenac and his officers meet with the chiefs of the five tribes in Iroquois territory. But Frontenac responded with the same kindly dismissiveness that he had used with the Huron and Ottawa.

"It is for the father to tell the children where to hold council, not for the children to tell the father," said the royal governor. "Fort Frontenac is the proper place, and you should thank me for going so far every summer to meet you."

Count Frontenac told Decanisora that the Illinois were also his children, and that he expected his entire family to be on good terms with one another. Then, in his characteristic blending of sternness with flattery, the royal governor declared his visitor a great chief of the Iroquois, commissioned him with sharing these words of peace with his countrymen, and bestowed upon Decanisora a sumptuous belt of wampum, a gold-trimmed jacket and silk cravat, beads for his wife, crimson fabric for his young daughter, and a shiny new musket. The Iroquois departed for Oswego convinced of their own importance and eager to show off these tokens of the royal governor's esteem.

Frontenac's appeasement of the Iroquois, if not exactly a Pyrrhic victory, was, at best, a temporary one. Father Jean de Lamberville, a prominent Jesuit who acted as missionary to Onondaga, the Iroquois capital, warned the royal governor not to become complacent regarding his hold on the Iroquois. When Decanisora and his warriors returned from Montreal, Lamberville wrote a letter reminding Frontenac that the Iroquois feared no one, least of all the undermanned French, and had added nine hundred warriors to their ranks by adopting the hardiest captives from other tribes. The priest's unease at what he had observed led him to believe that the Iroquois intended to "pounce all at once upon Canada, and overwhelm it in a single campaign."

While Frontenac was dealing with the Iroquois and other crises, his principal domestic enemies, who were high-ranking clergymen, dispatched a stream of venomous letters to Louis XIV, decrying the governor's imperial ways and enumerating his many transgressions, both real and imagined. But the king was no fool. Aware of the jealousy that had stricken his representatives in Canada, as well as the inherent difficulties of ruling over a wilderness, Louis XIV was content with issuing the sort of moderate reproofs that a headmaster dispenses among unruly but talented schoolboys. Of all the lies, half truths, and semi-valid complaints leveled against Count Frontenac, the accusation that finally exhausted the king's patience turned out to be the most accurate. The royal governor was charged with using the services of the *coureurs de bois*, who were already regarded as lawless ruffians by the crown, to divert a large portion of the fur trade to his own accounts. Before these pelts could be shipped downriver by the Indians, these bushrangers intercepted them close to the source, exacting a certain number as gifts, or tribute, on behalf of Count Frontenac. Employing surrogates to trade on his behalf, Frontenac also received a hefty share of the beaver skins that did reach the market, usually at favorable terms.

These practices irritated Louis XIV. In a letter to Frontenac in 1680, the king wrote, "I shall hold you answerable for bringing the disorder of the *coureurs de bois* to an end throughout Canada. . . . The bishop, the ecclesiastics, the Jesuit fathers, the Supreme Council, and, in a word, everybody, complain of you."

Unwilling to change course, Frontenac instead plied his influential friends at Versailles with letters of his own, asking them to intervene on his behalf with the king. In raucous meetings with his rivals at Quebec, Frontenac was known to raise sticks and canes to threaten them, an escalating bitterness that occasionally led to swords being drawn though no actual blows were struck. Each side was as guilty as the other of interdicting the fur trade and piling up profits; it was all a matter of continuing without one's rival being able to do the same. Among the most damaging charges was the treasonous notion that both the royal governor and his enemies were trading furs to the English, for the advantages of a better price. And Frontenac was accused of spreading rumors that a deadly plague had struck Montreal, diverting the Indians from the annual fair and inducing them to sell their beaver skins at a low price upriver.

Finally, in 1682, after nearly a decade of unrest and intrigue, the king relieved Count Frontenac of his duties, ordering him to return to France. Before departing, Frontenac put all his complaints down on paper. He was mostly correct in asserting that the Jesuits were continually hacking at the roots of his governorship, intent as they were in profiting from the fur trade themselves and extending their authority over spiritual matters to the disposition of earthly ones. Frontenac noted that the ecclesiastics controlled nearly two-thirds of the most desirable land in all of Canada; that they employed a network of spies that reached all the way from Onondaga to Versailles; engaged in brisk trade with the English; and manipulated the Indians through their access to them in the mission villages. History would bear out most of these charges, but they did not assist Frontenac in the moment.

For all his failings, the king, and even Frontenac's enemies knew he was a man of quality, with a rare aptitude for taming the wilderness and the mercurial savages who populated it. Count Frontenac had a peerless ability to understand the inner workings of an Indian's mind; when to cajole and when to reprimand; how to motivate them to harass his enemies; and how to stymie their own violent impulses toward the French. He had a knack for redressing the haughtiest Iroquois chief with a remarkable simulacrum of the Indian's own bombastic rhetoric, then bestow trinkets on his wife, and get down on the floor of the chateau to play with his children. Frontenac had a keen sense of what people wanted; from him, certainly, but also from their struggle with the hardships of life. Even the roughest class in the New World respected and admired him; the *coureurs de bois* saw neither an orator nor statesman when they encountered Frontenac, but a professional soldier who had made a living with his sword, cheating death on a multitude of occasions.

Despite frequent bursts of temper, Frontenac had a sharp wit and didn't always take himself and his office too seriously. When a woman he was in conflict with delivered a petition in the form of a bawdy poem, Frontenac replied with some ribald verse of his own. Sensing an opportunity, the petitioner attempted to discredit the royal governor by including this correspondence in a legal matter being heard by the Supreme Council. Rather than erupting in outrage, which might have been expected,

Frontenac was amused, levying a small fine and then distributing the money among the women's children.

Count Frontenac had barely sailed away on the St. Lawrence River when his replacement as governor, Joseph-Antoine Le Fèbvre de La Barre, a sixty-year-old former judge, wrote to the king bragging that he planned to subdue the Iroquois with his sword, instead of more rhetoric. But he concluded his boast on a timid note: he must have more soldiers as soon as possible, or all of Canada would be lost.

At La Barre's first council with the Iroquois, before forty-three of their chiefs and sagamores at Montreal, the new governor neither boasted nor threatened. Instead, La Barre heaped gifts and flattery on the enemy he had pledged to destroy. Toward the end of their meeting, he roused enough courage to ask the Iroquois why they had attacked the Illinois against the king's wishes, resulting in a slaughter that included some Frenchmen who were with them. When the Iroquois orator said, "Because they deserve to die," La Barre dared not rebuke him, and it became clear to French military officers in attendance that Frontenac may have been discharged too hastily.

During this time, the English had taken over the principal Dutch colony, renaming it New York, and installed Colonel Thomas Dongan as governor, a well-born Irish Catholic who spoke French and was destined to be the next Earl of Limerick. A capable statesman, Dongan's appointment was a further impediment to French expansionism, since he had early on convened a meeting in Albany with the five tribes of the Iroquois League. Dongan's men dug a pit outside the council-house, and the Iroquois and the English threw ceremonial hatchets into the hole, covered them up, and agreed to peace between the Iroquois and the English of New York, Maryland, and Virginia.

At this gathering, Dongan informed the five tribes that La Barre planned to make war on them, showing the Indians a letter the French governor had sent to him, begging the English to stop selling guns to the Iroquois. These revelations convinced the Iroquois to place themselves under the Duke of York's banner and to refrain from making a treaty with the French unless Dongan gave his consent. Within a short time, La Barre's pompous blundering had reinforced his enemies on both sides, while drawing the English and the Iroquois closer together. The Jesuit missionary, Lamberville, who was still living among the Iroquois at Onondaga, wrote to La Barre saying that the Seneca were jubilant at the prospect of war with the French, who would be "stripped, roasted, and eaten" despite their reputation for having salty flesh.

Although La Barre engaged in a good deal of saber rattling, he refused to mount a campaign against the Iroquois. Of course, the Indians interpreted this as a sign of weakness. Urged by the Supreme Council to move against the Iroquois before they grew too powerful, La Barre finally assembled several hundred Canadian militia and a horde of savages, including the Abenaki, Algonquin, Huron, and converted Iroquois. After a lengthy, difficult trip upriver, the army disembarked at Fort Frontenac, where La Barre made the mistake of bivouacking in a swampy area plagued by hordes of mosquitoes. Soon after, malaria struck the encampment, killing several men and causing a great number to become ill, including La Barre. In this debilitated state, the French expedition dropped any pretense of war and offered the Iroquois a parley. La Barre and a small escort paddled across the lake and occupied a vacant field, where they invited the Indians to meet with them. But this camp also fell into sickness. Slumped in an armchair, the royal governor attempted to lie, saying he had left the main army at Fort Frontenac and had traveled here with only his personal escort, as a show of good faith. But one of the Iroquois who spoke French had overheard the truth about La Barre's depleted expedition.

Speaking through an interpreter, La Barre announced that the king had ordered the Iroquois to make reparations for the French traders they had beaten and robbed; to repudiate their budding alliance with the English; and to free the captives they had taken in their raids against the Illinois and Miami. If they failed in any of these tasks, the governor warned, he and his army had been ordered to attack them.

Now it was the Iroquois's turn. On this occasion, a wily Onondaga chief known as Garangula, or "Big Mouth," who was skilled in both reasoned argument and sarcasm, was chosen to represent the five tribes. When the interpreter fell silent, Big Mouth rose to his feet and paced up and down, finally coming to a halt in front of La Barre. The Iroquois chief was a striking figure: long-jawed, loose-limbed, keen-eyed, and rough-humored, his face streaked with war paint and a thatch of feathers sprouting from his scalp. After an opening round of pleasantries, Big Mouth fixed his gaze upon La Barre and in a loud, triumphant voice said, "Listen,

Onontio. I am not asleep. My eyes are open; and by the sun that gives me light I see a great captain at the head of a band of soldiers, who talks like a man in a dream. . . . I see Onontio raving in a camp of sick men, whose lives the Great Spirit has saved by smiting them with disease."

In a typical burst of sarcasm, Big Mouth added that he and the other warriors had disarmed the Iroquois women, children, and old men who had planned to attack in their stead, thereby avoiding the destruction of the French encampment. But when the Indians' laughter had died away, the Iroquois chief grew serious.

"We have the right to go whithersoever we please, to take with us whomever we please, and buy and sell of whomever we please," said Big Mouth. "We have knocked the Illinois in the head, because they cut down the tree of peace and hunted the beaver on our lands. We have done less than the English and the French, who have seized upon the lands of many tribes, driven them away, and built towns, villages, and forts in their country."

The truth of Big Mouth's oration hung in the fetid, mosquito-strewn air. Soon afterward, the French soldiers withdrew, trembling with fever as they packed into canoes and bateaux and drifted on the current toward Montreal. Author of a fragile peace, the royal governor had made several burdensome concessions and received next to nothing in exchange. His allies, the Huron, Ottawa, Ojibwa, Pottawattamie, and Fox, many of them having traveled a thousand miles to kill and eat the Iroquois, were now told to go home empty handed. They did so, filled with disgust at the weakness and chicanery of the French, more willing now to consider trading their furs at Albany instead of Montreal. Informed of this debacle, Louis XIV wrote to La Barre, ordering him to return to France.

The prospects of New France were dimming. Colonel Dongan had claimed all the land south of the Great Lakes for New York; the English of Hudson Bay were siphoning off the fur trade of the northern tribes; and the Bostonnais frequently raided the coastline of Nova Scotia by sea, disrupting and co-opting Canadian fishing stations there. Outraged by La Barre's shameful peace treaty with the Iroquois, Louis XIV replaced him with the Marquis de Denonville, a colonel of the dragoons with thirty years' experience as a professional soldier. To bolster Denonville's effort, the king sent five hundred troops aboard the new governor's ship when it sailed for Quebec. But in the sort of calamity that often attended such matters, nearly a third of these soldiers died of fever and scurvy during the voyage.

Both Denonville and his English counterpart in New York, Thomas Dongan, understood that the stakes were high. If the marquis failed to make the right decisions, New France would never amount to more than a single fortified town on the St. Lawrence River; and if Dongan bungled his attempt to turn the Iroquois and Abenaki against his rivals, the English hold on the New World would be limited to a few villages clustered along the Atlantic shoreline. (Both men had limited manpower, though the English population of New York, at eighteen thousand settlers, was a third larger than the French colony.) In the diplomatic fashion of the time, the rival governors, in the midst of their intrigues, maintained a correspondence by mail, their letters full of mutual, chivalrous flattery. When the marquis sent the English colonel notice of his arrival, Dongan, writing in French, wrote back, "Sir, I have had the honor of receiving your letter, and greatly rejoice at having so good a neighbor. . . . I have a very high respect for the king of France, of whose bread I have eaten so much that I feel under an obligation to prevent whatever can give the least umbrage to our masters."

The tenor of their correspondence was to change rapidly. In one letter, the French governor denounces his counterpart for supplying rum to the Iroquois, to which Dongan, now writing in English, responded, "Certainly our Rum doth as little hurt as your Brandy, and, in the opinion of Christians, is much more wholesome." When the marquis complained in another dispatch that the English were relentless in their efforts to agitate the Iroquois, Dongan, on the advice of his superior, King James II, wrote a placating note in return, and enclosed a gift: "Sir, I send you some Oranges, hearing that they are a rarity in your partes." Denonville replied, "Monsieur, I thank you for your oranges. It is a great pity that they were all rotten."

Denonville sent a more urgent and straightforward letter to his king, insisting on additional fighting men, *materiél*, and gold, stating that he would rather go to war than suffer from the thousand tiny wounds the enemies of France were inflicting. In June 1687, Louis XIV sent Denonville what he required, noting that it would not be expedient to attack the English, but instead, ordering him to assault the Seneca. Learning of this plan from some Canadian deserters, the governor of New York informed the Iroquois of the impending attack. Adept at choosing their allies as the occasion demanded, the Iroquois swore their allegiance to King James II and received ample gunpowder and lead in return.

The die was cast: The French would march against the Iroquois. But the initial action of this war took on a foreboding tenor. When Denonville and his army reached Fort Frontenac, they discovered that fifty-one local Iroquois, friendly Indians from nearby villages who hunted and fished to supply the French garrison, had been taken prisoner. They were lashed to a row of posts inside the fort, bound by the neck, hands, and feet, and exposed to the dense swarms of mosquitoes that appeared in late June. Shortly after Denonville arrived, so-called "Christian" Indians allied with the French began torturing the captives by burning their fingers and taunting them. Denonville saved the prisoners from death, if only for the horrible fate of being shipped downriver to Quebec and finally to Versailles, where they were enslaved alongside convicts and Huguenots in the royal galleys. It was an inauspicious beginning to the campaign, but the marquis could not risk any of the captives informing their relatives across the lake of his presence there.

During the night, one of the Iroquois prisoners managed to loosen his bonds, gain entrance to a nearby blockhouse, and jump from a second floor window to the ground. He was alarmed by what he saw outside the fort, and ran to warn the Seneca of Denonville's impending attack. Encamped outside the palisades were two thousand combatants, including French regulars, rowdy groups of *coureurs de bois*, and a large number of Indians who had been converted to Catholicism. Several months earlier, communicating by post, the marquis had also ordered French officers in charge of the fort at Michillimackinac and others among the Illinois to meet him at Niagara in early July, bringing along as many *coureurs de bois* and friendly Indians as they could find. The distance was so great and the logistics so improbable that the marquis had little hope of assistance. So the French military commander took it as a sign of divine providence when three separate forces, crossing a thousand miles in heavy weather from disparate points, converged at Irondequoit Bay within hours of one another. Now ready to take the field, Denonville had three thousand fighters at his disposal, nearly a quarter of the French population in Canada.

The encampment on a spit of land that demarcated Lake Ontario from Irondequoit Bay was as teeming, garish, and horrible as a painting by Hieronymus Bosch. Their tents arranged in rows under the banner of the marquis, the four battalions of French regulars and militia were commanded by the *noblesse* in their elegant, well-tailored uniforms. On their perimeter was the unruly bivouac of the *coureurs de bois*, who milled around spitting and cursing and greeting each other with roars of delight. Lying just beyond were the bark lean-tos and animal hide wigwams of the Christian Indians, and occupying a nearby swamp was a mob of untamed Indians babbling in various tongues and carrying an array of crude, terrible weapons the likes of which had never been seen. But for the stag horns and animal skulls perched on their heads, and the ox, lynx, raccoon, and shredded beaver tails dangling from their naked haunches, they wore nothing but pieces of iron jewelry, and the clan signs of the deer, fish, and bear they had painted on their torsos.

Two days later, the French expedition decamped, marching in the swelter of a July morning toward the Seneca village. Wading through the tall grass and clumps of brush, the army was led by two groups of *coureurs de bois*, who lacked military discipline but were familiar with the territory and constitutionally fearless. On their left flank was a band of Iroquois converts from Saut St. Louis and the Mountain of Montreal, urged on by the floating black specter of their Jesuit master. On the bushrangers' other flank were the savages from the upper lakes, with their horns and tails and infernal weaponry. Behind this vanguard of eight hundred men came Denonville and his French regulars, each of the four battalions of uniformed soldiers alternating with detachments of Canadian militia in their handspun clothing and buckskins. The heat was oppressive. Denonville had stripped to his blouse and sword, and later wrote, "It is a rough life to tramp afoot through the woods, carrying one's own provisions in a haversack, devoured by mosquitoes, and faring no better than a mere soldier."

Scouts returning from a patrol said that the Iroquois village was lightly defended, the occupants so unaware of the army's presence that women were tilling an adjacent cornfield. Unfortunately for Denonville's advance guard, this was a trick to make the French abandon their caution and rush toward the village. The heavily wooded terrain had narrowed into a gorge, causing the three prongs of the vanguard to squeeze into one long column. When they did, three hundred Iroquois waiting in ambush leaped from a shallow defile, most of them naked but for swaths of war paint. They were armed with swords and knives and hatchets, screaming in a great din, and fell upon the first column of invaders. But the initial cohort of rangers and Indians was so large the Iroquois mistook it for the entire force. In an effort to finish the battle quickly, a second wave of Iroquois, concealed behind the *coureurs de bois*, attacked their flank. They were unaware that the marquis and several battalions of regular troops and militia were right behind them, and their carefully planned ambuscade brought a mixed result. Fighting converged on all sides, and the thick forest, the din of musket fire, and the war whoops and shouts, echoing across the intervale where the engagement took place, confused both invaders and defenders. Patches of gun smoke drifted among the trees and hovered over the rank grass, limiting visibility.

It was a double ambush. As the second Iroquois war party attacked the *coureur de bois*'s flank, Denonville and the first battalion of French regulars closed on the Seneca from behind. To the tattoo of their drums, they waded into a bloodbath that consisted of screaming Indians and shaggy bushrangers discharging their rifles at close range, wrestling on the ground with dagger and hatchet, and springing from tree limb to tree limb, flinging arrows and musket balls into the chaos below. Ear-piercing shrieks mingled with cries of mortal agony, and the stench of mutilated flesh, like that of a slaughterhouse, spread over the field. Approaching the intense and bloody fighting at the bottom of the gorge, several French officers lay face down in the weeds, frightened into paralysis. Already, six or seven hundred fighters, many of them naked, be-horned, and bellowing in pain or blood lust, were crowded into the thickly forested gorge. The first group of militia to descend into the ravine, commanded by an officer named Berthier, took one look at the carnage and wheeled around, scrambling back the way they came.

His sword upraised, the Marquis de Denonville ran down the slope into the midst of the fray. Ordering Berthier to turn his corps around, Denonville shouted to the nearest drummer boy to play the charge. Now supported by a few resolute officers, Denonville moved among his troops and militia, ordering them to stand together and go forward, striking or shooting at anyone who looked like a threat. As more French troops poured into the defile, the Seneca grabbed their dead and wounded, disappearing among the trees.

In that quarter-hour, Denonville acquitted himself well. But the fatigue of their long march, the rising heat of midday, and what he had just observed regarding Iroquois tactics convinced the marquis not to pursue his enemy into the forest. Considering the ferocity of the battle, the French casualties were light; a half dozen men were killed outright in the ambush, and twenty more were seriously hurt, including one of the Jesuit priests who had not shied away from the bloodiest fighting. At least forty Seneca were killed, and sixty grievously wounded, according to a Christian Indian who was taken prisoner by the Iroquois and later escaped.

Due to the oppressive heat, as well as the precarious state of several wounded soldiers, Denonville told his officers to make camp adjacent to where the battle had occurred. That decision led to the marquis and his command staff witnessing the barbarity of their Indian allies, who quartered many of the Iroquois corpses like butchers' meat, boiled them in kettles, and gorged on their enemies' flesh. Some of the Iroquois dead had their limbs sliced open, allowing the conquerors to drink the warm blood. Denonville noted that among the lake tribe Indians, the Ottawa demonstrated the most cruelty, a trait he found particularly loathsome since they had shirked the actual fighting, only to return for their devilish sport when the battle had concluded.

The next day, the marquis deployed his troops in their previous formation, advancing on the famous Seneca town where so much barbarity had taken place. But all that remained was a smoldering ruin, filled with freshly dug graves, snakes, and other creatures, the Iroquois having burned it before retreating into the bush. The departing Indians had left behind vast stores of corn and pigs, which the French plundered, growing sick on the green corn and the poorly cooked meat before destroying what remained. His Indian allies melting away, the marquis decided not to pursue the Iroquois into the wilderness, and he and his troops decamped for Niagara, where they built a stockade on the strip of land between Lake Ontario and the Niagara River. Denonville left a hundred soldiers to protect the fort, while he and the rest continued on to Montreal.

It was a somber journey, far short of the triumphant return that Denonville had envisioned. Before the campaign, a converted Iroquois told the marquis that the only way to defeat the Seneca was to burn out and destroy them, like wasps. If he merely overturned the nest, his enemy would return again and again to sting him. Although Denonville had begun his campaign like a worthy successor to Count Frontenac, full of brio and daring, he had ended up like La Barre, doubting himself and his mission.

Hearing of these events, the governor of New York, Colonel Dongan, seized on the opportunity to reprimand the Iroquois, summoning them to Albany to denounce their practice of accepting Jesuit missionaries into their villages and holding councils with the French. In support of Dongan's efforts, King James II issued a decree that all the five tribes of the Iroquois League were British subjects, and as such protected from incursion or subjugation by force of arms. A testy exchange of letters ensued between the colonial governors of New France and New York. Denonville repeated his claim that all the territory occupied by both the Iroquois and the lake tribes, thousands of square miles that were rich in beaver furs, belonged to Louis XIV on the grounds of prior discovery and its present occupation by Frenchmen. To this, Colonel Dongan replied that "a few loose fellowes rambling amongst Indians to keep themselves from starving" did not grant ownership of the land to the French.

The agitation of the Seneca and the other Iroquois tribes strangled the fur trade for two years. Meanwhile, the troops garrisoned at the newly constructed Fort Niagara suffered from malnutrition and the constant threat of enemy patrols, with death and disease reducing their number from one hundred men to ten or twelve. Denonville was forced to abandon the stockade, which emboldened the Iroquois to such a degree that every French town above Three Rivers was transformed into a prison for its inhabitants, who were afraid to venture out. Iroquois war parties appeared frequently, torturing and killing those found outside the palisades. As foretold, the wasps had returned, and their stings were deadly.

In aggregate, Denonville had an advantage in manpower over the Iroquois, though his meager forces were deployed all over the territory, and the enemy usually knew their whereabouts. The marquis therefore considered a two-pronged attack on the Iroquois, moving against the Onondaga and Cayuga with one army, and attacking the Oneida and Mohawk with another. While he pondered the necessity of crossing through British territory to execute this plan, Denonville was surprised to learn that the Iroquois had approached the commander at Fort Frontenac with an offer to renew the peace. Always savvy and calculating, Big Mouth, the loquacious Iroquois chief, had recently set out for Montreal accompanied by a half dozen Onondaga, Oneida, and Cayuga sachems, and well over a thousand warriors. He left this immense war party at Lake St. Francis as a bargaining tool, and continued on to Montreal with his delegation and a small escort.

In his meeting with the royal governor, Big Mouth began by informing Denonville that more reckless Iroquois leaders, convinced of the French colony's vulnerability, had devised a campaign to make war against all the small farming towns and settlements. They planned to kill the livestock, burn the crops, terrorize the settlers until they retreated inside their stockades, and then attack the starving garrisons at the forts. The logic of this gambit startled Denonville. Continuing with his speech, Big Mouth said he had prevented his countrymen from executing their strategy because of his loyalty to Onontio. Furthermore, the Iroquois League was a friend to both the English and the French, though subject to neither, with Big Mouth also instructing his host that the five tribes had never been defeated in war.

The marquis was in a difficult position. He already knew that the army of warriors at Lake St. Francis had killed several converted Indians and planned to wreak further havoc, but he decided to keep his own counsel. Agreeing to sign a document that allowed the Iroquois to remain neutral in the disputes between the English and French colonies, Denonville looked on while Big Mouth drew tiny figures of birds and various animals on the treaty, representing his and the other Indians' signatures. To conclude these deliberations, Big Mouth told the French governor that a more comprehensive delegation of the Iroquois leadership would soon appear in Montreal, leading to a formal declaration of peace.

As often occurred in the New World, a strange and bloody coincidence would intrude on all these plans. Working against the colonial leadership was the notion that, to a man, they were smarter than Big Mouth and all the other Indian leaders. Certainly, the Marquis de Denonville and his advisors underestimated the Onondaga chieftain and orator, but they made an even more serious miscalculation in dealing with Kondiaronk, known as the Rat. A well-respected warrior known for his prowess in battle, his quick wit, and his remarkable ability to see the long-term consequences of events as they unfolded, the Rat, being Huron, had declared for the French and hated the Iroquois, but would occasionally change his opinions as the situation dictated. In other words, he was a match for Denonville, the sophistical Jesuits, and the other dissemblers and charlatans who populated the territory and afflicted the Indians with their schemes. At the same time that Big Mouth had agreed to peace terms with the French, Kondiaronk was roaming the countryside near Lake Ontario with a large party of warriors, hunting for Iroquois scalps. During a stop at Fort Frontenac, the Huron chief was alarmed to hear about these negotiations, and that another Iroquois delegation was expected to pass by, on their way to finalize a treaty in Montreal. Pretending it didn't matter to him, the Rat left Fort Frontenac disturbed by this news. If the French and Iroquois were at peace, there would be very little standing between the lake tribes and their sworn enemies, the Iroquois, who wished nothing but their destruction.

Instead of paddling back to Michillimackinac, avoiding the Iroquois as he had been warned, the Rat and his warriors detoured to La Famine, where they set up an ambush and waited. After nearly a week, the Huron spotted several canoes nearing the place where they had concealed themselves. No sooner had the Iroquois, led by the famous chief, Decanisora, grounded their canoes on the beach than the band of Huron leaped out and fired upon their enemies. One of the Iroquois chiefs was killed instantly, along with a few warriors, and nearly all the rest were wounded. Having bound their hands and feet, the Rat strutted around the captives with his rifle and hatchet, boasting that Onontio, the Marquis de Denonville himself, was the one who had betrayed them. Taken aback by the news, the Iroquois insisted they were on a peace mission and meant to become friends of the Huron.

The Rat feigned surprise, and then railed against Onontio for manipulating the Huron into such a treacherous act. Of course, the ambush was the Rat's idea and had nothing to do with the French governor. But the Huron chief, still pretending to be angry, freed his prisoners, returned their weapons to them, and suggested they take revenge against Denonville.

Still weaving the strands of his plot, the Rat kept a single Iroquois prisoner, claiming his right to adopt an enemy warrior in place of a Huron killed in the skirmish. The Huron party made their way to Michillimackinac, and the Rat turned his prisoner over to the French officer in charge of that remote garrison. The peaceful intentions of the Iroquois were unknown here, and although the Iroquois prisoner tried to explain the situation, Kondiaronk insisted he was merely trying to save himself, and the French officer had the warrior shot. Then the Rat visited a nearby

Huron village and set free an elderly Iroquois prisoner, making sure to first tell the old man what the French soldiers had done to his countryman at Michillimackinac. Having thus engineered an ambush, an execution, and an escape, the intrepid Huron chief maneuvered the two nations back in conflict with one another, and again put the abundant resources and resolve of the French between his people and the mighty Iroquois League.

As a seat-of-the-pants act of realpolitik, the Rat's legerdemain proved that even a tiny lever could move the weight of history. During a violent thunderstorm on the night of August 4, 1688, a war party consisting of fifteen hundred Iroquois crept into the French town of La Chine, just above Montreal on the St. Lawrence River. Before dawn, the warriors, arranged here and there in small parties, brandished their hatchets and pole-axes, let loose a cacophony of bloodcurdling screams, and rushed into the settlement, burning and looting the homes, and bludgeoning, shooting, and stabbing everyone they encountered.

By the time the commander of the local garrison, a French officer named Subercase, had returned in haste from Montreal, the settlement was in flames and the Iroquois had withdrawn to a nearby forest. The streets of La Chine were strewn with the dead: men, women, and children mutilated beyond recognition, either sprawled in the dirt, or hung from posts where they had been hacked to pieces and burned. Hearing that the Iroquois were in a nearby copse of trees drunk on looted brandy, Subercase, now leading three hundred soldiers, militia, and well-armed settlers, resolved to march out from the town and attack them. But a cautious superior ordered Subercase and his men to withdraw just as they entered the woods, and after a brief, heated argument, the junior officer and his column retired to nearby Fort Roland.

Five hundred additional troops were already inside the stockade, though with orders not to advance. The next morning, a detachment of eighty soldiers from nearby Fort Remy marched toward La Chine to improve the garrison. The Iroquois, having recovered from their debauchery of the previous evening, moved into position for an ambush. With the French looking on from Fort Roland, the savages vaulted from their concealment, butchering all but a few of the soldiers who ran in terror before the onslaught.

The French troops and their commanders were immobilized by indecision, confusion, and fear. The savagery of the Iroquois method of warfare, enacted in plain sight of Fort Roland's stockade, was, no doubt, a horrifying spectacle. But the French were superior in both manpower and weaponry, and, after suffering years of ambuscades, feints, and parries, were confronted with a large number of Iroquois out in the open, fighting without the benefits of surprise and guile that made them so formidable. Denonville was nearby, inside the fortifications at Montreal with a large contingent of soldiers. Had he marched out and taken the field, with the troops from Fort Roland and militia from La Chine on the flanks, the marquis could have destroyed the Iroquois war party within a few days. But while the French cowered inside their palisades, the Iroquois ranged over the surrounding countryside, burning the houses and barns, pillaging food stores, and killing and scalping every white person they could find within a ten-mile radius of La Chine.

Big Mouth had warned the marquis of just such a strategy, where the Iroquois would drive the French inside their stockades, burn down the villages and settlements, eliminate their food supply, and then lay siege to the forts, starving them out. Denonville's personal reputation for courage, as well as his previous exploits as a military commander in the New World and in Europe, made his paralysis during the assault on La Chine particularly tragic. The opportunity for a great victory was there, but he shrank before the challenge.

After the Iroquois dispatched the column of soldiers, they made for their canoes, taunting the Fort Roland garrison before paddling across Lake Saint Louis with several dozen captives. That night, the Iroquois camped on the far side of the lake, ignited several large pyres, and tortured and burned scores of men, women, and children. Their pitiful screams carried across the lake to the survivors at La Chine, who gathered along the shoreline, weeping and gnashing their teeth.

Soon, the colony of New France would be threatened as much by the newly crowned king of England as the Iroquois uprising. During the English Revolution that same year, 1689, William of Orange, who plunged Louis XIV and his reeling monarchy into King William's War, supplanted King James II. Faced with two powerful enemies in the New World, when either the Iroquois or the English would have been difficult enough, Louis XIV had no choice but to recall the Marquis de Denonville. In recent years, the fluctuations in the stability and fortunes of the colony had vexed the king a great deal. The next royal governor would be faced with a series of Herculean tasks: regaining control of the fur trade throughout Canada; striking back at the Iroquois and the English; stabilizing the colonial seats of Quebec and Montreal; expanding westward as far as the Pacific Ocean; and establishing a claim on all the land drained by the Mississippi River and its tributaries. To accomplish any of these goals would take a near miracle, given that the preoccupations of the war in Europe prevented Louis XIV from committing additional troops or money to saving New France.

It would require an exceptional man to fulfill such obligations. The new royal governor must have enough confidence in his own ability to be undaunted by the prospect, but of adequate experience to reckon with its various dimensions. He must possess the vigor necessary to endure the trials of his office, as well as the placid habits of mind required of diplomatists and prelates. Onontio, as the Iroquois called him, would be called upon, at various times, to coax and compliment, to lavish gifts, and to raise the hatchet against his enemies with murderous intent.

As Louis XIV considered the soldiers, statesmen, and courtiers who thronged the suites of Versailles, pondering which of them might have the peculiar array of talents necessary for the position, his gaze fell upon an unremarkable figure, now seventy years of age, his fortune debilitated and his usefulness seemingly at an end. At length, the king's choice to succeed Denonville was summoned to the royal apartments, where a grim-faced assemblage of ministers and clerics awaited him. So, when he strode into the drawing room after his name, and undoubtedly found some of the royal advisors with their mouths agape, the lieutenant-general designee for the king in New France, Louis de Baude, also known as Count Frontenac, must have felt at least a modicum of satisfaction in resuming the title and position that had been stripped from him seven years earlier. Without hesitation, Frontenac accepted the commission, bowed to his sovereign king, and departed French soil for the last time.

Never one to hesitate, Count Frontenac picked up his wily maneuvering right where he had left off. Aboard the French ship taking him to Quebec was the legendary Cayuga chief, Ourehaoue, and a dozen Iroquois warriors who had been taken captive with him some time earlier, at Fort Frontenac. After being enslaved on the royal galleys, Ourehaoue and his tribesmen were being repatriated by Louis XIV as a gesture of good will. On the voyage to New France, the returning Onontio often entertained the Cayuga war chief in his stateroom, treating him with great respect and civility. When they reached Quebec, Frontenac hosted Ourehaoue at the chateau, where a friendship continued to develop between the royal governor and the influential Iroquois chief.

By mutual agreement, Ourehaoue dispatched three of his party to Onondaga with a message, informing his fellow Iroquois that the great Onontio had returned. The chief reminded his countrymen that Frontenac had never deceived the Iroquois, as his successors had done. If the five nations would renounce the English, and take up the hatchet against them, the great Onontio would continue to love them, in the manner that a father loves his children. And if the Iroquois would send a deputation to Fort Frontenac to hold council with the great Onontio, he would make good on his promise and release Ourehaoue and his warriors.

Upon his return to Canada, Frontenac had become aware of a possible alliance between the Iroquois, the English, and the lake tribes, who had mostly remained loyal to the French. Count Frontenac realized that such a union could mean the obliteration of the colony. He was also troubled by the news that the lake tribes had returned some Iroquois prisoners to their villages, along with an offer of peace. Soon after, Ourehaoue's messengers were sent back to Quebec, not in acceptance of the French invitation, but with a counter offer: release our countrymen, and *then* we will agree to a council. The messengers also said that the Iroquois had made peace with the nine tribes of the Michillimackinac, and would not lay down their tomahawks against the French until Ourehaoue and his warriors came home.

The greatest of the Onontios never mourned the dissolution of his plans, quickly moving on to devise another. Having decided to attack the English settlements as a show of strength, Count Frontenac put together three war parties, personally choosing the officers and a number of the men in each contingent. Two hundred and ten men, including ninety-six Christian Indians from the mission villages, gathered outside Montreal. Simultaneously, a party of French militia and their Indian allies totaling forty-nine combatants mustered at Three Rivers. And the final party, consisting of nearly a hundred Frenchmen, left Quebec in the middle of a terrible winter and journeyed on foot into Maine, gathering several hundred Abenaki warriors along the way.

Trekking in snowshoes over the frozen disk of Lake Champlain in their hooded coats and mittens, the Montreal expedition tramped through swamps and dense forest until they reached the palisades of Schenectady. They burned the English town, killed thirty-eight men and boys, murdered women and children by stabbing and bludgeoning them, and seized the local minister, hacking him to bits with pole-axes and hatchets.

Descending from Three Rivers, the French sortie against Cocheco was also a rout, culminating in the torture and killing of Major Richard Waldron. Continuing on to Salmon Falls in Massachusetts, the French and Indians killed or captured eighty persons; their commanding officer and thirty-six of his men hastened to join the third party coming from Quebec, then ravaging the Maine countryside on their way to attack the English fort at Casco Bay. Between the two French columns and the large number of Abenaki Indians who joined them en route, the party exceeded four hundred men.

At Casco Bay, the French war party burned the outlying settlement, lay siege to the fort, and, when the English asked for quarter, induced them to open the gates. The French took the English commander as their hostage, but turned the Indians loose on the women and children, who were murdered in significant numbers, while a few were taken captive. Before returning to Quebec, the French spiked the cannon, then torched the fort and what was left of the village, leaving dozens of corpses heaped on the ground.

Frontenac had announced his return. His bold forays against the English served to reinvigorate Canada's spirit, while raising the blood lust of the Abenaki, inciting them to continue their attacks on the English settlements. But perhaps Onontio's greatest triumph would come in defense of New France, as Sir William Phips, the New England–born wayfarer and adventurer, had been commissioned to raise a fleet of motley vessels and sail, first against Atlantic Canada, where the English prevailed, and then against the rocky precipice of Quebec. With thirty-two ships and twenty-two hundred men, Phips's armada enjoyed great success in Acadia without firing a shot, and then entered the St. Lawrence River on its way to the Basin of Quebec. The end of the French colony seemed near at hand.

Fortune favors the brave, and certainly Count Frontenac was lucky on several counts as Phips drew closer to Quebec. While in Montreal preparing for a retaliatory attack after the burning of Schenectady, Frontenac received word that an Abenaki Indian, arriving in Quebec from Maine, had reported a large flotilla of English ships heading toward the colony. This gave Frontenac time to prepare for the English invasion. Additionally, French border settlements (unlike their English counterparts, which sprang up irregularly across three hundred miles of wilderness) consisted of easily defended villages, bunched here and there along a ninety-mile stretch of the St. Lawrence. As the English fleet passed by, often hewing close to the riverbanks, French settlers and militia, urged on by their priests, fired devastating volleys into the enemy ships, killing sailors and militia alike. Beyond this sort of harassment, Phips suffered from an inexplicable delay when he stopped for three weeks within a few days' voyage of his objective, allowing the French to muster additional troops and strengthen their fortifications. Phips's hesitation would give Frontenac an opportunity to reach Quebec ahead of the armada, inspect its defenses, and use the people's unshakeable faith in him to bolster their confidence.

After traveling from Montreal by leaky bateaux and canoe, Frontenac disembarked on the quay and ascended Mountain Street toward the Upper Town on foot. As the lieutenant-general, now a white-haired old man, climbed the hill amidst a drizzling rain, a crowd of merchants, brewers, tanners, coopers, carpenters, gunsmiths, stave dealers, and wheelwrights spilled into the street. The air was filled with cheers and huzzahs, with billeted officers and soldiers of the garrison waving their caps; innkeepers and fishmongers and apothecaries wiping away tears; shop boys running alongside; and even his old enemies, the Jesuit priests, the bishop, and the intendant, emerging from their chapel to hail the deliverer of New France.

The town, situated on a promontory overlooking the river and flanked by sheer cliffs, was nearly impregnable. Cannons were mounted at strategic locations above the basin, and additional earthworks and revetments were constructed under Count Frontenac's direction. More importantly, nearly three thousand French soldiers, militia, and *coureurs de bois* from the surrounding territory had poured in, bolstering Quebec's garrison. For two days, Frontenac met with his officers, evaluated the city's defenses, and supervised their improvement. Then, near morning on the third day, having done all he could to prepare for the invasion, Frontenac and his advisors kept their eyes fixed on the rising waters of the basin. As the light came up, four large British war ships, followed by thirty assorted brigantines, sloops, schooners, and motley fishing vessels, packed with British regulars, militia, and sailors, crowded the St. Lawrence to the horizon. The enemy had arrived.

To the wonderment of the onlookers, Phips refrained from firing upon the town. Confident of his overwhelming advantage, the English admiral ordered his ships to drop anchor, and, by mid-morning, had launched a small boat containing his emissary and a flag of truce. Frontenac sent four canoes to intercept him, and, before reaching the quay, the English officer was transferred to one of the canoes, and then blindfolded and paddled ashore.

A pair of burly sergeants grasped the envoy under the arms and, accompanied by a French officer, led him by a circuitous route to the royal governor, forcing the British subaltern to climb over stone walls and barricades. As he attempted these obstacles, stumbling on the paving stones lining the hill, a raucous crowd of townspeople followed alongside, jeering the messenger as if he was playing a game of blindman's buff.

When his blindfold was removed, the Englishman found himself blinking in the torchlight of the chateau. Arrayed before him in the spacious chamber were Count Frontenac and a group of his senior officers, wearing their plumed cockade hats and dress uniforms trimmed with battle ribbons and gold braid. The messenger saluted Frontenac, handing over a letter from Phips. In it, the admiral offered the French his terms of surrender, allowing just one hour for a reply. Frontenac said that the English need not wait that long: "I will answer your general only by the mouths of my cannon." Then the English officer was again blindfolded and directed back through the garrison, where he could hear the beating of drums, rattling chains, the heaving of guns into their emplacements, and other sounds of martial readiness.

Rather than a brisk volley from Phips's cannons—the sort of gambit that had made his reputation as a buccaneer in the West Indies—the admiral retired below decks to ponder his options. He was stymied by the response to his ultimatum, having fully expected the French to surrender. All that day, Phips met with his council, and, at sundown, their deliberations were interrupted by the noise of a military band and a great cacophony of voices erupting from the Upper Town. When Phips asked a French prisoner about the meaning of this uproar, he learned that the governor of Montreal, a man named Callieres, had arrived along with eight hundred men, including several battalions of French regulars and a rowdy band of *coureurs de bois*, eager for a fight. "You have lost the game," said the French prisoner.

The English decided to land a substantial number of men at nearby Beauport and attack the flank, while Phips's armada fired upon the ramparts from the basin. But it wasn't until the next day that Phips sent thirteen hundred men ashore, and simultaneously began a cannonade against Quebec's fortifications. Amidst the terrific roar of the batteries on land and on the water, the bitter stench of gunpowder filled the air, and vast clouds of smoke obscured the enemies' view of one another. French sharpshooters and militia repelled three attempts at a ground assault, and most of Phips's artillery fire, despite producing a great, echoing roar, fell harmlessly against the rocky promontory. The New Englanders were stubborn and resourceful fighters but possessed very little discipline and were no match for the experienced French troops.

Within a few days, the English fleet was defeated. Having expended all his ammunition and seen his ground troops shot to pieces, Phips withdrew beyond the range of the French guns to repair his battered ships. (French scouts were surprised to find the admiral himself, who had once been employed as a carpenter, high on a scaffold patching holes in his flagship.) An exchange of prisoners ensued, and then Phips and his armada sailed away, never realizing that if they had arrived a week earlier, before the French garrison had been reinforced, or remained in place for another week, exhausting Quebec's food supply, the English would have prevailed.

The Jesuits and the Récollet friars had prayed throughout the ordeal, later claiming that the headwinds and tides that had delayed the English fleet, their harmless barrage, and the icy weather that hindered their ground attacks, were all signs of God's favor. And though the banner of the Holy Virgin was carried in procession through the town, and the bishop sang *Te Deum* in the cathedral, when the peasants and the gentry, the tradesmen and their apprentices, the Ursuline sisters and the Jesuit fathers got down on their knees that evening, they included a prayer for Count Frontenac, whose luck, timing, and tactics had saved the entire colony from ruin.

King Louis XIV prized what his royal governor had done, enclosing two thousand crowns in a letter he sent to Frontenac, congratulating him for the defense of Quebec. (In a subsequent note to one of the king's ministers, Frontenac said that he appreciated the monarch's handwritten commendation more than the money.) His personal wealth aside, Frontenac had become increasingly concerned about New France's fur trade and the Iroquois's strenuous efforts to disrupt it. With their own territory hunted bare, the Iroquois required an increasing supply of beaver pelts to keep them continuously replenished with liquor, firearms, gunpowder, and shot. But collective dread turned to joy when the lake tribe Indians and *coureurs de bois* appeared at the annual fair in Montreal with 165 canoes laden with beaver furs. The colony was once again flush with money, at the exact hour of its greatest need.

Count Frontenac employed this newfound wealth to prosecute his half of King William's War, including the use of blood money. By decree of the royal governor, twenty crowns were paid to anyone bringing in a white male prisoner, and ten crowns for a white female. (This policy saved many lives among the English, since it induced the Indians to bring many of their captives to New France instead of just killing them.) After being sold to the French, adult captives were put to work in the settlements, and most of the children were converted to Catholicism and raised by the nuns. On the other hand, the French also paid ten crowns for a scalp, creating a brisk source of trade for the lake tribes, Abenaki, and converted Iroquois.

One scalp looked the same as another, and it was impossible to tell whether the victim was an enemy or an unsuspecting friend. Therefore, brutal murders committed in the name of the king were often rewarded with scalp money. Also, the bounty for a scalp was the same as for a female captive, and it was easier to transport the former to Quebec than it was the latter. As a result, women and children often fell under the scalping knife, and quarter was seldom given.

Looking to strengthen ties to the converted Mohawks and the Indians of the lake tribes, while further separating both groups from the Iroquois League, Frontenac organized a force of one hundred soldiers, a seasoned band of *coureurs de bois*, and more than five hundred Indians, with the intention of assaulting three prominent Mohawk villages. The war party traveled deep into Iroquois territory, killed and captured a large number of Mohawks, and, in the midst of a driving snowstorm, fought off a column of Englishmen who had pursued them. Conditions were so desperate, the level of supplies so low, that the English commander who agreed to have breakfast with his Iroquois scouts reneged when they ladled up the hand of a dead Frenchman from their soup kettle.

After a long march complicated by illness and starvation, the French survivors returned to Montreal, and their claim of victory over the Mohawk loosened another deluge of beaver skins that had been jammed up at Michillimackinac for three years. The descent of these furs brought another much-needed infusion of capital. And for his ingenuity and resolve in this matter, Count Frontenac was named "Father of the People" and "Preserver of the Country."

While Frontenac battled the Iroquois for control of the west, he maintained a second front with the English border settlements in New Hampshire and Massachusetts, and with Acadia, which included New Brunswick, Nova Scotia, and nearly all of Maine. Key to his strategy of keeping the English at bay was the cultivation of the Abenaki, the river Indians of the Androscoggin, the Kennebec, the Penobscot, the Saco, the St. Croix, and the St. John. These tribes produced effective warriors, nearly matching the Iroquois in ferocity and courage. Count Frontenac and his ministers encouraged the Jesuit fathers to live among the river tribes, preaching the gospel from their crude altars, and exhorting them to prey upon the English in the name of Christ. This way, the French were able to fight the English by proxy, without risking their men or munitions, and thereby saving lives and money. Therefore, it's no surprise that Frontenac became incensed when he learned of peace negotiations between the Abenaki and the Bostonnais.

Frontenac's reaction to the increasing trade between the English and the Abenaki was to order the aforementioned raids on York, Wells, Oyster River, and other towns, as well as the blood-drenched mayhem inflicted upon their citizenry. Here the Abenaki were used as blunt instruments against the English, since through an accident of geography they occupied the vast forests between Frontenac's chateau and the border. Frontenac succeeded in galvanizing all of Canada through these actions, which had the added benefit of drawing his Indian allies closer. In Quebec, he had occasionally raised the ire of the clerics by allowing a group of swaggering young officers to stage plays for their amusement, and certainly he had a theatrical streak himself. At a grand council of Christian Indians, the aged Frontenac once took up the hatchet and proceeded to stamp and whoop and scream until the collection of savages rose in unison and joined him in the war dance.

But one incident in particular demonstrated Count Frontenac's strange influence over those he considered his "children," as well as the old man's durability and vigor. In 1696, just a few months before the Abenaki raid on Haverhill, an army of two thousand French regulars, militia, and their Indian allies, commanded by Frontenac and accompanied by a fleet of heavily laden bateaux containing rockets, artillery pieces, mortars, and bundles of fusees, undertook the demanding, month-long journey to Onondaga, the Iroquois capital. On this occasion, there would be no talk of peace. At the age of seventy-six, Frontenac crossed Lake Ontario and then oversaw the arduous task of dragging the bateaux and canoes against the current and along the grassy siding of the Oswego River, as the vast army inched its *matériel* upriver.

After two weeks of skirting rapids and hacking through the underbrush, one evening at dusk they reached a steep set of falls, where the boats and heavy munitions were to be portaged along the margin of the forest. It took several hours to get the cannon and mortars uphill by means of wooden rollers. As this work continued into the night, Frontenac began to disembark from his vessel when the mission Indians, shouting and chanting in ecstasy, hoisted him up, canoe and all, and carried him on their shoulders. In the torchlight, their shadows ranged along the darkened wall of trees, the naked, be-feathered Indians and their beloved Onontio, followed by the trim marching figures of the royal guard.

It was impossible to keep an army of this size a secret. So when the French reached the vast Iroquois town, which the English had helped reinforce with double palisades and other military defenses, all they found was the smoking hilltop where it had once stood. Having learned that the great Onontio was coming to make war on them, the greatest of the Iroquois tribes had burned their capital and fled into the wilderness. And if the Iroquois had again melted away before Frontenac's advance, as they had before Denonville's, they were sufficiently impressed to dispatch an embassy of several chiefs to Quebec to beg for peace. Once more, Frontenac received the approbation of the king for his efforts, as well as the

Military Order of St. Louis. For the time being, he had driven away the wolf that loitered at the Chateau's doorstep.

Frontenac continued his aggressive campaign against the English settlements. Though by using the Abenaki to fight this war—and the curiously bloodthirsty Jesuits to harangue them—the royal governor ceded control over their penchant for bludgeoning, torturing, and scalping their victims, including women, children, and infants. The typical mission Indian carried a set of rosary beads on these expeditions, prayed frequently to the Virgin Mary, and wore a crucifix on a thong around his neck, but he offered no parley and granted little in the way of Christian mercy. Now a Catholic, he remained a savage and was just as likely to torture and burn his enemies as he was before his conversion.

Frontenac's cold-blooded policies would eventually reap what they had sown. His grand scheme to push the English back over the Piscataqua River never came to pass, and his vicious raids against the settlements created a stubborn adversary from those who had been content to live in peace. As the seventeenth century neared its end, the intersection of a crude but growing economy with the exigencies of the fur trade combined with the ambitious fury of the Iroquois and Frontenac's clever plotting to upset the balance of the New World. As often is the case when societal forces collide, many innocent people in New England and New France were bankrupted, burned out of their homes, injured, crippled, killed, or otherwise displaced. They were caught in the maw of something much more powerful than themselves: a ruthless, invisible, and pervasive tide that ruined the lives of thousands of people while making the fortunes of but a few.

And thus the village of Haverhill, which for one day became the fulcrum of this devastating power, was raided by the Abenaki. Houses were burned, farm animals slaughtered, and innocent settlers fell under the hatchet. Of the helpless few taken captive, they labored on through strange country, each in his or her peculiar fashion imagining what trouble still lay ahead.

CHAPTER VI

The Tomahawk and the Knife

Goodwife Duston could smell the Merrimack River. Although snow had fallen again, covering the fields, and the air was brittle and cold, occasionally she detected an odor of damp vegetation, like an airstream of moisture that enveloped them, and then slipped away. On they went, an endless round of bogs, dales, ravines, and ridges, gully after gulch, across kettle ponds rimmed with ice and hedge-bound enclosures still buried in snow. But passing through these vaporous clouds brought a keen sense of homesickness that stopped up Hannah's throat.

Having lived by the river, Duston was sure it was nearby, though their route, which was long and arduous, had taken them over land and they hadn't seen the Merrimack for several days. In the fortnight or so they had been traveling, their party had grown smaller. One of the Haverhill captives had fallen behind, never to be seen again, and another was found dead one cold, rainy morning. The only evidence they had been among the party were the scalps dangling from a warrior's belt and the homespun breeches worn by another Indian.

Goodwife Duston had lost count of the days after being stricken with fever, which she survived only because it coincided with a stopover that the Indians spent hunting and setting traps. They screeched and whooped long into the night after shooting a deer and snaring a rabbit, throwing the offal aside for their captives. The next day, they entered strange country that included long stretches of open ground alternating with large, heavily forested hills, containing no sign of any inhabitants and very little game.

During Hannah's illness, neither the Indians nor their captives had anything to eat for two days. Here, as close as she dared come to the fire, Goodwife Duston lay shivering with the ague-fits, not quite awake, her mind twisting and teeming with phantasmagoria. Intermittently, she was aware of Mary Neff sitting beside her, and of Sam Lenorson, who dug up a few, half-frozen groundnuts and tried to get her to eat. But she lapsed back onto the ground, re-entering her daydreams while the others kept watch over her, insisting she would soon be well.

Their situation grew so desperate that the Indians gathered up the bones of what appeared to be a dead horse or mule, scalding them in the fire. Duston and the other captives watched in revulsion as maggots and other vermin crawled from the jagged ends of the bones, dropping one by one into the flames. After some time, Bampico crushed the bones in a stone mortar, boiled the resulting powder along with a fistful of yellow lily roots, and the Indians drank the broth, never offering any to the captives.

After her fever subsided, and they had traveled another day or two, Hannah's strength began to return. In fact, her illness seemed to cleanse her of several woes, among them the lethargy of childbirth that kept her from escaping the Duston homestead, as well as the general sense of doom that had threatened to overwhelm her. At such a distance from the white settlements, the Indians relaxed their watch on the captives, knowing the English had no option but to continue along with them. And through Sam Lenorson's cheerful exertions, Hannah and Mary Neff were able to find things to eat, which they believed was a sign of God's favor.

Now, having gained something from the thin, cold air, as well as the morsels of food that Sam Lenorson procured for her with clever, improvised traps, Goodwife Duston became quite equal to her old self, before the hard childbirth, the laying-in a week, and the murder of her dear innocent Martha. Even over difficult terrain, Hannah was at little risk of falling behind the youngest and strongest of the Indians. In their behaviors and occasional remarks, her captors had made it plain that if Duston and Neff continued along, they wouldn't be harmed. In the evenings, by the fire, Bampico would often ask Duston how much her family would be willing to pay for her release. To set the Indian's mind on something other than mayhem and murder, Duston replied that she was worth twenty pounds, which created a hubbub among the Indians.

With the comfort of home far behind them, the captives trudged along a well-marked Indian trail that led into a pine forest. The freshwater smell of the river was strong here. A depression in the snow that spanned a half dozen feet delineated the trail, and when they had trekked over a mile along this trough, the fir trees grew thick and round and members of the party, in small groups, were able to take shelter under the low-hanging branches. Dusk had arrived. Beneath the sweet-smelling thatch, the pine needles were soft and mostly dry, and Hannah and her two companions banked them into narrow piles the size and shape of feather beds. For a short while, they had some privacy in their little den.

They ate some dried meat that Sam produced from his belt, and then prayed out of I Samuel: "The bitterness of death has passed." Abundant snow fell during the night, but insulated by the fan-like branches and tufted needles, they passed comfortably to the morning, when feeble shafts of light reached into their shelter. Hannah was the first to emerge, the snow cascading over her bosom as she disturbed the branches, adorning her in white. Immediately she came face to face with her master, who was bare-chested and clad in his bloodstained leggings and moccasins. The warrior was scratched along his torso from the nettles and undergrowth, his face blackened by soot, and his long black hair, which grew on the left side of his head, was stiffened with bear grease and sweat. He smelled of entrails and campfire smoke and, a short distance away, a waist-high column of steam rose from where he had just urinated in the snow.

A few days earlier, a portion of the captives had been diverted from the rest by a group of Indians that met them on the trail and included squaws and children. Here the party that contained Hannah Duston was reduced to seven captives, among them Mary Neff, Sam Lenorson, and Hannah Bradley, guided by a half dozen of the warriors who had raided Haverhill. Another twenty miles passed under their feet in relative tranquility, but the Indians, especially the one who confronted Hannah now, had mercurial temperaments. Danger lurked whenever they were near, and it was not uncommon for these savages to murder any Englishman who displeased them, merely on a whim.

Speaking to her now, the warrior in his halting English told Goodwife Duston that her children, separated from her in the early moments of the raid, had all been killed. Her husband had abandoned them, riding over the hill alone, the children scattered in his wake, crying out and stumbling in the underbrush. Her master said that another band of warriors carried off the Duston children, and later that day had roasted and eaten them. But their work was still incomplete, the Indian said. When Duston and her companions had been forced to run the gauntlet, and then sold to the French, Hannah's master said, he and the other warriors in their party would return to Haverhill and kill Thomas Duston.

Goodwife Duston made no reply. Spitting on the ground, the Indian said they still might decide to kill her and the other settlers, carrying only their scalps back to the French. He added that Duston and her companions would never be saved; the English had not followed them, and in any case, it took their leaders several months to decide whether or not to send out the militia. By that time, the captives would be far away, or dead.

So saying, the Indian stalked off toward the campfire, while the frontierswoman diverged the other way, trampling the drifts under a gray sky that presaged more snow. A clear layer of ice had formed on a nearby creek and Hannah punched through it, drenching her neck and brow with the icy water. She drank two handfuls, making her throat ache. At this moment, lying by the creek, dozens of miles from the home that had borne her, she reaffirmed her belief that, since her life was no longer protected by any law, neither that of man or God, she was unrestrained by any law to strike back at her oppressors, if the circumstances required and allowed it.

Returning to the pine grove, Goodwife Duston observed the Indians gathered in prayer by the campfire. Kneeling on a cleared patch of ground, each warrior adorned with a crucifix, they murmured in unison, telling their beads as Duston's master waved his arm over the fire, clothing them in smoke. It struck Hannah that these savages knelt to pray three times a day; they venerated the same Christian God worshipped by their captives, yet they murdered pregnant women, infants, and children, burning them alive, scalping them, butchering their flesh and boiling it in kettles. There was but one way to deal with such an abomination, and Duston must have felt it sinful not to pray for victory over these pagan idolaters, who had sullied God with their image making and perverted his will.

Mary Neff and Sam and the other ragged captives waited in a clearing just beyond the camp. Presently the Indians rose from their morning devotions, ate palmfuls of Nokehick from their deerskin pouches, and kicked out the fire. Hannah and the others were given heavy bundles to carry and urged on through the woods. Calling the English lad to him,

Bampico distributed a small amount of corn meal to Sam, indicating he should divide it with Duston and Mary Neff. They then proceeded with this reduced cavalcade out of the grove, across a snow-scattered meadow, and into low, open country bounded on three sides by trees.

They could hear the river as they passed through the grove of trees. Laboring under her burden, Hannah emerged onto the bank and there was the familiar sight of the Merrimack, nearly a half-mile across where it rounded a knoll and ran noisily over some rocks. The wind, sweeping down from the trees, roiled the water into shifting patterns of black and gray, and broken rafts of ice extended from each bank. On the far shore, the trees grew right to the river's edge, their empty branches tangled in a profusion that scratched against the gunmetal sky.

With the river expanded past its banks into the forest, the torrents of snowmelt rushed past, spreading over the bottomland that surrounded them. Off to Hannah's right, the file of Indians wound out of the trees onto the icy shoal and began crossing the river. For a quarter-mile stretch, the Merrimack churned into low rapids and dropped several feet, pooling at the terminus of the fast water. From Hannah's vantage point, it appeared that the Indians were stepping directly on these jaunty whitecaps, somehow buoyed by the current. But as Goodwife Duston and the other captives approached, they saw the natural ford that traversed the river in that location, augmented by a pathway of flat stones that the Indians took care to rearrange during times of low water.

At length, the entire party of Indians, agile and sure-footed in their moccasins, reached the western bank of the Merrimack and clustered there, waiting for the English to join them. Glancing at the churning water and each other, the captives sat on the bank and removed their shoes, which they hung about their necks. Sam led the way, having crossed many such rivers during his captivity, with the rest following behind him. The footing was unsteady, and the water, pushing against their knees, ranged from two to three feet deep and was numbingly cold. As Duston passed from rock to rock, her skirts, which had been split into pantaloons on their first remove and banded about her ankles, became heavy with water. The current sucked at her feet, dragging them away from the proper line, and she tripped, staggering and lurching over the slippery, uneven rocks. From the other bank, the Indians jostled each other and pointed, doubled over with mirth and hooting like children.

Upon reaching the embankment, the captives wrung out their skirts and trouser legs, laced up their shoes, and remounted their deerskin bundles. The Indians had moved off through the snow, following an untrammeled path that hewed to the riverbank heading north. Reluctantly, the captives fell in behind, their lower garments stiffening in the cold, as lightweight crystals of snow descended on the landscape. All morning and into the gray hours of afternoon, the Indians and their captives plodded on through the falling snow, watching it accumulate on the hedges and trees bordering the trail.

They continued on, steadily and perseveringly, the trail sometimes running along the bank of the river. Other times, the path searched farther west, into territory that was exposed to the weather, with nothing but a few hedgerows dividing the landscape into twenty- and thirty-acre parcels that were rapidly filling up with snow. Each of these tracts was bisected by creeks or scarred by gullies and ditches filled with brambles that narrowed their passage. It was a forlorn territory, marked by the occasional ruin of an Indian village or fishing station, but these were far between. Sam's master told him it was the land of the Pennacook, who were once led by a great Bashaba named Passaconaway, whose people had been killed off by war and disease or otherwise scattered. More than any other they had passed through, the country bore a haunted look, with snowflakes as large as a baby's hand dropping onto the skeletal trees and an absence of critters and birds. Even the figures moving across the landscape, the Indians and their captives, were nearly indistinguishable, wrapped in clothing taken from the dead they had left behind and dragging along their weapons and other appurtenances.

Always they returned to the bank of the river, the sound and scent of which never escaped them for very long. In the failing light, the party issued from a stand of timber into low, flat country where, up ahead, the snow had been trampled down over a large area. The river appeared through the trees lining the bank, so wide and placid it resembled a lake, the far shore obliterated by the low sky and distance. Through the dropping snow, Hannah could make out a cluster of figures waiting for them by the tree line. They were wrapped in their mantles, huddled together near a small campfire on the edge of the woods. For the first time since that morning, Duston's master spoke, pointing to the ground with his axe and telling the captives to wait. One by one the figures across the meadow rose up, shook off their torpor, and began to walk out from beneath the trees.

It was a party of seven or eight warriors, none of whom Duston had seen previously, though they wore the markings of a river tribe. In the middle of the field, Sam's master and two other warriors held council with these strange Indians. While they were talking and gesticulating, a young warrior nodded his head at Bampico's command, running back to where the English were crouched in the snow. Wading into the knot of captives, he began separating them by force, pushing Goodwives Duston and Neff and Sam Lenorson to one side with his lance, while glowering at them and making a low sound in his throat. The other captives, including Hannah Bradley, were prodded to their feet; the Indian gestured ahead with his pike, indicating that those four souls were leaving, while the rest were to stay where they were. Goodwife Bradley crossed the patch of snowy ground that separated them and pressed Duston's hand, then was shoved along by the young warrior and hastened to join the others being taken away.

Prowling behind them, the young warrior drove the four captives to the parley in the middle of the field, where they were briefly examined by the strange Indians, and then, joined by three of the warriors who had assaulted Haverhill, this contingent headed north, into the trees. For a few moments, young Sam's master, Bampico; Duston's master; and the young warrior stood near the tree line, one or the other occasionally gesturing to the east, in the direction of the river. The two older Indians took a burning ember from the fire and lit their tobacco pipes. After a final, brief exchange, the young warrior picked up his lance and deerskin bundle, setting out after the other party at a dead run.

During this interval, when Goodwife Duston realized that the group of captives had been permanently sundered, and that she and her two friends were now in the possession of Bampico and her own master, Hannah urged her kinswoman and the boy not to lose heart, saying that she had longed for this moment. There in the forbidding country of the Pennacook, Hannah stated her resolve to escape their tormentors, while begging her friends to assist her in these efforts. Time being short and their circumstances dire, Neff and the boy pledged their loyalty to the endeavor, and the three settlers agreed to carry out their plans at the earliest opportunity.

Duston's master beckoned to them, and the two women and the boy came up to the place where he was standing, With one Indian in front of them and the other behind, the captives made their way to the bank of the Merrimack, which lay just a hundred rods or so to the east, behind a stand of pines. When they cleared the trees, they found two squaws and a sturdy Indian boy waiting by the river. Below the cut bank at that location, two birch bark canoes were pulled up on a little beach that was crusted with snow. One by one, the warriors, the squaws, the Indian boy, and the three captives dropped off the bank and scrambled into the pair of canoes. The first vessel contained Bampico, Mary Neff, Sam Lenorson, and one of the squaws, and the other held Goodwife Duston, her master, the Indian boy, and the younger of the two squaws. With a squaw crouching in the bow and a warrior sliding the canoe over the snow before leaping in the stern, the two canoes pushed off and headed downriver.

Hannah marveled at the lightness and strength of the canoe, as the Indians paddled into the main channel and steered with the current. It was approximately twenty feet long, narrow in the beam, and rounded upward at each end. The vessel knifed through the water with its shallow draft and was constructed from one unbroken strip of birch bark cut from a single tree, fashioned over a strutted frame of white cedar. The long piece of bark was sewn over the ribs with cord made from black spruce root, the joints caulked with pitch and other resins. The floor of the canoe, where Hannah Duston and the Indian boy sat, was lined with close-set strips of cedar running lengthwise, and interior cedar ribs inversely arched from gunwale to gunwale. The canoe was etched along the prow with the clan signs of the tribe and propelled easily by just two paddles, each carved from a single piece of basswood. It was the first Indian canoe Hannah Duston had ever seen, this being her maiden voyage on the river, her previous experience limited to Pettee's ferry back at the settlement. For each of those crossings she was charged a penny, while the cost of her present excursion, as well as its destination, remained unknown.

It occurred to Hannah that, since she had been captured, they had trekked nearly a hundred miles, while turning back the calendar by a month. Here the river was wide and black, the trees that stretched along the banks rimed with frost, and the air tinged with the iron chill of February, though Hannah knew that fair April would set her foot down shortly. It was also the first time in many days that Duston was not forced to travel under her own power, which allowed time to examine her surroundings and consider the situation.

Alert to every chance for escape, Goodwife Duston studied the terrain to the left and right, without drawing her master's attention. She gauged the distance to each of the riverbanks, looking for Indian encampments or clues to where they were heading. Mist rose in little columns from the smooth black water, and passing through these vapors momentarily obscured the location of the other canoe. Duston weighed her chances of slipping overboard and swimming for the nearest bank, or throwing the squaw over the gunwale and fighting for mastery of the canoe, neither of which appealed to her. The Indians were a formidable challenge, and the water was cold enough to rob her of breath.

Duston could smell her master's burning tobacco as he paddled steadily along. The barrel of the Indian's musket rested on the thwart beside her. Duston was tempted to grab for it, but kneeling in such an awkward position limited her movement. Even if the gun was loaded there was only one ball to be fired. She thought about clubbing her master with the gun butt and then firing at the warrior in the other canoe, but their varying speeds and the unsteady platform made success unlikely. The report of the gun would also reveal their location, and she feared they might be in proximity to an Indian village. From what she had seen, there were Indians all around, which had emboldened the ones she was traveling with. Occasionally, the squaw, who was in the bow of the canoe, struck Hannah on the forearm or knee with her paddle, chortling to herself as they went along.

The other canoe was just ahead of them, on the westerly side of the channel. Looking over at Mary Neff and their young charge, Sam Lenorson, who was indistinguishable from the Indian boy squatting beside him, Goodwife Duston must have felt a pang of helplessness. It's likely this emotion had not arisen in the previous segment of the journey, focused so much on living moment to moment as they all were. But Duston also recognized that the Merrimack, for all its twists and turns, led back to Haverhill, and whatever disposition a just and merciful God had left her beloved husband and children.

The river was higher than she had ever seen it, a mass of swelling black water that rose beyond the tree line. Suddenly Hannah felt a tap on the shoulder and the Indian boy, kneeling right behind her, uttered something in his own language and pointed off to the left. A trio of ducks had swooped in, gliding a foot above the water, parallel with the canoe. When the Indian stroked with his paddle and then turned it up, the duck's wings and the shaft of the paddle flew along at the same height and speed. The boy grinned at Hannah, repeating what he had said.

Gazing downriver, Duston could make out what looked like a shadow bisecting the channel on the western side. Allowing the current to pull them along, the Indian canoes approached this dark shape, steering toward it. The mass was a small, triangular island lodged at the confluence of the Merrimack River and an adjoining stream. The other river dropped through a narrow gorge, passing on either side of the island in low rapids before spilling into the Merrimack.

Just as the canoes met the water flowing past the island, the Indians dug in their paddles, fighting upriver like sturgeon, with the darkened mass off to their left. Intermittently, Duston's canoe banged against a submerged rock or tree limb, but the Indians were as confident and agile on water as they were on land, allowing only a wavelet or two to lap over the gunwales. They darted against the current, moving left or right to take advantage of little eddies in the channel. Gaining the rapids, their canoe passed the tip of the island, hung in the drift for a moment, and then wheeled left, running downriver for a short distance. Just behind them, the other party completed the same maneuver, bobbing in the spray. A few paddle strokes, and both canoes grounded themselves on a sandbar beside another that was already there.

Having nothing to occupy her hands, Duston had surveyed the island from several vantage points as they paddled toward it, battled against the current to surpass it, and then landed on the beach. The narrow end of the island was aimed upriver—the Indians referred to this stream as the Contoocook—leaving a shoal encased in a sheath of dark, matted ice, spotted here and there with knurls of driftwood, river detritus, and hardened snowdrifts curved side by side along the point like scales on a fish. Here they disembarked, splashing through ankle deep water so cold it burned their skin. Goodwife Duston stumbled on some rocks and the Indian boy reached out his hand, steadying her.

The low-lying section of the island, containing signs of an old Indian fort and ruined palisade, was covered with a skein of rotten snow that made the footing uncertain. Overall, the island comprised about two and a half acres and was pitched above the surrounding territory, offering views in every direction. The motion of the river over an age, splitting, as it did, on both sides of the island, had eroded the original land mass until it stood above the current, a raised triangular wedge covered in scrub trees and gorse with a six-foot embankment all around. A skirt of ice extended irregularly from the lower bank, running out between ten and twenty feet until truncated by the rushing black water of the channel.

The squaws and the Indian boy emptied the canoes and, hoisting the deerskin bundles, made for a column of smoke that twisted up from the undergrowth. Rising ground led through some birch trees to a rectangular bluff that formed the base of the triangle. This headland stood nearly thirty feet above the river, marked by two large hemlock trees and a meadow that the Indians had cleared of snow, trampling the ground with their moccasins. Another squaw and half a dozen Indian children, ranging from age four or five to their early teens, had been preparing for their arrival for some time, as a fire was eating its way along a trench that had been dug. The brazier was four feet long and a couple of feet across, filled with pulsating coals that had been ignited hours earlier. With darkness sifting through the trees along with the snow, the warriors used their hatchets to cut down three birch saplings of equal length. While Bampico stripped off the bark with his knife, sharpening one end of each sapling and leaving an abbreviated fork on the other, Hannah's master ranged down slope to the lower part of the island. There was the quick, sharp report of his hatchet, and the Indian, his pipe still clenched his teeth, returned with a birch pole that was approximately twice the length of the saplings.

In the clearing, Bampico drove the sharpened end of the first sapling into the ground, and, arranging all three in a straight line, marked off six feet, plunged the second one in; then, pacing off an equal distance, the third. The other warrior, assisted by the boy from the canoe, was again searching the wooded portion of the island. Soon they returned with armfuls of eight- or nine-foot switches, along with several long, fanlike hemlock branches. They trimmed all these to roughly the same length, and Bampico placed the skinny birch pole in the crotchets of the saplings.

The two warriors, instructing the boy, rested one end of the switches against the horizontal pole, canting the other end at a forty-five degree angle to the ground, making a triangular space. To complete the shelter, they used the long strips of birch bark to weave all the switches and half of the spruce branches into an impermeable roof, taking the rest to pad and insulate the floor beneath. Then they hung a piece of deerskin from the ridgepole, closing part of it off.

All this was accomplished in a short time. The Indians placed the bulwark of interlaced branches to the wind, and the open side of the shelter leeward, facing the fire, so the inhabitants could warm themselves while the smoke trailed away. As the snow faltered, the air warmed slightly, and a cold rain began to patter the ground, Duston realized there wasn't any room for the captives in the hut, though the Indians, with growing conviviality, did not seem to begrudge them a place by the fire.

The blaze had been constructed so that it burned from one end, heading slightly downward, to the other, leaving the trench filled with ashes in its wake. One of the squaws had been down to the water's edge to retrieve a string of alewives caught that day, and hung through the gills on a switch. She laid this across the middling coals, and as the alewives browned on one side, the squaw and the Indian boy took up the overhanging ends of the switch and turned them over, broiling the fish evenly.

Huddled beyond the fire, the aroma of broiled fish causing their stomachs to rumble, the captives remained silent as the little encampment bustled around them. Opening the deerskin bundles, the squaws clucked and cooed over the bounty they contained, pulling out silver brooches and belt buckles, spools of ribbon, a mortar and pestle, pewter dishes, a compass, packets of gunpowder and shot, and sundry other items. Eyeing the squaws from across the fire-trench, Hannah checked herself when one of the women drew out the large piece of woven cloth that had been hacked from her loom. It represented over a hundred hours of labor, and when the squaw who had struck her with the canoe paddle draped the cloth over her shoulders, wiping her mouth with it, allowing the edges to wallow in the dirt, Goodwife Duston sat in the drizzling rain, her gaze fixed on the squaw, but her countenance blank.

Hannah's master tugged open the last parcel and took out a bottle of English rum. Spearing an alewife with a pointed stick, the Indian uncorked the rum, took a long draught, and proceeded to eat the entire fish—tail, gills, eyes, and all. Bampico soon joined him, and the two warriors, ignoring the squaws and all of the children except for the boy who had come up with them, puffed on their tobacco pipes, ate a mess of the alewives, and swapped the bottle of spirits back and forth.

The younger children took their portion of the supper that had been provided and crawled into the shelter, out of the rain. As usual, none of the food was offered to the captives, and Sam Lenorson's attempts at foraging over the barren island, in the darkness and rain, produced nothing besides the inner bark of a yellow poplar tree. Potting some river water, Sam Lenorson shredded two handfuls of the bark and rested the pot on the fire. With the two warriors preoccupied with the rum, the Indian boy, who had remained outside with the squaws, leaned over and tossed a fistful of Nokehick into the boiling pot. Sam encouraged his companions to drink this poor soup, which tasted bitter, but helped them recover a portion of their strength.

The bottle growing light, the two warriors began to stomp up and down beside the fire, growling and yelping as they capered about. Seated nearby, two of the squaws chanted along with them, beating on a log with sticks they found lying in the snow. When Goodwife Duston leaned over the fire to retrieve the boiling poplar root, one of the squaws left off drumming, stuck her hand into the cold end of the fire, and threw ashes in Hannah's face. Blinded for a moment, Duston groped around for a handful of snow and rubbed it in her eyes, causing them to water but leaving soot and bits of charcoal on her face. The squaw laughed and then rejoined the chanting, while the two Indians leapt over the fire-trench, whooping and hollering at the night sky.

It was plain to Hannah that they had crossed, or were about to cross, a threshold of some kind; the Indians had loosened the strictures attached to captivity a few days after the raid on Haverhill, but what had happened here was more significant than that. Beside the fact that Duston had witnessed her first drunken Indian, which must have been unsettling for it made these savages even more volatile, reaching the encampment ignited something in her captors that was unprecedented. For the first time on the journey, children were present, squaws, even the island itself, with its tall embankments, ruined fortifications, and strategic views of the river, had a mystical air about it, a power that seemed to embolden and rejuvenate the Abenaki. The presence of strange warriors also meant that other Indian towns were close by, and, with the arrival of fishing season, the Merrimack soon would be thick with canoes, strung across with nets, and studded with weirs. Undoubtedly, Goodwife Duston's hopes for an escape or rescue were slimmer than they had been since the first moments of the raid.

Straight-backed and vigilant, Duston sat beside the fire, gazing at the silver threads of rain that billowed over the headlands and the river below. Sam Lenorson was flat on the ground, asleep. Mary Neff dozed against Hannah's shoulder, and the squaws finally crawled into the hut and fell asleep. Still, the two Indians frolicked about, arguing over the diminished rum and grabbing at the charred fish heads and other scraps lying on the ground. The bottle of spirits finally overturned and empty, the Indians collapsed to their knees, and then their haunches, mumbling and chuckling over the pile of English goods they had upended.

Bampico fell over on his back, snoring loudly. The other Indian, who had proposed a game of chance to divide the spoils, poked Bampico with the handle of his axe, drilling him in the ribs and complaining. When the prostrate Indian failed to awaken, the other warrior, soaked by the rain and flecked with ashes, turned his attention to Duston, who was seated across the fire-trench. Laughing softly, he brandished his axe, shaking it back and forth. Captor and captive looked into each other's eyes for the last time.

With some difficulty, the drunken warrior got to his feet and lurched about the other Indian, nearly stomping upon his face. After a few clumsy attempts, he managed to reach over, grasp Bampico under the arms, and drag him into the shelter. Inside the maw of the hut, the Indian rummaged among the sleeping figures, laughing and muttering to himself. After awhile, the camp fell silent, but for the rain pattering on the trees, or an occasional burst of snoring.

For quite some time, Hannah remained upright, staring into the recesses of the hut. Nothing stirred, except for the sound of the river going past. At a late hour, Goodwife Duston stood up, as though she had been called to some task. By now the rain had stopped, and the sky had turned cold and clear. Having removed the dead man's coat and leather jerkin she wore, along with her own apron, bodice, and attached sleeves, Duston stood bare-armed in her shift and gown.

Kneeling by Goodwife Neff, and then the boy, Duston touched a hand to Mary's shoulder and jostled Sam's elbow, and her countrymen sat up, rubbing their faces and yawning. While they grew accustomed to the surroundings, Duston padded around in her stocking feet, here and there stooping to retrieve a pair of hatchets and her master's pole-ax, which had been left by the fire. No one spoke, until Duston came around again and whispered some final instructions. Then the trio passed over the smoldering fire-trench in unison, Neff and Sam Lenorson armed with hatchets and Goodwife Duston wielding the pole-ax.

Like theatrical players appearing on a stage, they stepped to the edge of the hut, with Duston to the right, Mary Neff in the center, and the boy on the left hand side. The Indians were asleep, with their heads toward the fire-trench, a warrior positioned at each end, and the squaws and children lined up between. The children's limbs were tangled, and their breathing was deep and regular.

The pole-ax in her right hand, Duston motioned to the others to ready themselves. Snoring unevenly, Duston's master lay in his filthy leggings and mantle, his scalp lock twisted into a fantastic shape. He looked unapproachable and fierce, even in repose. Duston straddled the Indian and raised the axe. Raised it with the arm that had broken ground with a spade, and carried the hod. The arm that had chopped a month's worth of firewood. That had lifted the calf, built fences, and hauled water from Little River. The arm that had cuddled Martha to her breast, and the hand that had stroked the infant's cheek.

The arm that held the axe descended in a terrible swift blow, the weight shifting to the balls of Duston's feet, and the heavy stone blade smashing against the Indian's forehead. There was a muffled crack, quickly followed by two more such noises as Mary Neff and the boy struck their victims. Looking down for a moment, Duston saw an abundance of clear fluid mixed with bright red blood flowing from the Indian's ear and nose. He gasped once, and fell silent.

Duston immediately sprang to her left, toward the next prone figure, the squaw who had doused her with ashes. Around her, groans of agony erupted from the other victims. Without hesitation, Duston swung the pole-ax up in a great arc and, taking the haft in both fists as the blade plummeted toward the earth, drove the stone into the squaw's right temple, obliterating her ear. Back in Haverhill on their farm, Thomas Duston had preceded the butchering of a cow by striking its skull with an iron bar, and the squaw's head made that same dull thud followed by a cracking noise.

Beside Hannah, young Sam dispatched Bampico in the exact manner he had been instructed, and Mary Neff swung the hatchet and incapacitated one of the squaws, who breathed rapidly and shallowly, with an abundance of dark red blood pouring from her mouth.

The stench of death filled the hut. By working in concert, Duston and her companions had decimated their captors in a matter of seconds, but the labored breathing, shifting feet, and cracking sound of the blows roused the others, who started up in alarm. Two of the children bolted from the shelter, followed closely by the remaining squaw. Mary Neff hacked at the squaw's arm when she leaped up, breaking it above the elbow. Still leaning over his master, Sam Lenorson appeared dazed. Duston spoke sharply to him and the boy regained his senses, joining Mary in pursuit of the fleeing Indians.

Crouched against the rear of the hut, the Indian boy who had been friendly to Hannah gazed at her in disbelief. But she raised her hand in a calming gesture, shook her head, and backed away, indicating that the boy should stay where he was. Then Duston swung the bloody axe to her shoulder and crossed back over the fire-trench. What was occurring beyond the upland resembled a scene from the lower reaches of hell.

With the two warriors lying dead on the bluff alongside the mangled squaws, the lower portion of the island quickly became a killing field. Looking upriver, the island sloped to a low, flat plain that dropped from a width of just ten or twelve rods to the narrow point where the canoes were beached. Besides a thin mix of birch, oak and young hemlock trees, and a few clumps of undergrowth, there was very little cover, just a stubbly meadow concealed by snow and the broken palisade that marked the old fort. This, in turn, was ringed by an abatis of stunted trees and thorn bushes. Mary Neff ran down one of the escaping children, threw her weight on the girl's back, and rode her into the wall of shattered tree limbs and thorns. While the girl hung there in the bracken, Neff chopped at her skull with the hatchet.

The wounded squaw, angling along the embankment, hurried past Neff and her victim, only to have Sam Lenorson run at her, knocking them both to the ground.

Swinging wildly, the boy split open her thigh with the blade of his hatchet, but the squaw was heavier than he was. To the boy's amazement, she sprang up and ran away, heading back up island. At the same time, Duston chased down a teenage boy near the ruined fort and thrust at him from behind, distending him over the pickets. On the boy in an instant, Duston struck him twice with her axe, crumpling his skull. Here and there, blood was scattered in gobbets over the snow. Four of the Indian children lay heaped up, and soon Mary Neff had another cornered in the ditch that preceded the headland, the teenage girl mired in the loose snow to her hips, as the former captive waded toward her with the hatchet above her head.

The anguished cries and wailing diminished, as the ranks of the survivors grew smaller. Duston spied the wounded squaw limping along the near bank, cradling her broken arm and once again trying to reach the canoes. Heading her off, Duston rushed forward with axe raised, screaming in bloodlust. Dodging behind a tree, the squaw eluded the full weight of the blow, but still received a wound to the ribcage that bled through her mantle. She tried to reverse course, going back toward the encampment, but Sam leaped out from the underbrush, chopped at the Indian as she squirmed past, and badly injured her free arm.

Duston had resolved that all the Indians on Sugar Ball Island must be killed, or their plan would have little chance of success. She had indicated to her accomplices that the one boy should be taken alive, but that no quarter should be given to the rest, who themselves had not granted any. Thus it was with a singular determination that she and her companions pursued the remaining squaw, driving her this way and that, as they took chinks from her flesh and broke her small bones.

Finally, Duston trapped the squaw on the headland, near the shelter where the bodies were piled up. The squaw, barely able to stand, groped along the bank for something to fight with. As she bent over, Duston brought the full weight of the pole-ax down on her shoulder, then recoiled, aiming the blade at the squaw's chest. But the squaw went reeling toward the edge of the bluff, grabbing at tree branches and scrub. Duston's roundhouse swing landed in the small of her back, knocking the squaw over the embankment. She fell thirty feet, skidding down the slope, bumping over the exposed tree roots and shale, and landing in the river with a splash. Immediately the black ribbon of current whisked her away.

Turning from the bank, on her way to complete whatever business still needed to be done, Hannah glanced into the shelter. The boy she favored was not inside, nor anywhere about. Bodies were strewn all over the island, and down near the old palisade Mary Neff was doubled over, retching into the snow. Sam Lenorson was nearby, perched on a stump with his head in his hands. Only then did Hannah spy another Indian boy, perhaps twelve years old—the same age as her son, Nathaniel, who, for all she knew, was dead—stealing along the bank toward the canoes. Duston rushed past her companions, reaching a dead run as her feet struck the narrow point that extended from the island. The boy was less than thirty feet from the canoes when she overtook him, using her size to hurl him onto the rocky beach. Pinning the boy there with her foot against his buttocks, she crushed his skull with one blow from the axe, and then collapsed on the ground a few feet away. With that final swing of the axe, Duston felt like she had freed herself—that something that had bound her had been severed.

After a lost moment or two, Duston got up and refreshed herself at the river, rinsing the blood from her hands and bathing her face and neck. Passing up island to the bluff, she told Goodwife Neff to safeguard the canoes. By the smoldering fire, Hannah gathered up what few supplies remained with the Indians: the gun her master had carried, an old blanket, two pouches of Nokehick, and some powder and shot. Paying little attention to the carnage she had inspired, Duston put on the clothes she had discarded earlier, and then sat on the ground and traded her ragged shoes for a pair of moccasins taken from one of the dead Indians.

Rejoining Neff and the boy, Duston sank two of the canoes by smashing through their birch bark hulls with her axe. She eased the remaining canoe a little farther onto the shoal, loaded in three paddles and their meager supplies, and leaned the musket up in the bow. It was still quite dark. With the clearing sky it had grown much colder, and steam rose from the gaping wounds of the two corpses lying nearby. The river ran past in a chorus, and soon Mary Neff and the boy were sprawled beneath the Indian blanket and gone to sleep

Stirred by an elation she had never known before, Duston gathered up her skirts and kept vigil, watching both sides of the Contoocook where it split to accommodate the island. The far banks, overgrown with trees and bracken, were no more than a few rods away on either side, providing easy vantage points for an Indian scout to observe them. Duston longed for morning so they could get underway, but knew it made them more vulnerable to being spotted.

Beyond the headlands, the Merrimack overspread the horizon, as dark and powerful as the waterways of the Old Testament. The river presided here, as both obstacle and deliverer, greater even than the stars and the sky. Sure of that, and equipped with the knowledge that Indians were lurking all around, Hannah Duston squatted by the canoe, waiting for first light.

CHAPTER VII

The Fate of Other Captives

The night after being separated from Goodwife Duston and the others, Hannah Bradley, now a captive of the Indians who had bartered for her at Pennacook, was seated by the fire in their encampment. This respite concluded another miserable day of being forced to travel at a blistering pace, ever northward, heading for the mission villages in either Acadia or Quebec. By that time, the war party had marched another five or six miles since departing the vicinity of Sugar Ball Island. Now that the Indians could envision receiving payment for their efforts, they had taken to feeding Bradley and the other captives. Tonight it was alewives the Indians had netted out of the river, which the captives were roasting on sticks when an unexpected visitor burst into the camp.

The intruder was a squaw, dressed in a wet, filthy skirt and mantle, suffering from a number of wounds, and drenched to the waist in blood. As an Abenaki, she was quickly recognized, wrapped in a blanket, and brought over to the fire. The Indians listened as the squaw explained what had happened to her, occasionally interjecting a question when their guest paused to devour the fish she had been given. Though one of her arms was broken and the other mangled and bloody, indicating the squaw had fought off her attackers and escaped under duress, she told her story in a quiet, even tone.

But the Indian woman grew excited when she revealed the deep gashes on her head, shoulders, and back, pantomiming someone wielding a tomahawk. Pulling aside her long black hair, the squaw exposed several wounds, most of which she had attempted to close up with the wool from a handful of rattlesnake weed. Blood was caked on her mantle and in her hair, and her broken arm had swollen to twice its normal size.

Only when the battered squaw uttered the name of Hannah Duston's master, and the Indians seated around the campfire reacted with surprise, did Goodwife Bradley realize what might have occurred. No doubt, Bradley and the other captives were astonished when it became clear that Hannah Duston, or perhaps Duston and Mary Neff, had assaulted the squaw, nearly extinguishing her life. The fact that the squaw had traveled on foot, alone and badly injured, meant that other Indians in their party had not been so fortunate.

In her condition, dazed by blows to the head, doused in the river, with a broken arm and bleeding from her wounds and from dozens of cuts, the squaw was describing for the other Indians a furious struggle that had ended in death for several of the participants. Who had or hadn't survived was an open question, though it seemed plain that the two warriors who were leading the party had been either killed or incapacitated. Bradley surmised that if these men had prevailed or even survived the fight, they would have been there to describe it for themselves.

Hearing of these travails, the strange Indians grew animated, several of them gesturing toward the captives, who were seated together on the other side of the fire. Through listening, watching the reactions of the Abenaki, and other subtle divinations, Hannah Bradley felt certain a massacre had taken place, and that Goodwives Duston and Neff had escaped and were at liberty in the countryside. This both cheered and frightened Bradley, revealing, as it did, the scope of possibilities inherent in the situation, including perhaps the arrival of her own delivery. There was also the specter of the Indians, having taken these developments as an omen, killing their captives, either as retribution, or as an investment in their scalps.

For Bradley, despite what she had gleaned, could not have known that Goodwife Duston, covered in blood and still carrying her master's pole-ax, was nearing the final act of her saga. For Duston, her captivity would turn out to be, in the end, a journey of a lifetime that occupied a mere fortnight. On the other hand, Hannah Bradley's experiences with Indian captivity had started long before the March 15, 1697 raid on Haverhill, and would stretch years into the future: an odyssey that involved several members of her family and was, in its own way, as remarkable as the events surrounding her more famous neighbor, Hannah Duston.

Two years earlier, in late summer 1695, Joseph Bradley and his wife, Hannah, were living on Parsonage Road in northwest Haverhill, the same remote part of town where the Duston farm was located. Abenaki raiding parties terrified the frontier that summer, attacking Exeter, New Hampshire, on July 7th, where they killed two settlers. On August 5th, the Indians bypassed Haverhill and assaulted Billerica, Massachusetts, killing ten settlers and taking five captives. Shortly after that, a party of Indians, lurking on the outskirts of Haverhill, wounded two members of the Whittaker family, and then surprised eleven-year-old Joseph Whittaker and fifteen-year-old Isaac Bradley, Hannah's young brother-in-law, who were laboring in the fields near the Bradley homestead.

Young Bradley and Whittaker were taken prisoner. Forgoing the kind of havoc they had sown in Billerica, killing settlers as they found them and burning down their houses, on this occasion the Indians seized the two boys and took them into the forest. Immediately they set out at a stiff pace, heading northward, without further excursions about the village.

Joe Whittaker was a rather slow and clumsy boy, shambling along in a man-sized body. It took considerable prodding to keep him on the move, and several times young Bradley was forced to intervene on his behalf, pleading with the Indians to spare his life. Isaac Bradley was a small, light-limbed, vigorous lad who had little difficulty keeping up and whom the Indians prized right away. Good-humored and enterprising, Isaac stayed close to his friend, soothing and encouraging him. When the situation demanded it, Isaac assisted the Indians in gathering food, setting snares and traps, and scouting for game. His efforts were appreciated on all sides.

After several days of walking through dense, mosquito-infested forest, the party reached an Indian village on the shore of an enormous lake. Passing through vast fields of Indian corn, Bradley and Whittaker were confronted with the glittering plain of Winnipisogee, or "Lake-land," the largest body of fresh water either of them had ever seen. When the wind swept down from the mountain range to the north, Winnipisogee was roiled by waves two feet high, the whitecaps stretching as far as the eye could see. The lake ended in a stone weir that divided the village in two, channeling the bass, salmon, shad, and sturgeon into submerged wicker cages, or else landing them in knee-deep water, where they were dipped out with nets or speared.

Here Isaac and Joseph were adopted by an Indian family consisting of a warrior, his squaw, a few young children, and a pack of five or six dogs, which were indispensible for hunting. By the time the leaves on the surrounding hills grew crimson, russet, and gold, the boys had acquired enough of the Indian dialect to hold a conversation. And when snow began to fall on the peaks to the north, Isaac learned that his master intended to get a winter's worth of labor from the two young captives before marching them to Quebec in the spring. In Canada, Isaac Bradley and Joe Whittaker would be sold to the French, allowing their master to profit twice from their captivity.

Exhausted by trying to improve the lives of his master's family while suffering the degradation of his own, Isaac conspired with Whittaker to devise a means of escape no later than the first days in April. Young Bradley feared that if they traveled into the wilderness that lay beyond the mountains, he would never again see his dear brother, Joseph, or his family. Isaac's frame had grown emaciated under the strain of a poor diet and all that work, and if he and Joe Whittaker were to undertake the perilous journey to Canada, only to be forced into more strenuous exertions there, Isaac was certain he would end up, unremarked upon and forgotten, in an anonymous grave.

Winter brought unrelenting snow, a cap of ice on the lake over a foot thick, and the threat of starvation, the family being reduced to an occasional fish caught through the ice, squirrels or a woodchuck trapped in a snare, and parched corn that was buried in a cache beneath their wigwam. They avoided disaster when the boy's master, hunting on snowshoes, killed and dressed a moose at a considerable distance from the village. The captives were required to trek through the wilderness for half a day, pulling the carcass back through the snow on a wooden sled.

After this ordeal, coming as it did when Isaac was in a weakened state, he suffered from a terrible fever. For several days, he lay delirious on the floor of the wigwam, near the point of death. Only the attentive care of his master's squaw kept him alive. To assuage young Bradley's fever, she hooded him with a blanket so he could inhale the smoke from burning the dried leaves of a red cedar tree. A chowder made from the head of a bass and several handfuls of Nokehick boiled in a kettle of water warmed the boy's digestion, and he was encouraged to chew on a piece of dogwood bark to alleviate his aches and pains.

Isaac's recovery coincided with the arrival of spring, and the boy's desire to escape grew even keener than before, while the return of his youthful strength made it seem possible. During young Bradley's illness, his sleeping place had been moved next to the squaw's, so he was not able to talk with Joe as frequently. Pretending to remain ill while marshaling his energy, Isaac began to have doubts regarding Whittaker's ability to endure another difficult trip. Every morning, an hour before sunrise, their master roused Whittaker with a kick to the ribs and they would exit the bark wigwam, the boy glassy-eyed and somnolent, dragging himself to the day's work. Considering all this, Bradley fixed the date for his escape in mid-April, soon returning to his labors along the weir and among the corn hills without revealing his plan to Whittaker.

A rising sense of guilt creeping over him, Isaac decided to approach Whittaker on a fine April morning, when they were sent to fetch water from the lake. Certain they couldn't be overheard, Bradley told Whittaker he meant to leave the wigwam that night and make his way toward Haverhill. Whittaker begged his friend to take him along. But Joe Whittaker was a heavy sleeper; in fact, he liked sleeping over every other pleasure, and Bradley, reminding him of that, said he was afraid his companion would have difficulty staying awake until the appropriate hour, thus endangering the attempt. Being caught in the midst of an escape was certain death, and Bradley realized the chances of success were much greater if he went alone. But Whittaker swore he couldn't bear living among the Indians any longer and prevailed upon his friend to take him along, and finally, Isaac agreed.

That night, Bradley lay by the pulsating coals of the fire as the hours passed. Snores erupted from the figures beside him, none louder than the ones arising from Joe Whittaker, over by the wall. But Isaac couldn't sleep, his mind agitated by the dangers he faced in getting up and leaving the wigwam, and then the long, pathless journey back to the settlement, which he had to undertake without the appropriate clothing and supplies. In this way, Isaac remained motionless until the fire had gone out, practicing over in his mind the actions he would perform to extricate himself from his blanket, the wigwam, and the Indian village.

Long after midnight, Bradley rose to his elbows and glanced around. The only sound was the regular breathing of the Indians, and Joe's abrupt snoring. Looking through the smoke-hole above him, Isaac gauged the position of the stars, folded back the edge of his blanket, and stood up. As he had long envisioned, the boy passed among the sleeping Indians with a light tread. He lifted his master's fire-works from where they hung against the wall, and removed some bread and a parcel of moose meat from a basket near the fire. Bearing these away, Isaac raised the deerskin flap and slipped outside, glancing up and down the silent row of wigwams. Stars wheeled across the night sky, and the moon, obscured by a cloud, suddenly emerged, illuminating the vast, glimmering lake.

Isaac felt a strong urge to be going. But the boy had made his promise, and, just as his father and mother had taught him, he intended to keep it. So, depositing the flint and awl and the moose meat among a grove of trees, Isaac again crept past several wigwams, re-entering the one where he had lived for the past eight months. It was a dreadful business, since his every instinct resisted going back there. Stepping over his master's sleeping form, Isaac knelt beside Joe Whittaker, surveyed the assembly of Indians, and then waited for a break in his friend's snoring before touching him on the shoulder.

The boy didn't stir. Again Bradley waited for what seemed the right moment, and gave Whittaker's arm a gentle shake.

"What do you want?" asked the other boy, rolling onto his side.

When Whittaker spoke, it echoed throughout the wigwam like a clap of thunder. Immediately, Bradley retreated to his old sleeping place, covered himself with his blanket, and pretended to snore. Any moment, he expected their master to awaken and begin groping for his hatchet.

The night stretched toward dawn. In the woods beyond the settlement, hunting for game or setting his traps, Isaac Bradley had always relied on intuition, and here his most powerful urge had been to go alone. Now, because of his good nature, he faced more privation and enslavement, perhaps even death. Shortly before the light came up, Isaac decided to abandon Joe and slip away on his own. With no one rising to challenge him, Bradley came to his feet and exited the wigwam, going quickly to where he had hidden the supplies. While he was busy there, Isaac heard footfalls coming from behind him.

Whirling around, Bradley was, at once, relieved and somewhat alarmed to see Joe Whittaker, his hair in a shock, mouth hanging open, and his eyes widened in fear. Barely glancing at him, Isaac took up the stolen provisions and followed the large stones that made up the fishing weir, going along the stream that emptied from the lake and ran gurgling into the forest, heading south. Little more than an hour remained before the Indians would arise to begin working. Lacking a compass or map, the two fugitives started running down the path that had originally brought them to the village, trying to put as much distance as possible between them and their master before he realized they were gone.

Bradley and Whittaker had traveled just three or four miles when light began delineating the branches of the trees, and sketching in the details of the footpath and surrounding countryside. Pursued by the encroaching daylight, the boys ran another mile or so before Isaac, spooked by the well-worn path, veered into the woods, urging Joe to come after him. The heavy timber, exposed shelves of rock, and abundant deadfall slowed Bradley down, as well as his concern for Whittaker, who was already near to giving up.

Picking his way along a ravine, Bradley took advantage of his companion's slow progress to scramble onto higher ground, but he still couldn't see anything but trees and undergrowth. When his breathing ceased to ring in his ears, Bradley heard a noise, both silvery and sharp, that came sweeping in from a distance and competed with the trilling of insects and snatches of birdsong. For several moments, Isaac waited atop the shale heap, listening intently. Soon the noise had clarified itself: it was a pack of dogs, trailing a scent and quickly drawing closer.

Isaac knew that he and Joe were the objects of the hunt. He gestured for the other boy to make haste, not utter a word, and follow him into the deepest tangle of bushes. The melody of the hounds increased, penetrating the gloom where Bradley and his companion now found themselves. While Whittaker sat on a log, spent by his efforts, Isaac cast here and there in the shadowy glen, trying to find a place they could conceal themselves, though he knew the dogs could find him in a rainstorm, at night, and on highlands blasted by the wind. He had seen them pull down a moose in the darkest portion of a swamp, having run after it for half a day.

With the dogs nearby, crashing through the bracken, Isaac's gaze fell on the log where Joe Whittaker had collapsed. Seeing it was hollow, he encouraged his friend to wriggle inside, and then, with a quick glance up and down the ravine, crawled in after him. Their hearts beat wildly against the interior of the log.

Stunned by the rapidity with which the dogs were approaching, Bradley considered running for a nearby stream, with the hope it would mask their scent. But it was too late. The clamorous music of the dogs surged up the ravine, and from where he was situated inside the hollow tree, young Bradley saw a half dozen, narrow-flanked hounds enter the dell, each of them long and slim with a fox's pointed head. They were trotting straight for Bradley and Whittaker's location. Just then the lead dog let out a single cry that electrified the others, bringing them to the opening of the log, where they rioted in celebration. All seemed lost.

Bradley scrambled from the hiding place. Up the ravine, just out of sight, he could sense the Indians coming toward him. The pack of dogs belonged to their master, which was a stroke of luck, for when Isaac called to them, calming their excitement, they recognized his voice and stopped barking. Walking forward on their bellies, the dogs crouched by the fallen tree, panting and wagging their tails. Motioning for Whittaker to stay hidden, Bradley took the moose meat from the pouch he had stolen, dangling it in front of the hounds. Then he reared back and threw the pieces of meat as far as he could, raining them down on the undergrowth.

The dogs ran off in pursuit of their meal. Retreating inside the hollow tree, Isaac remained motionless as the Indians came up, the moccasins of three warriors and a boy visible through the aperture of the log. The Indians loitered there, mulling over the behavior of the dogs, which had been pursuing a line that went straight along the ravine. Now they were scattered in the underbrush, acting as though various members of the pack had each discovered something, though not necessarily what they were after.

Had one of the Abenaki bent down and peered inside the log, Isaac knew that would be the end of things. But while the Indians paused beside them, conversing in low voices, the seconds passed in a strangely attenuated fashion. Death was close at hand.

Giving a command to the dogs, Isaac's master turned back up the ravine, with the others following, and then the dogs passed by the log, going at a trot. When the Indians had departed, still tracking along the ravine, Isaac and Joe began shaking so violently that the rotten interior of the log sifted down on them. They had been within inches of getting bludgeoned by their master's tomahawk.

All that day they sheltered inside the log, too frightened to come out. It grew warm inside such tight quarters, and the boys regretted the loss of their food, as neither had eaten since the afternoon of the previous day. When the piece of forest Isaac could see grew as dark as the log's interior, he ventured out. The woods were quiet, just the usual night sounds of chirrups and hooting that penetrated the canopy. The Indians had gone south, which was the direction the two boys also needed to go; to avoid coming upon their enemies in the darkness, Isaac decided to strike out eastward. With their stomachs empty and spirits low, Bradley and Whittaker rummaged among the tree roots and hedgerows in the dark, trying to find their way.

At sun-up, too exhausted and hungry to go on, the boys dug up some ground-nuts, pulverized them, and mixed the resulting mash with water from the stream. Deeming it too risky to build a fire, or do much scavenging, the boys hid themselves beneath a rocky outcropping, where they slept in fits and starts throughout the day. Again they set out in darkness, and failing to encounter any sign of their master or other Indians, Bradley once more turned their course south, toward Haverhill.

A night's walking brought them to a succession of low green hills. Feeling their pace too slow and their progress meager, young Bradley resolved to travel all that day and at night, too, a prospect that Whittaker did not find enlivening. Phlegmatic in temperament, Whittaker insisted on frequent rest breaks, testing his friend's patience. The territory that surrounded them was Indian country, and the longer they remained there, especially in daylight, the more likely they were to be spotted, recaptured, or killed. But toward evening on the third day, the boys' fortunes and Whittaker's condition improved when, as they were avoiding a swamp, Isaac noticed a covey of pigeons roosting in some bushes. He carried a few smooth stones with him, and carefully taking aim, he pegged one of the stones as hard as he could, knocking a pigeon to the ground. Now they would have meat. Further exploration of the weedy slough led Bradley to discover a turtle, as big as a frying pan, which he bashed flat with a large rock.

Still uneasy about starting a fire, they plucked the birds' feathers and picked away the turtle's broken shell, eating the meat raw, though they gagged on it, and bathing in a creek that ran into the swamp. Thus refreshed, the travelers harvested some pond lily roots, ate a fistful of them, and used the rest to dampen and preserve what was left of the meat, which Isaac carried along with him.

Soon they fell into a rhythm, despite Whittaker occasionally pulling against the yoke, and after numerous rocky scrambles and rest stops, and slight changes of direction, with the typical variations in pace of an energetic, nearly full-grown lad, and a lethargic boy, the two found themselves, on the sixth day, following a well-marked Indian trail. Believing their fortunes had improved, they walked for several miles without any encumbrances until, sometime after dark, they drew near to an encampment of some sort. They heard voices, and crawling to the brow of a hill, the boys looked upon a dozen strange Indians painted for war and seated by a large fire, their muskets and pole-axes and lances piled up beside them. The fugitives gazed down at the camp with astonishment. Exhausted though they were, flight was a necessity; if the young travelers remained in the vicinity, the warriors would kill them just for sport.

The party of raiders was directly in their way. Going as fast as they dared, Bradley and Whittaker retreated from the hill, back the way they came. By avoiding the path, the boys were torn by nettles and thorns, every step taking them farther away from Haverhill, and home. In the morning, they arrived at the same creek they had rested by a day earlier, hidden in a small copse of trees. Here they sprawled upon the grassy bank, the hard, uneven terrain having bloodied their feet, and the latest misfortune having dashed their hopes. Under the bower of trees, the two boys gripped one another by the elbows and started to cry, each possessed by thoughts of their family and friends, and the myriad comforts of life in the settlement. It was the low point of their ordeal.

Isaac Bradley had no desire to revisit the Indian town on the Winnipisogee, only to be whipped and beaten by their master, and subjected to an even more difficult journey, for the purpose of being sold to the French, still less to be taken prisoner by these other warriors, to face a new gauntlet of horrors. Bracing his young companion around the shoulder, Isaac dragged Joe along with him in a southeasterly direction, hoping to avoid both parties of Indians. Sullen and unresponsive, Whittaker stumbled over the tiniest obstacles in their way and frequently sat down on the ground, where he refused to budge.

This made slow going, but the boys endured another day of travel and then one more night. On the morning of the eighth day, Whittaker collapsed beside the stream, saying that he would not take another step. Bradley pleaded with him, but the younger boy refused to get up. Giving his companion an opportunity to rest and perhaps change his mind, Isaac busied himself along the creek, returning with a generous harvest of cattail shoots and other edible plants. But he found young Whittaker just as he had left him, face down in the weeds and breathing heavily, one arm caught awkwardly beneath him. Despite all of Bradley's efforts, Whittaker ignored his friend and wouldn't eat or drink any water. He buried his face in the mossy bank, and remained silent and motionless for quite some time. He had reached the end of his strength.

Moving a short ways off, Isaac sat for a while, eating the lily roots and cattails and drinking from the creek. He reckoned his course by the position of the sun, and, pocketing a few cattail shoots and rinsing his neck a last time, Isaac picked up and continued his journey without saying farewell. Sentimentality was a luxury on the frontier, though Bradley regretted abandoning his friend so much that he fell into despair.

Isaac endeavored to maintain a brisk pace, going along the creek, stooping beneath fallen trees, and scrambling over rocks, but walking grew difficult and his heart was like a stone in his chest. An hour into his trek, the stream entered a grove of pine trees, and Isaac stared with amazement at what lay just ahead. In the clearing was an English farmhouse, the construction not quite finished and the premises uninhabited, but, convinced that he had reached one of the settlements, Isaac turned around and went back upstream, dodging bushes and darting over brambles, intent on reviving Joe Whittaker by whatever means necessary.

Isaac's zeal was such that he shrank the previous hour by several minutes, arriving at the creek bank faster than he thought possible. There he found his companion still lying among the weeds. Joe Whittaker was only half conscious, his eyes rolled back in his head. Through Isaac's persistent efforts, Whittaker sat up and tried to speak. Massaging his friend's limbs and conjuring up images of farmhouses and Englishmen, Isaac coaxed the boy to his feet, where he swayed and stumbled. Grasping Whittaker by the arm, Isaac led him downstream, the two of them weaving like drunkards, first in one direction, toward the woods, then staggering into the creek, where they upended themselves on the slick rocks, banging their knees and elbows.

Just a few minutes after they started along, Whittaker's legs gave out, and he toppled over. Young Bradley was forced to yank the boy up by his armpits, balance Whittaker's unsteady feet upon a rock, and maneuver himself around front. With a heave of his legs, Isaac lifted Joe up and carried him on his back. They had not gone very far before the pair had to rest again, and continuing this way, puffing and wheezing, the boys traipsed on through the forest until it grew dark.

A chill descended through a grove of well-spaced pines, where stumps and piles of sawdust indicated many of them had been cut down. Emerging from the tree line, Isaac's feet struck upon the hard pan of a road, covered in gravel and dropping through an array of cultivated fields to where it terminated at the entrance to a fort. On the evening of the ninth day since leaving the Indian village, Bradley had succeeded in reaching Saco, Maine. They were hailed from the palisade, and men bearing torches and muskets rushed out to meet them. Young Bradley and Joe Whittaker fell down in the dust, and the militia recognized that, despite the boys' grimy clothing and matted hair, they were English, and carried them into the fort.

Whittaker burned with a fever that confined him to the garrison for several days. Isaac fared better. Once he had eaten a meal of cornbread and venison, and slept until morning, young Bradley, now rested and equipped with a sack of provisions, walked another forty miles to Haverhill. Over those months, Hannah Bradley had given up her husband's brother for lost, and must have been confounded by the sight of the rank, emaciated boy who appeared in the village that spring. When told it was Isaac, Goodwife Bradley joined her neighbors in giving thanks for his delivery from the Indians.

Less than a year later, twenty-four-year-old Hannah Bradley was in the possession of another band of wretches, laboring over snowy terrain north of Pennacook. After their meeting with the wounded squaw near Sugar Ball Island, the Indians had decamped early the next morning, spiriting their captives away, including Goodwife Bradley. Burdened with a heavy load and forced to move quickly, Bradley had no choice but to weather the harshness of her Indian masters. Steeped in the ways of the frontier, she knew enough to trudge along, keeping her own counsel.

By watching and listening, Bradley surmised that the captive uprising on Sugar Ball Island had upset the Abenaki, perhaps altering their plans. They were originally from Maine, now living among the mission Indians in Quebec, and loyal to the French. They were at a great remove from their own territory, surrounded by a barren wilderness. Even more sullen than usual, they gave terse, inscrutable commands and expected them to be obeyed immediately. It was clear the Indians wished to put as much distance as possible between their party and the avenging settlers who might still be nearby.

Within two days, Goodwife Bradley and the other captives had passed from the rolling terrain of the Merrimack River valley into the foothills of a great mountain range, the likes of which they had never seen before. After leaving the Indian camp near Pennacook, they entered a mostly uninhabited region, the mountains growing larger all around them, their peaks dusted with snow, even now, in April. Sometimes the bulk of these mountains rose before them so precipitously, crowding out the horizon, that at night when they camped, Goodwife Bradley felt like she was at the bottom of a deep pit, the only visible light shed by a handful of stars overhead.

So hemmed in by mountains it seemed impossible to continue, Bradley was impressed by the Indians' ability to locate and then traverse the gaps between them. At first, the party ascended toward notches that were visible from a distance, but as they climbed higher, into the scrub pines and snowfields, the Indians located narrow traces that meandered upward onto the high ground. These gullies were covered in snow, the footing uncertain and treacherous, but by picking their way along, the Indians stayed out of the harshest weather and thus avoided exposure to the winds raging above the tree line.

At this elevation, the air was so cold Hannah's breath grew short, emerging from her mouth in vaporous clouds, while the kettle ponds and sloughs were plugged with ice. Food was hard to come by, and sometimes the Indians camped for an extra night, out of the wind, fishing in the creek with hand lines while a few descended to lower ground, tracking a moose or deer through snow-covered meadows. With the Indians thus engaged, their prisoners were forced to huddle among the rocks all day, and the sky, which had been gray and laden with snow, cleared out for a brief interval. This opened up blue vistas to the horizon, and the captives must have been surprised by what they saw. A few miles north of their camp arose a mountain greater than all the others, a craggy, broad-shouldered massif draped in a thick mantle of snow.

The Indians called it "Agiocochook," or, the monarch of mountains. It dwarfed the entire range from every vantage point. Although the mountain was directly in their path, with notches visible on each side, after the hunting trip had concluded and there was meat for the camp, the Indians took pains to avoid the rocky slope of Agiocochook. By gestures and exhortations, they indicated that the summit of the mountain, shrouded again by a veil of clouds, was the dwelling place of the Great Spirit during his sojourns on earth, a prospect that clearly frightened them.

In fact, the Indians believed the summit of Agiocochook had been the meeting place of the Great Spirit and Passaconaway, the revered sachem of the Pennacook, an event that was witnessed, or at least reported by, their elders. At the appointed time, the great Bashaba bid farewell to his people, and then mounted a sled pulled by twenty-four giant wolves. Adorned in bearskin robes and whipping these beasts with a thirty-foot lash, Passaconaway roared through the woods above Pennacook and across the icy plain of Winnipisogee, the sled mounting into the sky trailed by a cloud of fire. The great chief sped over the treetops at the base of the mountain, screaming and lashing the gigantic wolves, ascending ever upward, until he and the sled were lost in the clouds atop Agiocochook.

Now, as the Indians and their captives trekked northward, descending into a river valley to the east, the Abenaki kept their eyes averted from the mountain, its misty peak hidden again by clouds. With everything covered in fresh snow, only the most trail-savvy Indians could differentiate between these pathways and the dead-end ravines and canyons that surrounded them. Here in the mountains, Goodwife Bradley understood that the only way to survive her captivity was to make it to Quebec, where she could perhaps be ransomed back to her family. Hannah also noticed that, over the course of their journey, the Indians had winnowed the group of captives down to the older children and the hardiest of the women, who were the most valuable as trade items. And though they often spoke rudely to Hannah Bradley and her companions, taking every opportunity to demonstrate their impatience and scorn, none of the captives were beaten or abused in other ways. Still, Bradley realized that if she tried to flee, she would be killed, and if she lagged behind her captors and their relentless pace, she would soon die of exposure, baffled by the mountain range that enveloped her.

Hannah Bradley knew what the Indians—especially these Indians—were capable of. From her dooryard on the morning of March 15th, as a portion of the Abenaki raiding party came screeching and whooping through the brush, Hannah had watched as her seven-year-old son Joseph and two-year-old daughter Martha were murdered with two strokes of a tomahawk. Their deaths were swift and without ceremony, done with the same heedless skill as a chicken dispatched by the fall of an axe. And in the terrible frenzy of that hour, Bradley's children went un-mourned, so urgent was her own survival and the myriad, almost instantaneous actions and decisions that attended it. Time was always short in the settlement, with all the work to be done, a pointed arrow that thrust itself forward to an ever-diminishing point on the horizon. But now, after the carnage of those days, with more terror all around, and the mountain passes and unpredictable weather as lethal as the Indians, Hannah came to reckon that nothing whatsoever remained behind her. Indeed, every distinguishable portion of the wilderness ceased to exist the moment she passed through it. There was no past, only the brief, wavering corridor of what lay just ahead, always closing in and growing narrower.

Even those moments that Goodwife Bradley anticipated and tried to prepare for, raw in their immediacy, jumped at her with such speed and violence she was robbed of breath. After the farm was ransacked and burned, she was taken captive at the point of a bloody lance, urged onward through the forest by the savages who killed her children. Bradley was walking only a few feet behind Hannah Duston when her neighbor's infant, Martha, was snatched away from Mary Neff and dashed to a pulp against apple tree. Other captives, especially those who couldn't keep up, were bludgeoned to death, and still more faltered during the march and were trailed after and dispatched with a pole-ax, or else they succumbed to exposure and were abandoned there on the ground, half frozen and covered in debris. And from her young relation, Isaac Bradley, Hannah had learned of the brutality and heartlessness of the Indians at Winnipisogee, and the many hardships and insults of his time among them.

Faced with this evidence, Goodwife Bradley went on, laboring over the frozen terrain without comment, hardening her heart toward the Abenaki, but also to a measurable extent toward her fellow captives, the idea of staying alive being such an individual pursuit. She even cast a dispassionate eye on her own losses, her own trouble. Her world was pain, and the ever-present vibrating shock of that pain was all she knew, or could expect from the life she was in. It was the same for the other captives, plodding along beside her in silence. No one complained, or even spoke of it.

At length, they entered a strange, elevated land beyond the mountains, half-covered with an immense pine forest, the trees marching in serried phalanxes toward the horizon. Still, Bradley kept on, eating what came to hand and sleeping on the ground, always resuming the trek northward. Eventually, the Indians came across a few bushrangers who were out hunting and trapping, a group of stout, whiskered Frenchmen in blanket coats and fur hats who traded brandy for some of the withered scalps the Abenaki were carrying. At this meeting, the Indians surprised Hannah by speaking French, and by how quickly they became drunk and took to muttering, crawling around in the dirt, and soiling themselves.

Bradley encountered more Frenchmen over the next few days, *coureurs de bois* moving along the sunken trails and waterways hunting for beaver, and other rough-hewn adventurers living in crude wooden lean-tos, many of them with scalps hanging from their lodge poles. There was a great number of Indians, too, gliding over the early rivers in their canoes, passing by in hunting parties of three or four warriors, and occupying a few small villages along the trail. The Abenaki raiders greeted their countrymen with aplomb, obviously proud of their English captives and the riches they would bring.

The snow grew deep as they approached a river the Indians called Arsikantegout, which meant "empty cabin place." Almost a month into the journey, Goodwife Bradley and the others were given snowshoes. Never having worn a pair, and forced to run in them when the terrain was flat, Hannah was plagued by severe cramps in her knees and ankles. The Indians referred to this discomfort as *mal a la raquette* and told her to chew on wintergreen, as well as blossoms of the pyrola weed that could be found growing along the embankment.

When the party reached the Arsikantegout River, which the French referred to as the Saint Francis, they found a channel of black water running between unsteady shelves of ice. Dividing into two small groups, the Indians and their captives scrambled into a pair of bateaux and pulled themselves across by means of a thick rope strung across the river. The Ste. Francis was considered the line of demarcation between Quebec and the frontier. Here the Indians rejoiced because they had reached the heart of Ndakinna, which translated to "our homeland."

Perched on a bluff overlooking the river, the Abenaki village was a smoky, smoldering collection of forty or fifty wigwams and their respective campfires, enclosed by a jagged palisade. At one end stood a large council house, as well as a stone church and bell tower, attended by two missionary priests. Upon reaching the town, Bradley and the other captives were met by the Jesuits, who instructed them to enter the church and thank God for preserving their lives. To the English Puritans, it was an idolater's church, filled with statues and graven images, and they were reluctant to comply. But the mission Indians threatened to knock the captives in the head if they refused to obey the priests, and so they went in.

Hannah Bradley was detained in Canada for several months. There is no record of her life there, but it is assumed she and the other Haverhill captives were sold to French landowners and made to labor on their behalf. Although the exact circumstances are unknown, Bradley regained her freedom on January 17, 1698, when she was taken aboard ship to Casco Bay in Maine and released. Soon after, she returned to Haverhill, where her husband Joseph and their sole remaining child, seven-year-old Mehitabel, were still living.

In the weeks after Hannah Bradley's disappearance, her husband, greatly alarmed by the mystery of his wife's ordeal and the murder of their two children, pondered which measures should be taken against such events recurring. To that end, he and some men from the village bottomed out a deep cellar hole near the ruins of his farmhouse. They sank four sturdy oak timbers, one at each corner, and built upon that foundation a steep, two-story garrison house, with a single door, narrow windows sectioned off with diamond-shaped pieces of leaded glass, and a central chimney with a slot for shoveling out embers. The walls were likewise constructed of square timbers chinked out with mortar, and after the house was enclosed, lined on the exterior with bricks. The upper story projected out from the lower one, with a ladder that could be pulled up in emergencies, and there were several gun ports throughout the structure, in the case of an Indian attack.

Enclosing a small area that included a garden, the building was surrounded by a tightly arranged eight-foot palisade with a single gate crisscrossed by strips of iron. Beside the gate was a raised wooden platform where a sentry could remain protected, yet with clear lines of sight beyond the wall. If the Indians were to return, an assault on the Bradley garrison would be a more difficult proposition than what they had encountered in the spring of 1697.

Between when Goodwife Bradley returned to the settlement and the winter of 1703, Joseph continued to make improvements to these fortifications, and, as the house was situated on the western edge of Haverhill, a contingent of local militia was detailed there. For nearly two years, ending that summer, the Indians remained absent from the frontier while the New England settlements enjoyed a peaceful interlude. But in August 1703, with the onset of the French and Indian War, five hundred Abenaki warriors and a handful of French soldiers commanded by an officer named Beaubassin attacked Wells, Maine, killing or taking captive thirty-nine settlers. Ranging two hundred miles along the coast of Maine and New Hampshire, the war party waylaid travelers, burned out farmers, and laid siege to the fort at Casco Bay. After a few skirmishes, Beaubassin was driven off when an English warship arrived in the harbor.

Beaubassin and his army withdrew to Quebec, but it was clear the French had once again engaged the mission Indians to harass the frontier. That fall, Abenaki raiders struck at isolated farmhouses and hamlets from Berwick in southern Maine to Hampton, New Hampshire, but these attacks subsided, as they usually did, when the winter snows arrived, burying the settlements and surrounding countryside, which made it difficult for a war party to approach and easy to track upon their departure.

Prudent settlers were vigilant at all times, though the late winter months were typically the most peaceful. An hour or so before dark on February 8, 1704, Hannah Bradley and several members of her household were occupied with chores within, and very near to, the safety of the garrison house. Hannah had struck up a blazing fire just outside her front door early that day, cultivating it to her appointed task by feeding in wood at certain intervals, then letting it burn down to white-hot coals. Engaged in soap-making, Hannah had collected wood ash all through the autumn and winter, and over the last two days had poured water over these ashes to leach out the brownish liquid containing the lye. The smell was so horrible, the lye was left boiling in the yard between the house and the palisade, while a kettle of leftover cooking fat and bits of gristle and other animal fats was simmering indoors over the chimney fire. The garrison door remained open as Hannah Bradley moved back and forth, trying to strike the right balance of the lye solution and fat boiling over the outdoor fire.

At the same time, Joseph Bradley and a militiaman named Jonathan Eastman were a half-mile away, splitting logs and stacking them in the wood lot. Also in the house, dipping candles and mending boots and other items was a hired woman, who kept watch over the youngest Bradley children, five-year-old Martha and two-year-old Sarah.

An afternoon snowfall had ceased, and eager to complete as much work as possible in the waning daylight, Hannah asked the sentry posted at the gate, a raw-boned youth named Jonathan Johnson, for help, since she was getting close to delivering her sixth child. Only happy to comply and relieve the tedium of his watch, the young sentry hung his musket on pegs above the fireplace and hurried back outside. When he re-emerged into the yard, Johnson was followed outside by little Sarah, who wandered over toward the boiling kettle.

After fetching a bucket from an attached shed, Johnson sallied out through the palisade gate, crossed the snow-covered meadow adjacent to the house, and descended into a hollow where the creek was located. After stamping a hole in the ice, Johnson filled his bucket, heading back toward the house with fresh water and the armload of wood Goodwife Bradley had requested.

Inside the house, with the front door open, Hannah was tending a large black kettle suspended over the chimney fire. On the left of the hearth, shaded from the fire by a wooden rack draped with Joseph Bradley's hunting clothes, was a diminishing pile of hardwood, as well as the animal fats and salt necessary to soap-making, which Goodwife Bradley was tending. Just then the young sentry passed through the gate, stomped across the tiny dooryard, and entered the house with his bucket of water and several pieces of hardwood to refresh the fire. Both arms being full, Johnson had momentarily left both the palisade gate and the door to the house wide upon, and an arctic blast of air followed him to the chimney step.

Unbeknownst to the inhabitants of the garrison, a small band of Abenaki raiders had been watching the house for most of the day, waiting for just such an opportunity. Stealing across the open ground between the forest and the palisade, half a dozen warriors, wary of the militia and casting glances left and right, accelerated as they drew closer, passing one after another through the narrow aperture of the gate without uttering a sound.

Just as he unburdened himself of the firewood, Johnson turned for the door and saw the Indians about to rush inside. Taking the loaded musket down from its pegs, Johnson whirled and fired; the abrupt report of the gun, puff of white smoke, and the acrid odor of the discharge were joined by the screams of the Abenaki as they crowded through the door. One of the warriors was heard to exclaim, "Now, Hannah, me got you." The first Indian to enter the house was struck by Johnson's musket ball and knocked to the floor, right at Hannah Bradley's feet. But the next two Indians rushed in, discharging their rifles, and the low-ceilinged room was filled with the haze of spent gunpowder, and the whooping and yelling of the Indians.

Screaming with fright, little Martha and the hired woman ran for the ladder dangling from the attic; the women lifted Martha overhead, following quickly on her heels before reaching the floor above, whereupon the woman pulled up the ladder and bolted the trap. With no access to the upper reaches of the house, the raiders made short work of the main floor.

The wounded Indian had become separated from his tomahawk by the force of the musket ball lodged in his shoulder. Dazed for an instant, he scrambled toward the fireplace trying to reclaim it, when Hannah Bradley, acting on instinct, lifted the boiling kettle from the hearth with a pair of tongs. Grasping his tomahawk, the Indian struggled to one knee. As his torso rose to waist-level, Bradley poured the steaming liquid onto his head, sloshing it into his eyes and open mouth; then, as the raider fell back, howling and flailing his limbs, she struck him with the iron kettle on top of the head as violently as she could. The smell of burning flesh added itself to the odor of gunpowder and the nauseating stench of the lye. The Indian screamed, writhing on the flagstones and tearing at his face, before he gasped aloud and died.

The warriors who had shot Jonathan Johnson grabbed him by the hair and the collar of his jacket and dragged him out of the house. As he lay moaning, the Indians bludgeoned the sentry's face into a pulpy mass with their gun butts and scalped him. Nearby, little Sarah was heaped up on the ground, her skull crushed by a pole-ax. Another Indian seized Hannah Bradley, who fought against being taken but was quickly overpowered. The savage hauled her out through the palisade gate and across the meadow to the tree line.

On this dim winter afternoon, spurred on by her new master, Goodwife Bradley was driven toward a little clearing north of the garrison house. Here the Indians rendezvoused with another small party of raiders, who had been waiting for them in a grove of trees with four shivering and disconsolate villagers. Thrust together and shoved onto the trail, soon the party was traveling through dense forest, stumbling over roots and stones hidden by the snow, and trembling in their household clothes.

Gloom deepened over the landscape, and in the minds of the prisoners. The attack had happened so suddenly there was no general alarm, and the daylong snowfall meant that nearly everyone in the settlement was indoors, unaware of what had occurred. Almost before she realized what was happening, Goodwife Bradley had been taken captive a second time.

On this occasion, Hannah suffered the additional complications of her unborn child and the perils of harsher weather. It was apparent these Indians had been afoot for several weeks, clothed in deerskin leggings, thick moccasins, and bearskin robes, as well as being outfitted with snowshoes. They carried pouches of Nokehick, dried pieces of moose meat, and a supply of tobacco. Being in precarious health of late, Goodwife Bradley had been confined to the garrison house for almost a month, emerging only on fair days to empty the slop-pots or bring in firewood. The deaths of Sarah and the young militiaman had come as a shock to her, as had the narrow escape of her other child. That winter, Hannah had spent every day in the steadfast company of her husband, and Joseph Bradley's absence, which had extended less than an hour, spoke to the cleverness of the Indians, as well as her own bad luck.

Added to these woes, the Indians again required Bradley to put on snowshoes, which she found hard to maneuver in, and to carry a deerskin bundle of such proportions that she staggered beneath the weight of it, toppling into a snow bank. The only assistance she received from her master was a rebuke, his foot banged against the tender portion of her ribs, and the expectation that a subsequent fall would precipitate being knocked in the head with his axe.

The Abenaki moved at a thumping pace for several days, never pausing to hunt, and often walking in shallow rivers to make it difficult for any would-be pursuers to track them. Hunched under her enormous parcel, Goodwife Bradley trudged along these stony creek bottoms, her feet numbed by the frigid water. Incessant snowfall, rugged terrain, and the bitter cold made it unlikely they were being followed. The wind blew so sharply, the Indians withdrew into their mantles until they resembled a procession of bears, walking on their hind feet. They ate handfuls of parched corn and drank from streams as they went along, which allowed the captives only a few moments to rip the inner bark from trees or dig in the frozen soil for wild onions and groundnuts. At night, Goodwife Bradley ate bits of dead skin from the underside of her feet, no doubt repulsed by the idea of devouring herself to survive.

On several occasions, Bradley fell behind the rest of the party, faltering in the drifts of new snow. She was burdened by the parcel of stolen goods, and further obstructed by the child she was carrying. Though Bradley expected to deliver her seventh child before the rising of the new moon, she was not treated any differently than she had been during her first captivity. The growing urgency of her condition evoked little sympathy from the Abenaki, who rarely glanced back to see if she was keeping up with them. Each day, following very little sleep and given only a strip of moose hide to chew on for breakfast, Goodwife Bradley tramped after the Indians, making what headway she could against the biting wind.

After three weeks, the column arrived at an Indian village in the middle of a trackless pine forest. Here Bradley's snowshoes were taken away, and she was made to travel in knee-deep snow until they reached another encampment. A squaw took pity on her and built a meager fire, after which she covered the expectant mother with a few hemlock branches. Suffering from lack of food, the endless sacrifice of her travels, and the agony of childbirth, Hannah Bradley delivered the infant without further assistance. Mother and child remained another fortnight in this location, while the Indians hunted the woods, drying the meat on their braziers. Suckling her child the best she could, Hannah was tormented by the scent of the cooking fires, having been given little to eat besides groundnuts. Furthermore, the abundant smoke meant the Indians were preparing to resume their journey northward, filling Bradley with dread.

After they had been in the village a few days, the squaw again visited her, this time in the company of a French priest. He was a large, coarse-looking man, with keen eyes in a narrow face, dressed in a long black cassock, a four-peaked black hat, and a crucifix dangling below his waist on a length of rope. He took another wooden cross from beneath his robe and began to pray over mother and child in what Hannah Bradley supposed was Latin. She had never heard it spoken before, only knowing it was the language of the idolaters, but she was familiar with Norridgewock Abenaki from twice being in captivity. So when the Jesuit used the squaw's dialect to send her for something, Hannah was even more surprised when the priest addressed her in English, telling her to proffer the infant for his blessing. He gave it, describing a cross in the air with his hand, and when the squaw re-entered the wigwam with a palm-sized chunk of moose meat, the Jesuit passed it to Bradley and exited as quickly as he had arrived, never once meeting her gaze.

And scarcely had the priest departed when Bradley's master, pacing up and down, forced the exhausted woman and her infant from their resting place. Just beyond the snow-laden camp, the entire party had mustered itself at the trailhead, outfitted in snowshoes and shouldering their deerskin bundles. By gestures and exclamations, the Indians convinced Bradley they would allow the child to live if one of them baptized the infant in the Catholic manner. Reluctantly, she agreed.

Seizing the child, Bradley's master withdrew his knife from its thong and carved a tiny, shallow cross on the baby's forehead. A stream of blood ran into the child's eyes, and it began to wail. The Indian thrust the howling infant back into its mother's arms, sheathed his knife, then struck down the trail with the other Indians, leaving Bradley to press a handful of snow against the infant's wound, hardly believing what she had just witnessed.

Onward they journeyed into a wilderness more remote and forlorn than what came before. The infant, forced to travel so soon and so roughly, scored by the Indian's knife, and complaining of hunger and other discomforts, mewled and cried throughout the afternoon despite Bradley's efforts to console it. Incensed that the noise would attract their enemies and frighten off game, Hannah's master circled back to mother and child, his gaze baleful and steady as he walked a parallel course through the trees. Bradley hugged the infant closer, keeping to the trail with her head angled downward.

At night, the Indians trampled over a small area, kicked away the snow, and lined the space with pine boughs. After they built a fire, Goodwife Bradley stayed as far away as possible, trying to nurse the infant and keep it quiet. But the child wouldn't suckle and its sobs, amplified in the stillness, echoed among the trees. Reaching into the fire, one of the Indians dislodged several embers with his pole-ax and crossed the intervening space with the coals balanced on the flat side of the blade. While the other savages looked on, grinning and jostling each other, Bradley's master took the child from her, tilted its head upward, and deposited two of the burning embers into its mouth. The infant gasped, choked, and screamed. Rushing forward, Hannah grabbed the child back from the Indian and retreated across the clearing.

The infant began to sob and then to howl, pitching its weak, shuddering voice above the other night sounds. Bradley cleared the deadened coals from the infant's mouth, tried to staunch the burns with crystals of snow, and paced back and forth, rocking the child against her bosom.

All that night the cries of the distressed infant haunted the woods. Before dawn, the Indians, hollow-eyed and menacing, had Goodwife Bradley on her feet and hurrying after them. Trail signs and other harbingers meant they were closing on their destination, as the well-traveled snow and bits of refuse indicated a large Indian village was nearby. That afternoon, while the Indians were eating from their stores, Hannah Bradley crept to the edge of the forest, swaddled the infant in her coat, and placed it on top of the deerskin bundle. Then she retreated a short distance for her daily ministrations. In a short while, Bradley returned, only to discover her child impaled upon a stick that thrust upward from the ground. Its eyes bulged open, and gobbets of blood trailed down the stake.

In New England, little time was provided for mourning, especially among the Indians. Most of them had taken up their weaponry and provisions, rejoining the trail at the point where they had left off, paying no attention at all to the murdered infant. As quickly as possible, Bradley wrapped the child in her shawl and, with little more than a narrow depression for a grave, covered it with snow and then followed the tracks of her master. Her face twisted into a horrible grimace, limbs moving automatically, Bradley departed the little copse of trees without a single look back, parting with her own heart's blood being such a commonplace thing in that time. Of her seven children, five were already gone: one dead at birth, and Joseph and Martha killed in the first raid on Haverhill; two-year-old Sarah was murdered in the second attack on the settlement; and now the unnamed infant, summarily deprived of its life in a nameless portion of the wilderness, far from any civilized place. The only thing for Hannah Bradley to do, in the face of such travails, was adhere to what she had left, and that required making it safely to the French settlements.

The war party reached the border in a few days, where Goodwife Bradley was sold to a French family for eighty livres. Hannah was provided with a narrow cot, and though her day was occupied from start to finish with unceasing labor, it was preferable to living with the Indians. Her new master treated her fairly, if brusquely, seeing to her daily needs and refraining from beating or striking her. Each morning, when Hannah milked the family's cow, she took scraps of bread from her pocket and sopped up what was left in the bucket, allowing her to regain her strength and vigor.

Just over a year later, in March 1705, forty-year-old Joseph Bradley received the news that his wife was in the possession of the French. Hardy and steadfast, Bradley had become accustomed to tragedy after the death of his four children at the hands of the Abenaki. He had also suffered the murder of his older brother, Daniel Bradley Jr., Daniel's wife, Hannah (Dow) Bradley, and two of their children, during the March 15, 1697 raid on Haverhill. Resolved to ending Hannah's second captivity, which, taken with their earlier period of marital separation exceeded three years, Goodman Bradley set out from Haverhill under dismal weather conditions. Passing through long stretches of hostile territory was easier alone than with companions, thus Bradley, taking his dog, piling his belongings on a stout wooden sled, and smoking his pipe for company, walked from the English frontier to Quebec, avoiding the most commonly used Indian trails. Snow fell during the day and even more often at night. But the dog could trot for hours, had a good nose, and like every other creature on the frontier that slept under a roof, heeded its master. Circling hills and fording rivers added days to Bradley's trek, and he arrived in New France in just over a month.

Packed among the items on the sled was a bag of snuff, which was a rare and expensive commodity, given to Bradley by the governor of Massachusetts, Thomas Dudley, for bestowal upon the governor of Canada, Phillip de Rigaud, the Marquis de Vaudreuil, with the former's compliments. The French governor looked favorably on this token, and, combined with a payment given to Hannah's master, Bradley was able to secure his wife's release. He booked passage on a ship sailing from Montreal to Boston, and when it reached port, husband and wife made the forty-mile trip to Haverhill on foot.

After reinforcing the garrison house, and being careful to have sentries always on watch, Joseph and Hannah resumed their life on the frontier. But that summer, there was additional reason for concern when several Indian raids were inflicted on the settlements. In early August, a roving band of Abenaki killed two Haverhill residents, Joseph Page and Bartholomew Heath, in the midst of their labors, while a boy in their company was able to escape. These incursions prompted Governor Dudley to order the reinforcement of Haverhill with "twenty able soldiers" from the Newbury garrison. But Haverhill's Colonel Nathaniel Saltonstall protested in a letter to the Newbury commander that the transferred militia were not experienced soldiers, "but boys, or children, not fit for service, blind in part, and deaf, and cross-handed."

Once again the New England frontier was quiet through the winter, but in the spring of 1706, the Indians attacked Oyster River, Dunstable, and Exeter, killing more than twenty settlers, wounding at least that many, and taking several captives. Despite Saltonstall's complaints, the Haverhill garrison houses were still undermanned, and in July, shortly after the raids on Exeter and Dunstable, a band of four or five Abenaki, painted for war and intent on a particular errand, approached the Bradley garrison beneath the light of a waxing moon.

Her family had been greatly depopulated by the Indians and by illness; and only Hannah Bradley, who was now thirty-six years old, her husband, and one of the Newbury militiamen were contained within the house when they noticed raiders stealing across the meadow. Having no knowledge of the Indians' strength, but seeing a quartet of Abenaki nearing the gate, Joseph and his two companions grabbed their muskets, secured the door, and peered out through the leaded window at the enemy. To give the inhabitants of the garrison a further advantage, Goodwife Bradley snuffed out the box-tin candles and threw a dirt-encrusted hearthrug over the fire. With a mixture of exasperation, ire, and deadly calm, Hannah took up an extra rifle, powdered the barrel, shoved the cartridge down, and pulled the tumbler back to half cock. She was certain the Indians meant to seize her again, and as Joseph went past with his gun, Hannah declared that she would die fighting rather than be taken captive a third time.

The settlers braced themselves as three Indians climbed over the palisade and rushed the garrison. Beating at the front door with pole-axes and the butt of their rifles, they had nearly succeeded in knocking it off the hinges when an Indian began to squeeze himself through the narrow space. Advancing with her musket, Hannah Bradley fired a ball into the Indian from close range, while shouting at him to go to the devil. The gun emitted a resounding boom in the small space of the house, and the Indian fell dead, with a large hole in his chest. Joseph Bradley and the soldier ran outside with their muskets cocked, but the other two Indians had already clambered over the palisade and disappeared.

Hannah Bradley stood in the doorway, reloading her musket and scanning the tree line. The only way to stop the Indians was to kill them. There would be no parley.

Chapter VIII

Escape from Sugar Ball Island

As light seeped in, revealing the narrow shoal, Hannah Duston rose from where she had squatted all night and woke her companions. While Mary Neff and Sam Lenorson prepared to depart, Hannah took up the loaded rifle and went along the embankment, searching for a place to launch the canoe. Snow covered the entire island, and, on the downriver side, the bluff dropped fifteen or twenty feet to the water, which was running fast and deep beneath the undercut bank.

Duston's limbs creaked from her previous exertions, as well as the torpor of a very cold night, and her ragged clothing was stiff with blood. A young boy's corpse, rigid as iron, was sprawled on the rocky shoal, and two more dead children were face down in the snow nearby, their mantles and exposed flesh specked with bits of frozen gore.

Walking along the riverbank, Hannah was certain that Indians were lurking all around, perhaps among the trees on the far bank, or gliding downriver in their war canoes, obscured by the rising mist. But Hannah made no attempt to conceal herself, or her intentions. The Abenaki were swift, merciless, and cruel, without any semblance of fear or restraint, ready to kill at a moment's notice. But none of this hindered Duston any longer. To meet the Indians on their own ground, Duston had herself become a savage, ready to inflict pain and death, or suffer it, as the circumstances demanded of her.

For the first time since her arrival, Duston had a clear view of the terrain and a grasp of their situation. Sugar Ball Island was shaped like an arrowhead, with the Contoocook River descending along a high-banked gorge and splitting at the sharp end of the island, then going equally along both sides, with the broad sweep of the Merrimack passing by the blunt end. The land mass was no more than a couple of acres, though like most things, it had seemed larger in the dark, with a rising headland on the downriver side and a low triangular dell covered in pines, hemlocks, birch trees, and scrub on the pointed end. The smell of death clung to the place, though it was very cold and the wind trailed from the northwest.

Ribbons of smoke fluttered up from the ashes of the fire-trench. Just beyond it, the two dead warriors and a pair of squaws were lying stiffly on the ground where Hannah and the others had killed them. Watery blood from their noses and ears streaked the grime on their faces, and the flesh around the eyes and the bed of their fingernails had an eerie, bluish tint. Duston stepped over her master's body without a second glance, making her way to the edge of the headland.

The island was steeply banked all around, but for the rocky strand that marked the lower end. From the bluff, Duston saw that the irregular skirt of ice protruding from the island had lengthened in the cold temperatures overnight. The shelf of ice, an inch or more thick, extended from the shoreline eight or nine feet to as much as a rod, making it impossible to launch a canoe directly into the swelling current of the Merrimack.

Duston gazed at the immense water-channel beyond the headland, probing for any sign of the Indians: smoke from a cooking fire, the low, narrow V of an approaching canoe, or a hunting party wending along the bank. Just upriver from the island, on the western shore of the Merrimack, was a great plain of snow fringed by trees that bordered the river. This marked the place where, the previous evening, Duston's master had parleyed with another band of Indians, trading Goodwife Bradley and the others for a rifle and some powder and shot. Even from a distance, Hannah could make out the rutted snow and other markings that showed the war party had been there. There was a trammeled spot in the middle of the clearing, and funnel-shaped grooves on the embankment indicated where the canoes had been pushed into the river. Duston couldn't say whether all the footprints were from the night before, or if there had been other Indians moving along the Pennacook trail.

Coming around a sharp easterly bend to sweep past the island, the Merrimack was twenty or thirty rods wide at that point, high black water that carried past the island with barely a sound. From horizon to horizon there was the Merrimack, the air filled with the smell of it and the river overflowing beyond the trees on either side. As the sun edged over the horizon, Hannah turned and descended back through the canebreak to where Mary Neff and Sam were stamping their feet and flapping their arms to stay warm. Not saying a word, Goodwife Duston strode over to the canoe, put the rifle back in its place, and, grasping the thwart with her right hand, dragged the vessel along the snowy embankment until she found deep enough water to hold the draft.

Never hesitating, Hannah plunged down the bank into the river, the canoe sliding along beside her. Duston's weight broke through the ice, and banging and slashing at the inch-thick skirt with her elbows and the canoe paddle, soon Hannah was immersed to her thighs in the freezing water. Beckoning to Sam and Mary to follow the snow-trough she had made down the embankment, Duston steadied the birch bark vessel while her companions eased over the gunwale and took their places.

Lenorson came amidships and Neff, taking up the other paddle, crowded herself into the bow to distribute the weight. Leaning hard on the stern, Duston raised herself over the gunwale and onto the rear thwart, wielding the paddle. Immediately the current sucked the vessel broadside, and Duston, who had never paddled before, flailed away on the right side and then the left, trying to keep them afloat and get the prow of the canoe pointed downriver. Immediately the rippling water threatened to overwhelm them.

The canoe, once entered, felt unstable and wobbly in such fast-moving water. The occupants, particularly Hannah and Mary, who were heavier than the boy, had to loosen their hips, shifting left and right to keep the craft steady. In less than a minute, Hannah, mimicking the way the Indian had steered the canoe, used short, powerful strokes to thread them into the current. But no sooner had Duston maneuvered the canoe into the channel, navigating as best she could among the submerged rocks, when she appeared to change her mind. Letting out a brief cry, Hannah turned her paddle into a pole, forcing the canoe sideways to the current. Once that was achieved, she worked at a frenzied pace, digging at the river with the paddle. The canoe barely avoided being swamped, and, with some difficulty, they turned back toward the island.

Instantly, the current drew them a fair distance past their entry point. They were just a moment or two from being thrown by the Contoocook into a much larger river, when Duston, paddling furiously, was able to smash the bow of the canoe through the ice, grounding it against the bank. Telling her companions to stay where they were, Hannah stepped into the current, waded alongside the hull of the canoe, and secured the bow by hauling it up onto the shore. She instructed Mary to keep the rifle trained on the opposite side of the river until she got back, saying it wouldn't be long.

With that, Duston clawed her way up the snow-laden bank, using roots and exposed rocks to support her weight. Gaining the crest, Hannah parted a tangle of brush and immediately headed up island. As she disappeared over the bank, Neff and Lenorson were puzzled by their return to the island, especially after there had been so much haste in leaving. While they stared at the other bank, watching for movement, neither of them could have guessed what task Hannah had left undone, or which item she had overlooked.

And Duston, having clambered onto the bank, glanced down island for a moment, then turned her gaze quick around, making her way through the hedges and scrub with a purposeful stride. Reaching the bluff, Hannah scrambled up the snowy ridge on all fours, saving the time she would have spent going around to the path. Blood hammering in her ears, Duston reached the flat top of the headland and stood erect, looking over at the black expanse of the Merrimack. The fire-trench smoldered from one end, and the beaten snow all around was marked by a host of scattered items: overturned kettles and spools of ribbon, fish bones, pewter dishes, empty rum bottles, and a tomahawk with a broken handle, all indicators of the desperate struggle that had taken place there.

Four corpses littered the ground, arms and legs flung over one another, the bodies half in and half out of the shelter. Going straight to where her former master lay, his bare arm thrust across his face, Hannah bent down and removed the Indian's knife from its deerskin thong. Even in the cold air, the body emitted a horrible stench, and it took a considerable effort to pry the Indian's arm away from his face, the limbs were so rigid. The savage's forehead was caved in, exposing a clotted mass of brains, and one of his eyes was missing. Blood covered the ground in places like a series of frozen black mats.

Kneeling on the corpse with the knife in her right hand, Duston reached down, grasped a fistful of the Indian's greasy top knot with her left hand, pulling it straight back. With the Indian's hair stretched tight, Hannah dug the edge of the knife into the top of his skull and began sawing all around. After hewing and cutting in this way, a large flap of skin and the clump of hair pulled away, until just a piece of knotted gristle held the scalp in place. The blade of the knife bumped against the skull with a grinding sound, until Duston was able to sever the last bit of flesh connecting the Indian's scalp to the bone. It was nothing more than dirty hair with a rag of flesh attached to it, not much blood, something that resembled a dead vole or rat, with the same foul smell.

Goodwife Duston knew how to handle a knife, being frequently engaged in skinning rabbits; beheading salmon or sturgeon; gutting and boning waterfowl, turkeys, and pheasants; and occasionally butchering and dressing a stag or broken-legged calf. And Duston had watched her dead master and the other Indians scalping her neighbors over the past fortnight, taking notice of how it was done. Though it was grim work, it was work with a purpose, and she carried it out with a grim, purposeful air. But like all other skills connected to frontier life, scalping took a great deal of practice, and Duston's first effort was a clumsy one.

Moving quickly, Duston removed the scalps of the other warrior and the two squaws, rooting among the discarded items and half empty deerskin bundles until she found something to wrap them in. Balled up amongst an irregular pile of sundries taken from Haverhill was the piece of broadcloth the Indians had cut from Hannah's loom during the raid. Wrapping the scalps in this, she retraced the steps she had taken a few hours earlier. Below the headland, Duston sliced through the forehead of the girl who Mary Neff had killed, and folded up the scalp with the others. Following various sets of footprints and blood trails, Hannah scalped all the rest, including the two corpses stretched over the palisade and the boy she had killed on the strand, coming away with ten scalps in all.

Hannah piled up her trophies in the cloth, tying it with a deerskin thong stripped from one of the corpses. After Duston cleaned the scalping knife in the river, testing its edge by drawing the blade across a smooth rock, she passed along the trail on the western side of the island. Coming upon the impressions she had made in the snow, Duston spotted the canoe rocking on the edge of the current. She tucked the bloody cloth under one arm, called softly to Mary Neff, and skidded down the embankment on her hip.

Wading into the river, Hannah traded places with Mary, who left the rifle leaning against the thwart and squeezed by young Sam into the bow. The scalping knife, jabbed into the gunwale when Hannah got in the canoe, and the leaking, half-opened bag of scalps, now piled up with their original supplies, made it clear to the others why Duston had returned to the island. Whether Hannah had scalped her enemies out of revenge, for a bounty from the Massachusetts governor, or to prove what she had done in killing the Indians, Neff and Lenorson remained silent. They were confident that Duston had her reasons.

Pushing off the embankment with her paddle, Neff freed the canoe, which immediately swung to, and re-entered the current. By means of a narrow, rocky chute that fell between the dense trees on one side and the island on the other, the occupants of the vessel bumped over hidden outcroppings and rocks, nearly losing the bundle of scalps overboard. Hannah dipped her paddle left and right, scraping the gunwales and striking against rocks so forcefully that the vibration numbed her wrists and hands. The river churned along on both sides, higher than the thwarts of the canoe. Fearful they were about to be capsized, and thrown into the roaring water, the travelers were propelled through a zigzag channel before they dropped over a final rocky shelf and were deposited, all in one movement, into the swollen waters of the Merrimack.

On the broad elbow of the river where the canoe was disgorged, a sliding mass of water stretched over a half-mile from bank to bank. With the wedge-shaped island off to their right, and the shore of the Merrimack low and weedy on the near side and raised into a bluff on the other, they'd entered a perilous new country. Glancing upriver and down, Hannah felt exposed on all sides, in danger of being spotted from a hundred possible vantage points. An arctic wind came from the northwest, roiling the water with a million glittering facets as the sun crested the horizon. Threatening snow, an encroaching armada of clouds drifted in from the west, mottling the blue sky.

Duston's pantaloons were sopping wet to the mid-thigh, and the air was so cold she couldn't stop her jaw from clattering together. Water had been thrown over the gunwales and was sloshing around in the bottom of the canoe, numbing her feet. Hannah moved them to and fro, draining first one moccasin and then the other, as she paddled as hard as she could. Therein lay the biggest obstacle to the settlers' flight; whereas the narrow channel of the Contoocook, descending in swift fashion, limited the pad-dler's effectiveness, making their way in the slow-moving Merrimack required so much energy that Hannah and Mary were soon bent over the thwarts, gasping for breath. In the middle of the river, the wind seemed to come from every direction at once, blowing the canoe sideways; while veering too close to shore carried them into long, rippling eddies that flowed against the main current, stymieing their progress. No matter how smartly they dug at the water surrounding them, how prolonged a joint effort they made, Duston and Neff's inexperience left them adrift just a short distance from where they'd entered the Merrimack.

After some trial and error, the paddlers found a rhythm and were able to eclipse Sugar Ball Island. As they passed, a little gray smoke trailed up from the headland, and birch trees tufted with brown leaves waved like rags in the wind. Only young Sam, who was turned around facing the stern, looked back at the smoke rising from the island, preoccupied by what they had done there.

Hannah kept them in the middle channel, equidistant to either shore, making it more difficult for a party of Indians to surprise them. In such high water, the current so forceful that uprooted trees were being swept along, there was a chance of being capsized, pulled under, and drowned. But the most pressing danger remained the stealth and cunning of the Indians. Over the past fortnight, Duston had watched one of the Abenaki kill a deer with his bow from three hundred yards. The arrow flew on a breath of wind, passing straight through the buck's neck before it knew what had occurred. Pump-handling at the river as Hannah and Mary were doing, their shoulder joints worn to the bone with paddling, it was equally debilitating to be always searching the nearby terrain with their eyes, wondering if there were Indians, how many, and how disposed they were to attack.

The other fear was chancing upon a war party paddling downriver. The Indians' familiarity with traveling over water, their speed, and their endurance made it possible for them to appear at any moment, overtaking the stolen canoe from behind, or moving faster upstream than the whites were capable of going with the current. As Duston and Neff grew wor-ried, paddling out of synch with each other, they appeared to meander in a circle, the river so wide and slow it was like being caught offshore on a vast lake. Here the river entered low flat country, winding among pine trees interspersed with snow-covered meadows. Soon they were being pushed to the western shore by a stiff headwind, making it seem like they were being blown back to the island—a disconcerting occurrence in this first hour of their escape. For over a mile, the river was broad and slow, featuring a high bluff where scouts could easily be observing them. Duston fretted that the turns and twists of the river would allow these Indians to retreat through the forest and set up an ambuscade downstream.

Crouched amidships, Sam Lenorson urged the others to pause for a moment and eat. Reluctantly they obliged, fortifying themselves with handfuls of Nokehick washed down with river water so cold it made their throats sore. Peering over the gunwale, Duston noticed that the depth of the river was less than two feet, the water clear and moving swiftly over a flat, sandy bottom that looked like it had been shaped with a trowel into perfectly symmetrical ridges. The banks had dropped to a level just above the water line, and Duston grew uneasy when she realized that a war party could charge out from the tree line, rush through the knee-deep water, and kill them all before she could load and fire a second shot.

Just then, Duston was startled when a hawk swooped low over the water, scanning the shallows for fish. Hannah grasped the paddle and doubled her stroke rate, encouraging Mary to follow suit. The flotilla of clouds had sailed across the horizon by now, encasing the sun, and a steady snowfall dropped on the trees along the bank, melted into the river, and clung in feathery piles atop the gunwales. Two miles from Sugar Ball Island, the Merrimack descended into a much narrower channel, with mossy rocks poking up between whitecap Vs made by the irregular river bottom. Larger rocks below the surface threw plumes of spray into the canoe, or else jutted above the surface, menacing and black. This stretch of river was bumpy and rough, but it offered a modicum of solace to Duston and her companions, because the rapids made it unlikely the Indians could waylay them, and the heavy snowfall, dropping over the pines, hid them from observers on the bank. Reduced to an occasional two- or three-stroke flurry, and more often using her paddle as a rudder, Goodwife Duston took account of their progress while catching her breath.

Having now experienced the twisting course of the Merrimack, its varying currents and backchannels, and the abundance of natural obstacles, Duston reckoned the foot miles they had traveled to the best of her ability, and then fixed her estimate at sixty or seventy river miles between Sugar Ball Island and Haverhill. Judging by the gauzy presence of the sun, obscured in the cloudbank, they had traveled approximately two miles in about two hours, a rate of speed that would expose the fleeing captives to a myriad of dangers. Hannah Duston's short time on the river had enumerated all the dangers of such travel, and the thought of spending two or more days in the stolen canoe filled her with dread.

Passing off to the right was a large flat rock that stood at least two feet above the current in the middle of the stream. The winter's ice had receded to the embankments on either side, but the rock was crested with snow at least a foot thick that extended all around, like the top layer of a cake. While those aboard the canoe stared at this oddity, the vessel running of its own accord through a shallow, fast-moving trough, there was an abrupt, jarring thump, and they stopped short, the water coursing past on both sides, nearly swamping the canoe. All three heads snapped around, their torsos whiplashed backward, and Mary lost the grip on her paddle, which fell into the river and went racing ahead of them on the current.

The canoe had struck a hidden rock, the presence of which had escaped Neff's attention, since a fan of water curling from the riverbed looked insubstantial enough, and they had passed through many of these already. With the bow jammed against the rock and the canoe stock-still in the middle of the river, torrents of water began to rush in, piling over Mary's knees. Hannah dug her paddle into the stream, groping for a purchase, and, striking a rock beside the canoe, pushed off with all her strength. Due to its marvelous buoyancy, the vessel shot to the top of the foam, continuing among the low rapids that flowed along this part of the Merrimack.

With only one paddle, the canoe was more difficult to maneuver, and Hannah fought to keep them nose-first in the channel. The icy water in the bottom of the canoe rose to their shins, and more rocks, both visible and likely, mined the river ahead. They jounced along for some distance, with Mary and young Sam attempting to bail out the canoe with their hands. At the end of the rapids, the Merrimack traveled over a shallow, pebbly course and Hannah, gazing past Sam and Mary, could see they were approaching a significant drop in the river. Nothing could be done about it, as the canoe, with three persons and one paddle aboard, sailed over a rocky ledge all at once, the bottom of the vessel taking the air, and then landed in the white water beyond the falls with a loud smacking noise.

Again, this wonder of Indian craftsmanship landed lightly and of a piece, maintaining its integrity and floating ahead on a much reduced current, with the bewildered travelers gaping at the venture. Here the Merrimack swelled to the horizon, an inland sea of water populated by clumps of bare-limbed trees. One of the eddies doubling back toward them contained the lost paddle, and Hannah made her way over and secured it, while Mary bailed them out with a kettle reclaimed from the Indians.

For a while, they remained nearly motionless in the channel, Hannah leaning over the thwart exhausted from paddling, with Sam Lenorson replacing Mary Neff in the bow of the canoe. Off to the right, dead leaves clung to the upper branches of the trees standing along the bank. The experience of passing over the falls had raised another concern. Duston knew there was a large set of falls in Pawtucket, approximately fifteen miles upriver from Haverhill that traveling Indians frequented, though a tiny English settlement was located there. What other falls existed throughout the long, remote passage that stretched ahead was unknown. And with the spring fishing season nearly upon them, when the shad and salmon would be running, the Indians were undoubtedly flocking toward the Merrimack in large numbers, to string their nets and rebuild the weirs after a long, damaging winter.

Having resettled themselves, with the only change being that Sam occupied the bow while Mary rested, the company set out in earnest. The river was a quarter-mile across, sometimes a little wider and running slow, at other junctures narrowing to a flat, shallow draft contained within the banks and moving somewhat faster, though still requiring a substantial effort by the paddlers. Long shelves of ice extended outward from the eastern bank, creating a solid, foot-thick obstacle that in several places covered half the river's width. This platform was sturdy enough to allow a party of Indians to advance to the water's edge, shooting their arrows and discharging their muskets straight into the canoe. Recognizing this, Duston and her companions hurried on.

Narrow, snow-covered islands also began to appear, some of them close to one bank or the other, or else dividing the river into equal channels. As they approached, Hannah gauged the current, the number of visible rocks and snags, and the possibilities of an ambush, deciding whether to navigate to the left or the right. Each island also represented a potential fishing station or watch house for the Indians, which caused the voyagers' apprehension to rise as they drew closer.

Upon reaching one of these islands—three or four rods wide and more than ten rods long, substantial enough to contain a small forest of pine trees and scrub—the whites shuddered when they paddled by the strand. There on a narrow beach, the remains of a campfire emitted a twist of smoke, which had been impossible to detect because of the low skies. Duston signaled Mary Neff to take up the gun, and without a word, she and Sam Lenorson paddled by the island without so much as a backward glance.

At times, the river was so wide it became a dimpled plain, gunmetal gray in the low light, with shifting white ruffles appearing here and there when the wind changed. Duston's hands were bleeding from her grip on the paddle, and her shoulders felt like they'd been wrenched from their sockets from the drops in the river, the weight of each stroke, and the continuous revolution of her arms. Amidships, Mary Neff slumped over the stock of the rifle, dozing in fits and starts. Finally, the light diminished to an evanescent fringe on the horizon, and the countryside grew dark, punctuated by strange hooting and other calls. The whites ate a little corn meal from their stores, and in brief whispers decided to stay on the river through the night.

The proximity of the abandoned campfire, just a mile or so back, and its clear indication they were not alone in the country, made traveling by night the only possible choice. Camping on shore would find them, in the morning, no closer to the settlements, relegated to completing the bulk of the journey in daylight, and prone to being discovered by a band of pursuing Indians. Or a hunting party might chance upon them, only too glad to exchange the pursuit of venison for their scalps.

Against Hannah's objections, Mary Neff declared that she would steer the canoe as they floated downstream, avoiding chunks of ice and what obstacles they encountered as best she could, while the others slept. If they passed any Indian encampments, or Neff saw anything out of the ordinary, she promised to alert the others. She and Duston exchanged places, and Mary rested the gun on the thwart that bumped against her knees. After keeping the first watch, Neff agreed to wake up Sam Lenorson, and they would alternate in that way until morning.

The canoe lurched over an object beneath the water, and Hannah started up. Sam Lenorson was in the stern, trying to maneuver the best he could, but they had been taken out of the main channel, drifting too close to shore. A steep, rocky ledge formed the western margin of the river, while on the other side, half the embankment had been eaten away by the current, the exposed roots of fir and birch trees hanging beneath the earth's crust like the tentacles of a great sea beast. Despite Sam's paddling, the canoe had struck one of the roots and jolted Duston awake.

It was still dark and quite cold, but Hannah felt better. Leaning against the thwart amidships, and covered with an Indian blanket that Sam had thrown over her, she looked up at the sky to get her bearings. In front of her, Mary Neff was asleep in the bow of the canoe, her head lolling over the gunwale. In this country the Merrimack was glossy and still, and the trees, flanking them on both sides, loomed overhead. Motioning with her hand, Duston gestured to young Lenorson that they switch places, feeling energetic after a little sleep. Having been transported a fair distance without any concern, the quality of her slumber being so sound, Duston again took up the paddle and her worries, setting about the task of regaining the middle of the river.

The river was quiet except for the parchment-tearing sound of the current running along the banks, and the occasional fir tree creaking onshore. An hour or more remained before the first rim of dawn, but all the snow in the woods and the stars wheeling overhead made navigating easy. Duston had little idea of where she was, or how many miles they had traveled, but was grateful to be making way, still undetected, far from Sugar Ball Island. Soon the boy was fast asleep, and Hannah was no doubt reminded of her own children, the varying lot of them, and could not help herself from wondering about their various fates. For just as Goodwife Duston had no idea what had become of Thomas and the children, she also realized that her husband and their brood, had any of them survived the attack, were equally unaware about what had become of Hannah.

Chances were slim on the frontier, generally, and the circumstances of the raid had narrowed them to a hair's breadth. Prior to this interlude on the river, Duston had not really taken time to consider what had occurred back in Haverhill, though it was not that surprising to her. Neither Hannah nor Thomas expected more out of life, which thus far had provided little comfort, an abundance of toil, and a hundredfold sorrows.

Several years earlier, Hannah and Thomas's three-year-old son John had succumbed to an illness; young Timothy's twin sister, Mehitable, died a few months after her birth in 1694; and Mary, tall and sturdy at fifteen years of age, had been taken by fever. Of the remaining eight children, from Hannah's teenage namesake to three-year-old Timothy, she dared not speculate which of her loved ones had fallen under the tomahawk and the scalping knife. If any of them had survived the raid, they'd already discovered Martha's corpse, the infant's head caved in by one of the savages, whose own skull was now broken into pieces, his life extinguished. That was the world they all knew.

At length, after a considerable pace-slackened drift, Hannah woke Mary Neff in the bow of the canoe and they resumed paddling. There was no real sunrise, the sky was so overcast, just an accumulation of light by degrees, and a corresponding drop in temperature. All that night, the river had been cold and damp, and their limbs were stiff from having the frigid water beneath them and the northwesterly wind on their necks. But where it had been a watery chill to that point, more damp than cold, what they felt at daybreak was the starkness of winter returning to the Merrimack. Hannah shivered even in the midst of paddling and longed to go ashore and strike up a fire.

The riverbanks dropped until they were nearly at water level. Close in, a legion of ghostly trees crowded both embankments, their thin, skeletal branches twisted together like withes, growing so close the trees formed a barrier between the river and the open, snow-encrusted meadows beyond. It was thrilling country, the river wide, dimpled, and black, slow moving, edged with protruding shelves of ice and arched over by leaden skies. Heaped up on the bottom of the canoe, young Lenorson stirred, rubbed his face to get the blood flowing into it, and gazed around at the landscape they had entered.

Snow lay everywhere in the woods, thrown up in great rotting bundles on the ridges overlooking the channel. The only sign that winter had passed was the snow receding from several trees, leaving a brown circle of earth at the base of the trunks. After another mile or so, the water ran clear, and the voyagers, peering over the gunwales, could make out thousands of round rocks lying side by side along the bottom. On either shore, the barrier of trees dropped away, the banks widened, and the river descended more sharply. The bottom turned to shale that was streaked brown and gray, and the water grew shallow, running swiftly until a thousand white curls of foam arched into the air. Coming around a final bend, the travelers sailed into a basin that stretched half a mile across. A great roar filled the air.

Less than fifty rods ahead, the Merrimack dropped over a large falls, obscured from view by spumes of diaphanous vapor. Canted between the banks at a thirty-degree angle, the smooth-flowing ream of water approached the precipice and thundered over, breaking into great powerful columns of foam. To avoid tumbling over the drop, Goodwife Duston and Mary Neff aimed the canoe at the nearest bank and paddled like devils, as the current pulled them toward the falls. Reaching the shallows, all three voyagers disembarked, the powerful force of the Merrimack sucking at their feet and legs. Stumbling as they dragged the canoe toward the embankment, they managed to reach the shoreline with the paddles and their supplies intact. A short distance away, the unbroken skein of water dropped over the falls and rioted along for a half-mile before going around another bend.

Neff and Duston lifted the canoe, found purchase on the slippery embankment, and, trudging in ankle-deep snow, began looking for safe passage around the falls. Each had witnessed boatmen portaging their craft when they reached the old fishing weirs at Haverhill, the small barges and bateaux often loaded on horse-drawn carts or rolled along the bank on pine logs. For as long as they could remember, the falls at Haverhill had teemed with salmon, sturgeon, and herring during the spawn that occurred in early April. There remained some villagers of long standing who recalled that the weirs originally belonged to the Pawtucket Indians, who had vacated the nearby hunting grounds when the settlement was established, but for a number of seasons leased back their fishing rights.

Now they were deep into Indian territory at Amoskeag Falls, a legendary gathering place since Passaconaway's reign. Sam Lenorson had heard the Abenaki mention it, saying the herring runs were immense, and that they wished to return after selling their captives in New France. For her part, Duston felt guilty of momentous crimes, as they hurried along with the stolen canoe, scanning the horizon for smoke or any other sign of an encampment. At the top of a rise, the whites became further alarmed when they found a portaging trail marked with an Indian gazette. This was a small weathered board hanging from a pine tree that depicted two men carrying a canoe alongside the falls. It was the first such carving they had seen during the entire trip, indicating this was a significant place for the Indians during the fishing season. In low water, the Indians would not need to portage their canoes; they would simply climb over the edge of the falls and hand the lightweight vessel down to their companions.

The path bowed outward, crossing a snowy field and heading into a grove of trees. Hauling the vessel across open ground, Hannah felt especially vulnerable, and though the canoe was a light burden, it wasn't meant to be carried very far, the distance to navigable water and the trajectory of the path causing the women to bump their knees and shins as they waddled along. Beneath the trees, a woodpecker opened up with a staccato burst, and the women nearly dropped the canoe and ran into the forest.

Behind them, Sam Lenorson carried the gun, with instructions to shoot only as a last resort, as the noise would attract every Indian within a mile of the falls. Though Duston had seen fish hawks gliding over the shallows, and intermittent schools of alewives had passed beneath the canoe, the great torrents of fish that would draw hundreds of Indians to the falls had not yet begun. But the nature of the migration was its suddenness, and Hannah feared that the converging Indians would catch them in the open, or along the riverbank, and she and the others hurried through the trees, the canoe banging against their hips.

A sudden twist in the path brought the fugitives through a grove of trees in sight of the large, churning basin that stood below the falls. There on the strand ahead of them were the half-broken frames of several wigwams, a blackened fire pit, and haphazard piles of the staves used to make fishing weirs. Going past, Duston knew this was the remains of last season's Indian village, reduced to debris by a long, cold winter, but soon to be reconstituted by the horde of savages due to arrive.

Hannah and Mary Neff raced toward the edge of the river, the canoe jogging along between them. Here the water ran fast and black, undulating over hidden rocks and other debris, and tipped with white crescents of foam. The falls were so loud Duston couldn't hear herself shouting to Mary Neff where they should put the canoe in, gesturing and waving her free hand to make herself understood. Hauling their bark into knee-deep water, Duston steadied the gunwale and they all scrambled in and immediately began paddling. The current below the falls was the strongest they had encountered, and while Hannah leaned hard on her paddle, trying to steer between obstacles, the river took them swiftly around the bend into new country.

When they had surpassed the clamor of the falls, eager to put additional miles between themselves and this Indian gathering place, they found the canoe delivered into flat, still waters that barely seemed to flow at all. Here the Merrimack was still and black as ink, so undisturbed it provided the weary voyagers with a perfect reflection of the canoe and its inhabitants. Making things worse, the river ceased its straight-banked trajectory as it meandered through wetlands on a serpentine course.

A series of ox-bow twists forced the river to turn back on itself again and again, tempting Duston to take the shortest route across these marshy spits of land, as one stretch of the Merrimack ran almost parallel with the next. But wading to the bank, unloading the gun and other loose items from the canoe, and portaging it across these lowlands, which were covered in grasses and dotted with iced-over pools, would be more cumbersome than staying in the channel and paddling around.

The tangled course of the Merrimack bringing their progress to a standstill, Duston became so preoccupied with the abrupt bends in the river and how easily the Indians could paddle up the channel or wade through the grasses to ambush them, that she and her companions failed to recognize the territory they had entered. By Hannah's own reckoning, at least forty miles remained between their position and the settlements, nearly all of it Indian country, but when the river began straightening itself, Duston recognized the open vale and low glacial hills. The curves in the river became gentle, the water lapping at the banks, and miles of open ground stretched away to a succession of drumlins on each side, the snow having retreated from the adjacent Indian fields through exposure to the sun.

Now the sun danced over the river in glittering facets, having eclipsed the fleet of dark clouds that hid it all morning. The wind had eased off, and an occasional songbird appeared on one of the linden trees growing along the bank. Toward late afternoon, overhanging trees again enclosed the river, and only glimpses of the sky were permitted from their location in the middle channel. The western bank had dropped away, leaving no definite shoreline, and the eastern side of the river accommodated a series of wooded hills that towered over them. Sailing under the bower of tree limbs sharpened their sense of hearing to a keen edge, making audible every fish that rose to take a minnow, and the claws of squirrels and chipmunks scuttling along the branches.

With darkness filtering through the trees like a fine black powder, the voyagers poled along in the shallow, still water, alert to every trill and chirrup, as well as the leaves rustling overhead. Passing the mouth of a brook that entered the channel on the western bank, Duston felt certain she heard something approaching them from downstream, perhaps the clunk of a paddle against birch bark and the whisper of human voices.

Fearing that a party of Indians would appear any moment, Duston tapped Sam on the shoulder, gesturing toward the nearby stream, and the youth, in turn, directed Mary Neff's attention toward the embankment. Stroking twice each on the left side, the two paddlers swung the canoe that way. Hiding upstream would be quicker than landing on shore to disembark, and Duston's first instinct was to avert their course from the oncoming party. The stream was no more than a rod across, running into the Merrimack between grassy banks, its slow-moving water about three or four feet deep.

Now more accustomed to paddling, Duston and Neff moved the shallow draft of the canoe upstream without too much difficulty. Hearts booming, they resisted the urge to pound away at the water, fearing the noise it would make, instead maintaining a steady stroke as they ascended the brook. When they had passed through the fringe of trees bordering the Merrimack, bent low over their paddles and curving with the stream across a long meadow, the voyagers felt reasonably sure they weren't being followed. Cattails lined both sides of the brook, screening them from view, and the dense thicket cut off any sounds emanating from the river.

On the far side of the meadow, they entered another grove of lindens, farther distancing themselves from the Merrimack. Now more than a half-mile from the mouth of the stream, Duston and the others meant to pause awhile and listen, but any slackening of effort would allow the current to push them back downstream. So they persevered in mounting the brook, gliding through the darkened copse of trees into another field, where they rounded a bend and were surprised to find a quiet solitary little house. Built into a rising mound of earth like an animal's burrow, the house stood among a clump of venerable oak trees, with a heavy door flanked by a pair of latticed windows, and a façade made from square timbers—most decidedly, an Englishman's house.

The proprietor of this establishment had scythed away the grass in front of the entrance, with a path of fieldstones leading downward to the edge of the brook. Held fast against the bank were two large creels made of willow branches and woven reeds, and as the voyagers drew closer, they saw a glimmering tangle of silver eels in each of these cages, flashing here and there in the diminished light. Amazed by their discovery, Hannah and the others held themselves in the current, their mouths thrust open in wonder.

While the travelers were thus engaged, a footfall sounded on the opposite bank, and looking round, Hannah Duston was confronted by the keeper of this property, a rough, keen-eyed, white-haired man of fifty or so years, carrying his rifle and snares in one hand, and a brace of dead rabbits in the other. While the canoe hovered there in the brook, the man swung the rabbits across to the other bank and draped the snares about his neck. Without addressing his visitors, he stepped lightly from the bank into the stream, the water up to his thighs and soaking the tails of his deerskin coat as he waded across. Hauling himself up after placing his gun and shot pouch in the matted grass, the man stood in front of his house, dripping wet, looking down into the canoe.

By now, the circumstances of each were plain to the other, this being the frontier and all the parties being white, though that was not immediately evident due to the ragged and bloody attire of the escaped captives, and the muddy frame and countenance of the settler. His name was John Lovewell and this was Salmon Brook, he said, located in Dunstable, Massachusetts. One look at the Indian canoe and Lovewell recognized his visitors' plight; he reached down to grasp Duston by the wrist, and with astonishing strength, handed her up onto the embankment.

Duston and her companions had not reached the settlements. In fact, Lovewell's cabin was the lone outpost in an unbroken wilderness that stretched from Sugar Ball Island to Pawtucket Falls. A former ensign in Oliver Cromwell's army, Lovewell was also a veteran of the legendary Narragansett Swamp Fight of 1675. Because of Lovewell's role in that battle, which ended King Philip's War against the English, the Indians in that vicinity respected the old militiaman and left him alone. Still, being just eight or ten miles downriver from Amoskeag Falls, which attracted strange Indians as well as familiar ones, Lovewell's cabin was dug into the earth and fortified with thick timbers, as substantial as any garrison house. If the voyagers were to ascend Salmon Brook another half-mile, they would find the burned out cabins owned by less fortunate settlers, Lovewell informed them.

The inside of the one-room house smelled of moss and tubers, freshly killed game, wood smoke, and other rank odors. A handful of coals were burning on the hearth and, with the approaching dusk, Lovewell closed the shutters to keep in the light, making it harder to spot the house. Three years earlier, a trading post had been established a few miles south, and Lovewell's served as a way station for furs brought downriver by the Indians. With the opening of the fishing season, which would arrive any day now, the fur trade would also begin. Lovewell advised Duston to travel all night, since the Indians rarely took to the river after dark, and with a day's hard travel, they might reach the tiny settlement at Pawtucket Falls by the following evening. Staying here any longer would not get them any closer to Haverhill.

Retreating to the canoe with a pouch of smoked eel bestowed upon her by their host, Duston, immediately repaying this kindness, gave Lovewell half of their Nokehick, scarcity being the principle of all things on the frontier. And with a wave from the bank, Duston and Neff got the canoe turned around, and paddled back downstream toward the Merrimack. Washing down into the river with the current, Duston banked to starboard and guided the canoe along the eastern shore, which was hung with shadows as darkness came on.

The voyagers devoured the meal that Lovewell had provided, listening to the night sounds echoing through the forest. For quite some time, Hannah and Mary paddled together, while Lenorson dozed. They moved steadily downriver, the channel wide and clear, with the darkness no hindrance to their speed. Then, as prearranged, Hannah changed places with Sam and curled up in the middle of the canoe and went to sleep.

When Duston awoke, the moon was out, reflecting off the flat black expanse of the river. Gesturing in silence, Mary, who had been in the stern with Lenorson now asleep in the bow, handed Duston the pouch of corn meal and traded her spot for Hannah's. Soon Neff was asleep. The water was clear of obstruction and running straight between tall, grassy banks, its length reflecting the moonlight. Occasionally a night bird flapped low across the water, or the wind, barely stirring all day, suddenly aimed downward in a blast, rattling the dead leaves on a cluster of oaks, and then passed away.

Hannah discovered that paddling once on each side of the canoe in a long, powerful stroke, then letting the paddle trail behind, where she used it as a rudder, allowed her to maintain the center of the channel. Huge oak trees leaned out from the banks, their immense branches nearly meeting overhead. The river carried them along at a fast rate, and this maneuver allowed Duston to conserve her strength; as she glanced back, the moon peeping between the branches left a phosphorescent trail of bubbles in their wake.

Hannah drew her knees up as the night grew colder, and with the sighs of her companions measuring the pace, she kept up the three-part motion of her stroke. Lovewell's remark about the Indians rarely traveling by night brought comfort to her, and for the first time since their flight from Sugar Ball Island, Duston had occasion to reflect on the magnitude of what they had done. Circumstances had allowed no time for common prayer, and Hannah's mind was so preoccupied with avoiding the Indians, especially during their initial flight, and then in the portaging of Amoskeag Falls, her attention had been diverted from the usual scripture passages that had eased her spirit during hard times.

In the quiet of those hours, Hannah determined the justification for the acts that her captors' brutality had forced her to perform. Hannah's father, Michael Emerson, who immigrated to Haverhill from Lincolnshire, England, while still a young man, had taught his children to read and write through the agency of bible study. Growing up near Primrose and Winter Streets, Hannah, the eldest of Michael and the former Hannah Webster's fifteen children, had received a good education through the diligence of her father and an abiding respect for the path that God had revealed to her. In this part of her life and every other, Goodwife Duston had never taken anything that God did not provide for her and thus felt her deliverance from the Indians was the action He had chosen. Duston recalled the story of Jael and Sisera, from the Book of Judges. In the old time, Sisera was the commander of a great army consisting of nine hundred chariots fitted with iron. For twenty years, Sisera and his army plagued the Israelites, and the people of Abraham beseeched God to assist them in defeating His enemy. The prophet Deborah told the Israelites that God would deliver his people from their oppressors, but that a woman would vanquish Sisera. After his army was routed and all his men had died by the sword, Sisera got down from his chariot and attempted to escape on foot. An Israelite woman named Jael welcomed Sisera into her tent, provided him with a skin of milk, and covered him with a blanket. Exhausted, he quickly fell asleep. Then Jael took up a hammer and drove a spike through Sisera's head into the ground.

Duston believed that her actions on Sugar Ball Island were equally righteous, and that the cruelty of the Indians and the desolation of the surrounding wilderness allowed her no alternative. In short, the fate of the Indians was preordained. A just God had exalted His servant and delivered the savages into Duston's hands, just as He delivered Sisera to the door of Jael's tent: "At her feet he bowed, he fell, he lay down; at her feet he bowed, he fell; where he bowed, there he fell down dead."

Having made her peace with what had occurred, Hannah did not dwell on it. She passed several miles before the channel opened up and the sky lightened to the east. The river was more than sixty rods wide, with a shallow, clay bottom that gave the water a yellowish hue. Neff and Lenorson, roused by the sun, each took some of the Nokehick and leftover eel for their breakfast, and Mary began paddling in tandem with Hannah.

Out of the hazy sunlight came the high-pitched drone of a million insects thronging in the trees along the banks. An occasional gust of wind created blue ridges in the channel, disappearing into black when the sun ducked behind a cloud. Their vessel was thrust forward on the current, and a watery, fecund smell swept in with the breeze. Winter seemed finally in abeyance. The mountains were far behind them, and the blue-walled ether of the sky rose up on both sides, meeting overhead. Two or three rocks broke the surface, and then a long, straight-banked portion of the river continued for over a mile before curving into the trees.

After flowing south for over forty miles, the Merrimack doglegged to the left, heading sharply east. This bend in the river marked the entrance to the lower Merrimack valley, near Tyngsborough, Massachusetts. Here and there granite ledges protruded from the banks, and as the river narrowed to forty rods, dropping to a depth of ten or fifteen feet, the voyagers passed a large, wooded island, encompassing seventy or more acres.

Having heard the Indians speak of this place, Sam Lenorson said they had reached Wicasuck Island, which had changed hands many times, most notably when Passaconaway's son, Wonalancet, sold it to the English in order to repay a debt incurred by his brother, Nanamocomuck. Later, the General Court of Massachusetts returned Wicasuck Island to the Pennacook, and when they were driven out, the area's first settler, Jonathan Tyng, was deeded the island as compensation for manning a garrison house in the vicinity.

Passing Wicasuck Island, the travelers glimpsed what looked like the ruins of an Englishman's cabin, but the island was so wooded and overgrown they couldn't be sure. A mile or so downriver, Hannah and the others could make out a farmhouse, a few outbuildings, and a patchwork of cultivated fields on a bluff overlooking the Merrimack. Here they dropped over a low falls without portaging. The homestead was located a half-mile from the river, too far off to justify beaching the canoe and inquiring of their exact whereabouts. Eager to reach Haverhill, they decided to stay on the river.

They paddled all that morning, changing positions in the canoe when fatigue or hunger required it. For long periods, the water was smooth and iridescent, broken only by the head of a turtle, making a V-shaped wake along the bank. By midday, they had reached Pawtucket Falls, carrying the canoe around by means of a well-worn path. Later that afternoon, the voyagers caught sight of a giant sturgeon, its dark shiny back rising and falling as it swam against the current. As the day wore on, Goodwife Duston heard the yelp of a dog before spotting a crew of white men who were floating several pine logs along the bank. The men told them they had reached the settlement of Andover, Massachusetts, fewer than ten miles from Haverhill. After Duston shouted who they were and where they had been, the settlers offered to send a galloper to Haverhill, announcing their presence on the river. The voyagers, again passing up an opportunity to stop and rest, continued on.

Vistas stretched ahead for over a mile, the sun drenching the eastern shore, illuminating every branch on the trees growing there, with the opposite bank wreathed in shadows. The river was a quarter-mile wide, the only sign of a current the blurring of the reflected trees cast down on its surface. The mix of fir and oaks grew so close together they formed a wall on both sides, the blue sky vaulting overhead with only patches of clouds floating along. Their weariness mingled with a growing excitement, the paddlers struggled on, the water as motionless as a lake.

The Merrimack, growing shallow again, had spent all day absorbing the light, and the paddlers could see quite clearly, though the trees astride the river had grown dark. A gull shrieked overhead, startling them, and then a voice—more voices—called out from shore. They had arrived at Haverhill. A gathering of settlers, including many of Duston's children, were walking along the bank, halloaing and waving their arms, near the place where Bradley's Brook emptied into the river.

Turning for shore, Duston and Mary Neff paddled with a renewed fury. In the shallows, Neff and Lenorson scrambled out, nearly overturning the canoe, and Hannah leaned over the gunwale, panting in exhaustion. A fallen oak tree, bleached white like a gigantic bone, lay across the outlet of the brook, its cragged roots upended against the sky. Goodwife Duston felt herself being helped from the canoe, her children spreading over the bank into knee-deep water.

Duston leaned over the canoe, handing out the rifle and hatchet while retrieving a bulky piece of cloth. Her husband, Thomas, was there, standing beneath a tree with his hat shading his eyes. He crossed over to the low point in the bank, and took the sodden bundle from his wife. Unfastening the thong that held it together, Goodman Duston looked down at the foul-smelling knots of hair, swaddled in the cloth that his wife had labored over.

Chapter IX

Samuel Sewall, Cotton Mather, and the General Court of Massachusetts

Hannah Duston's joy at finding Thomas and the children alive, though tempered by exhaustion and the murder of her infant, carried her through that day, supported by her husband and older children as she walked unsteadily along the riverbank. The Dustons' temporary lodging, for convenience and safety, had shifted from one of their remaining outbuildings to the Marsh garrison house, the family farm having been destroyed by the Indians. After first saying goodbye to Sam Lenorson, who was taken in by a local family until a messenger could be sent to Worcester, Hannah traveled to the Marsh garrison in a cart belonging to one of their neighbors.

Guided to the upper story of the house, Duston, assisted by her grateful, murmuring daughters, was fed a meal of roasted potatoes and salmon, bathed in tepid water, and wrapped in a clean blanket. She was given a fresh shift, petticoat, and underskirt against the nighttime chill, which still pervaded the garrison house despite a succession of warm, sunny days. Hannah also wore a gown made of a woven skirt, cotton bodice, and linen sleeves. Before it was dark, the former captive was helped into a bed near the dwindling fire and covered with a pair of quilts. Hannah slept all that night and nearly through the following day.

Except for a stroll at dusk, Goodwife Duston remained indoors, relating the story of her ordeal to her husband and the older children. The rifle and hatchet Duston had taken from the Indians were set aside, and

Thomas, after briefly inspecting the scalps, retied the bundle, placed it in a canvas sack, and stored the parcel in a heavy wooden box. The family ate a meal together, and again Hannah was put to bed early.

After two days of rest, Goodwife Duston emerged on a bright, temperate morning at the conclusion of the first week in April, clad in a pair of borrowed shoes and a neighbor-woman's cloak, all her own belongings having been incinerated in the fire. Renewed by the fresh air, nourishing food, and plenty of sleep, that morning Duston undertook a few light chores after praying with her family, giving thanks to God for delivering them from the Indians. But Hannah soon discovered that she had returned to a settlement quite different from the Haverhill she had known. Rightly preoccupied with her own survival and that of her two companions, Duston had given little thought to the greater impact of the March 15th raid, as well as the disposition of her family, neighbors, and friends.

During her initial stay at the garrison house, Goodwife Duston had been left alone but for the three militiamen standing guard, and the occasional appearance of Onesiphorus Marsh, who tended to the horses—including the Dustons' own—in the shed attached to the rear of the building. When she was able to begin moving about, Duston learned that Thomas and the children were hard at work near the site of their former home, planting the fields, clearing away the charred wreckage, and salvaging what they could from the outbuildings. Other than the land beneath the burned out farmhouse, the Dustons had been left with next to nothing. The loss had been devastating, and Hannah would soon learn that their privation in the wake of the Abenaki raid was shared by other good, hardworking families.

Fatigued by her walk down Pecker's Hill, Hannah rested on a stump while her children and Thomas worked through the forenoon. When the others stopped to eat potatoes and cornbread that their daughter Elizabeth had fetched down from the garrison, Thomas took his wife by the arm and they passed along the road that descended from their blackened cellar hole, along the edge of the plowed field, and through a hedgerow to the grove of trees beyond. Hannah knew where they were headed without being told, and after going across another meadow that had greened considerably in recent days, they came near to the west bank of Little River. In a clearing up ahead, Thomas pointed to a little mound of earth heaped up at the foot of an apple tree.

Hannah recognized the tree, and though the pile of earth yet lacked a marker, she knew this was her infant's grave. The wind blew lightly across the tops of the budding trees, and the smell of the river wafted in. Husband and wife stood by the apple tree and, after a few moments, Thomas replaced his hat on his head and they turned from Martha's grave and went back through the trees.

Later that week, Hannah would become further disquieted while accompanying Thomas to Haverhill's meetinghouse to pray with Reverend Benjamin Rolfe, and, since he was an educated man, to confer with him about the future disposition of their family. Along the way, Thomas and Hannah would pass the burned over cellar holes and blackened outbuildings and ruined conveyances of nearly a dozen homesteads. In every instance, many of the settlers who had occupied those farms had been bludgeoned or shot to death while attempting to save their families.

John Keezer; Keezer's aged father; and his son, George, were dead. Likewise, Thomas Emerson, his wife, Elizabeth, and their two children, Timothy and Sarah. Hannah and Joseph Bradley's children—Joseph, Martha, and Sarah—had all been murdered. So had Hannah Bradley's brother-in-law, Daniel Bradley Jr., and his wife Hannah, along with their two daughters. In all, twenty-seven residents of Haverhill had been slaughtered during the raid. Of the thirteen captured, only Hannah Duston and Mary Neff had thus far returned. The infant Martha, and at least four others, had been killed along the way, or died in captivity from hypothermia, starvation, or exhaustion. Hannah Bradley's whereabouts were unknown, but Goodwife Duston was able to give Bradley's husband, Joseph, a small measure of hope. Early on her first day in the settlement, she told the grieving Bradley that his wife had been alive a week earlier, when she was traded to another band of Abenaki near Sugar Ball Island.

After another short interlude, Hannah was back to doing chores and taking care of the children. Still, Goodwife Duston and her husband felt that her actions on Sugar Ball Island had certain significance in relation to the colony's recent trouble with the Indians, and resolved to talk to Reverend Rolfe about it. Early one morning, Thomas and Hannah Duston began their five-mile trip across the settlement to the parsonage by leading their horse through the woods. The cart path was filled with stones and ground level stumps, having recently been hacked out of the forest by Onesiphorus Marsh and his detachment with axes and adzes and made to run on the best possible line with the aid of a Gunter's chain, cutting a mile off the old route to the village. At the base of the hill, Goodwife Duston climbed upon the horse and the sojourners met Winter Street, crossed Little River a half-mile along, and turned right onto Main Street, which led down to the northern bank of the Merrimack River. Water Street ran eastward along this bank from the intersection with Main, and after crossing over Mill Brook, the Dustons neared the most populated section of Haverhill.

As Hannah and Thomas Duston went along Main, and then Water Street, toward the old meetinghouse, she astride the bulky, fifteen-hands horse and her husband walking along with the reins, the former captive was touched by the civility of her neighbors, who, despite laboring under their own grief in the wake of the Indian raid, left off these grim duties to approach the road. Some were digging among burnt timbers and wrecked farming equipment, coming through the gorse covered in soot, or else planting a new garden or mending a fence in a lot that lacked house or stable; but when the name of Hannah Duston passed from neighbor to neighbor, these hard-working settlers crossed the muddy pastures or hurried up a dirt lane to speak to the woman who had struck back at the Indians. Several tipped their caps, or praised God for delivering Hannah and Mary Neff; still others walked alongside for a short distance, inquiring of Goodwife Duston's health and that of her family, or, after a copious apology, requested a few details of what had transpired on Sugar Ball Island. Having heard about Duston's actions, and now, confronted with the Indian tomahawk and rifle that their neighbor had used, which Thomas carried along with him, they were emboldened to speak of these things, and to acknowledge Hannah Duston and thank her. The expressions of gratitude were universal, touching the Dustons' hearts as they plodded along toward their meeting with Benjamin Rolfe.

Water Street curved through the trees alongside the river, following the downstream course to the oldest part of the settlement. This consisted of three or four dozen substantial houses, arranged in close proximity along the bank of the Merrimack, with four well-developed roads running perpendicular to the main thoroughfare. Framed with timbers of white oak, and aligned with one another at the river's edge, the oldest homes in the village were two stories high, the second story lapped slightly over the other with a central chimney; several large, hinged double windows made of diamond-shaped panes of glass set in lead; and tall, steeply arranged gambrel roofs covered with shingles. All of these houses had survived the raid, since the Indians concentrated their attacks on the perimeter of the settlement. A few of the newer houses, built along the ox-common and interspersed among a few small cottages, were made of brick from Thomas Duston's kiln; he had been the principal builder for a handful of these structures and was in the process of constructing a two-and-a-half-story brick garrison house approximately a mile from the homestead the Indians had burned down on March 15th. His family would henceforth reside there, with a small detachment of militia provided by the town fathers.

The meetinghouse, and Benjamin Rolfe's parsonage, which he had taken over from the previous minister, Mr. Ward, was located on a rising patch of ground overlooking the river. The parsonage was a fine large house accompanied by several outbuildings and sheds, built on ten acres of meadowland and well situated with respect to the main highway. Behind the manse and stretching away into the forest were two hundred acres of upland that belonged to the parsonage. Opposite the minister's home on the other side of the road was the meetinghouse, erected in 1648, an unadorned one-story cabin only twenty-six feet long and twenty feet wide, set on a foundation of rough stones grouped together in piles. It constituted the hub of the village's spiritual life.

Haverhill's population now comprised more than three hundred persons, crowding the old meetinghouse on the sabbath to the point where people stood outside looking in through the windows. In recent months, a committee had been appointed to visit several neighboring towns to take the measure of other such buildings, with an eye toward building a larger structure akin to those in Beverly and Reading. Behind the current meetinghouse was the old burial ground, referred to by the English as "God's acre," squared off by an iron fence running between granite pillars. As Hannah Duston climbed down from the horse outside the parsonage, her vantage point allowed a glimpse of more than a dozen new graves, marked only by sculpted piles of freshly turned earth. These were the victims of the raid.

Benjamin Rolfe had taken over Haverhill's ministry in 1692, succeeding eighty-six-year-old Reverend John Ward, who was one of Haverhill's first settlers. It was agreed that Rolfe was to be paid the equivalent of forty English pounds a year in wheat, rye, and Indian corn, in exchange for preaching, visiting the sick, and advising the town fathers on educating the youth of the settlement, among other Christian matters. In addition to his annual salary, which soon rose to sixty pounds of grain equally divided among the three types, as well as fifty cords of seasoned firewood, upon Mr. Ward's full retirement from the ministry, Rolfe was granted the free use of the parsonage farm and adjoining acreage.

By this time, the entire settlement was aware of Hannah Duston's return and of her travails during the raid, her captivity thereafter, and of what had transpired upon Sugar Ball Island, with the local clergyman being no exception. Word had traveled along Primrose Street ahead of his celebrated visitor, and when Hannah had unfurled her skirts and Thomas Duston had cleared the mud from his boots with a stick, Mr. Rolfe was standing in the doorway of the parsonage, greeting the Dustons with a genial equanimity proper to his station. The parsonage was a two-story, six-roomed house, standing at the high point in the road and arched over by a copse of enormous oak trees. Securing his horse to the rail fence, Thomas Duston unfastened the Indian rifle and hatchet from their strappings behind the saddle and steered his wife up the front walk and into the quiet, wax-scented confines of the house. Rolfe was standing in the doorway of the parsonage, a tall, solidly built man dressed in black from head to toe. Bowing to his visitors, Mr. Rolfe led them into the parlor, a rectangular, low-ceilinged room decorated with portraits of the Reverend John Ward and his father, the Reverend Nathaniel Ward. The younger Mr. Ward had been born and educated in England, and, with others from Newbury, Massachusetts, had been instrumental in establishing the settlement of Pentucket in 1641, that name later being changed to Haverhill.

Rolfe's visitors were invited to sit down at a polished hardwood table, which was furnished with a jug of cider, some writing paper, a pen and pot of ink, and the minister's leather-bound Bible. After listening to Hannah's tale and reading from his Bible for several minutes, Mr. Rolfe inquired of Thomas how much he had lost in terms of real property, equipment, and stores due to the Indian raid and the subsequent burning down of his farmhouse and outbuildings. Upon some consideration Duston answered him. After dipping his pen in the inkwell, the minister wrote a few lines on a sheet of foolscap, asking Goodman Duston to produce the items he had brought along with him. Dutifully, Reverend Rolfe inspected the Indian rifle and then the hatchet that Goodwife Duston had used to kill the Indians. Before coming to Haverhill to assist Mr. Ward, Benjamin Rolfe had been assigned as chaplain to the garrison in Falmouth, Maine, during the tumultuous summer and fall of 1689. During his tenure, Rolfe had witnessed the savagery of the Indians firsthand and developed a passing knowledge of their weapons and tactics. After examining the rifle, he lowered the hammer to close the breach, passing it and the blood-stained hatchet back across the table.

After this was finished, Mr. Rolfe excused himself and stood up. Making it clear that he wished Thomas Duston to accompany him, Rolfe bowed to Goodwife Duston, asking for her leave, and the two men circled the table, exiting through the front door of the parsonage. Through an open window, Hannah Duston watched as her husband unfastened the canvas sack from the back of his horse. Placing it on the top rail of the fence, Thomas opened the bundle and Mr. Rolfe, dressed in a long black coat, black trousers, a twill waistcoat, and a stiff-collared shirt, leaned over with his hands clasped behind him, and inspected the contents of the sack. After a few moments, Duston closed the bundle, retied it to the saddle harness, and the two men returned to the house.

Now that Mr. Rolfe was convinced he had a thorough understanding of what had occurred, and after first informing Goodman Duston that the General Assembly of the Province of Massachusetts was no longer offering a bounty for Indian scalps, he asked his guest if they had anything else to add. In response to a question, Rolfe said that the Massachusetts government had ceased paying for scalps more than a year earlier, but that the governor of New France, Count Frontenac, had not stopped engaging in this practice. Satisfied they had fully explored the matter, Reverend Rolfe took up the pen, dabbed it in the inkpot, and, after taking up a fresh sheet of paper, began to write.

Hints of spring drifted in through the canted window. At length, satisfied with what he had written, and flapping the piece of paper gently to dry the ink, the minister handed this document to Mr. Duston, who scrutinized it for a few moments and gave it back. After clearing his throat, the minister read the petition aloud:

"To the Right Honorable the Lieut-Governor, and the Great and General Assembly of the Province of Massachusetts Bay, now convened in Boston.

"The humble petition of Thomas Duston of Haverhill sheweth: That the wife of ye petitioner (with one Mary Neff) hath, in her late captivity among the Barbarous Indians, been disposed & assisted by Heaven to do an extraordinary action, in the just slaughter of so many of the Barbarians, as would by the law of the Province which a few months ago would have entitled the actors unto considerable recompense from the Publick.

That tho' the (want) of that good law (warrants) no claims to any such consideration from the Publick; yet your petitioner humbly—that the merit of the action still remains the same; & it seems a matter of universall desire thro' the whole Province that it should not pass unrecompensed.

And that your petitioner having lost his estate in that calamity wherein his wife was carried into her captivity, render him the fitter object for what consideration the Public Bounty shall judge proper for hath been herein done; of some consequence not only unto the persons more immediately delivered, but also unto the generall interest.

"Wherefore, humbly requesting a favorable Regard on this occasion, your petitioner shall pray, &c.

"Thomas Du(r)stun."

Mr. Rolfe stood up from his chair, again dipped the pen in the inkpot, and extended it across the table. Duston, also on his feet, took up the pen, bent to the table, and signed his name to the petition. Examining the petition a last time, Mr. Rolfe imparted a few instructions. The three of them got up from the table, and upon receiving Reverend Rolfe's good wishes, they all prayed together in the foyer; then the visitors departed, returning to the Marsh garrison house by the same route, slowed once more by the knots of well wishers who intercepted them on the road.

After Goodwife Duston had further recovered, and her husband and family had done such work as they could to guarantee, at least, a modest harvest of corn and other crops to sustain them in the autumn, Thomas Duston and his wife planned a trip to Boston, taking along the signed petition, as well as the Indian rifle, hatchet, and the bundle of withered scalps. At that time, women had no legal rights after they were married, and Thomas Duston was therefore compelled to file the petition on his wife's behalf.

In the few weeks since Goodwife Duston's return to Haverhill, news of her feats on Sugar Ball Island had spread throughout the colony. Letters had arrived at the parsonage from Boston, written by such eminences as Judge Samuel Sewall and Reverend Cotton Mather, inquiring about Goodwife Duston's health and spiritual well being, as well as that of her family. When replying to these correspondents, Benjamin Rolfe informed Judge Sewall and Reverend Mather of Thomas Duston's intent to seek recompense for his wife's service to the colony by means of a petition to the General Court. In a second round of epistles, Sewall and Mather both invited the Dustons to call on them when they traveled to Boston, which Benjamin Rolfe estimated would be in the latter part of April.

As the crow flies, the distance from the Haverhill settlement to Boston was nearly forty miles. But the roads between the seat of the General Court of Massachusetts and the outlying settlements did not run true, and Goodman Duston and his wife, often riding pillion behind her husband to make up time, were likely forced to travel by a circuitous route, passing through the coastal villages of Newbury, Ipswich, and Salem. These rutted pathways ran through vast salt marshes and over hills that provided vistas of Cape Ann, as well as the glittering plain of the Atlantic Ocean. Alternately riding and walking, Thomas and Hannah traveled all day and all night, arriving at the intersection of the Boston and Cambridge roads at sunrise.

By this time, Boston was populated by nearly seven thousand souls, a vibrant seafaring town filled with gentlemen farmers, fishmongers, merchants, jobbers, soldiers, sailors, itinerant laborers of every description, and a sturdy crop of ministers, jurists, and scholars. Founded in 1630 under the leadership of John Winthrop, the second governor of the Massachusetts Bay Colony, the settlement had originally been called "Trimountaine," in recognition of the three hills that dominated the peninsula. That pear-shaped land mass, comprising just 783 acres, was approximately a mile across at its widest point and just short of three miles long, bounded by the Charles River to the north and the harbor to the east and southward, being connected to Roxbury and the mainland by a narrow isthmus. The harbor was protected by a string of barrier islands, and the trio of hills, especially the largest one, called Beacon Hill, offered great vantage points for observing any friend or foe approaching by sea.

The Indian name for this locale was *Shawmutt*, which had been variously translated as "living waters," "where there is going by boat," and "near the neck," all of which were appropriate. Another feature recommending Boston as the seat of colonial government was the spring at the base of the three hills. Compared to the brackish water of the Charles River, which often bedeviled the residents of neighboring Charlestown, the sweet, cold spring water was a boon to the growth of this new town, as well as an asset the Indians had long prized, since another variation of the Algonquin picture-name for Boston, *Shawomet*, meant simply, "a spring."

Like many other colonial settlements, the eventual English name of this valuable port, Boston, was chosen to curry favor with one of the principals of the Massachusetts Bay Company; in this case, Isaac Johnson, "the greatest furtherer of the colony," who emigrated to the New World from his home in Boston, Lincolnshire in England, and died in Charlestown, Massachusetts, on the very day of the renaming. The town sprang up along the irregular coastline of the peninsula, with several large, well-built houses grouped on the upper half of State Street, though hundreds more warehouses, churches, burial grounds, commons, and modest homes had been added in the decades since.

Although it's unlikely that Thomas and Hannah Duston were familiar with Boston, being so occupied with the daily challenges of life in the settlement, even if they had visited there previously, the sudden appearance of the town shortly after daybreak must have been an impressive sight. When they reached Roxbury and began crossing over to Boston on the mile-long strip of land called "the neck," the town lying ahead of them had shaken off the last vestiges of nighttime gloom and was demonstrating ample signs of life. Smoke from a thousand cook fires rose into a brightening sky, and the cries of teamsters and drovers echoed from the gloaming up ahead, while the silhouettes of various-sized ships eased out from their moorings along Windmill Point.

As they tip-tupped along on their horse, the roiling waters of the Charles River on one side and the expanse of the harbor on the other, Duston and his wife shared the narrow road with peddlers and jobbers pushing barrows filled with partially dressed game, including deer, rabbits, and an occasional moose; baskets piled with eggs; ragged stacks of beaver, otter, and marten pelts; pails of milk; huge wheels of cheese, and other goods produced or made in Roxbury and the other nearby settlements, all pressing toward Boston to sell their wares in the marketplace. Coming the other way, overloaded wagons and Johnny-carts that stank of fish, clams, and quahogs came racing pell-mell along the strand, forcing some of the peddlers to run their handcarts over the embankment into the cold shallow water of the bay, so intent were the fishmongers on profiting from their catch before it spoiled.

Clearing the neck and entering the town proper, Hannah and Thomas dismounted and led the horse along the increasingly hectic main road, dodging columns of militia; ornate coaches enclosing various eminences whose identities they could not begin to guess at; crowds of young men in rough tweeds heading to their places of employment in warehouses and along the waterfront; lone riders galloping over the cobblestones; and even a few Christian Indians, wrapped in deerskin mantles or blankets, gliding along the shoulder of the road. Several "praying towns," filled with Indians who had accepted the tenets of the Puritan faith, were in close proximity to Boston. Members of these tribes hunted in the dense forests beyond Roxbury and Dorchester and Charlestown, walking great distances to trade the fresh or cured meat for handmade and imported goods, as well as flour, sugar, barley, salt, and rum. Still, Hannah shuddered at the presence of these savages, her face drained of color, though she did not avert her gaze as they passed in knots of two and three Indians, or even a single, bold-faced warrior, a six-pointed stag thrown across his shoulders, its antlered head trailing blood down the Indian's mantle.

As they had been instructed by Benjamin Rolfe, when the travelers gained the peninsula and found themselves on Cornhill Road, Thomas began inquiring of passersby the whereabouts of Hull House, which was where Judge Samuel Sewall lived with his family. The Sewall residence was located on Boston's main thoroughfare, a few blocks west of the Town House—where the Dustons would deliver their petition to the General Court—and a block east of Boston Common. The Hull House, which was actually a substantial estate, comprised a large, timber-framed manse, a spacious garden, orchard, stables, coach house, pond, several outbuildings including a tenant farmer's cabin, and the two-story colonial treasury, all of these encircled by a spear-tipped iron fence. Sewall's late father-in-law, John Hull, who had served as the colony's mint master, originally owned all the land and the structures on it, inviting the young Sewall to share lodgings after the latter graduated from Harvard and married Hull's daughter Hannah, in 1676. It was said that when the pair were married, John Hull gave as a dowry Hannah's weight in "pine-tree" shillings, minted right there, on the property.

Just as everyone in town knew where Judge Sewall lived—the Dustons were soon tying up their horse at the intersection of Cornhill and Summer Street—the residents of Hull House, including Hannah Sewall, had been told of Goodwife Duston's ordeal among the savages and were eager to make her acquaintance. Judge Sewall's wife and Hannah Duston were the same age, thirty-nine, and like many of their contemporaries each had suffered an abundance of grief, though Hannah Sewall's children had died in their beds, rather than at the hand of the Indians.

The two women conversed in the large entry hall while Thomas stood nearby, his hat in his hands, waiting for Judge Sewall to descend from his study. After the cramped, drafty, Marsh garrison house, where Thomas and his children had been living while he built them a new home, the Haverhill farmer and brick maker was driven to wonderment by the assortment of rare items that filled the Sewall residence. Claw-footed mahogany chairs and brocaded settees laid over plush ornamental rugs woven in the Far East; hand-carved oak tables decorated with silver urns and vases; and sideboards filled with bone china, figured silver platters, tea sets, beakers, and goblets. Warmed by a central chimney, the main room on the first floor provided grand views of the harbor, and Duston's reverie at the passing of merchant ships and frigates was disturbed by a heavy tread on the stairs and then the master of Hull House's arrival.

Judge Samuel Sewall, then forty-five years of age, was a sturdy, middle-sized fellow with gray hair to his shoulders, a prominent nose, and a small, lively mouth. Given his station in life, and the trappings of his success as a prominent merchant, Judge Sewall wore a pair of well-polished boots, black trousers made from English wool, a white linen shirt with brass buttons, and a black woolen doublet, or short jacket. Around his neck was a russet-colored scarf, the ends falling to his waist, and he carried a wide-brimmed felt hat. Samuel Sewall looked the gentleman, from head to toe.

As Sewall approached, both his hands extended in greeting, Thomas Duston noticed a curious item among the mostly black, well-tailored clothes in the jurist's ensemble. Peeking out between the buttons of the judge's shirt, and visible to a small degree at his neck, was an undergarment that resembled an uncured goat hide or other animal skin. In fact, it was a hair shirt, also known as sackcloth, a rough garment worn against the skin as a sign of penitence and self-mortification.

Thomas Duston's minister, Benjamin Rolfe, had mentioned Sewall's habit of wearing sackcloth during their conversation, quoting Zechariah 3:1-5, "Lord, take away my filthy garments, and give me a change of raiment." Sewall's reason for seeking God's forgiveness in this instance—and for humbling himself in the eyes of his fellow sinners—was well known, even in the far-flung settlements. For Samuel Sewall had been one of the justices named to the Court of Oyer and Terminer in Salem, Massachusetts, that, five years earlier, had tried hundreds of men and women on charges of witchcraft. Sewall and his fellow judges, including, for a short time, Colonel Saltonstall of Haverhill, convicted more than thirty of these people as emissaries of Satan. Beginning with an innkeeper named Bridget Oliver Bishop, who was hung on June 10, 1692, at Gallow's Hill in Salem, over the next few months twenty of these poor souls were executed. Nineteen were hanged, and one man, Giles Corey, was pressed to death under the weight of large stones.

What Thomas and Hannah Duston had not known until Benjamin Rolfe told them was that Judge Sewall, hounded by the memory of these gruesome deaths and wracked with misgivings over his part in the tribunal, had offered a public apology for his role in the Salem witch trials. Less than four months earlier, on January 14, 1697, Sewall, his wife, two sons, and three daughters had attended services at Boston's Third Church, just a few blocks from their home. Seated in the first row of benches on the men's side of the hall—a position befitting his status in the community—Sewall was in good position to hand the minister, Reverend Samuel Willard, a piece of paper containing a note. Moments later, Willard nodded from the pulpit, and Sewall stood up and bowed his head, listening along with the congregation as the minister read the following: "Samuel Sewall, sensible that as to the guilt contracted upon the opening of the late Commission of Oyer and Terminer at Salem . . . desires to take the blame and shame of it, asking pardon of men, and especially desiring prayers that God, who has an unlimited authority, would pardon that sin and all other of his sins, personal and relative."

Since the tumult of the witch trials ended with the final executions on September 22, 1692, none of the jurists associated with the proceedings had forsworn his role in them. Only Nathaniel Saltonstall of Haverhill, whom Thomas Duston served under in the settlement's militia, expressed any public misgivings about the rightness of the court's actions. He had resigned from the Court of Oyer and Terminer a month after it opened, saying "I am not willing to take part in further proceedings of this nature." Back then, Thomas Duston had appreciated his neighbor's honesty and courage, and hearing of Sewall's more recent gesture—and now, meeting him in the flesh—Thomas undoubtedly responded to Sewall's warmth, the vivacity of his gaze, and the hospitality provided to him and his wife.

The Sewalls and the Dustons, husband and wife each, despite being from divergent backgrounds, had a great deal in common. The two men were born in 1652, although Samuel Sewall's birthplace was Bishopstoke, Hampshire in England, and Thomas Duston Jr. was born in Kittery, Maine; while Hannah (Hull) Sewall and Hannah Duston were born just a few months apart, in 1657 and 1658, respectively. The couples represented two different vantage points in the social strata but had considerable experience with the hardships of life, not the least of which was Judge Sewall's remorse over his part in the witch trials. Between the birth of the Sewalls' first child, John, in 1677, and the time of their meeting with Thomas and Hannah Duston, Samuel and his wife had buried seven of their twelve children, with their thirteenth child stillborn just a few months earlier. Four of the twelve Duston children, including the infant Martha, killed during the raid, were already lying in their graves.

So it was with a marked degree of human feeling and empathy that Judge Sewall led their guests to a long oaken table by the chimney fire. Ordained a minister, though a merchant by trade and disposition, Sewall led the group in reciting from scripture and then presided over a meal of johnnycakes, molasses, cornbread, fried herring, and cider. The women sat alongside the men, since Judge Sewall, besides his public expression of shame over the witch trials, which he had come to regard as a gross injustice, was known to espouse fair and equal treatment of the weaker sex. Sewall had also spoken out against slavery—in contrast to many other wealthy men in the colony, Sewall owned none—and believed, as had Reverend John Eliot before him, that the Indians belonged to one of the ten lost tribes of Israel and thus, like the Puritans themselves, were heirs to God's covenant.

Sometime after the meal, with the cider aiding their digestion, Judge Sewall asked Hannah Duston to describe her recent ordeal at the hands of the Indians. In a series of gentle questions, no doubt reflective of his long experience as a jurist, Sewall was able to gain a clear picture of the terror and suffering that this soft-spoken woman had endured, as well as the concentrated fury of her revenge. During this interval the servants kept away from the table and the house grew quiet, but for Hannah Duston's brief replies. Among the things Duston told Judge Sewall was that her master, whom she killed with his own tomahawk, had once lived with a minister in Lancaster, Massachusetts, where he was known as a praying Indian. At Judge Sewall's request, Thomas went outside to fetch the Indian's rifle, the tomahawk, and the bag of withered scalps, returning them just as quickly when the mistress of the house became indisposed.

What Hannah Duston and Samuel Sewall must have been thinking, as they sat over the breakfast table, regarding each other: the celebrated judge who had been acclaimed for his service to the Massachusetts colony and to God for his participation in the witch trials—what amounted to a great disservice he now believed, and a feat he was ashamed of—and this humble farmer's wife, who had been dragged from the bosom of her family by heathens, and yet had smote them amidst the howling wilderness. To her interlocutor, Hannah Duston was an angel of vengeance, striking out with a sword against the real and visible enemies of God.

Before his guests rose from the table, Sewall persuaded them to join him and his wife in singing Psalm 21.

The Lord shall finde out all
that are thine enemies:
thy right hand also shall finde out
those that doe thee despise.

Thou setst as fiery oven
them in times of thine ire:
the Lord will swallow them in's wrath
and them consume with fire.

Again the couples stood and prayed together, only this time for the infant Martha Duston, and for the soul of the Sewall's twelfth child, Sarah, who had died a few years earlier. While his servant was clearing the table, Judge Sewall took Goodwife Duston aside for a moment and gave her a valuable gift, the first of several she would receive from government officials and other important figures. Sewall's present was a sack of Connecticut flax seeds, and several thick sheaves, or "hands" as they were called, of retted flax stalks suitable for dressing and then being made into linen cloth.

Sewall walked his visitors to the door. Then the two men shook hands, and Thomas and Hannah Duston went out. Soon after they left, Sewall would make the first of two related entries in his diary:

1697. April 29. 5th day (Thursday) is Signalized by ye (the) achieve-ment of Hanah Dustun, Mary Neff, and Samuel Lenerson, who kill'd two Men, yr (their) Masters, & two Women and 6 others, and have brought in Ten scalps.

Two weeks later, still brooding over what he had seen and heard, Judge Sewall would record more details of his meeting with Hannah Duston.

Fourth day May 12—Hanah Dustun came to See us. I gave her part of Connectiuct [sic] Flax. She saith her Master, whom she kill'd, did formerly live with Mr. Rowlandson in Lancaster: He told her, that when he prayed ye (the) English way, he thought that was good; but now he found ye French way was better. The Single man shewed the night before, to Sam. Lenarson, how he used to knock Engl. Men on Ye head & take off thr scalps; little thinking that the Captives would make some of ye first Experiment upon himself. Sam. Lenarson killed him.

When they regained Cornhill Road, Thomas Duston discovered that the Sewalls had done them another kindness. Their horse had been watered, grained, and brushed, as they caught sight of a manservant going along-side the house with a feedbag and currycomb. On the periphery of their conversation with the Sewalls, Thomas and Hannah had been aware of servants moving among the adjacent rooms, orchard keepers and labor-ers passing by the broad-paned windows overlooking the harbor, and the occasional delivery or message brought to the side entrance. Now, amidst the increasing morning traffic, the Dustons, walking their horse by the reins, sensed the curiosity and approbation emanating from passersby on their way to the Town House. News of Hannah Duston's feats had traveled to Boston two weeks ahead of the woman herself, and the urgent cry of her presence had spread outwardly from Hull House that morning, causing people to stop along Cornhill Road or to emerge from other stately manses, or from merchants' shops, whispering that here was the woman who had killed the Indians. The town being so populated, and the marketplace so busy, not everyone knew, but enough passersby doffed their hats or bowed that still more people noticed the Dustons and inquired who they were.

As the travelers drew closer to the open square on State Street where the Town House was located, a strange thing occurred. Crossing the paved expanse where groups of sea-going men, traders, merchants, jurists, and ordinary townspeople were conducting the day's business, Hannah and Thomas passed by the stocks, where criminals and sinners were sometimes interred, and a large iron cage, bolted to the cobbles, that day housing a number of boisterous drunkards and reprobates whom the sheriff had arrested. Near the edge of the square, Hannah noticed an Indian gazing upon this commotion. The savage was tall and straight with a fierce visage, dressed in a greasy deerskin mantle and breechclout. Hannah started when she saw him; for a moment the two locked gazes across the intervening space. Without changing his expression and with no sign of haste, the Indian turned from the scene and walked down State Street toward the harbor, passing among the crowds of teamsters, tradesmen, and sailors.

Thomas asked Hannah what had startled her. The truth was, Goodwife Duston felt she knew the Indian, that he had not come from the praying towns but was an Abenaki. In fact, Goodwife Duston was sure this Indian was among the group of young warriors on the snowy plain where Hannah Bradley and the others were traded off by the Indians who had abducted them. But the savage had already disappeared among the hordes congregating at the lower end of State Street, and Hannah decided not to trouble her husband with the matter.

Boston's Town House, erected in 1657, was a three-and-a-half-story, wood-sided building, topped by a large chimney and two windowed spires contained within a widow's walk. The ground floor, consisting of a large wooden platform, twelve thick wooden pillars, and an enclosed shed, was open to the air on three sides; during market days, it was filled with fishmongers, farmers, and peddlers, selling great fish hauled up from the deep, seasonal vegetables and fruit by the bushel and peck, and salted beef, venison, and other sundries. Housed within the shed was a staircase leading to the upper chambers, including the House of Assistants and the House of Deputies, along with other county and town offices.

Tying his horse to the rail, Thomas Duston, accompanied by Hannah, took the petition that Benjamin Rolfe had written on his wife's behalf; the sack containing the scalps; the Indian rifle; and the hatchet, its edge still marked by a scrim of dried blood, and proceeded up the staircase. The General Court was in the first week of its quarterly session, when by order of the House of Deputies such petitions had to be filed. On the first landing, a pair of soldiers and the house doorkeeper inquired of the Dustons their business, opened the breach of the rifle, and looked into the canvas bag that held the scalps. It gave off a putrid odor, and the doorkeeper quickly shut it up again and admitted the visitors to the General Court.

The uppermost floor of the Town House was a stuffy, overpopulated warren of dim offices, narrow hallways, and paneled chairs where various dignitaries sat and entertained a host of petitions, applications, decrees, and complaints. Bulkheads of light slanted in through the closed windows, teeming with dust motes that swirled around the trouser legs of the men passing up and down. Loud voices filled the chamber, and it took Thomas Duston several minutes to locate the person Judge Sewall, who was a magistrate of the court, had referred them to. The speaker of the House of Deputies, Penn Townsend, who also served on the committee to deal with the Indians, was seated at a desk behind an oaken rail on a platform just outside the assembly room. A florid-faced man, dressed in black with a silk scarf knotted around his throat, sat at a lower desk in front of the speaker, behind a small brass placard that read "Clerke of the House of Deputies for the Generall Court."

More than two dozen petitioners besieged the clerk at the rail, a varied collection of land speculators, shipping clerks, sheriff's deputies, wholesalers, and touts, all clutching their writs and shouldering one another aside. Beyond them, the rail jutted outward just enough to accommodate a wooden table and three members of a screening committee, this body charged with deciding the relative merit of "all particular petitions and suites" before referring them to the House of Deputies.

Again, Goodwife Duston's reputation preceded her, and members of the committee stood up and pushed the most aggressive occupants of the queue away from the rail, allowing Thomas and his wife to draw near with their petition and the evidence they carried. These were given to the clerk, who examined them briefly, handing them back to Speaker Townsend, who donned his spectacles and began reading the document.

A jolt went through the crowd pressed against the speaker's dais, spreading down the hall to various offices and meeting rooms. Soon more well-dressed men jammed through the doors to the assembly hall. After hearing Thomas Duston's explanation of his petition, and exacting a fee of two shillings and six pence for considering it, Speaker Townsend's clerk unlatched the bar in the railing and motioned Thomas onto the platform. This allowed Townsend's committee to look more closely at Duston, as well as the items of supporting evidence. The petitioner's rough work clothes, muddy boots, and calm, self-possessed air made a distinct impression. One of the committee members read the document, taking particular note of its quality, while Speaker Townsend along with his clerk examined the rifle, hatchet, and the ragged, foul-smelling scalps. Finished with the petition, the committee member nodded his assent, and Speaker Townsend laid the rifle on the table, inked a nib, and signed the petition.

Penn Townsend shook hands with Goodman Duston. From his raised position behind the railing, the speaker bowed to Goodwife Duston, and a huzzah went up from the crowd. Over the din, the clerk informed Thomas that the "first reading" of his petition to members of the House would occur before the end of the week, and that the Dustons would receive word of the court's disposition by courier. Then members of the committee handed the rifle and other items over the banister, and Thomas and Hannah made their way out, to the sound of hearty greetings and approval.

Only one thing remained undone—to honor Cotton Mather's wishes, and visit the esteemed minister at his home. Coming back onto State Street, which was more populous now that noon had struck, the road was filled with clumps of horseshit and crowded with wayfarers of every sort—criers, hod carriers, butchers' boys, post riders, and soldiers—and rattling with carts and carriages of every description, along with deputies and assistants on recess, most of whom had learned of Hannah Duston's petition and were straining for a glimpse of her. Smoking was prohibited in chambers, and they stood along the foundation of the Town House, enjoying their tobacco as they nodded in Hannah's direction, voicing their sentiment at the occasion to those clustered around them. Eager to move along, Thomas unfastened the horse, and once more on foot, the visitors continued their tramp eastward, along Cornhill Road toward the town dock.

Reverend Mather lived two and a half miles away, on Hanover Street, a few blocks from the Second Church of Boston, where he was the pastor. As the Dustons approached the house, which had originally belonged to Captain Turrell, more townspeople began to recognize them, keeping a respectful distance but ceasing their activities long enough to watch the couple pass by. Captain Turrell's former residence was a two-story brick house that loomed over the street. Tying his horse to the wrought iron fence, Thomas leaned over toward Mather's door and sounded the knocker, which echoed within.

The servant who answered the knock called Reverend Mather to the foyer. At age thirty-five, Cotton Mather, one of the most well known personages in the Massachusetts Bay colony, was an oval-faced, long-nosed, serious-looking man, dressed entirely in black, with a sharp gaze and a stern, piercing manner. He invited his visitors into the house. Wearing a clerical gown and tight black skullcap, Mather possessed a dignified, nearly omniscient air. He greeted his visitors politely, though not with as much feeling as Judge Sewall. Mather seemed like a man on the verge of conducting an investigation, which undoubtedly would be borne out by Thomas and Hannah's later recollections to their friends in Haverhill. In spite of the delay it caused in resuming their journey, meeting Reverend Mather was a notable occurrence.

The son of the influential minister, Increase Mather, who was then president of Harvard College, Cotton Mather had an astonishing background, as well as the haughty manner that went with it. Admitted to Harvard at age eleven, graduated at fifteen, and in possession of a master's degree in divinity just three years later, Mather had already published several books, pamphlets, and broadsides on a wide range of topics, and had been preaching at his church in Boston's north end for twelve years. Mather's wife, the former Abigail Phillips of Charlestown, was delivered to the front room of the house to greet her husband's visitors and then retired. Among Mather's scientific interests were a belief in fasting, a moderate diet, and prolonged physical exertion as a means to good health. Thus, he congratulated his guests on their endurance in reaching Boston in a single day and invited them to be seated at a table that contained only his writing materials and a pitcher of water from the local spring.

Exactly what Thomas and Hannah Duston knew about Mather is unknown. Certainly, they were familiar with his reputation as a third-generation Puritan minister, community leader, and accomplished intellectual and writer. It seems likely that their minister and advisor, Benjamin Rolfe, had filled in some of the details of Mather's accomplishments in explaining their invitation. Still, it must have been intimidating to sit across from the great man in his own home, subject to his penetrating stare and a barrage of questions. Among the four hundred scholarly works he would eventually publish, Thomas Duston at least was aware of, but most certainly had not read, Mather's tract defending the judgments of the Court of Oyer and Terminer. Appearing four years prior to the Dustons' visit, *Wonders of the Invisible World* provided an unreconstructed and unrepentant view of the witch trials, including the many tortures and hangings, among other gruesome deeds. It also testified to the power of Satan and his plan to destroy New England's churches.

Working on behalf of his visitors, and increasing at least by some degree the cordiality of their host, was Mather's belief, parallel to his father's in this regard, that the Indians were often used as divine agents, varyingly of God and Satan: either to punish his wayward children for their sins in the former instance, or to inflict evil on the Puritans in the latter. Again and again, Mather dipped his nib in the inkpot, writing steadily as he transcribed and interpreted his visitors' account of the raid on Haverhill and its aftermath. Occasionally, he interrupted, first Thomas and then Hannah, stopping their testimony to add a new query in his slight stammer.

After two hours' effort, the water pitcher was empty and Cotton Mather had a rough draft of the first and only detailed account of what the Duston family had suffered during the last two weeks of March in that same year. All other versions of the tale would spring from this document, which Reverend Mather transformed into a sermon and published in three of his books: *Humiliations Followed by Deliverances*, 1697;

Decennium Luctuosum, 1699; and as "A Notable Exploit, Dux Faemina Facti," in his comprehensive Puritan history of New England, *Magnalia Christi Americana*, which would appear in 1702. The Duston story, as related and put down, would become a glowing footnote in the illustrious and controversial legacy of Reverend Cotton Mather.

In this document, Mather captured the essence of Hannah Duston's rationalization of her actions, stirring a debate that would echo throughout the works of other prominent New England writers for more than three centuries: "being where she had not her own life secured by any law unto her, she thought she was not forbidden by any law to take away the life of the murderers by whom her child had been butchered."

Fatigued by the journey and the excitement of their business, Thomas and Hannah thanked Reverend Mather for his kind attention. In April, the days remained short and the nights cold. Anxious to be going, the Dustons rose from their places and Thomas shook Cotton Mather's hand. Tarrying long enough to pray with Reverend Mather, husband and wife exited the house, unhitched their mount, and rode pillion through the streets of Boston. Several people took notice of them, and many others did not, and soon they had passed through town onto the neck and back toward Haverhill.

Little material exists regarding the ensuing lives of the three fugitives from Sugar Ball Island. Upon her return to Haverhill, Goodwife Duston received several more tokens of recognition for her actions in the face of the enemy, including the gift of three large pewter chargers from Governor Nicholson of Maryland. Within a few weeks, Thomas Duston would learn that his petition had been successful. The General Court of Massachusetts awarded fifty pounds to Hannah Duston, and twenty-five pounds apiece to the widow Mary Neff and Samuel Lenorson. Young Sam returned to his family in North Preston, Connecticut, and never saw his former companions again. Mary Neff remained in Haverhill, living with her son until her death, in 1722, at the age of seventy-six.

On October 4, 1698, Thomas and Hannah Duston welcomed their thirteenth and final child into the world, a daughter named Lydia. No doubt, the birth seemed another kind of victory over the Abenaki. Later that same year, the French royal governor, Count Frontenac, died in Quebec at the age of seventy-eight. But the conclusion of King William's War in 1697, and the death of New England's wily adversary shortly thereafter, did not signal the end of the colony's troubles. War and intrigue would rage along the frontier for several more decades, and Haverhill was not exempt from the horror and brutality of these incursions. During a winter raid in 1704, Hannah Bradley was taken captive a second time, as aforementioned; and four years later, Reverend Benjamin Rolfe, his wife, and youngest child were killed by Indians while trying to defend their home.

During these attacks, the Indians skirted the Duston residence, though they burned other nearby farms and killed some of their neighbors. Hannah Duston and the Abenaki did not speak the same language, but during her captivity, Duston had scattered vivid word-pictures all over Sugar Ball Island. The Indians knew what they meant. She fought the same way they did, asking and giving no quarter, and perhaps the Abenaki had seen enough of her.

Thomas Duston died on November 17, 1732, at the age of eighty. He named his widow as executrix, leaving all his real property to his sons, and to his intrepid wife, "all my Stock of Cattell . . . horses, sheep and swine & all my household goods and provisions." Hannah died in Haverhill in February of 1737, leaving behind eight children, sixty-two grandchildren, and two great-grandchildren. Although celebrated in her own time, and for more than two hundred years thereafter, Hannah Duston and her exploits would eventually fade into the darkness of history. As a result, the location of her grave remains unknown.

Acknowledgments

When the ghost of a story begins moving toward you, indistinct and shimmering in the distance, and someone else recognizes it, encouraging you to pursue this specter until it takes on weight and substance, you've either consulted another madman or are fortunate enough to have an imaginative and talented literary agent. Anthony Mattero of Foundry Literary + Media is just such an agent, helping me chase the spirit of Hannah Duston across literary hill and dale with the zeal of an escaped captive. I am grateful for Anthony's thoughtful advice, editing suggestions, relentless energy, and friendship; and the same for his colleague, Peter McGuigan, who co-founded the agency. Peter and I have been good friends and creative collaborators for many years, and though we sometimes fight like wild Irish brothers, those are the sorts of people I prefer to spend my time with.

At Lyons Press, acquiring editor James Jayo also saw shape and substance in Hannah Duston and was an early champion of this book. Editor Holly Rubino was insightful and enterprising as the story took shape, and her colleague, Ellen Urban, spent many hours on the *telephone* fine-tuning the manuscript—a lost art these days. Also, Sharon Kunz and Sara Given contributed many useful suggestions and did an enormous amount of work during the book's later stages. I am indebted to them all, and to editor Keith Wallman and Rowman & Littlefield publisher Jim Childs for their personal contributions to the book.

I have long noted the contributions to my work made by the staff at Nevins Memorial Library in my hometown of Methuen, Massachusetts. Some time ago, I decided to go beyond that and dedicate *Massacre on the Merrimack* to Nevins reference librarian Maureen Burns Tulley, whose enthusiasm for the project, diligence in hunting down rare materials, and frequent encouragement were absolutely essential to completing the book. Last summer, Maureen was diagnosed with cancer, and after a long struggle with the disease, my good friend and collaborator died just a few months ago. I'm glad that I had the privilege of knowing Maureen; of working with her on four of my books; and that I had the opportunity to tell her about the dedication. Maureen's devoted family, co-workers, friends, and the community itself will remember her patience, selfless hard work, good humor, wisdom, and generosity for many years to come. I will miss her.

Maureen's colleagues in the Nevins Memorial Library reference department were also incredibly helpful during the years I spent writing this book. Sharon Morley and Beth Safford, in particular, excavated dozens of tiny facts and details of the early colonial period that added a sense of reality to the narrative. Department head Kirsten Underwood, Sue Jefferson, Tatjana Saccio, and Ned Toomey curated an entire section of Duston materials within the library, which I accessed at various times throughout the process. Library director Krista McLeod, her husband Matt McKeon, and daughter Madeleine, history buffs and bibliophiles all, shared my enthusiasm for Hannah's story and helped me sort out how to tell it. Patricia Graham, also a Nevins librarian, historian, and Haverhill resident, has a large personal collection of books and ephemera related to Hannah Duston. Pat shared many of these rare materials with me and was the first reader of each chapter in the book. Pat's suggestions helped improve the authenticity of the story. Over the course of this project, I have also sought help from Nevins staff members Ellen Paine, Kathy Moran-Wallace, Sarah Sullivan, Tracy Pekarski, Loreen Augeri, Beverly Winn, Brian Winn, Ashley Brown, Cynthia Christie, Amy Dorsheimer, Carla Friedrich, Shirley Toomey, Barbara Lohmueller, Gladys Medina, Fran Magro, Rob Gentile, and Susan Juknavorian.

Energetic local historian Tom Spitalere accompanied me on several hikes through the Haverhill woods and along the banks of the Merrimack River. Tom's enthusiasm for the Duston saga was contagious. With Tom leading the way, I also chatted with several members of the Duston-Dustin Family Association at their annual gathering in Haverhill. Retired museum curator, Chris H. Bailey, the former genealogist for the association, is the 8th great-grandson of Hannah (Emerson) Duston and the 9th great-grandson of Joanna (Corliss) Hutchins (1650–1734), who was the younger sister of Mary (Corliss) Neff, Hannah Duston's nurse. Chris has been researching Hannah's saga and Duston family genealogy for decades. Through Chris's generosity and goodwill I was able to bolster my story with an array of facts that would've taken half a lifetime to uncover. I am in his debt.

Thanks to Haverhill Public Library Special Collections and the Memorial Hall Library in Andover, MA, where I spent many Sunday afternoons polishing the book. I am also grateful to the folks at the Haverhill Historical Society, which owns many significant Duston items and ephemera. My sincere thanks to Methuen historians Martha Welch, Atty. Matthew Kraunelis, Joe Bella, and my old Pop Warner football teammate, Dan Gagnon, for their insights and encouragement. To my students at Boston University, your intellectual curiosity, good humor, and open mindedness continue to inspire my work. My BU colleagues Bill Marx, Chris Walsh, Kate Burak, Lou Ureneck, and Bill McKeen are quick with a joke or to light up your smoke; and writers Chuck Hogan, David Daniel, Alex Beam, and Steve O'Connor provided much appreciated advice and perspective on the book. As filmmaker John Ford often noted, at the end of the day, it's a job of work.

I ground all my narrative writing in the physical world, and again on this book, I enlisted my teammates from the Vandals Rugby Football Club. In the late winter months, we undertook a series of lengthy snowshoe and cross-country ski treks along parts of the captives' routes through northern Massachusetts and central New Hampshire. Ken "Bubba" McIntosh; Mike Zizza and his son Anthony; Brad Hayman; "Surfer John" Hearin and his wife, Stephanie; Jason Massa; Atty. Todd Hathaway; honorary Vandals Susan Viscosi, Tammi Wilson, and Sarah Wilson; and Chris Pierce and his wife, Tanya, all pitched in enthusiastically, even when temperatures dropped well below zero and the wind picked up. "Piercey," as his friends call him, is akin to the Abenaki warrior, "Hope-Hood," also known as Wahowah, "the Indian-rubber devil," as one early historian referred to him. Like Hope-Hood, Piercey is skillful and resolute, traits on full display as we twice descended the trickier sections of the Merrimack River during the March thaw. Dangerously high water, unexpected rapids, floating sheets of ice, and overturned trees evoked nothing more than the occasional wisecrack from Piercey. In bitter cold temperatures and perilous conditions, Chris Pierce is the guy you want manning the other paddle, believe me.

Special thanks to Pete Olson for loaning his canoe and cold weather gear and providing helpful paddling advice. I'm also grateful to Dan Nudd, an employee of the local power company and a boating enthusiast, whose knowledge of the upper Merrimack River helped us avoid potential disaster in harsh circumstances.

Vandals rugby teammate Dr. Aloke K. Mandal, who is a board-certified surgeon and trauma specialist, explained the manner in which Martha Duston died, as well as how Hannah Duston and the others were able to kill their captors. Dr. Mandal's insight into these events proved far superior to his foot speed, and I'm thankful for his expert help in rendering these events on the page.

I never decide on a book project, title, or cover without first consulting my University of Florida rugby teammates, including Dr. John "Surfer" Hearin, "Stormin' Norman" Litwack, Dave Civil, Carlos Ballbe, Dr. Noel Carpenter, Dave Farwick, Ken "Wee Wee" Alabiso, Conrad Merry, Dr. Frank Merry, Matt Allen, Atty. Rob Kaplan, Brian Friedman, Greg "Psycho" Taylor, Mike "Yes! Yes!" Siskin, and Ken "Burr" Farrington; and from my Acadia University sporting days in Canada, Dag Fullerton, Ron Martin, and Sheila and Drew Cooper. At every phase of my career, I've also spent time discussing my plans with my family, which has offered support and advice across eight books. For Owen, Reese, and Shane Bower; Katie and Matthew Berry; Nick and Michaela Sparks; my brothers-in-law, John Berry and Jay Sparks; John and Jackie Atkinson; Scott and Mary Leonhart; Barbara Leonhart; Natalie Wermers; my siblings, Jodie, Jill, Jamie, and Patrick; and my son, Liam, thanks for always being there for me.

Endnotes

Chapter I: The Raid
Page

1   Caverly, 105–6. In the predawn gloaming of March 15, 2013, I was on or very near the spot just west of Little River in Haverhill where Thomas Duston had stood when he first heard the Indian raiders exactly 316 years earlier. Drifting westward over the trees was a faint cry that steadily grew louder, and I soon realized that the eerie sound of seagulls following the course of the river sounded very much like the Indian war cries described by Caverly: "It was here at Namskekat that the Pilgrims first heard the terrible war-whoop cry of the savage. . . . WOACH! WOACH! HA—HA—HA—HACK—WOACH!"

1   Bailey, 20. On November 4, 1679, Thomas Duston Jr. purchased "about 18 acres of upland" lying just west of Haverhill's Little River from Theodore Atkinson. The house he built on this lot was where the Duston family was living on March 15, 1697 when the Indians raided the settlement.

3   Chase, 185. The March 15, 1697 raid on Haverhill turned out to be "one of the bloodiest forays" in King William's War, when a party of approximately twenty Indians assaulted "the western part of the town."

3   Galvin, *MHC Reconnaissance Survey Town Report: Haverhill*, 11. At the time of the raid on Haverhill, the local Indians, the Pentuckets, who had mostly gotten along with the English settlers, "were likely extinct in the township."

3   Parkman, 268. The alleged motive for Indian raids on frontier settlements like Haverhill, which were sponsored by the French colonial authority to the north, was to "prevent the people of New England from invading Canada." As part of a mostly agrarian society, especially in towns like Haverhill, the English were little inclined to leave their homes on forays to Quebec.

4   Ibid., 277. The Abenaki raid on Haverhill, like those on Kittery, Wells, and York, Maine, were vain attempts by the French "to force back the English boundary."

5   Salisbury, 16. "In status-conscious England and its colonies, 'mister' was reserved for men of authority and learning, such as ministers, magistrates, and military officers, and was also applied to very wealthy merchants. But landowners who

218

lacked the status of either aristocrats or gentry . . . were addressed simply as 'goodman.'"

5 Russell, xi. In his book, *Indian New England Before the Mayflower*, Harold Russell begins by saying, "The word 'Indian' as used in this book refers to the native inhabitants of New England at the time Europeans first met them. It is a misnomer inherited from the earliest explorers and mapmakers of the New World, which they had hoped would be India. To call the natives 'Amerinds,' as some writers have done, merely compounds confusion, for Amerigo Vespucci was not the discoverer of either new continent." My decision to use the term Indians when referring to the tribes of New England (as well as other words, like "rod," or a distance of 16½ feet, as a unit of linear measurement) reflects the usage of the period.

5 Howe, 18–19. Demonstrating the remoteness of Duston's farm and underscoring the notion of seventeenth-century Haverhill as the edge of the frontier, just a few miles west of the spot where Thomas Duston first spotted the Indians is a pond still known as World's End. (Now within the boundary of my hometown, Methuen, Massachusetts, World's End was contained within Haverhill until 1726, when Methuen was founded.) Two white men were killed and a boy taken captive by another band of Indians near World's End less than a year after the March 15, 1697 raid.

5 Mather, 634–36. Mather's version of these events, reported in his book, *Magnalia Christi Americana*, is the lengthiest and most detailed of the three accounts Hannah Duston gave shortly after her return from captivity. These are the only known firsthand testimonies and form the basis of the narrative portions of this book, as cited in the notes below.

5 Chase, 179–83. Chase reprints Mirick's account of the abduction of Isaac Bradley and Joseph Whittaker from Haverhill in 1695, which I will detail in Chapter VIII.

6 Ibid., 197. The Duston homestead "must have been a small house, because the cellar was small." This is the testimony of Moses Merrill, an aged resident of Haverhill, visiting the Duston homestead site with Haverhill historian George Wingate Chase on September 8, 1860.

6 Lawson, 22. The colonists who resided in the outlying English settlements were "easy prey" for the marauding Abenaki, who were elusive and always on the move.

6 Russell, 188. Indian warfare was predicated on "three chief tactics: surprise, ambush, and stratagem."

6 Fuess, 144. Following other commentators, Fuess states that the Duston farm "was the first house attacked" by the Indians during the raid.

6 Chase, 95. Commenting on the "better sort of houses" in Haverhill at that time, the author says they were generally "two stories high, with upper story jutting out a foot or so over the lower. The roofs were generally high and steep, and hipped, or gambreed. The frames were of white oak, and . . . the beams of each finished room were left considerably in sight. The windows were from two and

a half to three feet long, one and a half to two wide, with squares like the figure of a diamond, set in lead lines and from three to four inches long. These windows were sometimes entire and sometimes in halves, and opened outwardly on hinges."

6   Mather, 634. "On March 15, 1697, the salvages made a descent upon the skirts of Haverhill, murdering and captivating about thirty-nine persons, and burning about a half a dozen houses."

7   Bailey, 18. Thomas Duston and Hannah Emerson were married in Haverhill on December 3, 1677. Their nuptials are recorded in Vol. 2, page 98 of Haverhill marriage records.

7   Ibid., 25. "Mary Neff, eldest daughter of the nine children of George and Joanna (Davis) Corliss of Haverhill. Mary was born Sep. 8, 1646 at Haverhill and was ten years older than Hannah Duston. Mary had been married Jan. 23, 1665 to William Neff who had died in Feb. 1688/1689. Mary was the mother of nine children born at Haverhill, seven of whom were still living and six were married at the time of her abduction. After their escape Mary Neff returned to Haverhill and lived with a son until here [sic] death there on Oct. 22, 1722." In a footnote, Bailey adds, "The Haverhill, MA vital records state William Neff 'went after the army and died at Pemaquid'."

7   Ibid., 19. According to Haverhill vital records, Hannah (Emerson) Duston was born on December 23, 1657 at Haverhill.

7   Lawson, 12. The Dustons, as victims of one of the most notorious "French-instigated attacks" during King William's War, were unfortunate in the location of their homestead, which was far from the town center. But Thomas Duston was lucky to be outdoors and on the move when the raiders struck.

7   Sprinkle, 18. Men like Thomas Duston were inured to the dangers of frontier life. From a narrative account, published in 1854, concerning a 1786 raid on a remote farmhouse in Virginia, the author says, "It was necessary that the head of the family should be hardy, fearless, capable of enduring labour and exposure without injury, and able by day or by night to find his way through the forest with the certainty which characterizes the wolf or the Indian. Familiarity with the use of the rifle and the tomahawk, was scarcely considered an accomplishment. It was necessary that every man should possess them. He did not know at what moment all his skill would be called into requisition in defending his cabin against the attack of the Indian."

7   Wilbur, 52. "Attacks on a village were rarely at night. The war party usually concealed themselves until daybreak when the enemy was in the deepest sleep. When the first dawn provided a measure of visibility the attack was begun."

7   Salisbury, 23. The author notes that Indians learned the technique of attacking and wiping out entire villages from the Pequot War in 1637. "The harshest criticism of the English destruction of the Pequot village had come from the then-allied Narragansetts, who complained that English warfare 'was too furious and slays too many men.' Given the memory of the Pequot War and the evident willingness of the English to attack, capture, and slay noncombatants, Indians . . . recognized the need to be equally ruthless."

7   Ibid., 68. In the account of her own captivity in 1675, Mary Rowlandson begins with a scenario nearly identical to the one reported by Hannah Duston. "On the tenth of February 1675, Came the *Indians* with great numbers upon *Lancaster*: Their first coming was about Sun-rising; hearing the noise of some Guns, we looked out; several Houses were burning, and the Smoke ascending to Heaven. There were five persons taken in one house, the Father, and the Mother and a sucking Child, they knockt on the head: the other two they took and carried away alive."

7   Bailey, 20. "Thomas (Duston) Jr. settled on land in Haverhill given to him by his mother in 1673 and a brick maker and farmer, by trade. The land was in the North Parish of Haverhill in the vicinity of present-day Dustin Square."

7   Chase, 185. The author includes an interesting footnote on the various spellings of the name Duston. "It was originally written *Durston*, and was changed to *Duston* about the time of above-named Thomas Duston. This is shown, not only by our Town Records, but by Duston's petition to the General Court, in June, 1697. In the heading of his petition (which is not in his own hand writing) the name is written *Durstan*, and it so written in subsequent proceedings on the petition. But his signature to the petition is "Du(r)*stan*," (or perhaps Du(r)*stun*). The letter "r" must have been interpolated subsequent to his first signing the petition, and we think it most probable that it was done by Duston himself, so as to make his signature agree with the name as given in the heading of the petition. We have adopted *Duston* in this work, because it is so written, in almost every instance, in our Town Records."

8   Wilbur, 79. In order to move freely during the raid, the attackers would have worn very little clothing, or in some cases, none at all. The author describes the breechclout as being made of "doe or seal skin. A yard and a half long, it was suspended from a belt or girdle with flaps hanging down in front and back. It was frequently the only garment worn by the men around camp."

8   Chase, 94. In 1677, Dustin built the house "in which he resided at the time his wife was taken prisoner."

8   Sprinkle, 21. It's hard to imagine now, but Thomas and Hannah Duston probably made the life and death decisions related to the Indian raid with a mere nod of the head or a single word. The account of the second raid on the Moore farm in 1786 includes this passage: "From his childhood [Captain James Moore] had been familiar with these dangers, and his wife as well as himself had grown up in the midst of them. . . . All had lived from infancy in the midst of dangers, and being accustomed to meet difficulties of every kind, every one possessed a determined self-reliance which could meet without dismay anything that might happen. Familiarity with danger hardens the mind against its terrors."

8   Mather, 634. "Ere (Hannah) could get up, the fierce Indians were got so near, that, utterly desparing [sic] to do her any service, (Thomas) ran out after his children; resolving that on the horse which he had with him, he would ride away with that which he should in this extremity find his affections to pitch most upon, and leave the rest unto the care of the Divine Providence."

8   Chase, 120. "An untrodden, and seemingly inexhaustible wilderness stretched itself between (Haverhill) and Canada, in which no smoke curled from the home of a white man."

8   Sprinkle, 26. James Moore, the hardy teenage son of Captain James Moore of Abb's Valley in 1784 Virginia, reported a "strange presentiment of the evil which was about to befall him" shortly after losing sight of his father's house and moments before he was taken captive by Black Wolf, a fierce Shawnee chieftain, and his band of raiders. Duston was as carefully tuned to the dangers of the frontier as young Moore and would likely have wasted no time in reacting to the danger.

8   Chase, 195. "This, in our opinion, makes it *certain* Duston did not reside on the east side of Little River when his wife was captured: and, as the deed is dated less than two months subsequent to the vote of the General Court, granting him fifty pounds for the scalps taken by his wife, it almost confirms the old and generally received tradition, that (a later residence known as 'Duston Farm' on the other side of the river from the house attacked by the Indians) was *bought with the scalp money.*"

8   Mather, 634. "In this broil, one Hannah Duston, having lain in about a week, attended with her nurse, Mary Neff, a body of terrible Indians drew near unto the house where she lay, with designs to carry on their bloody devastations."

8   Bailey, 11. "Thomas Duston was one of twenty-eight men who served as soldiers in the war between the Indians who were making a desperate attempt to extirpate the English which is commonly called 'King Philip's War'."

9   Bruchac, 2. Although the territory that includes present-day Haverhill, Massachusetts, was home to the Pentucket band, who belonged to the Pennacook tribe, the author makes the case that the raiders, who were Abenaki and considered mercenaries in service to the French, also had a legitimate claim on the land containing the Duston homestead. "The original Abenaki homelands reached far beyond the boundaries of Odanak. *Ndakinna* (meaning, 'our homeland') includes all of present-day New Hampshire, all but the southwestern corner of Vermont, and parts of northern Massachusetts, northeastern New York state, and southern Canada, encompassing important waterways like the *Kwanitegok* ('long river'—the Connecticut River) and *Merrimack* or *Morodemak* ('deep river') and thousands of fresh-water lakes. Although particular bands and families took responsibility for specific sites and resources, Abenaki people routinely travelled all over this territory for seasonal hunting and fishing and ceremonial gatherings."

9   Wills, 72. "By the mid to late sixteenth century, Northern Europe saw the development of the snaphance, or snaphaunce lock. (The term comes from a Dutch word for 'pecking bird.') In the snaphance, the cock held a piece of flint, which sprang forward on the trigger-pull to strike a piece of steel (the frizzen), sending sparks into the priming pan. A similar type of lock, the miquelet, appeared around the same time in Southern Europe. Technical refinements to both eventually led to . . . the true flintlock, early in the seventeenth century."

10 Hogg, 24. "The flintlock rapidly assumed the premier position. . . . in military firearms; here was a lock which was relatively simple, strong, not expensive, and as reliable as could be expected, and which put an end to the dangers of carrying burning slow match."

10 Chase, 157. Regarding Duston's skill in small arms warfare, the author notes that "almost every man was a soldier" in that place and time.

10 Ibid., 128. Thomas Duston had significant experience fighting the Indians. On August 26, 1676, Captain John Hull, "Treasurer of the Colony" (see note on Hull in Chapter IX), authorized the payment of seventeen shillings in cash to Thomas Durston [sic] of Haverhill, for his service as a soldier during King Philip's War.

10 Hogg, 24. "A good flint was generally considered to last for about fifty shots, after which it was generally discarded, since attempts to put a new edge on it were seldom successful. The actual fixing of the flint into the cock was quite a delicate matter."

10 Ibid., 25–26. The author describes the step-by-step process related to the proper loading of a flintlock rifle, which I used to recreate Duston's actions before mounting his horse in the orchard.

10 Mather, 634. "[Hannah Duston's] husband hastened from his employments abroad unto the relief of his distressed family; and first bidding seven of his eight children (which were from two to seventeen years of age) to get away as fast as they could unto some garrison in the town, he went in to inform his wife of the horrible distress come upon them."

10 Chase, 107. Duston's compulsion to help a neighbor in distress would have been more than a passing thought in that era. Chase notes that Puritan mores in the early decades of the colony indicated that "Not to do that which ought to be done, was considered as worthy of punishment, as to do that which ought not to be done."

10 Ibid., 198. "The distance from that point to the site of the old garrison house on Pecker's Hill, in an *air line*, is a fraction over one mile." This comment appears in a footnote on the page.

12 Mather, 635. "[Thomas Duston] overtook his children, about forty rod from his door: but then such was the agony of his parental affections, that he found it impossible for him to distinguish any one of them from the rest; wherefore he took up a courageous resolution to live and die with them all."

12 Wilbur, 52. Indian "assaults were every man for himself. Warriors took cover, dodged and leaped about on open ground." Only the bravest men "would rush into hand to hand combat" at the climax of the skirmish or battle.

13 Chase, 187. As the Indians pursued Thomas Duston and the children up the slope of Pecker's Hill, "Mr. Duston dismounted his horse" and "placed himself in the rear of his children." This indicates that Duston was on horseback, which proved a great advantage in getting his children to the garrison house.

13   Fuess, 144. Somewhere on the slope of Pecker's Hill, Thomas Duston dismounted, "and shielding himself behind his horse held the skulking Indians at bay until the young ones had all reached a place of safety."

13   Chase, 187. In a footnote, Mirick lends credence to the notion that Duston menaced the raiders with his gun, but didn't actually fire upon them: "The *Indians* pursued him all the while, but he kept in the rear of his little Flock, and when any of them came in reach of his Gun, he presented it at them, which made them retreat."

13   Ibid., 155. By 1690, Haverhill's selectmen had ordered six garrison houses and four "houses of refuge" to be constructed as a defense against Indian attacks.

13   Ibid. "One of the garrison houses was commanded by Sergeant John Haseltine. The house stood on the north side of the road, about halfway up Pecker's Hill, and a few rods northwesterly from that formerly occupied by Samuel Pecker. . . .This garrison was owned by Onesiphorus Marsh, sen." According to Chase's research, Haseltine had seven men under his command, including Onesiphorus Marsh Sr., and his son and namesake.

13   garrisonhouse.org/house.html. The description of the Marsh garrison house in Haverhill is based on that of "The 'Old Chelmsford' Garrison House" in nearby Chelmsford, Massachusetts. The Old Chelmsford Garrison House was built sometime between 1683, when Thomas Adams obtained the land in a grant from the town, and 1702, when a "saltbox" addition was made to the original building. This garrison house still exists as a museum and was a family home as recently as the 1950s. Just three local families owned the house over a three-hundred-year period, with the title passing to the Garrison House Association in 1959.

13   Chase, 157. The author quotes Mirick, saying that the Haverhill garrison houses of that era "had but one outside door, which was often so small that but one person could enter at a time." There were only two rooms on the main floor, and reaching the chamber above was achieved "by way of a ladder, instead of stairs, so that the inmate could retreat into them, and take it up if the basement-story should be taken by the enemy."

13   Ibid., 187. "We feel confident that . . . *Duston did not fire his gun*. Had he done so, his pursuers could and would have rushed upon him before he could possibly have re-loaded, and have made sure work of him. But by making a barricade of his horse, and reserving his fire—bringing his trusty gun quickly to bear against the blood-thirsty, but *cowardly* red devils, as any of them chanced to peep from behind a tree or wall—he took the most reasonable and effective method for keeping them at bay." This passage, contained in a footnote, refers to a concurring opinion in *History of New England*, London, 1747, by an author named Neal. On the other hand, Mather writes, "A party of Indians came up with him; and now, *though they fired at him, and he fired at them* . . ." [my italics; this passage is continued in a note below]. Given there is no evidence that Thomas Duston spoke directly to Mather of his own actions during the raid, and in concordance with Chase's and Neal's opinion and my own research into the mechanics of the flintlock rifle, it appears highly unlikely that Duston fired his gun at the Indians.

If he did so at all, he fired once, probably very near to the garrison house when there would be less of a need to reload quickly.

13   Mather, 635. "(Thomas Duston) manfully kept at the reer [sic] of his little army of unarmed children, while they marched off with the pace of a child of five years old; until, by the singular providence of God, he arrived safe with them all unto a place of safety about a mile or two from his house."

13   Bosman, 5. Captivity narratives such as the one prepared by Mather from Hannah Duston's account were "summary lessons of disaster experienced, set down to strengthen the Christian faith of the reader who was a settler in a land inhabited by a race whose savage ways were unfamiliar." These captivity narratives were immensely popular, and in the colonial period were printed in Boston and went through a great number of editions.

13   Chase, 193. Like many other commentators, the author states that Thomas Duston, who "heroically staked his life for his *children*," did not receive enough credit for his role in defending his family during the raid: "It was a father's love that nerved his arm, and not *revenge*."

13   Ibid., 200. The March 15, 1697 raid on Haverhill "was a terrible blow for the town. Some of its most useful citizens and promising youth were slain." Chase puts the number of houses burned to the ground as nine.

CHAPTER II: DISPOSSESSED
Page

14   Chase, 42. The connection between Haverhill and the great Bashaba known as Passaconaway is made clear in this early history of the settlement. "The Indian name of the region included within the present bounds of the town, was *Pentuckett*, and it was at one time the home of quite a numerous tribe of that name, who were under the jurisdiction of Passaconaway, chief of the Pennacooks. Their principal village is supposed to have been on the banks of Little River, not far from its mouth."

14   Parkman, 929. "The commission of De Monts, in 1603, defines Acadia as extending from the fortieth to the forty-sixth degrees of latitude, —that is, from central New Brunswick to southern Pennsylvania."

14   Meader, 22. "Thus was De Champlain the discoverer of the Merrimack River, although its existence was previously known, even under its present name, by the coast Indians and Europeans far to the eastward. Some accounts declare that De Champlain landed at the place of his interviews with the natives, which was undoubtedly what is now known as Rye Beach. If this was the case, he was unquestionably the first European to set foot on the soil of New Hampshire; but the fact may be considered as still in doubt whether or not he actually landed."

14   Howe and Mack, 13. Prior to the coming of the settlers, the Pentucket Indians made their home on the Merrimack River, near the mouth of Little River.

14   Chase, 20. "The earliest notice we find of the river Merrimack, is through the Sieur De Monts . . ."

15   Ibid. The northern Indians called this river the Merrimack, combining the words "merroh" or strong, with "auke," meaning place; thus "strong place." Other possible interpretations of the Algonquin word-picture for Merrimack are also described here.

15   Town of Merrimack, New Hampshire, Master Plan Update, 2002, viii–2. Origins of "Merrimack."

15   Braun, 105. There are no written records detailing the history of the northeastern tribes "from the centuries before the arrival of the Europeans." Furthermore, the written reports of the first European visitors "tell us only a small fraction of what we would like to know" and are rife with the prejudices of the correspondents.

16   Beals, 23–24. The great chief of the Pennacooks, Passaconaway, was most likely named "Papisseconewa" by his elders, from "Papoeis," meaning "child," and "Kunnaway," or "bear." Thus, the "son of the Bear" was probably "a powerful, fierce and gigantic youth."

16   Ibid., 13. "At this time the Pennacooks, around Manchester and Concord, were the strongest and most highly developed of the New England Indians, and their tribe the most developed one."

16   Chase, 30. "The Penacooks were the most powerful tribe in the whole region."

17   Pendergast, 147. Potter, following many early commentators, noted that Passaconaway, along with Samoset and other powwows, or medicine men, were sent into a swamp to conjure against the Pilgrims not long after they arrived in what would later be called Plymouth, Massachusetts.

17–21   Beals, 27. The author quotes the early historians Wood, Bouton, Belknap, Hubbard, and others on Passaconaway's remarkable charisma and extraordinary abilities to conjure, or at least create the illusion of the supernatural.

18   Ibid., 22. As chief and sagamore to three thousand Pennacooks, Passaconaway could field an army of five hundred "skillfull and cunning" warriors when the occasion demanded it.

18   Ibid., 26–27. An account of Passaconaway's skills as a conjurer from William Wood's *New England's Prospect,* published in London in 1635, when the Bashaba was still living.

18   Pendergast, 104. Passaconaway was believed by early historians to "have supernatural powers," which included making a dry leaf turn green, causing water to boil and soon after, turn to ice, and handling a live rattlesnake without harm. From C. E. Potter's *History of Manchester*, published in 1885.

18   Beals, 32. Beals, citing also Bouton's *History of Concord* and Drake's *Indians of North America*, notes that the word Mohawk is "an Algonquin word meaning cannibal."

18   Meader, 29. "The (Wheelwright) deed was signed by Passaconaway, the Sagamon of Pennacook; Runnawit, the Chief of Pawtucket; Wahangnonawit, the Chief of Squamscot; and Rowls, the Chief of Newichewannock, and properly witnessed."

19   Salisbury, 8. Passaconaway was certainly intelligent enough to realize he and his people faced a changing world. The author notes, "Altogether about twenty thousand English, mostly Puritans and Puritan sympathizers, moved to Massachusetts Bay and the neighboring colonies of Connecticut, Rhode Island, New Haven, and the older colony of Plymouth between 1629 and 1642, when the outbreak of civil war in England largely halted emigration."

19   Beals, 30–32. Several commentators note that the so-called Wheelwright Deed, handing over a huge parcel of Pennacook land to the English, was probably a forgery. "Whether the Wheelwright Deed is valid or not, it affords proof of the extent of [Passaconaway's] power and dominion."

19   Lawson, 4. Passaconaway "sensed the demographic and military power of the [English] and knew that armed resistance was futile."

19   Beals, 12. Given the power and ferocity of the Pennacook's enemy, the "Magua," or Mohawk, Passaconaway's powers of leadership and organization were integral to the tribe's survival.

19   Ibid., 6. Despite his best efforts, Passaconaway "seems to have exercised his powers in vain against the English," seeking in various ways "to conciliate their favor." From Nathaniel Bouton's *The History of Concord*, NH, published in 1856.

19   Belknap, Vol. I, 101.

20–21   Braun, 90–91. William Wood's famous description of the Indians from his 1635 book *New England's Prospect* is repeated here, and in many other histories, including Morton, Hubbard, et al., which are excerpted in Pendergast.

21   Russell, 39. The hardy and simple outdoor life of the Indians fostered good health and a kind of natural selection that weeded out the sick and those of weak constitution. "The life span was substantial: sixty, eighty, even a hundred years or more were recorded."

21   Chase, 90. Only thirty-five miles northeast of Boston, Haverhill remained a wilderness for three generations: "it seems almost incredible that nearly a century should intervene between the settlement of this town and . . . Pennacook, only forty miles distant. But so it was. Haverhill was a frontier town for more than seventy years."

22   Ibid., 31–33. Writing in 1860, the author had a low opinion of Indians, ranking them "far below the negro race," thereby exposing two distinct prejudices in one sentence. Chase went on to write, "Like the traditional Yankee, [the romantic notion of the Indians] are only and altogether creations of fancy."

23   Beals, 29. Shortly after the English arrived in Massachusetts, "a word from Passaconaway . . . would have swept our fore-fathers into the sea." But the great Bashaba of the Pennacooks knew that driving them out by force would be a grievous error.

23   Pendergast, 6. The author cites Thomas Morton's account: "In 1642, upon an alarm of an Indian conspiracy from Connecticut, the government sent a force of forty men to disarm Passaconaway."

23   Beals, 34. Passaconaway, though friendly toward the English, would not suffer from their prejudice without comment. When they captured his son,

Wonalancet, spiriting him to Boston, they ordered the great Bashaba to travel there immediately. Passaconaway was said to have replied through a messenger: "Tell the English when they restore my son . . . I will talk with them."

24   Salisbury, 8. With the treaty of 1644, "Massachusetts Bay had become the new tribute-collecting power in eastern New England."

24   Pendergast, 7. "At this period [the time of the treaty] Passaconaway was an old man—his age variously estimated from eighty to one hundred."

24   Salisbury, 19. According to the author, Daniel Gookin was "Massachusetts Bay's superintendent of Christian Indians." And since Passaconaway had purportedly converted to Christianity some years earlier, there's a plausible reason for Gookin attending his farewell oration.

24   Pendergast, 52. In note #7 Pendergast writes: "Gookin was appointed Superintendent of Indians at the time Eliot appeared at the Pawtucket Falls on the Merrimac. He was the author of *An Historical Account of the Doings and Sufferings of the Christian Indians of New England in the Years 1675-1676-1677*. He is also a valuable primary source."

24–25   Ibid. In note #8 Pendergast writes: "William Hubbard was the author of *The History of the Indians Wars in New England* (1671). He was present, according to his own testimony, at the farewell speech of Passaconaway."

24–25   Chase, 33. Some nineteenth-century historians thought little of the Indian's reputation for oratory: "They have been called eloquent. Never was a reputation more cheaply earned."

24–25   Russell, 20. The contemporary historian disagrees with Chase on this point. "At tribal sessions eloquence might be the decisive attribute. An able speaker drew admiration equal to that accorded the capable of body or even the brave warrior. At such general sessions unanimity was the objective, and time was taken to achieve it."

24–25   Beals, 40–41. Potter's version of the farewell speech of Passaconaway.

25–26   Braun, 99. Account of Indian burial practices in the early colonial period. Also in Pendergast, 36. This was originally taken from William Little's *The History of Weare*, New Hampshire.

26   Beals, 48. James Osgood's version of the funeral tribute to Passaconaway from his book *White Mountains*.

26   Hubbard and Drake, 75. "The other town is called *York*, formerly known by the name of *Agamenticus*, from an high Hill of that Name, not far off therefrom."

26   Johnson, 145. "Finally in June 1675, after Plymouth Colony's execution of three of King Philip's men for the murder of an informant, the Indian chief began his raids on settlements in a year-long war in which many native tribes sided with the settlers."

27   Wilbur, 99. In his brief account of King Philip's War, Wilbur also places the number of Indian casualties at five thousand.

27   Salisbury, 1. "In proportion to total population, the bloodiest and most destructive war in American history was neither the Civil War, World War II, nor the

Vietnam War. It was, rather, a conflict known as Metacom's (or King Philip's) War. . . ."

27   Ibid., 2. "Like the Civil War, Metacom's War was one in which peoples who had long coexisted rather abruptly concluded that they could no longer do so peacefully."

27   Pendergast, 127. The author, discussing Colonel Benjamin Church, notes in a caption beneath a portrait of King Philip's pursuer that he "was much more obese than this print implies. A soldier was constantly by his side to help his perambulation. He led the ambush which killed King Philip and ended the conflict."

27   Johnson, 145. King Philip's desecrated corpse was paraded through the streets of Boston under the authority of the Puritan leadership.

28   Pendergast, 126–27. This account of the "sham fight" of 1676 in Dover, taken from Potter's history of Manchester, New Hampshire, is identical to several others from various early historians.

28   Ibid., 39. Wonalancet, like Passaconaway, was "a friend of the English" and withdrew farther north, rather than fight the colonial militia after the treachery of the sham fight. Taken from William Little's *The History of Weare*, New Hampshire, 1888.

28   Beals, 68–69. Wonalancet and his people were hounded out of their territory despite their willingness to treat with the English. "All this trial and suffering had come to the Pennacooks simply because their leader, from conscientious scruples, was endeavoring to be non-partisan and peaceable."

28-29   Ibid., 70. Indians captured during the sham fight who were believed to have participated in King Philip's War against the English were marched to Boston, imprisoned, executed, or sold into slavery.

28–29   Ibid., 72. "This deception [of the sham fight] greatly enraged the Pennacooks and they pointed to it as an insult to their honor, for it had been under their hospitality that the 'strange Indians' had come into Dover, and the hosts helplessly looked on while their guests were swept away to death or slavery."

29   Pendergast, 126. After all his loyalty to the English, Wonalancet and his family were reduced to becoming wards of Mr. Jonathan Ting (also spelled Tyng) of Dunstable, subject to his permission to move about the settlement and surrounding country. This must have been humiliating for the great Bashaba of the Pennacook.

29   Ibid. After his poor treatment in this instance, Wonalancet "seems to have placed but little reliance upon the promises of the English."

29   Ibid., 73. In September 1677, Wonalancet departed for St. Francis in Quebec, compelled "partly by force and partly by persuasion" to leave Pennacook and break ties with the English.

29   Ibid., 74. Wonalancet and his diminished band made their home among the St. Francis Indians in Canada for many years, only returning to New Hampshire for short visits.

29   Ibid., 78. "In 1685 Kanacamagus succeeded to the throne of the Indian confederacy and brought with him a throng of restless and vengeful Androscoggins."

29–30 Pendergast, 130–31. Potter writes that Kancamagus, like his grandfather Passaconaway, was able to draw other Indians to him because of his charisma, intelligence, "superior skill and bravery."

29–30 Ibid., 131. Upon Wonalancet's removal to Canada in 1677, the warlike faction of the Pennacooks were led by the noted warrior, Kancamagus, who was Passaconaway's grandson.

30   Beals, 79. From Belknap: "The Pennacooks knew that the Mohawks were being hired to annihilate all the Indians from Narragansett R. I., to Brunswick, Maine."

30   Ibid., 80. Kancamagus first went to the English governor of New Hampshire for protection from the Pennacook's enemies. "Word came back from the Mohawks that they intended to kill all the Indians from Mount Hope to Pegypscott."

30–32 Purvis, 206. In *Colonial America to 1763*, Purvis notes, "from 1680 to 1741, the governorship of Massachusetts and New Hampshire were consolidated. New Hampshire's lieutenant governor or chief councillor [sic] often acted as the province's chief magistrate." Edward Cranfield served as New Hampshire's lieutenant governor from 1682 to 1685.

30–32 Beals, 80. The letters from Kancamagus, aka "John X. Hawkins," to Governor Cranfield are proof of the Bashaba's intelligence, logical thinking, and clarity.

31   Ibid., 81. Kancamagus cleverly mentions his "grant father," i.e., Passaconaway, in his second message to Cranfield, calling up memories of the great chief's loyalty to the English.

31–32 Ibid., 82. In his final letter to Cranfield's surrogate, Mr. Mason, Kancamagus makes it clear he understands the nature of English government: "*his* power *that* your power now."

32–34 Chase, 23. The English kings during this period enforced their own brands of Christian orthodoxy, and "could burn as heretics the favorers of Protestantism, and hang as traitors the supporters of the Pope."

32   Pendergast, 129. By signing the 1685 treaty with the English, Kancamagus indicated that he had assumed "the sagamonship of his grandfather" Passaconaway, according to Potter.

32   Beals, 84. The expiration of the treaty in 1689 brought about the start of King William's War.

33   Purvis, 206. The estimated number of white settlers in New Hampshire by 1700 was five thousand.

33   Parkman, 260. The French and English alike found enlisting the Indians as allies was, at best, a difficult and unpredictable proposition.

33   Chase, 31. Although generally disparaging in his comments about the Indians, Chase begrudgingly admits they had a remarkable "power of enduring hunger and weather."

33–34   Herr, 87. Herr's depiction of the US military's attitude toward the Montagnards, whom he calls "a kind of upgraded, demi-enlightened Annamese aborigine," forms an astute commentary on how the original inhabitants of North America were perceived and treated.

33   Chase, 19–21. Puritan authorities during the early colonial period—as well as many later commentators—condemned the Abenaki and other mercenary Indians as vicious slavers. But as early as 1605, the English explorer and trader George Weymouth "kidnapped five of the natives, who he hurried into bondage." In 1614, Captain John Smith "acted honorably with the natives," but his crewman and supervisor, a man named Hunt, "copied the vile example of Weymouth, and kidnapping upwards of twenty of the natives, sailed for Malaga, where a part (at least) were sold as slaves."

34   Beals, 84–85. Kancamagus, Mesandowit, Hope-Hood, and other notable warriors nursed grudges against the English colonial government and were not inclined to renew the treaty that expired in 1689.

34–36   Parkman, 111. The most dangerous aspect of relying on Indians as allies in a fight was that "they changed their minds every day," and would often turn "against each other or against their hosts."

34   Beals, 85. The warrior, Hope-Hood, also known as Wahowah, was "a tiger, and one of the most bloody warriors of the age," according to Belknap.

35   Pendergast, 138. Indians often gave some indication that they meant to attack a certain place or take revenge against an individual, sometimes out of carelessness but often out of custom. Captain Thomas Hinchman of Chelmsford, Massachusetts, learned of Kancamagus and Hope-Hood's plans to attack Cocheco and punish Major Waldron, and he wrote a letter that was routed to Governor Bradstreet of Massachusetts with the details.

35   Ibid., 138–40. The inefficient handling of Captain Hinchman's letter by colonial authorities is reminiscent of government indifference and bumbling that has contemporary resonance.

35   Beals, 89. After a warrior named Mesandowit, who felt some degree of loyalty to Major Waldron for past acquaintances, attempted to deliver a veiled warning to the feisty octogenarian, he withdrew and left the old soldier to his fate.

35   Caverly, 317. During a visit to Cocheco shortly before Waldron's murder, Mesandowit asked his host what he would do if strange Indians were to invade the fortified settlement. Waldron answered smugly: "I could assemble an hundred men by lifting up my finger."

35–36   Pendergast, 140–41. The attack on Cocheco took place on the night of June 27, 1689. As part of an effective ruse, several squaws approached the garrison houses within the settlement and asked for a night's lodging. All but one garrison admitted the Indians.

36   Parkman, 165. An account of Major Richard Waldron's murder during the raid on Cocheco mention that two squaws "begged lodging" in his palisaded house and were allowed entrance. Later, they slipped outside and unlocked the gates for the warriors.

36–37   Beals, 90. The Indians had the intention of making this "Richard Waldron's judgement-day" for his role in the sham fight and for his cheating ways as the owner of a prominent trading post.

36   Caverly, 318. Though an old man, Waldron fought back vigorously when the Indians invaded his private chamber, temporarily driving them back with his sword.

36   Pendergast, 140. When Waldron attempted to retreat to better arm himself, he was struck on the head. The Indians meant to stun him, not kill him, with that blow, having other torments in mind for the old trader.

36   Beals, 90. The author notes that many similar accounts of the death of Major Waldron appear in other historians' work, including Quint, Potter, Drake, Belknap, and Bodge. In each version, Waldron is tied to a chair and placed on top of a table while the Indians stick him with knives and jeer him.

36   Caverly, 318. The Indians cut off Waldron's fingers, taunting him that the fist that he would place on the scales when trading for beaver skins would no longer weigh a pound.

36   Pendergast, 141. From Potter's *History of Manchester NH*: "They then cut off (Waldron's) nose and ears, forcing them into his mouth; and when spent with the loss of blood, he was fast falling down from the table, one of them held his own sword under him, which put an end to his misery."

37   Beals, 92. Other residents targeted by the Indians were treated as roughly as Major Waldron: "The garrison of Otis, a partner of Waldron, was taken in the same way as the Major's. After the fray Otis was found dead in his chamber; some think he was shot while getting out of bed; others that he met his death while peering out of his window."

37   Pendergast, 142. For the survivor of the Cocheco raid, Potter uses the name Elizabeth Heard. Belknap refers to her as "a young woman."

37   Beals, 93. An account of the attack on Cocheco lists the casualties and captives. "In this one night there were twenty-three persons slain and twenty-five made captives. In all, six houses were burned, including that of Waldron, and the mill upon the lower fall."

CHAPTER III: THE SETTLEMENT
Page

38–40   Galvin, *MHC Reconnaissance Survey Town Report*, 7. Pawtucket Plantation was incorporated as the town of Haverhill in 1645, becoming the twenty-third incorporated township in the colony. (Topography, boundaries, population, settlement pattern, and other information about Haverhill, Massachusetts, its origins and its distinguishing features, including the Merrimack River, are drawn from this report.)

38–40   Vital Records of Haverhill, Massachusetts, 4. Haverhill was named in deference to one of the original settlers, Rev. John Ward, "who came from Haverhill in England."

38–41   Galvin, *MHC Reconnaissance Survey Town Report*, 6. The report notes that, "all Haverhill settlers during this period were ethnically English and exclusively Congregationalist."

38   Ibid., 1. Haverhill is "at 42 degrees 47' north latitude and 71 degrees 4' west longitude."

38–39   Chase, 30. The Merrimack Valley was home to the Pennacook Indians (which included the aforementioned band of Pentuckets), "the most powerful tribe in this whole region."

39   Galvin, 5. The Pentucket Indians subsisted on great runs of shad, salmon, and trout from the Merrimack River, up to and including the time when white settlers first arrived from Newbury, Massachusetts. The quality of the fishing made the location, especially near the mouth of Little River, where the Pentucket village was located, attractive to settlers.

39   Chase, 46–47. The author provides a facsimile of the deed signed by the Pentucket Indians, Passaquo and Sagahew, proxies for the great sagamore Passaconaway, ceding title to the parcel of land that became Haverhill.

39   Galvin, *MHC Reconnaissance Survey Town Report*, 7. "In 1642, the settlers obtained the deed from the Indians including a tract of land extending for 8 miles west along the Merrimack from Little River 6 miles east and 6 miles north. This tract in effect amounted to a triangular piece of land including what would later be set off as Methuen, Lawrence, and the New Hampshire towns of Salem, Hampstead, Plaistow, and Atkinson."

39   Chase, 47. The six Haverhill settlers who signed the deed with the Indians were John Ward, Robert Clements, Tristram Coffin, Hugh Sheratt, William White, and Thomas Davis.

39–41   Galvin, *MHC Reconnaissance Survey Town Report*, 7. House lots in Haverhill were granted proportionate to the settlers' wealth. Those with a net worth exceeding two hundred pounds received "the maximum house lot size of 20 acres."

39–41   Ibid. The original settlers of Haverhill "considered themselves the sole proprietors of the land," granting them the power to divide it any way they wished.

39   Braun, 53. The text includes an excellent illustration of a fishing weir similar to the one the Pentucket Indians would have constructed each year near the mouth of Little River.

39   Galvin, *MHC Reconnaissance Survey Town Report*, 3. The Indians' major transportation routes in the vicinity of Haverhill (including those used on the approach to Haverhill on March 15, 1697 and in retreat after the assault) emphasized water transportation and paralleled the Merrimack, Little River, and East Meadow River.

39   Chase, ix. The Merrimack is the fourth largest river in Massachusetts.

39   Ibid. Writing in 1860, Chase claimed that Haverhill was eighteen miles from the mouth of the Merrimack River in Newbury, Massachusetts.

39   Galvin, *MHC Reconnaissance Survey Town Report*, 2. This 1985 report fixes the
        distance between Haverhill and the mouth of the Merrimack River at thirteen
        navigable miles.

39   Chase, x. Chase mentions that Little River was so called to distinguish it from
        the "Great River," or Merrimack, and that its original name was Indian River.

39–41   Galvin, *MHC Reconnaissance Survey Town Report*, 7. Those potential settlers
        with a net worth less than two hundred pounds were given house lots "pro-
        portional to their value as well as proportional meadow and common planting
        grounds."

40   Chase, 60. Chase's account fixes Haverhill as the thirtieth town incorporated in
        Massachusetts, though the *MHC Reconnaissance Survey Town Report* probably
        based its conclusion that Haverhill was the twenty-third incorporated town by
        only counting those towns that remained in the commonwealth when state lines
        were redrawn in 1741.

40   Ibid., 152. Haverhill residents and other settlers of the frontier had to be vigilant
        at all times: "The people always went armed to their daily labor, and on the Sab-
        bath. . . ."

40   Ibid., 124. The author lists Ephraim Kingsbury as Haverhill's first casualty in
        King Philip's War. Kingsbury was slain in Haverhill on May 2, 1675 by Indians,
        most likely a band returning from a raid on nearby Andover.

40   Galvin, *MHC Reconnaissance Survey Town Report*, 11. "By 1675 Haverhill's
        population included three hundred white inhabitants plus 25 negro slaves." It is
        important to note that well-to-do English settlers had the means to keep slaves
        in seventeenth-century Haverhill. This is especially interesting in light of the
        fact that early historians often referred to members of Indian raiding parties
        as murderous slavers for their propensity for taking captives. (More than one
        descendant of Hannah Duston whom I talked with dismissed the Abenaki who
        took her captive as mere slavers.) I came across no evidence that the Duston
        family had slaves during this or later periods.

41–43   Bailey, 3. Chris H. Bailey, former genealogist for the Duston-Dustin family,
        was born in 1946 in Robinson, Illinois. A retired museum curator, Bailey is the
        eighth great-grandson of Hannah (Emerson) Duston, and the ninth great-
        grandson of Joanna Corliss Hutchins (1650–1734) who was the younger sister
        of Mary (Corliss) Neff, Hannah Duston's nurse and friend who was also taken
        captive from the Duston homestead. Mr. Bailey was generous in sharing his
        many years of research with me for the purposes of accuracy in this book. In
        his unpublished, book-length manuscript, Bailey says that the community at
        Northam, later called Cocheco and then Dover, where Thomas Sr. went to live,
        "consisted of a certain number of responsible citizens of good character and
        numerous others of a lawless type."

41   Ibid., 5. In 1650, the "Grand Jurie" of the Massachusetts General Court fined
        Thomas Duston Sr. and his wife ten shillings for missing church services. "As
        there were no future offences noted, we assume they were thereafter regular
        church attendees."

41 Ibid., 11. Thomas Duston Jr.'s experience as a soldier is proven with this notation: "Thomas 'Durston' was paid 17 shillings, 10 pence for his service" during King Philip's War.

42 Ibid., 20. On November 4, 1679, Thomas Duston Jr. bought "18 acres of upland in Haverhill" from Theodore Atkinson of Boston. "This deed was recounted in the *Essex Institute Historical Collections*, Vol. 70, p. 152."

42 Ibid. "It appears Thomas Duston's home built on the lot purchased from Theodore Atkinson was his home and that which burned at the time of the Mar. 15, 1697 massacre."

42 Ibid., 11. Thomas Duston Jr. was twenty-five years old and Hannah (Emerson) Duston was nineteen when they were married in Haverhill on December 3, 1677.

42 Chase, 155. At the time of the March 15, 1697 raid, Haverhill was protected by no fewer than a dozen palisaded and fortified structures, known as garrison houses and "houses of refuge."

42–43 I inspected the egress of the tunnel in the Duston garrison house, a brick structure still standing in Haverhill that was probably built in the months following the March 15, 1697 raid.

42–43 Chase, 188. Since the Indians most likely attacked from the north, or west, Thomas Duston directed his fleeing children to the south, and east. Therefore, the nearest garrison was that of Onesiphorus Marsh, on Pecker's Hill. This was located on the west side of Little River, which corresponds with Bailey's opinion of where the Duston house was located, on the parcel of land formerly owned by Theodore Atkinson of Boston.

42 Galvin, *MHC Reconnaissance Survey Town Report*, 1. The highest elevations along the coastal New England plain do not exceed five hundred feet, indicating that Pecker's Hill, at less than four hundred feet, would be a significant landmark on the horizon.

42 Chase, 203. During King William's War, "[From June, 1689 to May, 1698], five hundred and sixty-one persons were killed, eighty-one wounded, and one hundred and sixty-one captured by Indians, in Massachusetts, New Hampshire, and Maine, including Schenectady." (It is interesting to note that Chase includes only white, English settlers in his statistics.)

43 Caverly, 325. The June 26, 1696 attack on Portsmouth, New Hampshire, where Captain Shackford was able to counterattack successfully, also began with Indian assaults on homesteads "two miles out from the village"—a pattern that the Abenaki raiders would repeat in Haverhill less than a year later.

43 Chase, 33. The author's opinion of Indian virtues reflects his time, calling them "sullen, jealous, intensely vindictive, and ferociously cruel."

45 Mather, 635. The Indians burned the Duston home to the ground after taking Hannah, Mary Neff, and the infant captive.

46–47 Johnson, 91. In March, both Duston and Neff would have been fairly well dressed for the weather, although not prepared for a long trek and nights spent outdoors. The author notes that colonial women of this period usually wore a three-piece gown consisting of a skirt, bodice, and sleeves, with an apron over it. They also wore an underskirt of linen, or a petticoat, or both, with a shift beneath that, along with a kerchief, cap, and stockings. "Often a woman wore almost five layers of clothing."

46–49   Mather, 635. Mather picks up the story after Thomas Duston spirits the children away to the garrison house. "But [Duston's] house must in the meantime have more dismal tragedies acted at it. The nurse, trying to escape with the new-born infant, fell into the hands of the formidable salvages; and those furious tawnies coming into the house, bid poor Dustan to rise immediately. Full of astonishment, she did so; and sitting down in the chimney with an heart full of most fearful expectation, she saw the raging dragons rifle all that they could carry away."

46–49   Parkman, 278. Several Haverhill captives, probably those the Indians deemed unfit for hard travel, were dispatched quickly. Hannah Duston and Mary Neff "were dragged into the forest, where they found a number of their friends and neighbors, their fellows in misery. Some of these were presently tomahawked, and the rest divided among their captors."

46–47   Sprinkle, 29. The Indians punished defiance but respected courage, and Hannah Duston must have demonstrated prudence and a certain degree of stubbornness to survive the first minutes of the raid. In an account of the captivity of fourteen-year-old James Moore of Virginia in 1784, the author, a descendant, wrote, "[James] understood enough of Indian character to know that all his chance of faring well with them, depended on showing a spirit which would not quail at any appearance of danger, and which would resist everything like oppression." When one of the Shawnee attempted to grab his hat from his head during a rainstorm, Moore objected, and then struck the Indian. When the Shawnee pantomimed that he wanted to borrow the hat to protect the workings of his rifle from the downpour, the boy relented, and the Indian promptly returned the hat when the rain stopped.

47–48   Howe and Mack, 80. The estimable Methuen historian, a taciturn old Yankee I knew personally, writes of the household goods of the early colonial period, "Clothing was mostly home-made from sheep's wool and from the hide of animals, except what could be imported." Regarding the fact from Hannah Duston's account that she was taken by the Indians wearing only one shoe, there is strong support for my rendering of these events. The cold March weather typical of the region made it unlikely that Hannah would have been able to travel on foot for over a hundred miles in the snow, and most likely retrieved a shoe from one of several fellow captives who were killed by the Indians not long after setting out. Mack says, "Crude shoes were . . . made at home with no difference between the right and left feet."

47   Chase, 188. In a footnote, the author writes, "Mrs. Duston was barely allowed time to dress herself, and was even compelled to start on the long journey, at that inclement season, with but one shoe."

47   Fuess, 144. Hannah Duston only had time "to secure one shoe before starting on her terrible journey" and several other captives were killed shortly after they were taken from their homes.

48–49   Salisbury, 68. Rowlandson's 1675 account makes it clear that Duston and the other settlers taken from Haverhill most likely witnessed several horrors as they were led away: "Another there who was running along was shot and wounded, and fell down; he begged of them his life, promising them Money (as they told me) but they would not hearken to him but knockt him in head, and stript him naked, and split open his Bowels."

48–49   Mather, 635. "About nineteen or twenty Indians now led these away, with about half a score of other English captives; but ere they had gone many steps, they dash'd out the brains of the infant against a tree; and several of the other captives, as they began to tire in the sad journey, were soon sent unto their long home; the salvages would presently bury their hatchets in their brains, and leave their carcases on the ground for birds and beasts to feed upon."

48   Chase, 189. Soon after being taken captive, Duston and her companions were informed "the place of destination was Canada, where the Indian expected to obtain from the French a handsome sum for his captives."

48–49   Salisbury, 31. "(Mary) Rowlandson's narrative indicates that the Indians who captured English prisoners during Metacom's War tried to keep most of their captives alive, killing only those whose condition impeded their movements or who tried to escape." Since this policy held sway at the time of Hannah Duston's kidnapping (and various accounts make it clear that the number of captives grew smaller quite rapidly after the conclusion of the raid), it seems likely that one or more Haverhill captives were murdered almost immediately for impeding the movement of the raiding party during their withdrawal, as some may have panicked and tried to escape.

48   Bailey, 25. Mary Neff, who was born in 1646, was ten years older than Hannah Duston.

48–49   Ibid. "Samuel Leonard, alias Lenardson, son of Samuel and Deborah Leonard, had been born about 1683 at Bridgewater, MA and had been abducted in the autumn of 1695 when about age 12 at Worcester, MA where his family was then living. He had been with the Indians many months when Hannah Duston and Mary Neff were captured. After their escape young Samuel rejoined his family who by then had settled at North Preston (present-day Griswold), CT. He married about 1806 to Lydia Cooke, daughter of Richard Cooke of Norwich, CT. He died a young man on May 11, 1718 at Preston, CT, age 35, leaving a widow and five infant children." There are many different spellings of Lenorson's name, keeping with the practice of the time. In a footnote, Bailey refers to *Memorial and Genealogical, Historical, and Biographical, of Solomon Leonard, 1637 of Duxbury and Bridgewater, Massachusetts and some of his Descendants* as his source. Other accounts state that Samuel Lenorson was twelve years old at the time of the March 15, 1697 raid on Haverhill and had been captured approximately six months before that date.

48–49   Mather, 635. The murder of Duston's infant came in the midst of general carnage, as several other captives "were sent unto their long home" with hatchets buried in their brains.

49   Chase, 188. The infant Martha Duston was killed when one of the Indians smashed her head against the tree. Quoting Mirick, the author notes that it was an apple tree: "We have been informed by a gentleman that he heard his grandmother who lived to an advanced age, often relate this fact, and that she had frequently ate apples that grew on the same tree." The tree was located on the west side of Little River.

49   In order to gain a clear picture of the infant Martha Duston's death, I consulted with Dr. Aloke K. Mandal, a board-certified surgeon and trauma specialist. (For an in-depth explanation of the blunt force trauma suffered by Martha Duston, and by the victims on Sugar Ball Island, a more complete set of Dr. Mandal's opinions are contained in a note from Chapter VI.) Regarding the murder of the week-old Martha Duston, Dr. Mandal wrote in an e-mail: "So, there definitely would be some sort of muffled crack—think of a dull thud with just a bit of a cracking noise. That would be for an adult skull with the skull thick and the suture lines ossified. There would be more of a muffled thud and no cracking noise with the infant's."

49   Sprinkle, 43. Martha Duston was not the only infant murdered by this method. In an account of a 1786 raid on a Virginia farm by the Shawnee, the events described have a startling familiarity. "The infant was fretful, and was taken from the arms of her mother, her brains dashed out against a tree, and the lifeless body thrown away. What the feelings of the captive mother were under these accumulated trials cannot be imagined."

49   Whitford, 318. Thoreau and other writers mentioned that for many years after the March 15, 1697 raid, subsequent residents of Haverhill ate apples from the tree where Martha Duston's brains were dashed out. Whitford asks, "Does it imply a peaceful, flourishing farmstead inhabited by the children and grandchildren of the Dustins, or a ghoulish tendency in humans titillated by the recollection of eating the fruit of a tree accursed—and if so, does the reference hint at the Biblical apple which brought evil into the world?"

Chapter IV: A Forced March
Page

50–51   Parkman, 278. In his account of these events, Parkman refers to Duston as "a captive Amazon" and following Mather, Pike, and others, says, "The Indians had killed the new-born child by dashing it against a tree, after which the mother and the nurse were dragged into the forest, where they found a number of friends and neighbors, their fellows in misery. Some of these were presently tomahawked, and the rest divided among their captors." He writes that Duston, Neff, and Lenorson, at the very least, soon "fell to the share of a family consisting of two warriors, three squaws, and seven children, who separated from the rest, and hunting as they went, moved northward towards an Abenaki village, two hundred and fifty miles distant, probably that of the mission on the

Chaudière." Parkman is one of the few commentators to say that Duston's party "separated from the rest" before reaching Sugar Ball Island near present-day Concord, New Hampshire. The island appears to be the place—or near it—where the Abenaki divided their captives and split up.

50–81   Fuess, 18. "The Essex County drumlins belong to a somewhat vague group of something less than three hundred, of which not quite two hundred lie within the district itself. . . . Haverhill alone, including Bradford, has twenty, all except one important enough to be named."

50–81   Galvin, *MHC Reconnaissance Survey Town Report*, 3. By studying maps of the early colonial period and the traditional Indian routes through the Merrimack Valley, I was able to discover with a reasonable amount of certainty the path that the Abenaki used to spirit their captives from Haverhill to what was then called Pennacook, now Concord, New Hampshire. By comparing the distances that Duston reported, such as their forced march of approximately twelve miles that first day, with the total length of her journey (various commentators estimate it covered 100–130 miles over twelve to fourteen days), as well as the distance traveled by Mary Rowlandson between "removes" during her captivity twenty-two years earlier, I could discern likely places in the territory where the Indians and their captives stopped to hunt and rest. These routes were simpler to figure out by consulting documents like this regional survey prepared by the Massachusetts Historical Commission in 1985, which states, "Native American transportation routes in the Haverhill area likely emphasized water travel along the Merrimack River and its major tributaries, the Little and East Meadow rivers. Water travel along the Merrimack provided faster, more convenient, and at times probably safer travel from the coast westward to interior areas of Massachusetts, and eventually Central New Hampshire. . . . Land-based travel was also probably important linking interior areas with the Merrimack River and its tributaries, as well as land-based counterparts to riverine routes. Mainland routes through Haverhill likely found along the banks of major riverine areas noted above, providing links between the coast and interior as well as northerly routes. Secondary land travel extending to the town's numerous ponds, meadows and wetlands, likely spurred from major inland trails along the Merrimack River and its tributaries." By inspecting many of these locations on foot, the majority of which are still undeveloped forest areas in Haverhill and the New Hampshire towns angling northwest from there, I was able to pinpoint areas that would have provided fresh water, shelter from English patrols, and plentiful forage food and wildlife, including fishing areas, for the travelers.

50–81   Salisbury, 67. In "The Preface to the Reader" that opens Mary Rowlandson's account of her captivity, the unnamed writer (the author of the preface is believed to be Rev. Increase Mather) notes how difficult it would have been for a militia force to overtake the Indian war party and save the captives: "I may say, that none knows what it is to fight and pursue such an enemy as this, but they that have fought and pursued them: no one can imagine what it is to be captivated, and enslaved to such atheistical, proud, wild, cruel, barbarous, brutish (in one word) diabolicall creatures as these, the worst of the heathen; nor what difficulties, hardships, hazards, sorrows, anxieties and perplexities do unavoidably wait upon such a condition, but those that have tryed it."

50   Chase, 42–43. There is a common misconception that the Indians who raided Haverhill and surrounding towns on several occasions in the late seventeenth and early eighteenth centuries were the aggrieved native inhabitants who felt cheated of their land. There is no evidence to support this. The author notes that there were very few Pentucket Indians left in and around Haverhill, going back to the very beginning of the settlement. "We have now no means of knowing how many aborigines still lived here at the time of Mr. Ward's settlement (1640), but circumstantial evidence indicates that they were few in number. In but few of the early accounts of the native inhabitants is any mention made of any tribe or tribes at this place; and where mentioned, it is a remnant—the last few—of a once vigorous tribe. On the other hand, the wording of the deed (to Haverhill) and the small sum paid for the large extent of territory, strongly favor the conclusion that but two families of the natives (that of Passaquo and Saggahew, signatories to the deed) then remained."

50   Ibid., 71. Of the scarcity of Pentucket Indians in the vicinity of Haverhill, the author writes, "In one of the land grants of this year (presumably 1650) we find mention of a 'wigwam' in the town. It is also mentioned in 1660 and 1685. These are the only mentions or hints of the Indians, or of anything belonging to or done by them, that we can find in the early records of the town."

50–57   Ibid., 152. Despite their ferocity and control over those they had captured, early commentators are unanimous in their judgment that the New England Indians in the early colonial period refrained from sexually assaulting their female captives. Chase writes, "Such aged and infirm persons as were unable to perform a journey through the wilderness, were generally despatched. Infants, soon as they became troublesome, had their mouths filled with burning embers, or their brains dashed out against the nearest stone or tree. But we have one thing to record which speaks highly in their favor; that is, the modesty with which they generally treated their captive women. We do not recollect of but one instance where they attempted to abuse their chastity in word or action." Chase explains that exception in the following note: "This was in the case of Mrs. Hannah Duston, when her captors told her that she, and her companions, must be stripped naked, and run the gauntlet." (This was to occur when the Indians reached their ultimate destination, probably in Quebec.)

50–57   Salisbury, 27. Though the author is referring to Mary Rowlandson who was taken captive by the Narragansetts in 1675, the situation has an eerie parallel with Hannah Duston's. "The very shock of the attack and her capture, the death of one child and her separation from the rest of her family, and her entry into a mobile, generally hungry society of Native Americans at war combined to cut Rowlandson off from nearly all her worldly associations that, without her giving it a thought, had constantly reminded her of who she was and where she belonged in the world."

51–57   Mather, 635. Once in captivity, "Dustan (with her nurse) notwithstanding her present condition, travelled that night about a dozen miles. . . ."

51   Johnson, 90–91. The author gives a detailed account of the "three-piece gown," and other items of clothing worn by women during the early colonial period.

51   Salisbury, 70. No doubt more atrocities were committed as the Indians left the Haverhill settlement, as they decided quickly which of the captives would be easiest to manage on a forced march. In Duston's case, the trauma of seeing her infant and several other captives killed by blunt force is immeasurable. As the captive Mary Rowlandson was led away during the 1675 raid on Lancaster, Massachusetts, she was in a state of shock, later noting, "There was one who was chopt into the head with a Hatchet, and stripped naked, and yet was crawling up and down. It is a solemn sight to see so many Christians lying in their blood, some here, and some there, like a company of Sheep torn by Wolves."

51   Ibid., 95. Victims of these raids, some of whom had been surprised in transit to or from the settlements, were often discovered later, strewn across the landscape. Rowlandson writes, "As we went along I saw an *English-man* stript naked, and lying dead on the ground, but knew not who it was." Among the twenty-seven townspeople killed during the raid on Haverhill, it's very likely some were discovered near the settlement on the route the Indians took along Little River.

51–52 Parkman, 266. Noting that the Indians raiding the settlements of the English frontier, including Haverhill, were Abenaki, Parkman says they included, "the tribes from the Kennebec (River) eastward to the St. John (River)." These were the Canibas, or Kenibas; Sacos, Androscoggins, Sheepscot, Pequawkets, and the fierce tribes of the Penobscot, called the Tarrantines. "All these tribes speak dialects of Algonquin so nearly related that they understand each other with very little difficulty," Parkman says. It's important to note that these Indians were not the displaced Pennacook who had once lived along that stretch of the Merrimack River, but so-called "strange Indians" who had been converted to a rough brand of Catholicism by the French Jesuits, and whose fellow tribesmen had raided Cocheco and other settlements in the time of Kancamagus and Mesandowit.

51–52 Wilbur, 78. Descriptions of the way Algonquin warriors dressed their hair, including a quote from early historian William Wood on the subject: "other cuts they had as their fancie befools them, which would torture the wits of a curious barber to imitate."

52   Ibid., 73. "Abenaki—New England's northernmost tribe were hunters, not farmers. Untouched by the epidemics, these dread and cruel Tarrantines (as they were called by the tribes to the south) warred on the disease-ridden tribe called the Massachusetts."

52   Chase, 31–32. Even Chase, a harsh critic of the region's native inhabitants, notes the Indian's "power of enduring hunger and weather" and their particular brand of stoicism, including "fortitude under suffering." The Indians were famously inured to the cold and would have been cardiovascular marvels due to the stamina it took to complete these raids, and to move so swiftly and at such distances across the winter landscape of New England.

52–57 Mather, 636. "These two poor women were now in the hands of those 'whose tender mercies are cruelties. . . .'"

52 Wilbur, 77. "Painting of the face was common with both men and women. Red was the preferred color. It was also liberally spread over the body—and indeed, many of their possessions. The bulk of this paint was brought from the iron out-crops near Katahdin and elsewhere in central Maine. This love of staining the body red was the reason the early explorers called them 'red men'. . . . Men rarely used other decorative paints unless on the warpath. Every warrior painted him-self as he wished—always with the hope of frightening his enemies. He was an expert with background colors, figures of birds and animals, and particularly the clan symbols across his chest. Various colors, especially black, yellow and vermil-ion, were kept in small individual bags. There were also bags of fat, used to mix the dry pigments into a paste. These were contained in a larger bag and carried by both men and women."

52 Ibid. The Algonguin place name for the home of the Tarrantines—Androscog-gin—meant "fish-curing place."

52 I will describe the abduction and captivity of Isaac Bradley and Joseph Whit-taker, who were taken from Haverhill in 1695, in a later chapter.

53 Caverly, 21. Thomas and Hannah Duston's son Nathaniel was born on May 16, 1685. Most accounts list the age of Sam Lenorson, or Lenarson (among other spellings), who was already with the Abenaki raiders when they struck at Haverhill, as eleven or twelve years, and put the length of his captivity to that date somewhere between a couple of months and a year.

53 Bailey, 21. Commenting on the Indian who killed Martha Duston and his even-tual fate, the author includes this passage: "(o)ne John Marshall made the fol-lowing entry in his diary, dated April, 1697. . . . The chief of these Indians took one of the women captive when she had lain in childbed but a few days, and knocked her child in (the) head before her eyes, *which woman killed and scalped that very Indian*." (These are my italics.)

53–54 Salisbury, 78. About a mile northwest of the Duston farm, the country changes and becomes more wooded and hilly. No English homesteads existed beyond this point in 1697, and it's a natural place for the Indians to have paused briefly to take stock of their captives and themselves. Rowlandson states that once she and the other captives were hurried away from the settlement at Lancaster, the Indians put out a rear guard to protect against being followed by the militia. "For they went, as if they had gone for their lives, for some considerable way, and then they made a stop, and chose some of their stoutest men, and sent them back to hold the English army in play whilst the rest escaped: And then, *like Jehu, they marched on furiously*. . . ."

54–56 Wilbur, 79. When the raiders had put some distance between them and Haver-hill, they must have added warm clothing to what little they wore during the attack on the village. "Mantles or shoulder capes were fastened over the left shoulder and hung under the right arm to allow for full motion. On the trail, the mantle was secured at the waist with a belt. This belt was sometimes hollow to carry a supply of parched corn for the journey. . . . Mantles for cold weather were logically dressed with the fur intact. The furred side was worn next to the body. Bear, moose, deer, wolf, beaver, otter, fox, raccoon, and squirrel pelts were used.

But raccoon was the favorite, for when the skins were sewn together, the trailing tails gave a striking appearance. As for the deer mantle, a perfect tail or 'flag' was greatly admired. One bear, moose, or deer hide was large enough for a single mantle. The free right arm was covered with the whole skin of the bobcat."

54   Ibid., 80. The Indian version of trousers were "leg tubes of deerskin" worn by the men. "One of the most practical articles of clothing, they gave protection from the brush and brambles along the trail. . . . An oblong of hide was perforated down the two longest sides with a series of awl punch holes, then sewn with sinew to form a cylinder. One for each leg, each was suspended from the belt by lateral thongs, while the lower legging was tied under the foot. Each legging was decorated down its length and sometimes fringed. Decorated gaiters of hide or woven fiber held the legging snug below the knee." For winter moccasins "moose hide was sturdier (than deer hide) and usually preferred. Each moccasin was made from a single piece of hide, with only the sole added. . . . In foul weather, the flaps were raised to give added protection."

55   Wilbur, 77. Hannah Duston would have no doubt been taken aback by her close examination of her captors when they stopped to rest.

55–57   Salisbury, 78. Captives traveling in groups learned quickly not to complain. Mary Rowlandson recalled an English captive she met named Amy Joslin who was eight-and-a-half months pregnant: "She having much grief upon her Spirit, about her miserable condition, being so near her time, she would be often asking the Indians to let her go home; they not being willing to that, and yet vexed with her importunity, gathered a great company together about her, and stript her naked, and set her in the midst of them; and when they had sung and danced about her (in their hellish manner) as long as they pleased, they knockt her on head, and the child in her arms with her; when they had done that, they made a fire and put them both into it."

55   Parkman, 278. The author names the French mission of Chaudière as the likely destination of the Abenakis who raided and plundered Haverhill.

55   Ibid., 78. In his depiction of the March 15, 1697 raid on Haverhill and its aftermath, Parkman writes, "Every morning, noon, and evening, (the Indians) told their beads, and repeated their prayers. An English boy, captured at Worcester, was also of the party."

55   Ibid., 33. "A warrior could carry forty days provisions of 'no-cake' without inconvenience. It could be eaten with a little water, hot or cold. Each brave carried a small basket of Nokehick at his back or in a hollow leather belt about his middle—enough for three or four days."

56–57   Bailey, 25–26. About 1724 at the age of 67, Hannah Duston wrote a letter and asked to receive the full covenant of the Second Church of Haverhill. It was found in 1929 and made mention of her captivity. It is recounted below in full:
I desire to be Thankful that I was born in a Land of Light & Baptized when I was Young; and had a Good Education by My Father, Tho I took but little Notice of it in the time of it;—I am Thankful for my Captivity, twas the Comfortablest time that ever I had; In my Affliction God made his Word Comfortable to me. I remembered 43d ps.ult—and those words came to my mind—ps118.17. . . .I have had a great Desire to

come to the Ordinance of the Lord's Supper a Great While but fearing I should give offence & fearing my own unworthiness has kept me back; reading a book concerning Suffering Did much awaken me. In the 55th of Isa. beg. We are invited to come;— Hearing Mr. Moody preach out of ye 3d of Mal. 3 last verses it put me upon Consideration. Ye 11th of Matthew has been Encouraging to me—I have been resolving to offer my Self from time to time ever since the Settlement of the present Ministry; I was awakened by the first Sacram 'l Sermon (Luke 14.17) But Delays and fears prevailed upon me;l—But I desire to delay no longer, being Sensible as it is my Duty—, I desire the Church to receive me tho' it be the eleventh hour; and pray for me—that I may hon'r God and obtain the Salvation of my Soul. HANNAH DUSTIN WIFE OF THOMAS AETAT 67' (Bailey's italics).

56–57 Ibid., 25. In a footnote to the above letter Bailey notes, "In 1929 the document was found with others in a vault of the Center Congregational Church of Haverhill." The letter is notable for many reasons, not the least of which is that it is the only first person written account by any of the captives of the March 15, 1697 raid on Haverhill, albeit a brief mention. It also stands as a clear example of the way that Puritans in the early colonial era felt about the primacy of their relationship to God and their belief that sometimes He brought on great challenges and suffering, not from displeasure, but because of His love for us. Furthermore, it details the prayers and biblical passages that assisted Duston in enduring these trials, which I have included in this chapter.

57 Salisbury, 80. At the outset of her captivity, Mary Rowlandson compares her desire to return to her home in Lancaster, Massachusetts, to Lot's wife's decision to look back at Sodom, which resulted in her being turned into a pillar of salt. As a Puritan, Hannah Duston would have been familiar with the same biblical passages, and that same sense of guilt, unworthiness, and determination to soldier on. Rowlandson writes, "I went along that day mourning and lamenting, leaving farther my own Country, and travelling into the vast and howling *Wilderness*, and I understood something of Lot's Wife's Temptation, *when she looked back*." (The italics here are Rowlandson's.)

57 Ibid., 88. That first night, at least twelve miles from home, Duston must have had to keep her desire to run away in check. Rowlandson writes, "But when I was without, and saw nothing but *Wilderness*, and *Woods*, and a company of barbarous heathens: my mind quickly returned to me."

57–58 Dolin, 100. "With a flourish, and amid the firing of muskets, La Salle planted a flagpole, raised the royal arms, and claimed the (Mississippi) river, and all the lands drained by it and its tributaries, in the name of King Louis XIV. . . . While La Salle was traveling south, another Frenchman, Daniel Graysolon, sieur Duluth (originally "Dulhur"), went in the opposite direction, exploring the headwaters of the Mississippi, the shores of Lake Superior, and lands farther north. Along the way Duluth established posts and traded for furs with the Cree and the Sioux, earning him the title 'king of the *coureurs de bois*.'"

58–60 Parkman, 243. "All the vast and sundry regions" of North America where the French were engaged "had a character of its own" and yet fell under Count Frontenac's personal supervision, attesting to the energy and vision of this intriguing fellow, who was well into middle age when he first set foot in Canada.

59   Ibid., 245. "Inland Acadia was all forest, and vast tracts of it are a primeval forest still. Here roamed the Abenaki with their kindred tribes, a race as wild as their haunts."

59   Dolin, 10. The European fishing and fur trapping industries, which began in the New World in the sixteenth century, were inextricably linked. "With (European) fishermen on land for long periods of time, Indians began bringing furs to the fishermen's camps to trade. Since many of the fishermen returned yearly to the same location, the trade became cyclical, the Indians saving up their furs in preparation for the trading season, and the Europeans stocking up on trade items before leaving home."

59   Parkman, 266. "The name *Abenaki* is generic, and of very loose application. As employed by the best French writers at the end of the seventeenth century, it may be taken to include the tribes from the Kennebec eastward to the St. John." In this footnote, the author gives an instructive primer on these tribes, their locations, and their particular dialects within the broad parameters of the Algonquin language.

60   Ibid., 245. In describing the seasonal round of the Abenaki tribes, the author notes, "In habits they were all much alike. . . .They passed their days in that alternation of indolence and action which is a second nature to the Indian."

60   Dolin, xvi. "In time the fur trade determined the course of empire. It spurred the colonization of eastern North America, and the fierce competition to control the region's fur trade pitted European nations against one another, transforming the New World into a battleground and ultimately leading to the expulsion of the Swedes, Dutch, and French from the continent."

60   Parkman, 246. "A priest was often in the (Abenaki) camp watching over his flock. . . ."

60   Ibid. "The Abenaki missions were a complete success. Not only those of the tribe who had been induced to migrate to the mission villages of Canada, but also those who remained in their native woods, were, or were soon to become, converts to Romanism, and therefore allies of France."

60   Ibid., 247. The author notes that the Bishop at Quebec was so concerned about the growing Puritan influence throughout Acadia he wrote an impassioned letter to the king: "I pray your Majesty to put an end to these disorders."

60   Ibid., 251. The Abenaki not only controlled the passes through the wilderness, but the French provincial government "relied on them to fight its battles."

61   Ibid., 251. Villebon, as well as the Canadian military officers who accompanied him to Acadia, were instructed to join the Indian war parties, and to be "animated by no other desire than that of making profit out of the enemy."

61   Ibid., 252. Villebon's fort upon the St. John River was both a show of French military might in the region and a rallying point for the Abenaki.

61   Chase, 19. Cartier's stockade, built on a hill in Quebec in 1540, would eventually become the seat of the French colonial government in the New World.

61–62   Parkman, 255. Besides direct attacks on the settlements, the Indians also burned and pillaged remote homesteads and farms. Although Frontenac concluded that the amount of damage wrought by the Abenaki in outlying areas along the frontier during 1690 was impossible to calculate "another French writer says that they burned 200 homes," according to Parkman.

61   Ibid., 253. The wife of the murdered clergyman was allowed to go free, but when she returned to the Abenaki camp to beg them to release her son, who was made a prisoner, they warned her to leave and not come back. When she returned yet again, they took her captive and shortly thereafter the woman died of exhaustion on the trip northward.

62   Ibid., 255. The timing of the sloops and sailboats that reinforced the garrison at Wells couldn't have been better: just as the vessels dropped anchor, terrified live-stock was seen running through the adjacent forest.

62   Ibid., 256. A party of Indians intercepted an English scouting party that had the misfortune of returning to the village of Wells during the attack. "The sergeant in command instantly shouted, 'Captain Convers, send your men round the hill, and we shall catch these dogs.' Thinking that Convers had made a sortie, the Indians ran off, and the scouts joined the garrison without loss."

63   Ibid., 256. Even when the Indians offered Convers favorable terms of surrender, he replied, "I want nothing but men to fight with."

63   Ibid., 257. When the attempt to burn the sloops with the fire-raft was unsuc-cessful, the Indians tortured and killed an English prisoner named John Dia-mond. Before he died, Diamond told his captors there were thirty armed sailors among the three vessels (there were only fourteen), which kept the Abenaki from making a direct attack.

63   Ibid., 261. The Abenaki chiefs who visited the palace of Versailles came back to Maine "in gay attire, their necks hung with medals, and their minds filled with admiration, wonder, and bewilderment."

63   Ibid., 262. Parkman calls Father Thury as "wise as the serpent" for turning the jealousy of Taxous over the English peace treaty into the bloody attack on Oys-ter River that left more than a hundred settlers dead.

63   Ibid., 263. The "united force" of Indians that attacked Oyster River in July 1694 totaled 230.

63–64   Ibid., 264. One hundred and four settlers were killed at Oyster River, according to Parkman.

64   Ibid., 264. Although it was still dark when the Indians attacked Oyster River, there was a full moon that allowed the Indians to move about in the woods adjacent to the settlement.

64   Ibid., 264. Another settler with a fortified house, a man called Jones, also ben-efitted from an early alarm: he woke up when his dog began barking.

64   Ibid., 265. Villieu, writing in his diary regarding Taxous and his warriors' activi-ties after the Oyster River massacre: "They mean to divide into bands of four or five, and knock people in the head by surprise, which cannot fail to produce a good effect."

65   Ibid., 271. In a footnote, the author writes, "The famous Ourehaoue, who had been for years under the influence of the priests, and who, as Charlevoix says, died 'un vrai Chretien,' being told on his death-bed how Christ was crucified by the Jews, exclaimed with fervor: 'Ah! why was I not there? I would have revenged him: I would have had their scalps.'"

65–81   Russell, 94. Mary Rowlandson, a minister's wife, was "dragged from her home in Lancaster in the dead of winter amid snow and cold," forced to travel into western Massachusetts, southern Vermont, then back to Mt. Wachusett in central Massachusetts. Rowlandson marveled at the Indians' ability to move and survive under these harsh conditions, "where there was nothing to be seen but from hand to mouth."

65–68   Salisbury, 71. Rowlandson's account states that the Indians who captured her (and several others from Lancaster) did not stop moving that first day until they were sure the English were not following them. Once they did make camp, she remarks, "This was the dolefullest night that ever my eyes saw. Oh the roaring, and singing and danceing, and yelling of those black creatures in the night, which made the place a lively resemblance of hell."

65–73   Ibid., 81. The Indians were efficient scavengers. When they entered a deserted English field, Rowlandson writes, they rapidly fanned out and gleaned what they could, including ears of Indian corn, "ears of Wheat that were crickled down," ground nuts (indicating they can be found and dug up in winter and early spring), and "other sheaves of Wheat that were frozen together in the shock." That night, she ate a partially roasted horse liver before they grabbed it away from her, and one ear of raw corn.

65–81   Braun, 102. The authors' explanation of traditional Indian pathways leads one to believe that figuring out the route that the Indians and their captives (including Hannah Duston, Mary Neff, and Sam Lenorson) traveled from Haverhill to an area on the Merrimack River north of present-day Concord, New Hampshire, is not as difficult as it would seem. "The long-used trade routes among the tribes of the Northeast quickly became the main routes for the fur trade. Later, these same routes became roads traveled by the Europeans themselves, and today many highways still follow the ancient routes."

67–68,   Russell, 71. "In place of the colonial's flint and steel to produce fire, each Indian
78   carried, in a leather case at his wrist or in a woodchuck skin hung from his belt a Minerall stone . . . and with a flat Emeris stone tied fast to the end of a little stick, gently he striketh upon the mineral stone awel, within a stroke or two a spark falleth upon a piece of Touchwood . . . and he maketh fire presently' (Brereton)."

69   Salisbury 71. During what Rowlandson calls their "First Remove," the first encampment where they stopped several hours after the raid, the Indians feasted on "Horses, Cattle, Sheep, Swine, Calves, Lambs, Roasting Pigs, and Fowls (which they had plundered in the Town) some roasting, some lying and burning, and some boyling to feed our merciless Enemies." The Indians did not share these spoils with the English captives, and soon enough both captives and captors were on the verge of starvation.

69–73 Ibid., 78. Rowlandson writes, "The first week of my being among them, I hardly ate any thing; the second week, I found my stomach grow very faint for want of something; and yet it was very hard to get down their filthy trash. . . ."

70 Bailey, 26. In the letter that Hannah Duston wrote in 1724 at the age of sixty-seven (which was discovered in Haverhill in 1929 and is believed to be the only mention of her captivity in her own hand), she mentions the solace she took from chapter 14, verse 17 from the Gospel of Luke.

71–72 Russell, 36. It is likely that Duston suffered from an advance of frostbite or frost nip, as it's called, because of the time she spent walking with one shoe—and then a borrowed, ill-fitting one—in such adverse conditions. "When captive John Gyles froze his feet, the Indians told him to smear them with a fir balsam salve; in a few days they were well again. The Indians had poultices, and they were familiar with massage and adept at reducing swelling."

71–73 Salisbury, 29. Hannah Duston and Mary Neff would have been reliant on their companions, most likely the boy captive, Sam Lenorson, for assistance in living off the land. "English women . . . relied almost entirely on a much narrower range of largely domesticated foods, so that Rowlandson was virtually unable to locate foods or otherwise survive in the wild, despite having lived her entire adult life in central New England."

71 Mather, 636. Duston's master, who had most likely learned some English when staying with the Rowlandson family as a boy, would harangue Duston and Neff about their Puritan God. "Now, they could not observe it without some wonder, that their Indian master, sometimes when he saw them dejected, would say unto them, 'What need trouble yourself? If your God would have you delivered, you shall be so!'"

71–74 Salisbury, 74. Sam Lenorson's months of captivity and familiarity with the Indians in the traveling party and their folkways must have been helpful to Duston and Neff. In her account, Rowlandson states that after a few days of captivity she met a fellow Englishman, a soldier named Robert Pepper, who had been injured in battle some time previously. The Indians carried him for a day or more, concocting a poultice of oak leaves that healed his wounds. Pepper showed Rowlandson, who had suffered a glancing wound from a musket ball during the melee at Lancaster, how this was done. "Then I took Oaken leaves and laid to my side, and with the blessing of God it cured me also," says Rowlandson.

71–74 Russell, 35. The author says that the Indians were steeped in "native pharmacopoeia" and were "acquainted with cough and cold remedies, emetics, cathartics, diaphoretics, vermifuges, astringents, alteratives, stimulants, narcotics, and antiseptics—all from plant sources."

71–79 Sewall, 81. There is strong evidence that Hannah Duston's principal captor spoke English and that they engaged in conversation. The account of Duston's captivity that appears in Samuel Sewall's diaries is one of the three brief reports derived from Duston herself. "May 1, 1697. Hannah Dustin came to see us; I gave her part of Connecticut Flax. She saith her Master, *whom she kill'd*, did formerly live with Mr. Rowlandson at Lancaster: He told her, that when he pray'd the English way, he thought that was good: but now he found the French way was better." (The italics here are mine.)

72 Ibid., 96. Often threatened by her captors after pleading for something to eat, Rowlandson writes, "They told me I disgraced my master with begging, and if I did so any more, they would knock me in the head: I told them, they had as good knock me in the head as starve me to death."

72–73 Ibid., 33. "Not only did (Rowlandson) learn how to function in Indian society, but she also learned to live as an Indian, subsisting on miniscule portions of ground nuts, horses hooves, and other food that she would have found inedible."

72–73 Wilbur, 34. "Groundnuts (*Apios tuberosa*). Common in moist thickets, this climbing perennial plant has fragrant, chocolate brown flowers followed by bean-like pods. The tubers grow on thread-like roots and resemble potatoes— about the size of a hen's egg. The Indians roasted or boiled the groundnuts, or mashed them into groundnut cake. It was baked before the open fire on flat rocks. They helped the Pilgrims survive the winter of 1623."

72–73 Russell, 81. "The tubers of the Jerusalem artichoke were eaten either raw or cooked. Growing three or more to a plant, nutritious and heavy in starch, they added sweetness, body, and their special flavor to pottages of flesh or fish." Of groundnuts, he writes, "Henry Thoreau, a close student of things Indian, tells how he dug some one afternoon, nearly as large as a hen's egg, from six inches to a foot down. . . . Other Indians ate raccoon's fat with them."

73 Salisbury, 93. Rowlandson states that she was often so hungry she would willfully burn her mouth when offered a scrap of hot food.

73 Ibid., 33. "Certainly Rowlandson's most remarkable lapse from 'civilization' occurs . . . when, ravenous after eating her own measly portion of horse feet, she grabs another from the mouth of a starving child—not an Indian but an English child—and quickly devours it."

73–74 Ibid., 95. Hardy captives quickly grew tolerant of the meager food supply available to them. Rowlandson writes, "He gave me also a piece of the Ruff or Ridding of the small Guts, and I broiled it on the coals; and now may I say. . . . Is my spirit revived again." In a footnote, Salisbury explains: "That is, parts that were rough (difficult or distasteful to eat) or had been gotten rid of because they were considered inedible."

74 Mather, 636. Duston reported that she and her companions did enjoy some favorable treatment from the warrior who claimed her, though not enough to mitigate the horror of her experience: "but the good God, who hath all 'hearts in his own hands,' heard the sighs of these prisoners, and gave them to find unexpected favour from the master who hath lain claim unto them."

74 Russell, 198. The author notes that the Indians' well-constructed snowshoes "permitted a five-mile-an-hour steady gait."

74–78 Salisbury, 106. As they were led farther away from Haverhill, Duston and the other surviving captives no doubt passed through hunting grounds which, more likely than not, had been emptied of game by the Indians that winter.

The Abenaki, therefore, had to become even more resourceful in putting a meal together. Rowlandson describes how her captors found some old bones that had been picked over after a kill. The Indians "cut them to pieces at the joynts, and if they were full of wormes and magots, they would scald them over the fire to make the vermine come out, and then boile them, and drink up the Liquor, and then beat the great ends of them in a Mortar, and so eat them. They would eat Horses guts, and ears, and all sorts of Wild Birds, which they could catch: also Bear, Venison, Beaver, Tortois, Frogs, Squirrels, Dogs, Skunks, Rattle-snakes; yea, the very Bark of Trees."

74–79   Russell, 126. Once they had traveled a long way from the English colonies, the Indians would have taken more time to hunt and set traps for game. "In late fall, and again in late winter, hunting parties, well organized and held by experienced and skillful elders, were important events. Nearer home, traps and deadfalls, individually maintained and marked, secured the smaller animals in the months when fat, hide, and fur were at their best." The most common and often useful deadfall trap was a "culheag." It featured heavy logs or stones disguised by branches and moss arranged above a piece of bait, often just a handful of moldy acorns, or offal from a previous kill. The animal stuck its snout beneath the suspended objects to sniff at the bait, tripping the logs and stones. The animal's head was crushed, but the fur and meat were left in perfect condition.

75–81   Russell, 51. The author, and several other commentators, make note that the Indians "preferred a physically attractive spot for a settlement, even a temporary camp. Almost without exception the sites chosen . . . combined a number of advantages: an elevation with a pleasing outlook, yet defensible; protection from the north wind by a hill or copse of evergreens; a clear, flowing spring; and a source of firewood nearby."

75   Wilbur, 62. "An enterprising Indian could fence off the outlet of a stream with branches. Fish would have no trouble swimming through the fence opening. . . . But on the return, the current forced them against the branch barrier. By sight and feel, the fisherman could hook his spear prong under the fish and yank it to the surface."

75–81   Braun, 93. A list of edible wild plants available to the captives includes the ones mentioned here, and several others.

75–81   Ibid., 83. "New England natives were fond of the sweet, gelatinous roots of the common yellow pond lily, *Nuphar advena*, and often dried them for the winter. 'Long aboiling they taste like the Liver of a Sheepe,' Johnson wrote. They were eaten boiled or roasted. . . . Since muskrats were also fond of the roots, the natives let these busy creatures collect and store them, then raided the storehouses, being careful . . . to leave the animals a supply for their own use. They valued also, for eating raw and for cooking, the roots of the cattail, rich in protein, and the spring shoots of the marsh marigold, or cowslip, found in the mud of shallow ponds and backwaters."

76   Wilbur, 34. The Jerusalem artichoke "can be peeled and sliced for salads or cooked as a vegetable."

76   Russell, 87. The author notes that the Jerusalem artichoke is "nutritious and heavy in starch."

77   Russell, 44. Indian customs and respect for other living creatures would have been helpful to Duston and her comrades as they foraged for food during captivity: "If the muskrat's winter store of lily roots was raided, the beneficiary of the little animal's foresight must never take all but must leave sufficient to carry the muskrat family to the next season. The muskrats had gathered the roots: they were entitled to a living."

77   Johnson, 136. "The natives saw themselves as sharing the earth with other animals, whom they saw as brothers. . . . The hunter took only what was needed for survival, just as the wolf or bear killed only what it needed for survival."

79   Mather, 634. The author notes that Duston's captors, once convinced they were not being followed, paused often to recite their Catholic prayers. "In obedience to the instructions which the French have given them, they would have prayers in their family no less than thrice every day; in the morning, at noon, and in the evening; nor would they ordinarily let their children eat or sleep without first saying their prayers."

79   Salisbury, 89. The English felt very little Christian fellowship toward the Indians who had been converted to Catholicism by the French Jesuits. In a footnote, Salisbury writes, "Rowlandson fears the French in Canada because they are Catholic. Puritans regarded the Pope as the Anti-Christ and Catholicism as a form of spiritual slavery."

79   Mather, 635. Although the Indians prayed to a Christian God, they made it difficult for the captives to say their own daily prayers. "Indeed, these idolaters were, like the rest of their whiter brethren [Mather is referring to first the Indians, and then the French here; in particular, the Jesuit priests who converted the Abenaki and those of other northern tribes], persecutors, and would not endure that these poor women should retire to their English prayers, if they could hinder them."

79   Ibid., 50. The author points out a fascinating connection between two of the most compelling captivity stories in early colonial history: Hannah Duston's ordeal, and the kidnapping and ransom of Mary Rowlandson of Lancaster, Massachusetts twenty-two years earlier during Metacom's War. "Dustin also visited another well-known colonist, Samuel Sewall, who, in recording the meeting in his famous diary, pointed out a connection between New England's two best-known captives. Dustin told him that 'her Master, whom she killed, did formerly live with Mr. Rowlandson at Lancaster.' In this brief statement lies the only recorded evidence of contact between Rowlandson and Native Americans before her capture. . . . Apparently the Rowlandsons, like a number of other English families during the middle decades of the seventeenth century, had taken a young Christian Indian as a servant into their home, thereby gaining some labor while promoting the 'civilization' of a 'savage.' More than likely, the boy was one of the Christian Nipmucs from nearby Nashaway. Whether or not he joined the fight against the English in Metacom's War—and perhaps the attack on Lancaster—thereby reinforcing Rowlandson's hostility toward

Christian Indians, is not clear. In any case, he was one of many Indians who had fled north to begin a new life in Canada." In other accounts, the name given to Sam Lenorson's master—the Indian who instructed him on using a pole-ax or tomahawk—was Bampico.

79   Chase, 96–97. The author comments on this practice of Indians living with colonial families (including some who resided in Haverhill): "Many of these praying Indians lived in the families of the settlers, and labored for them; and were allowed many privileges previously denied them, as, for instance, the possession and use of fire-arms."

79   Mather, 636. Although the militia did not mount a campaign to rescue the Haverhill captives, Mather insists that prayer was integral to their deliverance. Referring to the biblical Hannah, Mather writes that Duston and her companions "had opportunities, together and asunder, to do like another Hannah, in 'pouring out their souls before the Lord.' Nor did their praying friends among our selves forbear to 'pour out' supplications for them."

79   Bailey, 21. In one of Samuel Sewall's diary entries for May 1697, he wrote, "Fourth Day May 12—Hannah Dustun came to See us. I gave her part of Connectiuct [sic] Flax. She saith her Master, whom she kill'd, did formerly live with Mr. Rowlandson at Lancaster: He told her, that when he prayed ye (the) English way, he thought that was good; but now he found ye French way was better."

79   Mather, 636. From the account Hannah Duston provided to him about what occurred during her captivity, Cotton Mather later wrote: "This Indian family was now travelling with these two captive women, (and an English youth taken from Worcester, a year and a half before,) unto a rendezvous of salvages, which they call a town, some where beyond Penacook; and they still told these poor women that when they came to this town, they must be stript, and scourg'd, and run the gantlet through the whole army of Indians. They said this was the fashion when the captives first came to a town; and they derided some of the faint-hearted English, which, they said, fainted and swooned away under the torments of this discipline."

80–81   Ibid., 85. The attitude of the Indians toward their captives varied day-to-day, even moment-to-moment. According to Rowlandson, "Sometimes I met with favour, and sometimes with nothing but frowns."

80–81   Ibid., 97. In another place, Rowlandson writes, "So unstable and like mad men they were."

80   Braun, 92. The authors list the wild plants available in late winter/early spring to the Indians on their journey toward Sugar Ball Island: fiddlehead ferns, marsh marigold shoots, cattail shoots, milkweed shoots, roots and groundnuts (which they would acquire using "simple digging sticks"), and possibly Jerusalem artichokes.

80   Salisbury, 105. Rowlandson writes, "The chief and commonest food was Ground-nuts: they also eat Nuts and Acorns, Harty-choaks, Lilly roots, Ground-beans, and several other weeds and roots, that I know not."

80   Russell, 79. When hard pressed, or passing through unfamiliar country, the Indians usually carried "Nokehick, or parched cornmeal. . . . so hearty that, eating it as he felt need, with a little water, an Indian could travel many days with no other food. Put in a long leather bag trussed at his back like a knapsack, so Wood records, the traveler needed to take only 'thrice three spoonsful per day, dividing it into three meals'."

80   Sewall, 81. From his May 1, 1697 diary entry after meeting with Hannah Duston: "The single man shewed the night before, to Sam. Lennarson, how he used to knock Englishmen on the head and take off their Scalps; little thinking that the Captives would make some of their first experiment upon himself. Sam. Lennarson kill'd him."

80   Salisbury, 101. By putting great distances between their party and the English settlement, some of the Indians grew more cheerful and extended a modicum of hospitality toward the English. But circumstances required that captives keep their guard up. Rowlandson reports that at the captives "Nineteenth Remove," the nineteenth campsite they had occupied since being taken from Lancaster, an Indian invited her to dine with him on "some Pork & Ground-nuts. Which I did, and as I was eating, another *Indian* said to me, he seems to be your Good Friend, but he killed two *Englishmen at Sudbury*, and their lie their Cloaths behind you: I looked behind me, and there I saw Bloody Cloaths, with Bullet holes in them."

80   Russell, 189. An Indian tomahawk was "'made of wood like a pole-axe (indicating a long handle) with a sharpened stone fastened therein. . . . The handle or pole was about two and a half feet long, and its deadly work was done 'by a knob at one end as round and bigge as a football (of that period) . . . one blow or thrust will not neede a second to hasten death'."

81   Salisbury, 71. "To add to the dolefulness of the former day, and the dismalness of the present night: my thoughts ran upon my losses and sad bereaved condition. All was gone, my Husband gone . . . my Children gone, my Relations and Friends gone, our House and home and all our comforts within door, and without, all was gone, (except my life) and I knew not but the next moment that might go too."

81   Salisbury, 82. Rowlandson commented on the smoking of tobacco among the Indians. "Then I went to see King *Philip*, he bade me come in and sit down, and asked me whether I would smoke (a usual Complement now adayes amongst Saints and Sinners) but this no way suited me. For though I had formerly used Tobacco, yet I had left it ever since I was first taken. *It seems to be a bait, the devil lays to make men loose their precious time*: I remember with shame, how formerly, when I had taken two or three pipes, I was presently ready for another, such a bewitching thing it is: But I thank God, he was now given me power over it; surely there are many who may be better imployed than to ly sucking a stinking Tobacco-pipe."

CHAPTER V: COUNT FRONTENAC AND THE REIGN OF TERROR
Page

82   Parkman, 15. The author notes that Frontenac had an "uncontrollable passion for the life of a soldier" and had two years of distinguished combat experience before turning twenty.

83   Ibid. Fearless in battle and crafty in his tactics, Frontenac was wounded several times, which led to rapid promotions.

83   Ibid., 16. Mademoiselle La Grange-Trianon's guardian, Madame de Bouthier, strongly objected to her marriage to Frontenac because of his financial position.

83   Ibid., 13. The Comtesse de Frontenac was as fearless as her husband, both physically and politically. The author recounts her adventures at Orleans during the civil war of the Fronde.

83–84   Ibid., 16. Apparently the Comtesse de Frontenac abandoned her child and her husband simultaneously, preferring the life of a favored lady of the royal court over any domestic role.

84   Ibid., 19. The port of Candia was "doomed," though Frontenac acquitted himself well in its defense.

84   Ibid., 21. Frontenac's son, Francois Louis, was killed "at an early age," apparently as headstrong though not as fortunate in such matters as his father.

85   Ibid., 18. Frontenac's plans for improving his estate at St. Fargeau were far beyond his means, which both reflected his personality and a persistent frustration with his lot in life. After visiting him there, the Mademoiselle de Montpensier wrote in her memoirs: "it would need the riches of a superintendent of finance to execute his schemes, and how anybody else should venture to think of them I cannot comprehend."

85–86   Ibid., 20. A contemporary wrote of Frontenac, "He was a man of excellent parts, living much in society, and completely ruined. He found it hard to bear the imperious temper of his wife; and he was given the government of Canada to deliver him from her, and afford him some means of living."

85   Ibid., 21. On the Comtesse de Frontenac: "Like her husband, she had little property and abundant wit."

85–86   Ibid., 22. Frontenac's initial assessment of Quebec appears in his journal, *Frontenac au Ministre*, 2 Nov., 1672.

86   Ibid., 23. Frontenac believed that "centralization," i.e., consolidating all the power in the king, "tended to level ancient rights, privileges, and prescriptions under the ponderous roller of monarchical administration."

86   Ibid., 24. In the speech Frontenac gave to the assembly he praised Louis XIV, though in his actions the headstrong new governor would soon run afoul of his king.

86   Ibid., 25. In his speech to the Quebec noblesse, Frontenac also equated the expansion of Canada with "extending the empire of Jesus Christ throughout all this land, and the supremacy of our king over all the nations that dwell in it."

87 Bailyn, 3. The author says that the Indians' "world was multitudinous, densely populated by active, sentient, and sensitive spirits. . . . [that] impinged on their lives at every turn."

87 Parkman, 28. In his note to a fellow cleric, the bishop included a "complete summary" of Colbert's return letter to Frontenac, indicating he had access to both ends of the correspondence.

87 Ibid., 29. Frontenac complained often that the Jesuits thought "more of beaver skins than of souls" in their dealings with the Indians.

88 Bailyn, 30. Fur trading was both a "cultural malignancy" among all the tribes, and "a specific virus, unmistakable in the case of the Iroquois."

88 Ibid., 20. The Iroquois confederacy was the most sophisticated political alliance in the eastern woodlands, "and militarily the most powerful and the most feared."

88–89 Ibid., 12. The Iroquois villages and hamlets were spread across a wide territory from 150 miles west of the Hudson River to Lake Ontario.

88 Ibid., 21. The Iroquois League was actually a council of fifty sachems who lacked "coercive power" over the tribes but were influential and respected.

88–89 Beals, 16. Concerning his battles with invading Iroquois, Passaconaway later stated, "that from his wigwam pole the most Mohawk scalps hung."

89 Bailyn, 14. The size of the hunting ground for an Iroquois village with a population of two hundred was 175,000 acres according to a study cited by the author.

89 Ibid., 21. These large Iroquois towns often included several dozen longhouses, each two hundred feet long and twenty feet high. They each contained several fireplaces, and multiple family compartments.

89 Ibid., 12. Iroquois towns were "extremely rare" since most Indian villages had populations of one or two hundred, with many bands smaller than fifty.

89–90 Russell, 186. The Iroquois became so powerful that many Algonquin tribes saw the coming of the English settlements as the much lesser of two evils.

89–90 Johnson, 138. Notes on the Iroquois warriors' hairstyle.

90 Parkman, 62. The Seneca could muster as many warriors as the other four tribes of the Iroquois together.

90 Ibid., 297. Under torture, the eighty-year-old Onondaga warrior taunted his captors until they stabbed him to death. "'I thank you,' said the old Stoic, with his last breath; 'but you ought to have finished as you began, and killed me by fire. Learn from me, you dogs of Frenchmen, how to endure pain; and you, dogs of dogs, their Indian allies, think what you will do when you are burned like me.'"

90 Russell, 45. Abenaki sachems sang, chanted, and danced along with the sacrifice of tobacco in an effort to drive the contagion from their village to the land of the Iroquois.

90 Ibid., 187. The Iroquois reputation was so great that sometimes they merely sent emissaries, or messengers, to collect tribute from other tribes, or face an invasion.

90   Bailyn, 31. The Iroquois considered cannibalism "a religious as well as a military ritual" that "served to propitiate the dominant spirits, ostensibly to gain military success."

91   Dolin, 98–99. The so-called "Beaver Wars" were so devastating to commerce that by the time the English took over from the Dutch in 1664, New France's fur trade was practically nonexistent.

91   Ibid., 13. Beaver fur became so popular that the European and Eurasian beaver, *castor fiber*, was hunted nearly to extinction, causing increased demand for pelts from the New World.

91   Ibid., 14. The extinct giant beaver was believed to reach seven feet in length and over five hundred pounds.

91   Braun, 29. Hunting for beaver probably coincided with the beginning of man's dominance in the New World, which predated the Early Archaic period.

91   Dolin, 21. Pemmican cakes made from smoked beaver meat, animal fat, and berries would remain edible for months, even years.

91–92   Ibid., 13. The European and North American beavers differ only in their number of chromosomes and some behavioral characteristics.

91–93   Ibid., 15. Beaver fur was made up of two kinds of hairs; long, coarse "guard" hairs, and the soft, wooly undercoat.

91   Ibid., 325. "Castoreum ranks in fame alongside other animal-derived fixatives, including ambergris from sperm whales and musk from the African civet cat."

92   Ibid., 14–15. The beaver tail was known to promote such "masculine virtue" that an English observer noted that if European women had been aware of it, they would have hastened the shipment of that one item.

92   Ibid., 14. A beaver's incisors never stop growing, therefore the constant abrasion of their labor adds to the mammal's health by keeping the teeth at a manageable length.

92   Ibid., 17. The notion of beavers as "workaholics" who are constantly engaged in building their dams and lodges is a myth. The beaver is a clever and efficient worker whose streamlined effort leaves significant time for play.

92   Ibid. Generations of beavers will work on repairing and maintaining the same dam; these range from a mere eighteen inches high and a few feet across to a thousand yards long and eighteen feet tall.

92–94   whiteoak.org/historical-library/fur-trade/the-beaver-fur-hat/. Beaver fur hats were fashionable in most of Europe from about 1550 to 1850. They were so popular they led to the extinction of beavers in Europe, and their near-extinction in Russia and Scandinavia.

93   Dolin, 22. The history of hat making is vague, so the origins of the beaver felt hat are not entirely clear. Chaucer was most likely remarking on a fashion that was quite common by that time.

93   Ibid. Until the seventeenth century, furs had to be sent all the way to Russia for processing, since the hatters there were the only craftsmen skilled in combing

the wool from the so-called "parchment" beaver. This long, extra step on the raw pelt's way to becoming a hat drove up the price considerably.

94   Ibid. The molding, blocking, dyeing, and shaping of a beaver hat, a process that seemed equal parts craftsmanship and alchemy, is certainly a lost art today.

94   Ibid. The main hazard of the profession was death from mercury poisoning.

94   Ibid. A "dyer's copper," which was a sort of cauldron, was large enough to accommodate up to a dozen top hats at one time.

94   Ibid. A finished beaver hat was sturdy enough to support the weight of a two-hundred-pound man.

94   Ibid. The stiffening and waterproofing of a beaver hat were the most closely guarded secrets of the hatter's trade.

94–95   Bailyn, 250. The Dutch market town of Beverwyck on the Hudson River, formerly known as Fort Orange, was a tumultuous place during the May 1st to November 1st fur trading season. Drunken Indians were commonplace, and "wild auctions" frequently saw items as disparate as houses, yachts, and canoes promised in exchange for incoming furs.

95   Russell, 185. The Narragansetts and Block Islanders had access to the most desirable shells and therefore produced the most popular form of wampum.

95   Braun, 93. Several commentators set the value of wampum at three purple beads (or six white beads) are equal to one English penny.

95   Wilbur, 84. Wampum was highly prized as both currency and ornament, but chiefs and sachems were most likely to wear it and then usually in modest amounts (King Philip of the Wampanoags being a noted exception).

95   Ibid., 85–86. King Philip was said to own a fortune in wampum, during an era when English merchants valued a "fathom," or six feet of purple shell beads, at twenty shillings.

95   Russell, 185. Another factor in the stability of wampum over time was the fact that "even the devil could not counterfeit it."

95   Bailyn, 25. The sheer difficulty of producing wampum limited their availability, which regulated them enough to act as currency.

96   Parkman, 64. The Ottawa feared, with good reason, that the stabbing death of the Seneca chief would become a *casus belli* leading to a war that would destroy their people and the fur trade.

96   Ibid. The Rat implored Count Frontenac: "Father, take pity on us, for we are like dead men."

96   Ibid., 63. It was certainly the Iroquois's plan to master the fur trade by conquering the tribes who controlled the hunting grounds and trade routes, and taking all the beaver pelts for themselves.

96–97   Ibid., 64. Frontenac was aware that the Huron and Seneca were jealous of each other, and "trying to make favor with the common enemy" at each other's expense.

97   Ibid., 32. Fort Frontenac stood on the site of present-day Kingston, Ontario.

97–98   Ibid., 65. In his correspondence, Lamberville, the Jesuit missionary to the Iroquois capital at Onondaga, spelled the famous Iroquois chief's name as Tegannisorens instead of Decanisora. In a letter to Count Frontenac, the Jesuit wrote, "Tegannisorens loves the French, but neither he nor any other of the upper Iroquois fear them in the least. They annihilate our allies, whom by adoption of prisoners they convert into Iroquois; and they do not hesitate to avow that after enriching themselves by our plunder, and strengthening themselves by those who might have aided us, they will pounce all at once upon Canada, and overwhelm it in a single campaign."

97   Ibid., 65. Decanisora expressed "pacific intentions" on behalf of the Iroquois toward the Huron and Ottawa, but Frontenac required the Iroquois to accept all the tribes as brothers that he, the royal governor, considered allies of the French.

97   Ibid., 65. Parkman writes of the murder of the Seneca chief, and the subsequent visit of Decanisora: "Perhaps on this occasion Frontenac was too confident of his influence over the savage confederates."

97   Ibid. Lamberville noted that the Iroquois had strengthened their numbers over a two-year period by adopting the fiercest and strongest of their captured enemies into their tribes.

98   Ibid., 51. Frontenac's chief colonial adversary, a functionary named Duchesneau, wrote to the king that the royal governor so dominated the fur trade that "only the smaller part of what the Indians bring to market ever reaches the people of the colony."

98   Ibid., 51–52. After sternly rebuking Frontenac, the king added, "but I am willing to believe that you will change your conduct, and act with the moderation necessary for the good of the colony."

98   Ibid., 54–55. Frontenac was accused of striking the teenage son of his rival, Duchesneau, and having the boy's servant beaten.

98   Ibid., 56. The king considered the selling of furs to the English "the most heinous offense" that Frontenac and his enemies accused each other of, since this practice defrauded the colony of revenue.

98–99   Ibid. The plague, according to Duchesneau, was nothing more than eighteen to twenty Indians "who lately had drunk themselves to death at La Chine."

99   Ibid., 58. Frontenac stated in his parting missive that the Jesuits, Sulpitians, the bishop, and the seminary of Quebec controlled the majority of the "good lands of Canada" and "that, in view of the poverty of the country, their revenues are enormous."

99   Ibid., 59. Indian tribes loyal to the French continued to respect Frontenac, their "Great Father," despite his "occasional practice of bullying them for purposes of extortion."

99   Ibid., 59–60. Even in the midst of bitter quarrels, Frontenac was capable of surprising his rivals with "a surprising moderation and patience."

100   Ibid., 66. La Barre was so conscious of his scant military experience that he insisted on being called *Monsieur le General* rather than *Monsieur le Governeur* by his underlings.

100   Ibid., 68. La Barre held his first council meeting with the Iroquois in a newly constructed church and imparted lavish gifts on them valuing more than two thousand crowns, which did not seem like a declaration of strength to either his countrymen or the Indians.

100   Ibid., 72–73. Colonel Dongan of New York was a shrewd negotiator and political tactician, arranging a peace with the Iroquois without openly exhorting them to attack the French.

100   Ibid., 73. For several years, the Iroquois had occasionally raided the border settlements as far south as Maryland and Virginia, killing settlers and looting their farms and villages. This activity threatened to cause a war between them and the nearest English colony, New York, which Dongan wished to avoid.

100   Ibid., 74. When Dongan revealed La Barre's letter to the Iroquois sachems, their orator remarked that the French governor "calls us his children, and then helps our enemies to knock us in the head."

100–101 Ibid., 77. Lamberville wrote to La Barre that the Iroquois looked forward to discovering if the French tasted "as good as . . . their other enemies."

101   Ibid., 82. During the expedition to attack the Iroquois, La Barre became so ill with malaria that it brought him "to the brink of the grave."

101–2 Russell, 20. Indians were not the rubes they were often made out to be. Eloquence, the author writes, was a decisive attribute in choosing a sachem, and skilled orators were usually considered the equals of the warrior elite.

101–2 Parkman, 85. In his speech to La Barre, the Onondaga chief Big Mouth stated outright that he knew the French had come to knock the Iroquois in the head and only refrained from doing so because of their illness. Still, he was smart enough to turn the French's governor's weakness into a more lasting advantage for the Iroquois League.

102   Ibid. Big Mouth told La Barre that even the old men of his tribe did not fear the French, and added the startling revelation that his people had begun guiding English traders to the lakes in their vicinity.

102   Ibid., 89. King Louis XIV wrote to La Barre: "Having been informed that your years do not permit you to support the fatigues inseparable from your office of governor and lieutenant-general in Canada, I send you this letter to acquaint you that I have selected Monsieur de Denonville to serve in your place; and my intention is that, on his arrival, after resigning to him the command, with all instructions concerning it, you embark for your return to France."

102   Ibid., 92. While the English pressed on all three fronts, the Seneca continued their attacks on the Illinois, which angered all the northern tribes and began to persuade them of New France's territorial weakness.

102–3 Ibid., 91. The Marquis de Denonville, known as a pious man, spent the entire voyage to the New World reading and praying while nearly a third of the soldiers traveling under his command died aboard ship.

103   Ibid., 92. The population figures of the two colonies were drawn from the 1685 Canadian census and a well-regarded history of New York, respectively.

103   Ibid., 96. In their first round of letters, Colonel Dongan noted his dissatisfac-
       tion with the departed French governor, La Barre, and with the machinations of
       the Jesuits. For his part, Denonville appealed to his rival's Catholic faith in his
       attempt to "come to an understanding" over the missionary attempts to convert
       the Indians.

103   Ibid., 99. Seething over the English agitation of the Iroquois, Denonville sug-
       gested to King Louis XIV that he buy the colony of New York, since the pur-
       chase "would make us masters of the Iroquois without a war."

103-7 Ibid., 106. After La Barre's failure, it was not a simple matter for Denonville
       to convince his Indian allies and even his own soldiers and bushrangers that he
       would attack the Iroquois. A pastoral mandate from the bishop and daily masses
       "for the downfall of the foes of Heaven and of France" convinced the army to
       muster and take the field.

104   Ibid., 107. The Indians who were with Denonville tortured the Iroquois captives
       at Fort Frontenac by puffing on their tobacco pipes until the ember began to
       glow, then jamming the fingers of the Iroquois into the red-hot bowl. The Iro-
       quois, believing this to be a harbinger of worse things to come, sang their death
       songs.

104   Ibid., 109. A large percentage of the 150 or more women and children held at
       Fort Frontenac along with the fifty-one captured warriors died from disease
       and distress. The escaped captive, besides warning his countrymen, helped save
       the life of the Jesuit missionary, Lamberville. When the Onondagas learned of
       Denonville's presence, they were convinced the priest had nothing to do with
       the planned attack and let him leave their village.

104   Ibid., 113. After six days of travel, Denonville and his men, occupying four
       hundred canoes and bateaux, approached the headlands of Irondequoit Bay just
       as another massive flotilla of canoes also arrived, bearing La Durantaye and his
       rangers and Indians.

104-5 Ibid., 114. On Irondequoit Bay, three Seneca warriors got as close as the edge
       of the tree line. They called to a converted Mohawk who was in the camp, ask-
       ing what the French intended to do. "To fight you, you blockheads," said the
       Mohawk.

104-5 Wilbur, 51. It would not have been considered treasonous for the Christian
       Mohawk to inform the Iroquois scouts that they were about to be attacked.
       Indian fighting traditions required that an attacking tribe forewarn an enemy.

105   Parkman, 115. Tramping alongside Denonville was the Chevalier de Vaudreuil.
       Recently arrived from France, Vaudreuil was assigned to command the eight
       hundred soldiers left behind to guard the colony, but not wishing to miss the
       campaign against the Iroquois, he had traveled alone to reach the army in time.

105-6 Ibid., 116. Though Denonville had trouble with his own men, the Christian
       Indians fought well, equaling or surpassing the Iroquois in their athleticism,
       ferocity, and determination at the battle of the gorge.

105-7 Ibid. Faced with such a bloody scene, Denonville was cool under fire and used
       his superior numbers to great advantage, routing the Seneca.

105–7   Ibid., 119. Historians later determined that the battle of the gorge took place near a town called Victor, and that the Seneca town, Gannagaro, was a mile and a half away on Boughton's Hill. Large amounts of charred corn and significant "quantities of Indian remains" were found there over a century after the battle occurred and for many decades thereafter.

106   Ibid. As was typical of the Indian fighting style, when the Iroquois ambushed the French vanguard they had a swampy area at their backs and dense trees from which to fire their rifles and muskets.

107   Ibid., 117. Denonville wrote in his journal that the Iroquois left twenty-seven of their dead behind, and carried off twenty more, as well as sixty warriors who were badly hurt. Some estimates of Indian losses were based on the number of freshly dug graves in the Iroquois cemetery the French encountered the next day.

107   Russell, 191–93. It's well documented that the tribes of the Iroquois League tortured their captives. Also interesting is the fact that the eastern Algonquin tribes used brutality against their enemies but did not employ systematic torture until after the Iroquois had begun invading New England.

107   Parkman, 118. After their assault on the Seneca, one of the Christian Indians remarked that the French were "good for nothing but to make war on hogs and corn."

107–8   Ibid. Denonville was troubled by the need to rely on his Indian allies. He wrote, "It is a miserable business to command savages, who, as soon as they have knocked an enemy in the head, ask for nothing but to go home and carry with them the scalp, which they take off like a skull-cap."

108   Ibid., 120. The most telling part of Dongan's instruction to the Iroquois was that they must unite with their enemies, the lake tribes, in order to drive the French out. Then the Iroquois and lake tribes alike were directed to bring all their beaver furs down to Albany.

108   Ibid., 121–22. Dongan was a lively correspondent, if not a stickler for grammar or standardized spelling. In another letter to Denonville, he wrote, "The King of China never goes anywhere without two Jesuits with him. I wonder you make not the like pretence to that Kingdom." Dongan also states that the natural boundaries insisted upon by the French are another questionable means of demarcation. "Your reason is that some rivers or rivoletts of this country run out into the great river of Canada. O just God! what new, farr-fetched, and unheard-of pretence is this for a title to a country. The French king may have as good a pretence to all those Countrys that drink clarett and Brandy."

108   Ibid., 125. The French soldiers at Fort Niagara were so depleted by illness and attacks that a large war party of Miami, who were friendly, had to man the stockade until a French relief column appeared.

108   Ibid., 127. Denonville knew that passing "through territory indisputably British" on his way to fight the Mohawks would be a violation of the treaty between the two governments; nevertheless, he asked Louis XIV to send him four thousand

soldiers to undertake this campaign. The king agreed that Denonville needed these troops but could not spare them.

108–9   Ibid., 129. Big Mouth realized that his negotiation with Denonville would have more force, and greater effect, if he was "at the head of an imposing force." The number of warriors was so large that the French officer charged with escorting Big Mouth to Montreal was frightened out of his wits.

109   Ibid. The Iroquois plan of attack included burning all the barns and grain depositories right after the harvest, threatening the entire colony with food shortages right as winter fell upon them.

109–10   Ibid., 130. Of the Rat, the noted French officer La Hontan wrote, "He is a gallant man, if ever there was one."

110   Ibid., 131. In his discussion with the commandant of Fort Frontenac, the Rat was clever enough to learn the route that the Iroquois delegation would take on their way to see Denonville.

110   Ibid. The Rat, after playing both sides of his deception, said to the captive Iroquois, "Go, my brothers. Go home to your people. Though there is war between us, I give you your liberty. Onontio has made me do so black a deed that I shall never be happy again till your five tribes take a just vengeance upon him."

110–12   Ibid., 135. Denonville and the troops garrisoned at Montreal were described as being in "mortal dread" of the Iroquois, who suffered very few casualties in several days of fighting.

111   Ibid., 132. Apparently, Kondiaronk was a good actor. When he told the elderly Iroquois warrior what the French soldiers had done to the Iroquois peace emissary who had been executed, the Rat was said to have adopted "a mournful air."

111   Ibid., 134. With his sword in hand, Subercase and his men were about to attack the Iroquois's drunken encampment near La Chine when a "voice from the rear" ordered him to retreat. It was the Chevalier de Vaudreuil, who had fought alongside Denonville in his campaign against the Seneca. He carried orders from the marquis that demanded his officers avoid risk and stay on the defensive.

112   Ibid. When the Iroquois tortured their prisoners, they were close enough to Fort Roland for the French to hear the agonized screaming of their friends, wives, parents, and children.

112–13   Ibid., 136. King James II was a staunch ally to France and a friend of Louis XIV.

113–14   Ibid., 145. Ourehaoue was allowed to send three of his warriors to Onondaga with a message from the Cayuga war chief that read, "The great Onontio, whom you all know, has come back again. He does not blame you for what you have done; for he looks upon you as foolish children, and blames only the English. . . . He will permit me, Ourehaoue, to return to you as soon as you will come to ask for me, not as you have spoken of late, but like children speaking to a father."

114–15   Ibid., 154. Frontenac wished to capitalize on the popularity of his return by striking a blow against his enemies. Since the Iroquois "seemed as invulnerable as ghosts," the French would instead mount three simultaneous campaigns against the English settlements.

114–15 Ibid., 173. Frontenac's strategy of the three war parties, besides their immediate effects, taught the Iroquois "that they could not safely rely on English aid."

115 Johnson, xix. The assault on the English settlement at Schenectady, New York, by the French war party in 1690 was one of the "two most notorious massacres of European settlers by Indians in the colonial Northeast." The other occurred at Deerfield, Massachusetts, in 1704.

115 Parkman, 169. As the French approached Casco Bay, a force of thirty English soldiers commanded by a green lieutenant named Thaddeus Clark sallied out to meet them. "A crowd of Indians" waited in ambush, killing them all except four men fast enough to run back to the fort.

115 Ibid., 178. Phips was experienced and courageous but "never gave proof of intellectual capacity," which certainly was a disadvantage in his contest with Frontenac.

116 Ibid., 267. In New France, "the settlers built their houses in lines, within supporting distance of each other, along the margin of a river which supplied easy transportation for troops." Ironically, the main part of the settlement in Haverhill, Massachusetts, was arranged this way, though it wasn't the case among the isolated farmhouses, most notably that of Thomas and Hannah Duston.

116 Ibid., 193. Bands of French militia followed the English fleet along the banks of the St. Lawrence, repelling them with "showers of bullets" whenever they tried to disembark.

116 Johnson, 65. In the mid and late seventeenth century, centers of population like Boston and Quebec would have large enough populations to support specialization in the trades. "A typical street would have taverns, rope makers, a barber shop, ship masters, merchants, joiners, stave dealers, shoemakers, blacksmiths, silversmiths, tanners, hatters, and apothecaries. . . ."

116 Parkman, 190. In addition to the twenty-seven hundred fighting men inside the fortifications, Quebec was bolstered by the "armed peasantry of Beauport and Beaupre, who were ordered to watch the river below the town, and resist the English, should they attempt to land."

117–18 Ibid., 194. Having conquered Port Royal without firing a shot, Phips thought he could do the same at Quebec, though looking up at the white banner emblazoned with the fleur-de-lis that hung from the Chateau St. Louis, "a suspicion seized him that the task he had undertaken was less easy than he had thought."

117 Ibid., 195. In his letter to Frontenac, Phips attempted to distinguish himself, and the English manner of fighting, from the "cruelties and barbarities" of the French and Indians.

117 Ibid., 177–78. Phips was believed to be one of twenty-six children born to the same mother in a primitive border settlement on the Kennebec. He was forty years old when his fleet invaded Quebec, and his previous adventures included quelling two mutinies aboard ship in the West Indies, one with his fists and the other with his cutlass. An energetic, adventurous man, he made a weak governor of Massachusetts, and it was said that he was appointed to that post only

because Increase and Cotton Mather, influential ministers who were father and son, thought they could manipulate him.

117–18 Ibid., 206. Phips's extensive cannonade, in particular, which killed only two or three people, was seen as "proof of divine intervention" on behalf of the French.

118   Ibid., 197. When Phips's officers asked their prisoner, a man named Granville, about the din arising from the Upper Town, the Frenchman replied, "It is the governor of Montreal with the people from the country above. There is nothing for you now but to pack and go home."

118   Ibid., 201. Baron La Hontan, an intrepid French officer present at the battle for Quebec, later wrote of the English ground troops, "They fought vigorously, though as ill-disciplined as men gathered together at random could be; for they did not lack courage, and, if they failed, it was by reason of their entire ignorance of discipline. . . ." In contrast, La Hontan expresses nothing but contempt for Phips's knowledge of tactics and preparedness.

118   Ibid., 204. Even before Phips decided to withdraw, the French were feeling a "pinch of famine" within the town's ramparts. The influx of soldiers and militia, though integral to winning the battle, had quickly used up Quebec's stores of meat and grain.

119   Ibid., 230. Upon receiving Louis XIV's letter praising him for defending the colony, Frontenac wrote to the king's minister Ponchartrain. Having passed the age of seventy, the royal governor noted his desire for a "post a little more secure and tranquil than the government of Canada."

119   Ibid., 185. When the Huron, Ottawa, Ojibwa, Pottawattamie, Cree, and Nipissing, along with the *coureurs de bois*, paddled down to Montreal with their beaver skins, the market value was estimated at 150,000 crowns. "The stream of wealth dammed back for so long was flowing upon the colony . . . when it was most needed. Never had Canada known a more prosperous fur trade than now in the midst of her danger and tribulation."

119   Ibid., 217. Although the payment of bounties on prisoners saved lives, the bounty on scalps more than compensated for it, since "the scalp of a Frenchman was not distinguishable from the scalp of an Englishman, and could be had with less trouble."

119–20 Ibid., 228. Frontenac called the attack on the Mohawk towns a "glorious success," but it was costly in munitions and morale. On the return trip, pursued by the English, they were forced to boil the moccasins of their dead comrades for food and several died of famine.

119   Ibid., 229. After Frontenac's victory over the Mohawks, two hundred canoes loaded with furs arrived in Montreal. These were hailed as "the last resource of the country" and were met with expressions of unbridled joy by the bankrupted merchants and farmers.

119   Dolin, 349. In a footnote, the author explains that the cross-border fighting disrupted the flow of furs during King William's War. "The Iroquois sided with the English and therefore were a prime target for the French, whose attacks resulted in a marked decrease in the amount of furs that the Indians brought to Albany."

120–21 Parkman, 234. One of Frontenac's spirited young officers, La Motte-Cadillac, wrote to a friend, "The winter passed very pleasantly, especially to the officers, who lived together like comrades; and, to contribute to their honest enjoyment, the count caused two plays to be acted, 'Nicodeme' and 'Mithridate'."

121 Ibid., 186. Frontenac was "half Indian at heart, as much at home in a wigwam as in the halls of princes."

121–22 Ibid., 296. Frontenac endured a trip of nearly a month to reach Onondaga and was sometimes so weakened by the ordeal that French soldiers carried him over the rugged ground in an armchair.

121–22 Ibid., 298. After finding Onondaga in ruins, Frontenac sent an officer named Vaudreuil and seven hundred men to the seat of the neighboring Oneidas to ensure their offer of peace was genuine. Vaudreuil and his men destroyed the Oneidas' maize fields and, per Frontenac's orders, took several chiefs as prisoners.

122 Ibid., 271. The author refers to the Jesuit Father Bigot who lived with the Kennebec Indians, and the seminary priest, Father Thury, who worked among the Penobscot, as "apostles of carnage" for their zeal for encouraging Indians' attacks on the English.

CHAPTER VI: THE TOMAHAWK AND THE KNIFE
Page

123 Parkman, 277–79. Duston's exploits are depicted as a keen example of "stubborn settlers" holding their ground against French brutality. Parkman also refers to Duston as "A Captive Amazon" in his chapter headnote.

123 Salisbury, 78. No doubt, Hannah Duston's constitution was adversely affected by the horror of captivity, and the physical shock of hard travel, especially in light of her recent childbirth. In her own recollections, former captive Mary Rowlandson wrote, "We came about the middle of the afternoon to this place; cold and wet, and snowy, and hungry, and weary, and no refreshing, for man, but the cold ground to sit on. . . . My head was light and dizzy (either through hunger or hard lodging, or trouble or all together) my knees feeble, my body raw by sitting double night and day, that I cannot express to man the affliction that lay upon my Spirit."

123–24 Bosman , 9. Chroniclers differed on how far Duston and the other captives were forced to travel, as well as how long it took. Mather wrote that Duston walked "an hundred and fifty miles, more or less, within a few days ensuing." Nathaniel Hawthorne called it a hundred miles. The poet and writer John Greenleaf Whittier, who lived in Haverhill, estimated the distance at between seventy and eighty miles. According to Todd (and my own travels between Haverhill and Hannah Duston Island, as it's now called, by car, and on foot, and on a bicycle), the historian and poet Robert Caverly was "probably the most correct" in saying that the "march lasted fifteen days, covered seventy-five miles and ended at the junction of the Contoocook and Merrimack Rivers."

123   Sprinkle, 43. Indians would circle back and murder any captive who fell behind. Mary Moore, who was taken by the Shawnee in Virginia in 1786, saw most of her family murdered during, and shortly after, a raid like the one the Dustons had endured in Massachusetts decades earlier. "John was a feeble lad, and finding him unable to bear the fatigue of the journey, at the rate they were traveling, he was suffered to fall behind with one of their number, on the second day. When out of sight of the company, his head was split with the tomahawk; and the bloody scalp hanging in the belt of him by whom he was murdered, told the mother what had been the fate of her son."

124   Salisbury, 106. Duston would have marveled at the things the Indians would eat in order to survive the journey. Rowlandson noted that their diet included, "Tortois, Frogs, Squirrels, Dogs, Skunks, Rattle-snakes; yea, the very Bark of Trees," and related the story of scalding old bones "to make the vermine come out."

124   Wilbur, 56. Deadfall traps, or culheags, were often heavy enough to crush a bear under its weight. The bait was arranged near the far end of the deadfall, resulting in a crushed skull for a large animal, but preserving the fur and flesh. In the months that he spent with the Abenaki, the captive Sam Lenorson would have seen the Indians use culheags, snares, deer drives, and other trapping methods for the purpose of killing game.

125   Salisbury, 93. After the brutality of her early captivity, Mary Rowlandson noted that the Indians relaxed their vigilance and occasionally shared food and a modicum of good will.

125   Salisbury, 70. Rowlandson writes, "The *Indians* laid hold of us, pulling me one way, and the Children another, and said, *Come go along with us*; I told them they would kill me: they answered, *If I were willing to go along with them, they would not hurt me.*"

125   Ibid., 83. Their unfamiliarity with the territory beyond the settlements was another reason English captives did not often try to escape. As Rowlandson noted, "I was utterly hopeless of getting home on foot, the way that I came. I could hardly bear to think of the many weary steps I had taken, to come to this place." Arriving at the Merrimack River made the decision to attempt an escape a logical one for Hannah Duston, as she knew it led back to Haverhill and the other settlements.

125–6   Ibid., 97–98. Rowlandson was often asked, including by a council of sagamores, how much money her husband would be willing to pay for her release. The bewildered captive was reluctant to name an amount the Indians would deem too small, lest they kill her and be done with it; she was also afraid to speak of a "great sum" because she "knew not where it would be procured." Rowlandson eventually settled on twenty pounds, which pleased her captors.

124   Sprinkle, 32. There is little doubt that the captives' austere early lives and deepseated piety were critical to their survival. Fourteen-year-old James Moore was taken captive by the Shawnee in 1784, two years before the other members of his family were either slain or taken captive by the same band of Indians. A monograph about James Moore's ordeal published by family members in 1854 could just as easily have been referring to Hannah Duston and her companions.

"During the time of this solitude he often engaged in prayer, and found much comfort in it. Few incidents show the value of early religious instruction more clearly than this does. The good seed had been sown by parental care, and now it bore fruit in circumstances where it was much needed."

125–26 Salisbury, 85. Rowlandson states that one Indian family that she resided with during her captivity included a kind squaw who gave her some food, and a warrior "who when he had found me (in their wigwam), kicked me all along." She was vexed by the Indians' changing moods.

125–26 Ibid., 87. Rowlandson's son was also a captive, though often not included with her party. When she inquired of an Indian where her son was staying, the warrior replied that his master had roasted the boy, and that he had eaten a piece of Rowlandson's son "as big as his two fingers." But Rowlandson wrote that "the Lord upheld my Spirit" in the face of this grim report, since she had already concluded that the Indians were addicted to lying. Duston was likewise subjected to the Abenaki's mean-spirited behavior and duplicity.

125–26 Ibid., 105. During Rowlandson's captivity, the Indians scoffed that "the *English* would be a quarter of a year getting ready" to pursue the captives into the wilderness.

126–27 Parkman, 111. Duston was right to be wary of the raiders throughout her captivity. The author writes, "They were of a race unsteady as aspens and fierce as wild-cats, full of mutual jealousies, without rulers, and without laws; for each was a law to himself."

126 Mather, 635. Duston's master and the other Indians in his party are described as idolaters and persecutors, who "would not endure that these poor women should retire to their English prayers, if they could hinder them."

126 Salisbury, 71. Rowlandson's master would often taunt her, saying that the Indians meant to kill her husband "as he came homeward." No doubt Hannah Duston's captors were irritated by Thomas Duston's heroic actions during the raid on Haverhill.

126 Mather, 636. Commenting specifically on Hannah Duston after interviewing her, Mather wrote, "Being where she had not her own life secured by any law unto her, she thought she was not forbidden by any law to take away the life of the murderers by whom her child had been butchered."

126 Whitford, 321. Whitford interprets Mather's comment in the previous note: "The context in which these words appear suggests that Hannah is not seeking vengeance but invoking the Old Testament law of 'an eye for an eye', which, for people who consciously formed their legal system upon Biblical law, represented not revenge but justice."

126 Bosman, 6. In his thoughtful introduction, Glenn Todd notes that Mather, cloaking his account of Duston's predicament in biblical allusions and "poetic shading," is intent on providing justification for her actions. As Todd writes, "a conclusion can be drawn: Even God's law, which states 'Vengeance is mine,' did not extend to the lawless frontier."

126 Parkman, 272. Jesuit priests taught the Christian Indians the rites of the Catholic Church, "but they left the savage a savage still."

126 Parkman, 180. Humility was not a virtue among New England puritans, and Hannah Duston would certainly have felt morally superior to the "papists and pagan idolaters," both French and Indian, who oppressed her.

126–27 Mather, 635. Bampico's occasional kindness toward the captives would prove his undoing, while providing them an opportunity to escape. Mather saw this as a sign of divine intervention on behalf of Duston and her surviving companions. "God . . . heard the sighs of these prisoners, and gave them to find unexpected favour from the master who hath laid claim unto them."

127 On March 23, 2014, accompanied by my friend, Chris Pierce, an expert paddler, I took a cold-water canoe trip from Hannah Duston Island, several miles downriver to Bow, New Hampshire. Not much about the island and surrounding environment, which is still quite rural, has changed since Duston took her trip and described it to Cotton Mather. The river, the island, and the conditions in late March were how I describe them in this and a subsequent chapter, and accurately reflect the conditions that Duston would have encountered. Chris Pierce and I took a second overnight canoe trip in late March 2015, again on the northern section of the Merrimack.

127 Approximately five river miles south of Sugar Ball Island, which is now referred to as Hannah Duston Island, there's a natural ford known as Sewall's Falls, with a dense pine forest lining both adjacent banks. During an uncomfortable canoe trip downriver from the island on March 23, 2014, when the water was at its highest flow rate of the year, I made a note that the water at the ford was only a couple of feet deep, making it the only shallow crossing we would encounter all day.

127–40 Bruchac, 2. The place where Duston and her companions ended up, which included Sugar Ball Island, was Pennacook territory. The author described Pennacook as an Abenaki word meaning "place of ground-nuts."

127–28 Salisbury, 94. The Indians, proud of their athleticism and familiar with the wilderness, mocked Rowlandson as she attempted to ford the Baquag River: *"the water was up to the knees, and the stream very swift, and so cold that I thought it would have cut me in sunder. I was so weak and feeble, that I reeled as I went along, and thought there I shall end my dayes at last, after my bearing and getting through so many difficulties; the Indians stood laughing to see me staggering along: but in my distress the Lord gave me experience of the truth, and goodness of that promise, Isai. 43. 2. When though passeth through the Waters, I shall be with thee, and through the Rivers, they shall not overflow thee."*

128 Russell, 94. The Indians could fast for days, while maintaining a swift pace along the trail. Mary Rowlandson marveled at their ability to survive on the move in harsh conditions, and no doubt Hannah Duston felt the same way.

128 Howe and Mack, 15. It was common to find meadows in remote hunting regions, even among dense timber, which the author describes as "an occasional spot burned over by fires set by the Indians. The meadows were, many of them,

cleared and covered, with a tall and dense growth of grass. The Indians were accustomed to burn the grass in the fall, that they might more easily catch the deer resorting to them to feed on the young grass in the spring."

129–31 Russell, 162. The writer quotes a Jesuit missionary named Le Jeune, in *Jesuit Relations*: "Let us say with compassion that they pass their lives in smoke, and at their death fall into the fire."

129 Caverly, 18. The surviving captives from the Haverhill raid were separated into two groups as they approached Sugar Ball Island: "before they reached the island, the tribe divided into two parts: the one with several captives (among whom was Hannah Bradley, whose brief biography will appear on a subsequent page) continued still farther onward to another place; while the other company, with Mrs. Duston, Neff, and Samuel, crossed over in their birch canoes, to dwell, at least for a night, on the island between the safe surroundings at the junction of these two beautiful rivers."

129 Chase, 308–9. Evidence that Haverhill captive Hannah Bradley accompanied Duston, Neff, and Lenorson as far as Sugar Ball Island (before continuing on with a different group of Indians) is provided by a deposition, filed on behalf of Mary Neff. In 1738, the aged Neff, like Bradley and Duston before her, wished to acquire land from the General Court of Massachusetts in recognition of her feats against the Indians. In support of Neff's petition, Bradley wrote, "The deposition of the Widow Hannah Bradly of Haverhill of full age who testifieth & saith that about forty years past the said Hannah together with the widow Mary Neff were taken prisoners by the Indians & carried together into captivity, *& above penny cook the Deponent was by the Indians forced to travel farther than the rest of the Captives.* . . ." (My italics.) After her petition was accepted, Hannah Bradley was granted "two hundred and fifty acres of land . . . located in Methuen." (At the time of Bradley, Neff, Lenorson, and Duston's captivity, Methuen was part of Haverhill. It was incorporated as a separate town in 1726.) Neff's petition resulted in a grant of two hundred acres of land.

129 Mather, 636. Duston must have told Mather that she had been planning her revenge and escape for some time before an opportunity presented itself. As they gained Sugar Ball Island, Mather writes, "[Duston] heartened the nurse and the youth to assist her in this enterprize."

130 Russell, 195. The birch bark canoe was the New England Indians' "crowning achievement of handiwork," especially considering that the tribes did not employ any "wheeled vehicle" or "beast of burden." Separating the single, twenty-foot strip of bark from the tree without puncturing or scoring it was the first step. The finished canoe, caulked tightly with natural resins and sewn with tamarack root, weighed as little as sixty pounds and easily carried four grown men.

130 Wilbur, 64–67. Stands of fine paper birch in Maine and New Hampshire were often referred to as "canoe birch." The construction of a single canoe was a meticulous process that involved several people, resulting in a durable vessel that could last for decades.

130   Russell, 102. Warriors often traveled great distances to find a suitably large birch tree, skinning the bark off during the spring thaw. The women of the tribe did the "sewing, caulking, and pitching the bark and shaping it to the ribs."

130–31 Pendergast, 36. Early historian William Little stated that some canoes weighed as little as forty pounds, could be portaged around falls and rapids, and could safely carry five warriors.

130   Chase, 13. Peter Pattee, or Pettee, as he was also called, was a colorful character in Haverhill's early days. He was refused official recognition as an inhabitant of the town on several occasions, beginning in 1676. Apparently, Pattee was sent up before the local court "for being absent from his wife for several years," as well as "for having another wife in Virginia." Despite these travails, Pattee was named a Haverhill constable in 1680 and was listed as the operator of "Pattee's Ferry" in Haverhill as late as 1710.

130   Ibid., 110. Ferry rates were "three pence an horse, and a penny a man." Ministers were allowed to ride for free, and those coming to worship on the sabbath were also allowed free passage, according to Haverhill records from the latter part of the seventeenth century.

132   I visited Hannah Duston Island, now connected to the mainland by a railroad bridge, and home to one of the two statues commemorating Duston and her feats, several times in 2013, 2014, and 2015, including in late March, when Duston engineered her escape. The island has been described as containing as few as two acres and as many as four. When I walked around the island and made notes on March 23rd and 29th, I estimated the size of the island as a little over two acres. It was nearly covered in snow at that time, with very little under-growth and sparse oak, fir and hemlock trees. One can survey the entire island from any spot on it, and in late March it was covered in snow and lacking in any dense trees or other concealment. Returning in late June, when the water was very low, the island appeared to have doubled in size and was covered in such dense undergrowth that I couldn't pass through it without a cutting tool.

132–33 Salisbury, 92. Rowlandson noted that in foul weather, the Indians "quickly got up a Bark Wigwam." The fact that Duston and her companions were able to dispatch five adult Indians and five children with very little resistance meant that their victims must have been in close proximity to one another, most likely crowded into a hastily erected shelter like the one I describe.

133–34 Lawson, 86. In July 1784, historian Francis Belknap undertook an expedition to the Great Mountain (later named Mount Washington) with several others, including Captain John Evans, an explorer, hunter, trapper, expert backwoods-man, and former colleague of Major Robert Rogers. In Belknap's account, Evans quickly constructs a shelter like the one described here. Rogers, who gained international renown as an Indian fighter, guerilla, and commander of Rogers' Rangers, was born in Methuen (then part of Haverhill) in 1721. Rogers' rang-ers, and certainly his officers, learned their woodcraft from the man himself, and there's little doubt that Rogers learned his from the Indians of the Merrimack Valley.

134   Russell, 165. Once the captives were brought to Sugar Ball Island, their diets may have improved, however slightly. The author notes that "From late March to mid-April comes the month called 'Namossack Kesos, the time of catching fish,' before field work commences."

134–36 Bruchac, 4. Duston and her companions probably benefited from their captors being in a relaxed state upon reaching Sugar Ball Island. This pattern occurred on other occasions during the long series of wars between the two frontiers. On October 1, 1759, Robert Rogers and a contingent of his rangers conducted an infamously bloody raid against an Abenaki village located on a bluff overlooking the St. Francis River in French Canada. They had been sent there by General Jeffrey Amherst, at least in part to punish the Indians for their harassment of the English frontier, which had gone on for decades. Rogers later wrote that his men were able to infiltrate the village just prior to daylight, since the Indians had exhausted themselves "in a high frolic or dance" earlier that night. Having reached Sugar Ball Island, an Indian stronghold since the time of Passaconaway, who used it as a summer residence, the Abenaki would certainly have let their guard down, providing Duston and her companions the opportunity they had been waiting for.

135   Sprinkle, 29. When James Moore was taken captive in Virginia, the Indians nearly starved along with their prisoner. "In this condition, they resorted to an expedient for relieving the cravings of hunger which dire necessity had taught the savage. They took the inner bark of the yellow poplar from near the root, boiled it, and drank the decoction with evident benefit."

135   Salisbury, 87. When Rowlandson was being held captive and deigned to sit by the Indians' fire, a squaw took offense to her boldness: "In this place, on a cold night, as I lay by the fire, I removed a stick that kept the heat from me, a *Squaw* moved it down again, at which I lookt up, and she threw a handfull of ashes in mine eyes; I thought I should have been quite blinded."

135–36 Ibid., 104. Rowlandson recalled being in her master's village when the Indians were drinking liquor, singing, hopping about, "and knocking on a Kettle for their musick." Later that night, her master vacillated on his promise to sell Rowlandson back to the English, frightening her greatly. It was her first experience with a drunken Indian, and Rowlandson was so vexed she didn't sleep for the next three nights. Parkman notes that the Abenaki were often paid with brandy, and the Jesuits were complicit in keeping the Indians supplied with liquor.

136   Johnson, 91. Under the conditions they found themselves in, Duston and the others would have clothed themselves in whatever the Indians discarded upon killing some of the other captives. Johnson describes the "five layers" of clothing that a woman usually wore, and it is very likely Duston shed some of these to give her arm free play, before assaulting her captors.

136–40 Todd, 7. Hannah Duston's feats were celebrated in her lifetime, and it wasn't until a century had passed that her actions on Sugar Ball Island became subject to intense moral scrutiny. As time passed, chroniclers including "the historians—all men—have, like Nathaniel Hawthorne, tended to expand Thomas Duston's role and denigrate Hannah," writes Todd.

136–40 Whitford, 323. Taken in its entirety, and considering the separate experiences of Hannah and Thomas Duston, the saga "came to epitomize the two commonest border stories—one, that of Indian captivity and deliverance, the other, that of the successful defense of family and fort. Had [Hannah's and Thomas's] roles been reversed, their story might never have attracted more than local attention." However, up to, and including, the nineteenth century, "as the role of woman and mother was softened and sentimentalized . . . Hannah became an increasingly embarrassing national heroine."

136–40 Bosman , 9. In his introduction, Todd notes that Hannah Duston never became as familiar as Daniel Boone, Davy Crockett, or Pocahontas when it came to folk heroes. Never completely forgotten, Duston was eventually replaced in the pantheon of American heroines by "less troublesome, newer names, like Belle Starr, Boxcar Bertha, and Bonnie Parker . . . when an example was needed of a woman who could not be contained by the cultural limitations of her sex. Hannah with her hatchet embarrasses, an overkill that elicits a facetious tone from commentators, much like the voice of Hawthorne."

137 Johnson, 67. A woman in colonial New England "was allowed to do almost any work her husband did." Given her frontier circumstances and large family, there's little doubt that Hannah Duston was physically strong, mentally tough, and spiritually resolute. Early images of Duston, including the two statues erected in her honor, depict her as a tall, powerfully built woman (though no portrait or other representation of what she actually looked like has ever been discovered).

137 Salisbury, 101. Duston must have gotten some satisfaction from her resolve to strike back against the Indians. Rowlandson writes of the Indians, "They made use of their tyrannical power whilst they had it: but through the Lord's wonderful mercy, their time was now but short."

137 Bailey, 21. The author transcribes one of the four known contemporary accounts of Hannah Duston's ordeal, recorded in the diary of colonist John Marshall. In it, there is strong evidence that the Indian who murdered Duston's infant by smashing her head against the tree was the first Indian she killed: "The chief of these Indians took one of the women captive when she had lain in childbed but a few days, and knocked her child in (the) head before her eyes, *which woman killed and scalped that very Indian.*"

137–38 In an exchange of e-mails, I described the assault upon the Indians by Duston, Neff, and Lenorson to Aloke K. Mandal of Los Angeles, California, MD, PhD, whose expertise is in general surgery, surgical oncology, transplantation surgery, trauma surgery, and critical care. Dr. Mandal is board certified by the American Board of Surgery. Here is an edited version of that exchange:

> Atkinson: *Would striking the human skull in that place with that sort of force make a sharp sound, a dull thud, etc.?*
>
> Dr. Mandal: *The best way I would describe it would be a "muffled crack." I don't know if you ever have heard someone getting hit by a car, it is a "dull thud," but there is something ominous to it. With broken bones during*

a youth rugby match, I hear a dull thud, while standing by the touchline, but those around it say they hear a crack when a bone has been broken. If you need to imagine how it might sound, try banging a ball peen (i.e., the hatchet), against the following layers: a folded wet towel (skin/soft tissue), over a 1/4" plywood (skull), on top of a half a cantaloupe (brain). The melon would provide the same dampening effect as the brain would. So, you'd definitely hear a sharp sound, but it would be dampened. The skull is spherical, which has implications on the force required to crack it. The "average" man can exert 900 pounds of force with a 5 lb. ball peen (i.e., hatchet), which is in the range of force for being able to cause a skull fracture. So, there definitely would be some sort of muffled crack—think of a dull thud with just a bit of a cracking noise. That would be for an adult skull with the skull thick and the suture lines ossified. There would be more of a muffled thud and no cracking noise with the infant's.

Atkinson: *Struck swiftly without warning, would the victims have emitted any involuntary cries or groans, or any other noise?*

Dr. Mandal: *There is something called agonal breathing or agonal gasps. We usually see that after cardiac arrests and a deep breath. Some time you get very shallow breathing movements but no gas exchange.*

Atkinson: *Would there be an abundance of blood? If so, from where: the wound site, or eyes, ears, mouth, etc.?*

Dr. Mandal: *I think from the above, we can surmise that there would have been a skull fracture. In which case, there would be clear fluid (cerebrospinal fluid) most likely mixed with blood (shearing forces to the central veins—dark red blood—or direct impact to the side of the head which ruptures the middle cerebral artery— bright red blood) coming from the nose and ear.*

137–40 Mather, 636. Duston gave her account of what occurred on Sugar Ball island directly to Cotton Mather, and he was clear in expressing it, though he added a biblical justification for what, many years later, became a controversial subject: "While they were yet, it may be, about an hundred and fifty miles from the Indian town, a little before break of day, when the whole crew was in a dead sleep, (reader, see if it prove not so!) one of these women took up a resolution to imitate the action of Gael upon Siberia; and being where she had not her own life secured by any law unto her, she thought she was not forbidden by any law to take away the life of the murderers by whom her child had been butchered. She heartened the nurse and the youth to assist her . . . and all furnishing themselves with hatchets for this purpose, they struck such home blows upon the heads of their sleeping oppressors, that ere they could any of them struggle into any effectual resistance, 'at the feet of these poor prisoners, they bow'd, they fell, they lay down; at their feet they bow'd, they fell; where they bow'd, there they fell down dead.'"

137 My exploration of the island, Mather's account, and Dr. Mandal's notes on the method by which Duston and her companions killed their captors, makes it

plain that an initial assault on the two warriors made the most sense, and that the disturbance caused by that would have scattered the other Indians. But there was nowhere to go and no place to hide, and the massacre of the women and children would by necessity have been systematic and bloody.

137–40 Caverly, 390. During a speech that Robert B. Caverly gave at the dedication of the Hannah Duston statue on "the island Contoocook" on June 17, 1874, the historian and poet stated that, in the nasty border war between the French and the Indians on one side, and the English settlers on the other, "there were blows to take, as well as blows to give." Caverly added that, by capturing Hannah Duston, the Abenaki "'had been waking up the wrong passenger.'"

137–40 Todd, 5. Captivity narratives were immensely popular in colonial America. Cotton Mather, who heard it directly from the source, published three versions of Hannah Duston's story, including *Humiliations followed by Deliverances* (1697); *Decennium Luctuosum* (1699); and in his ecclesiastical history of New England called *Magnalia Christi Americana* (1702). Mather's *Good Fetch'd Out of Evil: A Collection of Memorables Relating to Our Captives*, which was published in 1706 and included the Duston story, sold one thousand copies in the first week after its printing.

137–40 Bailey, 27. After an initial period when Hannah Duston was celebrated for what she did on Sugar Ball Island, historians and other commentators began questioning whether it was necessary to kill the women and children who were present. The author, a direct descendant of Duston, notes that "even Cotton Mather in his earliest accounts seemed to wrestle with moral justification of the killings. The truth is that three centuries later we do not have enough facts and cannot know the actual situation in which the captives found themselves and the fear they probably had for their own survival." Bailey goes on to postulate that the children on the island "were at least teen agers" who may have taken part in the abduction and torture of these, or other, English settlers. Calling the Abenaki slavers and mercenaries, Bailey notes that the Indians weren't protecting their homes or livelihood. "As a descendant, I would like to believe that my 8th great grandmother's actions were justified, but I must conclude we cannot know for certainty if this was the case as we do not have enough genuine facts about the actual circumstances to be the final moral judges."

138 Mather, 636. Mather's account of what Hannah Duston had told him addresses the notion that one of the Indian children was spared intentionally: "Only one squaw escaped, sorely wounded, from them in the dark; and one boy, whom they reserved asleep, intending to bring him away with them, suddenly waked, and scuttled away from this desolation." The notion that the former captives would spirit away a prisoner of their own makes sense for several reasons: a boy would be easier to manage on the return journey than a captive warrior or squaw; he spoke the language of the other Indians in the vicinity and might be useful in that regard; Sam Lenorson spoke at least a modicum of the Abenaki language and could talk with the Indian boy; the Indian boy, in turn, could be ransomed back to his own people, or perhaps traded for an English captive. The Indian boy, who was an eyewitness of what occurred on the island, would

serve as proof that Duston's story was true, should they make it back to the settlements.

138–39 Chase, 308. Hannah Bradley's 1738 deposition in favor of Mary Neff's petition for a grant of land from the General Court of Massachusetts offers additional key facts in support of what actually occurred on Sugar Ball Island. After Bradley was separated from Duston, Neff, and Lenorson, she was taken to an Indian village or encampment that must have been fairly close to where her fellow settlers were being held: "The next night but one there came to us one Squaw who said that Hannah Dustan [sic] and the aforesaid Mary Neff assisted in killing the Indians of her wigwam except herself and a boy, herself escaping very narrowly, shewing to myself & others seven wounds as she said with a Hatched on her head which wounds were given her when the rest were killed, and further saith not."

139 Caverly, 21. Hannah Duston's son, Nathaniel, was born May 16, 1685, and would have been twelve years old at the time of the Haverhill raid. He was one of Hannah and Thomas Duston's thirteen children (including Lydia, who was born in 1698), three of whom died young, before the raid.

140 Chase, 190. In a footnote, the author states, "After performing the bloody work, Mrs. Duston gathered up what little provisions there were in the wigwam,—taking the gun of her dead master, and the tomahawk with which she killed him—and, scuttling all the canoes except one, she embarked in that, with Mrs. Neff, and Lennardson, on the waters of the Merrimack, to seek their way to Haverhill."

140 Chase, 191. According to Chase, the gun that Duston took from her dead master "continued in possession of the male line [of Dustons] to the year 1859, when it was presented to the *Duston Monument Association* of this town [Haverhill, MA]. At that time, the gun was the property of Mrs. Lucia H. Dustin, widow of Thomas Dustin, of Henniker, NH." The author's "disinterested efforts to procure the musket for the association" were recognized on July 9th, 1859, and Chase includes a partial transcript of the minutes of that meeting.

CHAPTER VII: THE FATE OF OTHER CAPTIVES
Page

141–67 Peters, 80. Among the most striking revelations provided in Peters's genealogical look at her family history (which can be perused in the Haverhill Public Library Special Collections room) is the assertion that the first complete history of Haverhill, which contains some of the earliest and most detailed accounts of both Hannah Duston and Hannah Bradley's captivity among the Indians, was actually written by a more famous author than the otherwise unknown B. L. Mirick. Peters contends that *The History of Haverhill*, which was published in Haverhill in 1832, and which is known as Mirick's, was compiled by John Greenleaf Whittier; upon his leaving Haverhill he placed his work in the hands of his friend and assistant, Mirick, who shortly after published the work in his own name, giving Whittier no credit whatever. "When Whittier heard of this dishonest transaction he caused an announcement to be printed several times in the then Haverhill newspaper giving a true account of the case: the compiler has seen a copy of this announcement." Whittier (1807–1892), the Quaker poet and writer, was perhaps Haverhill's most famous resident. The author of the epic poem, *Snow-Bound*, Whittier wrote about Hannah Duston in his first book, *Legends of New-England in Prose and Verse* (1831), which includes a version of the Duston story entitled "The Mother's Revenge." In his excellent introduction to Richard Bosman's illustrated book, *Captivity Narrative of Hannah Duston*, Glenn Todd writes that Whittier "transformed Hannah (Duston) from a rude seventeenth-century settler to a temporarily insane, saintlike mother—a figure in keeping with attitudes toward women in the nineteenth century." The John Greenleaf Whittier birthplace, which houses a curator/caretaker as well as a great deal of furniture and other items from Whittier's lifetime, is a popular historical destination in Haverhill.

141–67 Chase, 180. Chase quotes directly and extensively from Mirick's account of Hannah Bradley and Hannah Duston's captivity experiences. Since the only copy of the Mirick book available to the public (in the Haverhill Public Library Special Collections room) is quite fragile, I often used Chase's transcription to quote Mirick to avoid further damaging the book. At intervals, I cross checked against the original 1832 Mirick text to make sure the Chase book was faithful and it was.

141 Bailey, 26. Hannah Bradley, originally Hannah Heath, the daughter of John and Sarah (Partridge) Heath, was born in Haverhill, Massachusetts, on May 3, 1673. Hannah Heath was married to Joseph Bradley (1664–1727) on April 14, 1691 in Haverhill. John Heath Jr., Hannah Heath's younger brother, was the eighth great-grandfather of Chris Bailey, the author of the unpublished book-length manuscript, *Dustons & Dustins in America*, which I reference here. Bailey, a retired museum curator now living in Florida, is also a direct descendant of Thomas and Hannah Duston.

141–42 Ibid. On June 23, 1739, just over a year after Hannah Duston's death, Hannah Bradley referenced the events in this chapter in a deposition she gave to Joshua Bayley, Justice of the Peace in Haverhill. In her statement, Bradley attests that she was in the party of settlers that included Hannah Duston and Mary Neff, who "were taken prisoners by the Indians and carried together into captivity above penny cook (now Concord, NH), the Deponent who was by the Indians forced to travel further than the rest of the Captives and the next night but one there came to us one squaw who said that Hannah Duston and the aforesaid Mary Neff assisted in killing the Indians of her wigwam except, her self and a boy, her self escaping very narrowly. Shewing to my self and others seven wounds as she said with a Jatchet on her head which wounds were given her when the rest were killed and further saith not."

141–42 Ibid. The escaped squaw who Hannah Bradley mentioned in her deposition was seriously wounded; therefore, the Indians who took Bradley must have been fairly close to Sugar Ball Island when the squaw caught up with them.

141–42 Russell, 37. More often than not, the "medicine men" among the Indians were actually elderly, or older, women steeped in medical lore that had been "passed down in the family from grandmother to mother to daughter and kept private."

141–42 Ibid., 36. The Indians used spider's web, prince's pine, and the wool of rattle-snake weed, all commonly available, as styptics to staunch bleeding.

143 Chase, 179. The Bradleys lived "near the northerly brook" and the Whittakers lived "due west from Bradley's," which places them in the same remote part of town as the Dustons, just west of Little River.

143 Ibid. A "Doctr Bradstreet" received compensation from the town for the care he provided two children of Abraham Whittaker injured in the 1695 raid on Haverhill.

143 Ibid. Joseph Whittaker and Isaac Bradley were laboring in "open fields" near the Bradley house and were easy targets for the prowling Abenaki.

143–49 Fuess, 143. The editors state that Bradley and Whittaker's Indian masters on Lake Winnipesaukee "treated them kindly and taught them the native language," although it's clear the boys were taken captive by force and used as laborers.

143 Russell, 143. Ancient Indian corn fields, often arranged in small "hills," were discovered throughout New England, including on the shores of Lake Winnipesaukee.

143 Ibid., 125. The Indians constructed stone weirs at the outlet of Lake Winnipesaukee, which is now the site of Weirs Beach, a popular boating and tourist destination.

143 Ibid., 163. When the shad or herring were running, as many as one hundred Indians rushed to the weirs to spear or dip out the fish, empty the wicker baskets, and begin curing the catch on smoldering fires.

143 Belknap, Vol. I, 67. "In their (the Indians') capital fifhing (fishing) places, particularly in great Offapy and Winipifeogee rivers, are the remains of their wears, conftructed (constructed) with very large ftones (stones)."

144 Chase, 180. Isaac Bradley knew from conversations that his master often had with a neighboring family that the Indians meant to take the captives northward and ransom them at a French village or garrison. Once they left the shores of Winnipesaukee, their chances of escaping to Haverhill would be greatly diminished.

144 Russell, 180. In this region, hunting on snowshoes continued all winter, when the depth of the snow made it easier to track moose and deer, and more difficult for them to run away when spotted.

144 Ibid., 37. Indian women collected the herbs, leaves, twigs, buds and other supplies for their curatives well in advance, dried them, and stored the medicines for future use.

145–52 Chase, 180. While a captive of the Indians at Winnipesaukee, Isaac Bradley feared that "a deep and unbroken wilderness, pathless mountains, and swollen and almost impassable rivers, lay between them and [Haverhill]." Going on to Canada would make their return almost impossible.

145   Mirick, 80. Isaac Bradley waited until the day he meant to escape to tell Joseph Whittaker, saying, "I'm afraid you won't wake."

146   Ibid. The night of his attempted escape, Isaac Bradley must have been discouraged when Joseph Whittaker began to "snore lustily" and then refused to get up when Bradley tried to rouse him.

146   Ibid. Bradley's departure from the wigwam must have been carefully thought out, as he was able to remove some provisions only by stepping over his master and the other Indians.

146–48 Wilbur, 57. Early European visitors to the New World thought that Indian dogs were tame foxes or coyotes. The Indians used dogs for hunting, to rid the camp of mice and garbage, to warn of intruders, and as an emergency food supply.

146   Chase, 181. Joseph Whittaker's loud, abrupt reaction to being woken up in the wigwam was an "egregious blunder," according to Chase.

146   Ibid. It appears that Isaac Bradley, more frightened than ever, planned to abandon his sleeping friend, before Whittaker followed him from the wigwam the second time.

146–48 Russell, 56. The dogs used by the Indians "were likely to be slim, with foxlike heads and the look of a wolf." They were "extremely sagacious," and would obey hand signals and low-voiced commands from their masters. They were especially useful in running down moose or deer, and so light they could stay above the crust of the snow when hunting.

147–48 Mirick, 81. When the boys' Indian master woke in the pre-dawn hour, he "was astonished to find his prisoners had escaped, and immediately collected a small party with their dogs, and pursued them." It did not take the dogs long to come upon the boys, who had concealed themselves in a hollow tree.

148   Chase, 181–82. The Indians did not notice "the employment of their dogs" until they had passed by the hollow log, which was key to the boys remaining undetected.

149   Ibid., 182. Isaac Bradley and Joseph Whittaker "lay in the log during the day, and at night pursued their journey, taking a different route from the one travelled by the Indians."

149   Ibid. Bradley and Whittaker stayed hidden throughout the second day, but thereafter traveled day and night toward Haverhill. At this point they were "obliged to subsist on roots and buds."

149–50 Ibid. After killing the pigeon and turtle, they carried the leftover "fragments of their unsavory meal" for further sustenance on the trail, adding some groundnuts and lily roots to their stores.

150   Ibid. Deeply alarmed, Bradley and Whittaker fled the Indian camp and spent the entire night backtracking to where they had been the day before. At the end of this trek, they were bruised, disconsolate, and bloody.

151   Ibid., 183. Bradley could not convince Joseph Whittaker to accompany him and left him beside the stream and continued on. Later he admitted his despair over the decision.

151-52 Ibid. Isaac Bradley carried Joseph Whittaker on his back at least part of the way to the fort at Saco, Maine.

152   Ibid. Upon returning to Haverhill, Isaac Bradley told Joseph Whittaker's father about his son's condition and whereabouts and the elder Whittaker made the trip to Saco to bring young Joe home.

152   Giorgi, 11. The author, a Heath-Bradley descendant, agrees with Bailey and others that Hannah (Heath) Bradley was born on May 3, 1673 in Haverhill, Massachusetts, and died there on November 2, 1761. Hannah married Joseph Bradley in Haverhill, on April 14, 1691.

152   Bailey, 26. Between 1691 and 1717, Joseph and Hannah Bradley had eleven children, all of whom were born in Haverhill.

153–54 Lawson, 22. The Indians' northern route through the White Mountains, which they used to take their captives to Quebec, ran through dense forest along the traces that paralleled local streams and rivers.

154   Beals, 49. The Indians would hunt and trap in the mountain passes, but seldom ascended the highest peaks, especially Agiocochook, which they held in great regard as the earthly home of the Great Spirit.

154   Ibid., 50–51. Describing Passaconaway's mythical journey to the summit of Agiocochook, the author reprints "some stanzas from an old poem, 'The Winter Evening,'"

"A wondrous wight! For o'er 'Siogee's ice,
With brindled wolves all harnessed three and three,
High seated on a sledge, made in a trice,
On Mount Agiocochook, of hickory,
He lashed and reeled, and sung right jollily;
And once upon a car of flaming fire,
The dreadful Indian shook with fear to see
The king of Pennacook, his chief, his sire,
Ride flaming up towards heaven, than any mountain higher."

154   Ibid., 49–50. Passaconaway was believed to have "screamed with ecstatic joy" as he flew over the shoulders of Agiocochook (later called Mount Washington): "Fitting finale was this to the life of a kingly and prophetic man, and as well deserved was his triumphant translation as was the reputed one of the prophet Elijah."

154   Heath, 238. Along with Parkman, Caverly, Chase, and many other commentators, the authors note that the Indians rarely, if ever, abused their female captives. This was done as much for reasons of commerce, as on moral grounds, if such grounds existed in this conflict. "If the women were physically or sexually abused by the Indians, the French would not pay as much, as for the not abused."

155   Giorgi, 11. Hannah Bradley's two young children were killed in the March 15, 1697 raid, where she and Hannah Duston, Duston's infant Martha, and Mary Neff were taken captive. Joseph Bradley (Jr.) was born March 9, 1692, and was seven years old when he was killed. Hannah Bradley's daughter, also named Martha, was born September 3, 1695, and was just two years old when she was killed, most likely just a few minutes before the infant Martha Duston was murdered by the same Indians.

155–67   Ibid. The author, a direct descendant of Hannah (Heath) Bradley, writes, "The Bradley and Heath families suffered much from the Indians."

156   Parkman, 387. In Reverend John Williams' account of his captivity after the 1704 Abenaki raid on Deerfield, Massachusetts, which shares many of the characteristics of the assault on Haverhill just a few years earlier, he wrote of being given snowshoes as they approached Quebec and made to run in them. This caused Williams serious discomfort, but the Indians were afraid that an early thaw would make river crossings extremely perilous.

156   Russell, 36. Wintergreen contained aspirin and, along with pyrola weed, was a common Indian remedy for muscle and joint pain.

156   Bruchac, 2. The Abenaki called the St. Francis River both "Arsikantegout," which means "empty cabin place," as well as "Alsigontekw," or "place of shells." The names stem from a 1691 Mohawk attack, and a plague that occurred there in 1700, respectively.

156–57   Ibid., 1. "Town histories depict the Abenaki as violent foreign marauders, who attacked for no reason, conveniently forgetting to mention the broken treaties and boundary violations of English settlers in Abenaki territory."

157   Ibid., 2. Many of the so-called mission villages in Canada, where converted Indians fell under the dominion of French priests, were arranged around a central square, and included the council house and a stone church.

157   Parkman, 388. Since the mission of the Jesuits who were living among the Indians included converting nonbelievers into Catholics, the French priests would insist that English captives observe the rites and rituals of the church.

157   Bailey, 26. Hannah Bradley was released from her captivity near present-day Portland, Maine, ten months after she was taken from Haverhill.

157   Peters, 60. At the close of her first captivity, Hannah Bradley was taken to Casco Bay (now Portland) in Maine aboard an English ship called the *Province Galley*. The author quotes the journal of Captain Phillips, from the Mass. Archives: "The names of the Captives Rec'd at board the Province Galley from the Indians No 5 Hannah Bradley of Haverhill." Apparently, Joseph Bradley booked passage on the same ship, from Montreal to Boston, on the conclusion of her second captivity in 1705.

157   Ibid., 56. Mehitable was the only child of Joseph and Hannah Bradley who survived the March 15, 1697 raid on Haverhill. They would eventually have eight more children, though the Indians would murder two of them, Sarah and an unnamed infant, during Hannah's second captivity.

157–58 Slots that resembled a mailbox door were created in the wall beside the chimneys in most garrison houses. People taking refuge learned to first put out their own cook fires, which prevented attacking Indians from using embers from the fireplace to burn down their houses. After the raid was over, neighbors departing the garrison would pick up a burning coal from the pile that had been deposited through the slot, allowing them to restart their fires when they returned home.

157–58 Parkman, 268. Garrison houses were typically built of solid timbers, not just planks, and constructed with help from men living within a mile's radius or more, since they would all gather there in times of trouble.

158 Ibid., 365. The attack on Wells occurred on August 10, 1703, when "Thirty-nine in all, chiefly women and children, were killed or carried off, and then the Indians disappeared as quickly and silently as they had come, leaving many of the houses in flames."

158 Ibid., 367. One of the objects of these raids was to keep the English settlements from pushing farther north, certainly, but also to keep the Abenaki engaged in defending what the French saw as the boundary between the land they claimed, which was a vast parcel, and the little strip along the northeastern seaboard occupied by the English.

158 Ibid., 368. In addition to raids on Casco, Wells, and other nearby settlements in the late summer and fall of 1703, small parties of warriors, acting as individual units, created havoc along a two-hundred-mile stretch of the frontier, killing and scalping women, burning a prisoner alive, and taking captives in Black Point, Berwick, Hampton, and York.

158 Penhallow, 23. Prior to assaulting Joseph Bradley's garrison in Haverhill, the Abenaki raiders had been involved in a bloody fight with the militia at Berwick, Maine, led by Captain Brown. While repelling the attack, the English killed nine Indians and wounded many more. This "so enraged the wretches, that at their return they executed their revenge on Joseph Ring, who was then a captive among them, whom they fastened to a stake and burnt alive; barbarously shouting and rejoicing at his cries."

158–61 Peters, 69. It seems clear that the Abenaki raiders watching the Bradley garrison allowed Joseph Bradley and Jonathan Eastman to pass by them while they waited for an opportunity to take Hannah prisoner. Certainly, one object of the raid appeared to be the recapture of Hannah Bradley.

159 Chase, 216. Hannah Bradley was boiling soap when the Indians attacked the garrison house by filing through the open gate in the palisade. For details of colonial soap making, including the necessity of boiling the lye outdoors because of the stench, see www.ehow.com/about_4566250_soap-making-colonial-times.html.

160 Chase, 212. The author quotes one of the Indians as saying, "Now, Hannah, me got you," as they rushed inside the house, citing as his source, "one of her descendants."

160   Ibid. Bradley poured the contents of the boiling kettle onto the Indian wounded by Jonathan Johnson, "a soap-*orific* that almost instantly brought on a sleep, from which he has never since awoke."

160–161 Parkman, 368. Several commentators, including Parkman, observed, "the man who should have been on the watch was killed." He is referring to Jonathan Johnson, who wounded the first Indian to enter the garrison house but had left his normal post by the gate.

161   Peters, 71. The author quotes the papers of Samuel Sewall from the Massachusetts Historical Society Archives, who related that Hannah Bradley was within six weeks of delivering her baby when she was taken captive the second time. The Indians "made her put on Snow Shoes which to manage requires more than ordinary agility."

161   Fuess, 147. During the 1704 raid on Haverhill, Hannah Bradley was one of five captives taken from Haverhill by Abenaki raiders.

161   Chase, 210. At the time of her second captivity, Hannah Bradley, who was nearly eight months pregnant, "was in delicate circumstances and in slender health," which makes her fortitude under such duress even more remarkable.

161   Ibid. Her Indian masters required Hannah Bradley to carry a "heavy burthen, too large even for the strength of man."

162   Ibid. Hannah Bradley later told her family that "she subsisted on bits of skin, ground-nuts, the bark of trees, wild onions, and lily roots" on the trek to Canada.

162   Peters, 70. The author, a descendant of Bradley who spent many years compiling a genealogical record of the family, contributes many surprising details to the record of Hannah Bradley's tripartite ordeal. Bradley wore a pair of snowshoes given to her by the Indians. Short on food in mid winter, she chewed on dried strips of moose hide to extract what protein she could. Peters also says that three weeks elapsed from when Bradley was captured on February 8, 1704 and when she gave birth to an unnamed child.

162–63 Parkman, 368. Hannah Bradley was "safely delivered of an infant in the midst of the winter forest."

162   Belknap, Vol. I, 227. Famine was a serious threat to those in captivity, since "the Indians when they caught any game devoured it all in one sitting, and then girding themselves round the waist, travelled without sustenance till chance threw more in their way."

162   Peters, 73. According to Sewall, who was a contemporary of Hannah Bradley and Hannah Duston, when Bradley gave birth to an infant during her captivity, she was left outdoors with only a small fire and some hemlock branches provided by a squaw.

163   Ibid., 70. Shortly after giving birth in the Indian village, Hannah Bradley was visited by a missionary priest, most likely a Jesuit, who gave her something to eat, but "never condescended to meet her eyes." This snub was undoubtedly a result of Bradley's Puritan beliefs, as each religion distrusted those belonging to the other.

163   Parkman, 480. Since many accounts have Hannah Bradley taken to the village
        of Norridgewock, on the Kennebec River in Maine (the French considered this
        the border between Acadia, a territory which then comprised Nova Scotia, New
        Brunswick, and a large portion of Maine), it seems likely that she was visited
        by the famous Jesuit priest Sebastian Rale (sometimes he is referred to as Rasle,
        or Rasles). Rale was born in Franche-Comte in 1657 and was sent to the mis-
        sion villages of New France in 1689, when he was thirty-two years old. By 1704,
        when Rale was forty-seven, he was with the Abenaki of the Kennebec.

163   Ibid., 482. Father Rale was "of a strong, enduring frame, and a keen, vehement,
        caustic spirit. He had the gift of tongues, and was as familiar with the Abenaki
        and several other Indians languages as he was with Latin."

163   Chase, 211. After resuming their journey, the Indians promised they would
        allow Hannah Bradley's infant to live if it was baptized "in their manner." But
        taking the child from her, they "baptized it by gashing its forehead with their
        knives. The feelings of the mother, when the child was returned to her with its
        smooth and white forehead gashed with the knife, and its warm blood coursing
        down its cheeks, can be better imagined than described."

164   Parkman, 383. Camping after their raid on Deerfield, the Indians cleared away
        the snow and laid down a blanket of spruce boughs to avoid sitting and sleeping
        directly on the frozen ground.

164   Ibid., 368. The author follows Mirick (Whittier), Fuess, Caverly, Chase, and
        many others in recounting the episode where the Indians punished Bradley's
        child by putting hot coals in the baby's mouth. This method of torture is also
        mentioned in several other captivity narratives.

164–65 Ibid., 384–85. One or more of the Abenaki may have killed the Bradley infant,
        whose sex is unknown, to save it further torment. Reverend John Williams, in
        an account of his captivity after the raid on Deerfield, noted that the Indians
        killed several prisoners, including an infant and an eleven-year-old girl, after a
        few days on the trail. The Indians considered this a form of mercy rather than
        cruelty, since the captives were unable to keep up and would otherwise suffer
        "lingering death from cold and starvation."

164   Mirick, 109. Hannah Bradley's unnamed infant being "piked upon a pole" by
        the Indians is derived from a manuscript attributed to a Reverend Abiel Abbott.
        This anecdote is repeated by Fuess in Volume I of *The Story of Essex County*, and
        elsewhere. One account asserts that the child, after having its mouth burned by
        the embers, died of starvation.

164   Chase, 212. Murdering the infant may also have been intended as revenge
        against Hannah Bradley for killing one of the warriors during the Haverhill
        raid.

165   Penhallow, 46. Hannah Bradley was probably eager to reach Quebec once she
        saw there was little chance of escape. French treatment of English captives was
        "as various as their tempers and constitutions, but scarce a day passed without
        some act of cruelty" by the Indians who had taken prisoners.

165   Parkman, 484. Parkman, writing in 1876, when the west was still being fought over, observed, "The English borderers . . . regarded the Indians less as men than as vicious and dangerous wild animals. In fact, the benevolent and philanthropic view of the American savage is for those who are beyond his reach. It has never yet been held by any whose wives and children have lived in danger of his scalping-knife."

165   Montes-Bradley, 2. This well-researched genealogy by a descendant of Hannah Bradley lists each of Bradley's children and the means by which the child died. Five out of six of Hannah Bradley's children died before 1706, four of them at the hands of the Indians.

165   Chase, 211. Hannah Bradley's habit of soaking a few crusts of bread in milk while tending to the family's livestock appears here and in several other accounts, as well as the price of eighty livres the Indians received for her.

165–66 Fuess, 147. The French family that purchased Bradley from the Indians was cooperative in either releasing her or selling her back to Joseph Bradley when he reached them in Canada.

165   Mirick, 110. Joseph Bradley was "accompanied only by a dog that drew a small sled" on his trek to Canada to secure his wife's release.

165–66 Chase, 211. The bag of snuff was meant to ease Bradley's negotiations with the French and was probably difficult to obtain. Chase and other commentators also include the detail of husband and wife returning to Massachusetts aboard ship, rather than undertaking yet another journey through Abenaki territory.

165–67 Giorgi, 11. Joseph Bradley, married to the former Hannah Heath, was the son of Daniel and Mary (Williams) Bradley. Joseph was born on February 7, 1664, in a section of Haverhill known as Bradford, or in Rowley, Massachusetts, and died on October 3, 1727.

166   Peters, 55. Joseph Bradley's brother Daniel Bradley Jr. was killed by the Indians who raided Haverhill on March 15, 1697, when Joseph's wife Hannah, Mary Neff, and Hannah and Martha Duston were also taken into captivity. Daniel Bradley Jr., his wife, and two of his children were slain and his farmhouse burned to the ground. In the same raid, the Abenaki carried off two other of Daniel Bradley Jr.'s children, Daniel and Ruth. Ruth was able to return to Haverhill, though the date and circumstances are unknown.

166–67 Ibid. While Joseph Bradley's wife was in captivity the first time, he served in the Duston garrison house that was finished in April 1697, shortly after the fateful raid. Therefore, he had significant experience in the militia and in defending a garrison.

166   Chase, 213. In a letter from Haverhill's Colonel Nathaniel Saltonstall to Colonel Thomas Noyes of Newbury, the former expressed both indignation and disgust at the poor quality of the militia sent to reinforce his garrison houses. At one point, Saltonstall wrote, "*To take boyes for origginally prest (sic) men, and they hired too,* I know not ye regularity of it." (Italics included in original text.)

166   Ibid., 216. Although the Indians approached Bradley's garrison house with caution and stealth, they were visible to those inside because of the moonlight.

167   Mirick, 112. The first Indian tried to squirm through the opening of the par-
       tially unhinged door before Hannah Bradley shot him at close range.

167   Ibid. The Indians were able to force the garrison door partway, "and when one of
       the Indians began to crowd himself through the opening, Mrs. Bradley fired her
       gun and shot him dead." The other Indians saw him fall and withdrew.

CHAPTER VIII: ESCAPE FROM SUGAR BALL ISLAND
Page

168–90 Bouton, 52. In 1652, the General Court of Massachusetts ordered a survey
       to ascertain the northern bounds of the colony. Captains John Sherman and
       Edward Johnson of Watertown, Massachusetts, and surveyor Jonathan Ince of
       Cambridge, Massachusetts, "together with several Indian guides" traveled up the
       Merrimack River "to find the most northerly part thereof, which the Indians
       told them was Aquedocktan, the outlet of Winnepisiogee." By August 1, 1652,
       the surveyors had "decided the head source of the Merrimack 'where it issues
       out of the lake called Winnapusseakit (Winnipesaukee, as it's now spelled)' to
       be in 'latitude forty-three degrees, forty minutes and twelve seconds, besides
       those minutes which are allowed for the three miles north which run into
       the lake'." Bouton fixes the total cost of the expedition at eighty-four English
       pounds.

168–72 Caverly, 20. Following several other commentators, Caverly notes that, after
       scalping the Indians, Hannah Duston left the island in the sole remaining
       canoe, "yet soon returned, took off the ten scalps, taking also with them an
       Indian gun and tomahawk."

168–72 Dr. Aloke Mandal noted that rigor mortis occurs approximately three hours
       after death, and then at approximately twelve hours, during decomposition, the
       rigor mortis subsides. Bloating will begin to occur then, but how long it lasts is
       dependent on temperature after the twelve-hour period. The colder the envi-
       ronment, the longer the bloating will last. After violent trauma, like that suf-
       fered by the Indians killed on Sugar Ball Island, there will be bloody discharge
       from the ears and nose. Cyanosis in dark-skinned individuals would be seen
       in their nail beds. For further reference, see www.emedicine.medscape.com/
       article/1680032-overview#aw2aab6b6.

169   Chase, 190. In order to make their escape, Duston scuttled "all the canoes but
       one", and she and her companions "embarked in that."

170–71 Ibid. Duston and her party had "not proceeded far" downriver "when she has-
       tened back with her companions to the scene of death" upon Sugar Ball Island.

171   Ibid. Although Duston is believed to have taken the hatchet she used to kill her
       master back to Haverhill, Chase states, "This was some years after lost in the
       woods, near Mr. Dustin's." At the very least, Chase's account casts doubt over
       the claim that the hatchet currently in the possession of the Haverhill Historical
       Society in Haverhill, Massachusetts, is the one that Duston used on Sugar Ball
       Island.

171–72 Russell, 193–94. Early New England writers did not mention the taking of scalps as war trophies. Apparently, scalping developed, or at least increased in frequency, as a proof of death to assist in the collection of bounties, either from the French colonial government or the English. The first known reference to scalping appeared in the Oxford English Dictionary in 1670.

171–72 Caverly, 19–20. The author describes the method of scalping used by the Indians, and that Hannah Duston most likely used on her former captors. "This feat is performed by the savage as follows: Placing his foot on the neck of his prostrate victim, he twists the fingers of his left hand into the scalp-lock; and then, cutting with a knife in his right hand a circular gash around the lock, he tears the scalp from the head, and fastens it to his girdle with a yell of triumph."

171–72 Belknap, Vol. I, 103–4. The author, reflecting other commentators in the eighteenth and nineteenth centuries, states that the Indians were not the sole perpetrators of cruelty and terror during the colonial period. "Yet, bad as they were, it will be difficult to find them guilty of any crime which cannot be paralleled among civilized nations."

171–72 Ibid., 104. "We are struck with horror when we hear of (the Indians) binding the victim to the stake, biting off his nails, tearing out his hair by the roots, pulling out his tongue, boring out his eyes, sticking his skin full of lighted pitchwood, half roasting him at the fire, and then making him run for their diversion, until he faints and dies under the blows which they give him on every part of his body. But is it not as dreadful to read of an unhappy wretch sewed up in a bag full of serpents and thrown into the sea, or broiled in a red hot iron chair, or mangled by lions and tygers after having spent his strength to combat them for the diversion of the spectators in an amphitheatre?" After enumerating the above, Belknap includes a uniquely American form of torture: "confining a man in a trough, and daubing him with honey that he may be stung to death by wasps and other venomous insects."

172 Wilbur, 52. Although Duston's actions on Sugar Ball Island are barbaric by contemporary standards, it's interesting to note that Indian women "took a more active part than men" in torturing and disfiguring captive or dead enemies.

172 Bouton, 44. Duston "hastened back to the scene of death, took off the scalps of the slain, 'put them into a bag, and, with these bloody witnesses of their feat, hastened again on their downward course to Haverhill'." Bouton, echoing Mirick (Whittier), Chase, and others, puts Duston's motive for scalping her victims as proof of what had occurred—and not merely revenge—"fearing lest her neighbors . . . not credit her story."

172 Little, 113. In his account of the massacre on Sugar Ball Island, Little says that Hannah Duston "did up the scalps, fresh and bleeding, in a towel, took all the arms, what food they wanted, the best canoe, and scuttled the others to prevent pursuit, and started down the river."

172 Fuess, 145. Duston transported the Indians' scalps in "a piece of linen she had brought from home at the time of her capture," which corroborates several other

accounts concerning the broadcloth torn from her loom during the March 15, 1697 assault on Haverhill.

172   Peters, 66. This author, and several authors, write that it's unlikely Hannah Duston knew that the paying of bounties for scalps by the Massachusetts colonial government was "in abeyance." Peters reasons that it seems probable Duston was unaware of this, or else she wouldn't have been so "foolhardy" to return to the Indians' camp and "perform such a gruesome deed."

172   Little, 56. Although the General Court of Massachusetts was no longer paying for scalps in 1697, the French colonial government under Count Frontenac was doling out bounties to the Indians and *coureurs de bois*. By 1723, Massachusetts had reconsidered their policy and began paying one hundred English pounds per scalp.

172   Bailyn, 502–3. The author notes that the Indians used barbarous acts such as burning, dismembering, and scalping their victims as part of their "search for reciprocity in warfare and diplomacy," whereas the Europeans co-opted these practices in the service of domination over the Indians. Even the "gentle Pilgrims" eventually took up scalping.

173–90   In late March 2014, exactly 317 years after Hannah Duston, Mary Neff, and Sam Lenorson departed Sugar Ball Island in one of the Indians' birch bark canoes, I took a similar cold-water canoe trip from that starting point, accompanied by Chris Pierce, an experienced paddler and my partner on a number of outdoor adventures. The description of the river and the surrounding countryside in this chapter is based on my impressions recorded in a notebook during our expedition, and via Chris's photographs and video taken during that trip.

173   Chase, 190. Despite the inclement weather, Duston and her companions were "thinly clad."

173–74   Thoreau, 262. Unaccustomed to river travel, Duston and her companions "handled their paddles unskillfully, but with nervous energy and determination."

174   Bouton, 542. The Merrimack "is formed by the confluence at Franklin [New Hampshire] of the Pemigewasset and Winnepisogee branches, receives on the northern line of the town [Concord, New Hampshire] the Contoocook River from the west, and thence flows, gently and gracefully meandering. ..."

174–90   On the day Chris Pierce and I floated the Merrimack, the air temperature on the river was thirty-four degrees with a nineteen mile per hour northwesterly wind. According to Chris's GPS, the wind chill factor lowered the "real feel" temperature to twenty-three degrees. It was cold.

175   Chase, 190. The trio of escaped captives made their way downriver "each alternately rowing and steering their little bark."

175–90   Thoreau, 263. During his own trip on the Merrimack River, Thoreau estimated the distance between Sugar Ball Island and Haverhill as sixty miles.

175   Dan Nudd, who works for a local power company located near Hannah Duston Island and frequently boats that section of the Merrimack River, warned me about Sewall's Falls, which we would encounter approximately two miles

downriver from our starting point. The drop was only a few feet, but balancing the canoe upon landing in the slower water below the ledges took a little doing.

175–90 Disembarking from the canoe in high water at the conclusion of our trip, Chris Pierce fell into the river up to his armpits. Quickly climbing out by grabbing a branch on an overhanging tree and slinging himself onto the embankment, Chris stripped to the skin and changed into another set of high tech clothing we'd brought along in a dry bag. At the time, Chris noted that hypothermia would have occurred very rapidly if he'd remained in the water. As it was, he grew pale, with chattering teeth and blue lips. In order to recover, Chris volunteered to run a mile down the road in heavy boots to retrieve one of our vehicles.

175   Bouton, 540. Bouton writes, "Above Sewall's Island is a considerable fall" and the river in this vicinity is "subject to *freshes*, or overflows of the banks from . . . sudden meltings of snows, the whole adjacent interval is sometimes covered with water as far as the eye can see."

175   Thoreau, 263. During his trip down the Merrimack River, Thoreau noted the presence of several species of wildlife that Chris Pierce and I encountered on our trip, including a "fish-hawk" and geese that "fly over with a startling clangor."

177–78 Chase, 191. Duston and her companions "continued to drop silently down the river, keeping a good look-out for strolling Indians."

178   Ibid. To make their trip without stopping to rest, the escaped captives took turns paddling and steering: "in the night two of them only slept, while the third managed the boat."

178   Thoreau, 263. Near Amoskeag Falls, Duston and the others encountered an abundance of Indian sign. "Sometimes they pass an Indian grave surrounded by its paling on the bank, or the frame of a wigwam, with a coals left behind, or the withered stalks still rustling in the Indian's solitary cornfield on the interval."

179   Ibid., 262. In the pre-dawn darkness, using her paddle as a rudder as their canoe drifted on the current, Thoreau speculated that Hannah Duston's thoughts turned to the fate of her husband and surviving children. "(T)hey forget their own dangers and their deeds in conjecturing on the fate of their kindred, and whether, if they escape the Indians, they shall find the former alive."

180–90 Whitford, 317. The most distinctive feature of Thoreau's account of the Duston saga is that he "spends more imaginative energy on their journey home than he does on their capture and escape." Whitford also notes that, by 1832, "Hannah's heroism was being questioned even in Haverhill."

180–82 Little, 113. The author mentions the necessity of portaging the canoe, most likely at the great Indian fishing place, Amoskeag Falls, located in present-day Manchester, New Hampshire, saying "they carried round the falls" and "shot the rapids."

180   Bailey, 11–12. A detailed account of Thomas Duston and Hannah Emerson Duston's thirteen children: three who died before the March 15, 1697 raid on

Haverhill; the infant Martha, who died in the early minutes of the attack on the Duston homestead; and Lydia, who was born October 4, 1698. Caverly and others offer most of this same information.

180–90 During our river trip, the many small islands, often thickly wooded, seemed a likely hiding place for fugitives. On our second trip, Chris Pierce and I spent an uncomfortable night camping on one of these islands, where the temperature dropped to 18 degrees.

181 Beals, 21. Passaconaway kept his "royal residence" near Amoskeag Falls, on the site of present-day Manchester, New Hampshire.

181–83 Russell, 111. Amoskeag Falls was a revered gathering and fishing place for the Pennacook during Passaconaway's reign. By the close of the seventeenth century, when Duston arrived there, the April runs of salmon, sturgeon, and herring "brought together the members of many tribes." Therefore, several dangers were attached to the escaped captives' arrival and portage around the falls.

182 Belknap, 67. "The paths which served (the Indians) for carrying places between rivers, or different parts of the same river, are frequently discovered in the cutting of roads, or laying out of new townships" in the New Hampshire of Belknap's time.

182 Ibid. Such "gazettes" were a "mark of direction" for Indians passing through a region. Though not very common, pictographs of this sort were found in the vicinity of the Winnipesaukee River, "on which was depicted a canoe, with two men in it."

183 Thoreau, 263. The escaped captives were still far from safety when they reached Amoskeag Falls: "Every withered leaf which the winter has left seems to know their story, and in its rustling to repeat it and betray them. An Indian lurks behind every rock and pine, and their nerves cannot bear the tapping of a woodpecker."

183 Ibid. Thoreau notes that the escaped captives never got off the river, "except to carry their canoe about the falls."

183–84 Bouton, 540. Below the falls, the Merrimack twists along a circuitous route, "sweeping easterly, southerly, and westerly to form a respectable ox-bow near Sugar Ball bluffs."

184 Thoreau, 128. The basswood tree, which Thoreau identifies as *Tilia Americana*, also called the linden, or lime tree, with its broad, rounded leaf, was unique to the Merrimack River in the vicinity of Salmon Brook.

184 Ibid. Along this stretch of the Merrimack, the eastern bank "rose abruptly here and there into wooded hills fifty or sixty feet high," while the western edge of the river dropped away to accommodate the mouth of Salmon Brook.

184–86 Ibid., 130. Old John Lovewell's "house was said to be the first which Mrs. Dustan reached on her escape from the Indians."

184–86 Ibid., 129. According to Thoreau, as a young man Lovewell had been an ensign in Oliver Cromwell's army. He settled alongside Salmon Brook in Dunstable in 1690.

184–86 Ibid. During Thoreau's trip on the Merrimack River, he ascended Salmon Brook and learned from a haymaker working along the bank that silver eels had once been abundant in the vicinity. The old-timer pointed out some sunken creels at the mouth of the stream. Thoreau also discovered signs of the first white settlers and the "dents in the earth where their houses stood" including that of Old John Lovewell.

184–86 Pendergast, 67. From *The History of Hillsborough County, New Hampshire* by E. Hamilton Hurd: "Fifty years before the Scotch settlers came to Londonderry, and seventy years before any other town of Hillsborough County outside of 'Old Dunstable,' had a white resident there were log cabins on the banks of Salmon Brook a little above its junction with the Merrimack."

184–86 Ford, 60. This account reiterates the claim that the first white settler who Duston and her companions saw after their escape was John Lovewell of Dunstable, Massachusetts. They probably reached his crude garrison house on March 30, 1697.

185–86 Parkman, 506–7. John Lovewell Sr., was "a person of consideration in the village (of Dunstable, Massachusetts), where he owned a 'garrison house,' had served in Philip's War, and taken part in the famous Narragansett Swamp Fight" in 1675.

185–86 Thoreau, 129. In 1697, "Old" John Lovewell, whose father Captain John Lovewell, a renowned Indian fighter who died along with the great warrior Paugus in the 1725 battle of Lovewell's Pond, lived about one mile upstream from the Merrimack on Salmon Brook.

186   Pendergast, 64. Although Thoreau says that John Lovewell Sr. "cut a handsome swath at a hundred and five," and lived to be 120 years old, Kimball Webster, in *The History of Hudson*, NH, published in 1913, writes, "the statement that John Lovewell lived to the great age of 120 years has repeatedly appeared in print. It is one of those peculiar traditions that the curious seize upon without investigation. It is admitted that he died about 1752, and it is equally certain that his age did not exceed 102 years." If Webster is correct, then John Lovewell Sr. was forty-seven years old when he encountered Hannah Duston on Salmon Brook.

186   Fuess, 128. A trading post was established in Dunstable, Massachusetts, in 1694, though for many years the Indians resisted a larger settlement in that location.

187–88 Bailey, 26. In a letter that Hannah Duston wrote in 1724, when she was sixty-seven years old, she asked to receive the full covenant of the Second Church of Haverhill. This letter mentions Duston's captivity and was unknown until 1929, when it was discovered in a vault at the Center Congregational Church in Haverhill. That church was subsequently torn down to make way for a parking lot. In the letter, Duston notes she had "a Good Education by My Father."

187–88 Ibid., 27. In this letter, Duston makes it plain that the scriptures gave her courage—and provided her with justification—during her ordeal, stating "In my Affliction, God made his Word Comfortable to me."

187–88 Mather, 636. Mather, who was one of the few educated men who spoke with Duston personally about her ordeal, compared it to Jael's actions against Sisera from the Book of Judges in his *Magnalia Christi Americana*. In Mather's retelling of Judges 5: 27, he changes the pronoun "she" to "they," reflecting the role that Mary Neff and Sam Lenorson played in the revenge upon the Indians, as well as the fact there was more than one victim: "at the feet of these poor prisoners, they bow'd, they fell, they lay down; at their feet they bow'd, they fell; where they bow'd, there they fell down dead."

188 Ibid., 636. Concerning Hannah Duston's possible moral or legal culpability for her actions on Sugar Ball Island, Mather writes, "being where (Duston) had not her own life secured by any law unto her, she thought she was not forbidden by any law to take away the life of the murderers, by whom her child had been butchered."

188 Whitford, 324. Whitford, an associate professor in the English Department at the University of Wisconsin–Milwaukee, writing in 1972, had this to say about Mather's interpretation of the events: "Cotton Mather justifies Hannah's killing of her Indian captors on two grounds: the legalistic argument, which, one suspects, is the justification advanced by Hannah herself, and the providential argument, which served Mather simultaneously against his Catholic foes abroad and his political foes at home."

188 Thoreau, 72. The Merrimack River has a "clayey bottom, almost no weeds, and comparatively few fishes" in the lower valley, along with a yellowish tint.

188 Ford, 7. This description of the geography of the lower Merrimack River valley creates a vivid picture. "An imaginary line from Haverhill to the island of Sugar Ball would serve as the hypotenuse of a right-angled triangle formed with the leg and base of the Merrimack."

188–89 Thoreau, 99. Near the "Horseshoe Interval" in Tyngsborough, where the downstream current bends sharply to the southeast, the banks narrow to forty rods and the depth of the river is approximately fifteen feet.

189 Beals, 53. Beals notes that Wonalancet sold his "own home" on Wickasuck Island in 1663 to repay his brother Nanamocomuck's debt.

189 Thoreau, 90. In 1676, Jonathan Tyng wrote to the colony for aid, stating that he "lived in the uppermost house on Merrimac River, lying open to ye enemy, yet being so seated that it is, as it were, a watch-house to neighboring towns." According to Thoreau, Wickasuck Island was granted to Tyng in 1683, after the Indians departed.

189 Ibid. The Tyng farm was close to Wickasuck Falls.

189 Ibid., 92. The Algonquin word for the Merrimack was often translated as "River of Sturgeons." Thoreau and his brother toyed with the idea of netting or gaffing one of these great fish as it swam beside them, but it was so powerful they feared it would capsize their rowboat.

190 Ibid., 93. Thoreau explains that "they who are on the water enjoy a longer and brighter twilight than they who are on the land, for here the water, as well as the

atmosphere, absorbs and reflects the light, and some of the day seems to have sunk down into the waves."

190   Mirick, 91–92. Hannah Duston and her companions arrival at Bradley Brook was "totally unexpected by their mourning friends, who supposed they had been butchered by their ruthless conquerors. It must truly have been an affecting meeting for Mrs. Duston, who supposed that all she loved—all she held dear on earth—were laid in the silent tomb."

CHAPTER IX: SAMUEL SEWALL, COTTON MATHER, AND THE GENERAL COURT OF MASSACHUSETTS
Page

193–98 Chase, 154. At a town meeting on January 20, 1690, Haverhill residents voted to award Reverend Benjamin Rolfe, formerly of Newbury, Massachusetts, "forty pounds per annum in Wheat, Rye and Indian" to assist the settlement's aged minister, Mr. John Ward. Rolfe had begun preaching in Haverhill in the closing weeks of 1689.

193   Ibid., 198. At least nine houses were burned to the ground, and twenty-seven Haverhill residents murdered during the March 15, 1697 raid.

193   Caverly, 15–16. The list of those slain during the Abenaki raid of 1697 is taken from Mirick, and town records.

193   Peters, 56. His own family in ruins, Hannah Bradley's husband Joseph was serving in the militia detachment assigned to the Marsh garrison house on Pecker's Hill when Hannah Duston returned to Haverhill.

193–94 Lawson, 56. The frontier road builder had "an intuitive sense of direction, of lines of ascent and descent, of what appeared to be soil that would be sufficiently hard and stony to withstand the sudden freshet. His tools were an iron-headed axe fitted to an ash handle, an adze of the same construction, and a compass to gauge direction."

193   Ibid., 57. The Gunter's Chain, which was invented by Edmund Gunter (1581–1626), an English mathematician and astronomer, was used as a measuring tool in road building.

194–95 Chase, 95. The "better sort of houses" in the old Haverhill village were constructed in the manner that Rolfe's home is described, usually with one central chimney and "bricks laid against the inner partition." These were "covered with clay, and then clay-boards, (since corrupted to clap-boards)." The well-built homes were shingled, while one-story cottages built prior to 1690 had thatched roofs.

195–98 Since Thomas Duston had little schooling, and Haverhill's list of citizens from this period did not include any lawyers, it's likely that the most educated person in the village, Reverend Benjamin Rolfe, assisted the Dustons in writing their petition seeking a reward from the General Court for the Indian scalps.

195 Bailey, 10. Since Thomas Duston "was the only person in the extant lists to erect more than one house, it is likely he was erecting houses for others, perhaps brick houses since he . . . operated a brick making business."

195 Chase, 67. The original Haverhill meetinghouse, built in 1648, "stood facing the river upon the slight elevation or knoll, about midway between the south and the north bounds of Pentucket Cemetery." It was a one-story building, twenty-six feet long and twenty feet wide, and used for public worship.

195 Ibid., 91. In a November 1660 town meeting, ten acres of meadow and two hundred acres of upland were allotted for the construction of a parsonage for "Mr. Ward and his successors."

195 Ibid., 173–75. The dimensions and cost of a new meetinghouse in Haverhill were the subject of vigorous debate for several years. Residents finally agreed on a cost—"four hundred pounds in money"—and dimensions of "fifty feet long, forty-two feet wide, and eighteen feet stud." The building was completed by October 24, 1699.

195 Galvin, *MHC Reconnaissance Survey Town Report*, Haverhill, Report Date: 1985, 11. Haverhill's population was "about 300 white inhabitants plus 25 negro slaves" in 1675. Between that year and 1708, the settlement's population grew slowly because of frequent Indian attacks. "Over 60 Haverhill residents were killed in this period, particularly in 1697, the worst year for attacks."

195 Chase, 167. By the close of 1692, Benjamin Rolfe was hired to take over Haverhill's ministry from Mr. John Ward, who had held the position for nearly fifty years. Ward died on December 27, 1693, at the age of eighty-seven.

195-96 Ibid., 162. By November 1692, Reverend Rolfe had been "granted the free and full improvement of the Parsonage farm and meadow . . . so long as he continued in the town as their minister."

195–97 Ibid., 154. In a footnote, the author mentions that Reverend Benjamin Rolfe was attached to the English militia in Falmouth, Maine, from July 14 to November 14, 1689.

197 Bailey, 21–22. In September 1694, the Massachusetts legislature authorized the paying of fifty English pounds for each Indian scalp taken. This fee was reduced to twenty-five pounds in June 1695 and was revoked altogether on December 16, 1696. Given the circumstances of his wife's captivity and escape, Thomas Duston "apparently believed an exception would be granted and took his wife to Boston, arriving May 21, 1697." By the old standard, Hannah Duston and her companions would be shortchanged four hundred pounds for the ten Indian scalps.

197–98 Caverly, 38–39. The first publication to include Thomas Duston's petition to the General Assembly of Massachusetts was Caverly's 1874 edition of *The Heroism of Hannah Duston, Together with the Indian Wars of New England.*

197–210 Bailey, 22. Thomas Duston was required to post the petition on behalf of his wife, Hannah, since she had very few rights under the law as a married woman.

199   Ibid., 22 Bailey notes that Chase and others list the date that Thomas and Hannah arrived in Boston to present their petition as April 21, 1697. Bailey appears to have based this change of date on information he discovered in the Massachusetts archives, including the fact that Duston's petition was acted upon, in the affirmative, by vote of the legislature on June 8, 1697, a more reasonable gap between the reading of the petition and the decision of the assembly.

199–200   LaPlante, 51–52. The roads between Newbury and Boston were well trodden, and the proximity of the coastal towns to one another provided travelers with greater security when they ventured out from the more remote settlements.

199–213   Ibid., 11. A map of Boston provided here, which notes the location of all three places Hannah Duston was known to visit on her trip, corresponds with more detailed maps from the period contained in the Massachusetts Historical Society and Boston Public Library databases.

199–200   Galvin, Historical Data relating to the Counties, Cities and Towns in Massachusetts, 21. Boston was founded in 1630, having previously been called Trimountaine.

200   Bacon, 2. The "neck" as it was called, which connected the town of Boston to Roxbury and mainland, was a mile long. Later, much of the surrounding wetlands were filled in, allowing multiple points of access to the growing city and dramatically increasing its land mass.

200   Wilbur, 72. The Algonquin place name, Shawomet, is here translated as "a spring," and "place to which boats go."

200   Bacon, 1. "Shawmutt," or "living waters," reflects the practical nature of Algonquin "picture names."

200   Ibid. The order that founded Boston was "passed by the Court of Assistants sitting in the 'Governor's House'" on the opposite side of the Charles River, in Charlestown, Massachusetts, on September 17, 1630.

201   LaPlante, 12. The original Sewall home had been built by Samuel's wife Hannah's grandfather, the blacksmith Robert Hull, around 1635, according to the author, who is Judge Sewall's great-great-great-great-great-great granddaughter.

201–2   Ibid. The ground floor of the Hull House included two large halls, a kitchen, and a "long hearth."

202–6   Ibid., 285. Samuel Sewall entered Harvard at age fifteen, in 1667. He earned his BA four years later and his MA in 1674. During that year, he met Hannah Hull.

202   Bacon, 21. The dowry of the "mint master's daughter Hannah" was "her weight in pine-tree shillings."

202   LaPlante, 81–82. Hannah Hull's dowry was five hundred English pounds, a "massive sum," considering that a minister's annual salary was, on average, sixty to eighty pounds, plus a certain amount of corn, wheat, firewood, etc. The author repeats the story from Nathaniel Hawthorne's *Grandfather's Chair* about Hannah's weight in pine-tree shillings, calling it "fanciful," but given other evidence of the five-hundred-pound dowry, she does not dispute Hawthorne's story outright.

202   Chase, 154. In contrast to Hannah Hull's dowry, Rev. Benjamin Rolfe was paid "forty pounds per annum in Wheat, Rye, and Indian" in 1690, to assist the failing Rev. John Ward.

202   LaPlante, 285–86. Hannah (Hull) Sewall's first child, John, died at seventeen months of age, in 1677. A year before the Dustons' visit, her thirteenth child was stillborn. Between those, the Sewalls buried six other children.

202   Ibid., 21. Hull House contained an impressive collection of furniture and objects imported from England and the Far East by Robert Hull, Edmund Quincy, and Judge Sewall, who regularly did business with other merchants in England, Spain, and the West Indies.

202   Johnson, 89–90. By law, what colonists could wear was dictated by the net worth of their estates. Gold or silver lace, buttons, great boots, etc. were forbidden unless the wearer's "visible estate" exceeded the value of two hundred pounds. Thus, Judge Sewall and Thomas Duston would have been dressed quite differently, even if Duston had managed to acquire brass buttons or a pair of great boots.

202–3   LaPlante, 202. Some Puritans wore sackcloth to church as a sign of humility and penitence. Sewall's habit of wearing a hair shirt as an undergarment was closer to the Catholic sense of this item as "an instrument of self-mortification."

203   Ibid., 202. Sewall had been studying the passage from Zechariah and praying for a "change of raiment" shortly before his meeting with Thomas and Hannah Duston. Certainly, this scriptural passage and Sewall's reasons for self-mortification were known to Rev. Benjamin Rolfe, one of the most prominent citizens in Haverhill and the community's spiritual leader.

203–4   Ibid., 152. The Court of Oyer and Terminer opened on the second floor of the Town House in Salem, Massachusetts, on June 2, 1692.

203   Ibid., 152–53. Although Bishop was accused of supernatural crimes, among them "nursing imps" from her "'preternatural teat'," her persecution and execution were probably motivated by more ordinary reasons. She allowed gambling in her tavern, and often remained open past the hour set for curfew.

203   Ibid., 170. Corey remained silent during his trial and throughout the preparation for his execution. Under the laws of the Massachusetts colony, if a defendant refused to make a plea, he would "preserve his last will and testament." By enduring a grim ordeal that took over forty hours to kill him, "Corey succeeded in protecting his land and possessions from the sheriff, who had ransacked the houses and barns of many other convicted witches. Without a plea from Corey, the sheriff had no legal justification for invading his property," ostensibly saving it for his heirs.

203   Ibid., 199–200. After his unexpected public confession during services at Boston's Third Church, within a week Sewall experienced "spiritual relief" for the torment that had been growing worse in the years since Oyer and Terminer had concluded its heinous business.

204 Bailey, 19. Hannah (Emerson) Duston was born in Haverhill, Massachusetts, on December 23, 1657.

204 LaPlante, 285. Samuel Sewall was born in England on March 28, 1652. His wife, Hannah, was eighteen when they were married on February 28, 1676.

204 Bailey, 7. Thomas Duston Jr. was born "about" 1652 in Kittery, Maine.

204 LaPlante, 285–86. In 1697, the surviving children of Samuel and Hannah Sewall were Samuel Jr., Hannah, Elizabeth, Joseph, and Mary. A fourteenth child, Judith, was born in 1702.

204 Caverly, 21. Including the infant Martha, who was killed during the raid, the Duston children who had died prior to 1697 were Mary, John, and Mehitable.

204 LaPlante, 5. Samuel Sewall "published an essay affirming the fundamental equality of sexes" at a time when Puritans believed that only the bodies of men would be resurrected in heaven. In June 1700, Sewall also wrote and published what is considered America's first anti-slavery pamphlet, *The Selling of Joseph, A Memorial*.

204 Ibid., 215. Like some early colonial era thinkers, Sewall believed that the Indians might be "of Jacob's posterity, part of the long since captivated ten tribes, and that their brethren the Jews shall come unto them." However, it's unlikely given Hannah Duston's recent experiences among the Indians that Sewall brought up this matter during their meeting.

205 Ibid., 189. In July 1695, two years before his meeting with Hannah Duston, Sewall had commented on the policy, implemented by Count Frontenac, of paying for scalps in a letter he wrote to a relative in England: "As several captives escaped inform us, our heads are set (priced) at a certain rate by the governor of Quebec, as the foreskins of the Philistines were of old."

205 Johnson, 22. In 1640, a committee of Puritans translated the Psalms from Hebrew into everyday English, collecting them in *The Bay Psalm Book*. They removed the lyricism and poetry of other translations, believing those to be "popishly seductive." The Psalms were rendered in singsong cadence, without musical accompaniment.

205 LaPlante, 29–30. Psalm 21, which "describes God's destruction of his enemies," was sung by Sewall and the congregation at his two-week-old son Henry's funeral on December 24, 1685.

206 http://resources.osv.org/explore_learn/document_viewer.php?Action=. Old Sturbridge Village. OSV Documents—Early New England Farm Crops: Flax. Flax was a troublesome but valuable crop in colonial America, as it reduced dependence on imported linen. Southwestern Connecticut was a hub for raising flax during this period, and Sewall's connections as a merchant would have assisted him in securing this light, durable, long-lived fiber for making linens on his estate instead of buying linen shirts from abroad.

206 Bailey, 21. The author transcribes the two mentions of Hannah Duston's visits from Samuel Sewall's diary, with parentheses marking his editorial interjections. These accounts match several other mentions of Sewall's two known diary entries on the matter.

206 LaPlante, 68–69. One of the most remarkable documents to survive the American colonial era, Sewall's diary spanned fifty-six years, from December 1673 to October 1729 (one volume, 1677–1684, is missing). The original fourteen volumes of Sewall's diary, which LaPlante calls "an internal record of his spiritual career," are in the Massachusetts Historical Society in Boston.

207 Salisbury, 87. After the ordeal of her own captivity, Mary Rowlandson wrote of later seeing the very Indians who had oppressed her: "*Mine eyes have seen that fellow afterwards walking up and down Boston, under the appearance of a Friend-Indian, and severall others of the like Cut.*" Indians professing to be friendly were able to move about the colony in this era, due to the Puritans' wish to convert them.

207–9 Dalton, 21. Boston's original Town House, where Hannah Duston's petition was granted, burned down in 1711, was rebuilt, and was destroyed again by fire in 1747. The structure that replaced it, known as the Old State House, still exists.

207 Ibid., 22. A detailed drawing of the first Town House is contained on this page in the official history of the Massachusetts General Court.

208 Ibid., 13–14. In 1636, controversy over a missing sow led to the first bicameral legislature in United States history, when the General Court of Massachusetts decided that such cases would be decided by "the consent of the greater part of the magistrates on the one part, & the greater number of the deputyes on the other part."

208–10 Ibid., 27. Beginning in 1644, the General Court decreed that petitions had to be filed during the first week of each quarterly session, noting "the many and great inconveniences by this Courts taking in of petitions which are presented from time to time ... often times towards the close of the Court." Therefore, it stands to reason that the Dustons were instructed to carry their petition to Boston during the first week of the spring session.

208 Ibid., 15. The first doorkeeper of the House of Deputies, Samuel Greene, was appointed on May 30, 1644, with the salary of "two shillings per day, with diett and lodginge."

208 LaPlante, 116. Samuel Sewall was named a magistrate of the General Court of Massachusetts in 1689.

208–10 Dalton, 449. Penn Townsend served as speaker of the House of Deputies in the General Court of Massachusetts from 1696 to 1697. Nathaniel Byfield, who may have served as his clerk, succeeded him in 1698.

209 Ibid., 27. In 1638, a screening committee was first appointed to sort through the petitions before the court and determine their importance and viability.

209 Ibid. At least in part to discourage frivolous suits, the General Court established a filing fee of two shilling and six pence for "petitions of a 'common and ordinary nature'" beginning in 1648.

209 Ibid. Orders issued by the House were copied within ten days of the end of the session and subject to "the speedy & certeine conveyance thereof to those to whome they are especially directed unto."

210   Ibid., 28. Smoking was banned in General Court chambers in 1646, with viola-
      tors subject to fines of six pence per pipe-full taken.

210   Drake, 161. A "Captain Turrell" had built and originally resided in Cotton
      Mather's house in the north end of Boston, on Hanover Street.

210   LaPlante, 46. Mather is described as having a "rounder face than his father," a
      sizeable nose, and "large, intense, widely spaced eyes."

210–11 Mather Project, http://matherproject.org/node/36. Cotton Mather's father, Rev-
      erend Increase Mather, was president of Harvard College from 1685 to 1702.

210   Ibid. Cotton Mather would also receive an honorary Doctor of Divinity degree
      from Glasgow University in 1710.

211   Ibid. Mather's notions about diet and exercise, as well as the avoidance of smok-
      ing, were eventually published in his medical handbook, *The Angel of Bethesda*, in
      1723.

211–13 Bosman, 6. Cotton Mather was a third-generation American Puritan "who took
      all knowledge as his province."

211   LaPlante, 168. Mather did not feel many of the regrets that Sewall struggled
      with regarding the witch trials. When Martha Carrier of Andover, Massachu-
      setts, was hanged as a witch, Mather called her a "rampant hag" and then added,
      "The Devil promised her she should be queen of Hell."

211   Mather Project. Mather was noted for his "adolescent stammer" when he stud-
      ied medicine at Harvard.

211–12 Bosman, 6. Hannah and Thomas Duston's account appeared in three works by
      Cotton Mather and was entitled, "A Notable Exploit, Dux Faemina Facti."

212–13 Caverly, 391. On June 17, 1874, at the dedication of Hannah Duston's statue on
      "Island Contoocook," previously called Sugar Ball Island, the author and histo-
      rian remarked that the Indians, in choosing Duston as a potential victim, "'had
      been waking up the wrong passenger'."

212   Bailey, 25. Sam Lenorson died on May 11, 1718, at Preston, Connecticut (later
      renamed Griswold) at the age of thirty-five. He left a wife and five young chil-
      dren. His widow, Lydia, remarried in 1720.

212   Ibid. Francis Nicholson, who was governor of Maryland when he sent Hannah
      Duston a gift of three pewter chargers, lived from 1655 to 1728.

212   Ibid. Mary Neff was born on September 8, 1646 in Haverhill, and died there on
      October 22, 1722.

212   Parkman, 308. Frontenac died in Quebec on the afternoon of November 28,
      1698. Callieres succeeded him as royal governor.

213   Chase, 219–20. Benjamin Rolfe, his wife, and youngest child, Mehitable, per-
      ished when a trio of militia assigned to defend them fled from the Indians.
      Rolfe fought the raiders alone and was wounded through the arm when he
      attempted to barricade the door. Fleeing through the house, he was overtaken
      beside his well and killed with a hatchet. Two other of Rolfe's children were
      "saved by the courage and sagacity of Hagar, a negro slave," who hid them under
      tubs in the cellar when the Indians ransacked the house.

213   Bailey, 10–14. Thomas Duston Jr. was born in 1652, most likely in Kittery, Maine. He died in Haverhill, Massachusetts "shortly before November 17, 1732, aged about 80."

213   Ibid., 11–15. Hannah Duston was born December 23, 1657 and she "probably died in February of 1737 . . . after being ill for eight weeks and five days."

213   Ibid., 19. Hannah Duston may have been buried in a private family plot, but was more likely interred "in Haverhill's old Pentucket Cemetery" under a wooden marker that has long since disappeared.

Bibliography

babel.hathitrust.org/cgi/pt?id=loc.ark:/13960/t55d96d9g;view=1up;seq=11.

Bacon, Edwin M. *Boston: A Guidebook.* Boston: Ginn & Company, 1903.

Bailey, Chris H., ed. *Dustons & Dustins in America, Information on Thomas Duston, the Emigrant,* compiled by Harold D. Kilgore and Cecil D. Duston, 1938. Edited by Chris H. Bailey, 2009. Unpublished book-length manuscript.

Bailyn, Bernard. *The Barbarous Years: the Peopling of British North America—The Conflict of Civilizations, 1600–1675.* New York: Vintage Books, 2012.

Bancroft, George. *History of the United States of America from the Discovery of the Continent.* Boston: Little, Brown and Company, 1860 (numerous editions).

Beals, Edward Charles, Jr. *Passaconaway in the White Mountains.* Boston: The Gorham Press, 1916.

Belknap, Jeremy. *The History of New-Hampshire Comprehending the Events of one complete Century and seventy-five years from the discovery of the River Pascataqua to the year one thousand seven hundred and ninety,* Volumes I–III. Haverhill Public Library Special Collections, Haverhill, MA, originally published by Bradford and Read, Boston, 1813.

Bosman, Richard. *Captivity Narrative of Hannah Duston: Related by Cotton Mather, John Greenleaf Whittier, Nathaniel Hawthorne and Henry David Thoreau, four versions of events in 1697, interspersed with thirty-five wood-block prints.* Introduction by Glenn Todd. San Francisco: Arion Press, 1987.

Bouton, Nathaniel. *The History of Concord, From Its First Grant in 1725—To the Organization of the City Government in 1853. With A History of the Ancient Penacooks.* Haverhill Public Library Special Collections, Haverhill, MA, originally published by Benning W. Sanborn, Concord, NH, 1856.

Braun, Esther K. and Braun, David P. *The First Peoples of the Northeast.* Lincoln, MA: Lincoln Historical Society, 1994.

Bruchac, Marge. "Reading Abenaki Traditions and European Records of Rogers' Raid," www.vermontfolklifecenter.org, August 2006.

Caverly, Robert B. *Heroism of Hannah Duston: Together with the Indian Wars of New England.* Boston: B. B. Russell & Co., Publishers, 1875.

Chase, George W. *History of Haverhill, Massachusetts, From Its First Settlement, In 1640, To The Year 1860.* Haverhill Public Library Special Collections, originally published by the author, Haverhill, MA, 1861.

Coleman, Emma Lewis. *New England Captives Carried to Canada*. Portland, ME: Southworth Press, 1925.

Cronan, Francis W. *Red Sunday: The Saltonstalls, the Dustons, and the Fighting Ayers. Merrimack Valley History*. Decorah, IA: Anundsen Publishing Company, 1965.

Dalton, Cornelius, et al. *Leading the Way: A History of the Massachusetts General Court 1629–1980*. Boston: Office of the Massachusetts Secretary of State, Michael J. Connolly, Secretary, 1980.

Dolin, Eric J. *Fur, Fortune, and Empire: The Epic History of the Fur Trade in North America*. New York: W.W. Norton & Company, 2010.

Drake, Samuel Adams. *Old Landmarks and Historical Personages of Boston*. Boston: Roberts Brothers, 1881.

Drake, Samuel G. *The Book of the Indians of North America*. Boston: Josiah Drake Antiquarian Bookstore, 1833.

Dwight, Timothy. *Travels in New England and New York*. London: W. Baynes and Son, and Ogle, Duncan & Co., 1823.

ehow.com/about_4566250_soap-making-colonial-times.html.

Elson, Henry William. *History of the United States*. New York: Macmillan Company, 1904.

emedicine.medscape.com/article/1680032-overview#aw2aab6b6.

Ford, Helen deN. *The Starshine of Mrs. Hannah Duston*. Nevins Memorial Library Special Collections, Methuen, MA.

Fuess, Claude M., ed. *The Story of Essex County*, Vol. 1. New York: The American Historical Society, Inc., 1935.

Galvin, William Francis. *Historical Data relating to the Counties, Cities and Towns in Massachusetts*. Boston: New England Historic Genealogical Society, 1997.

Galvin, William Francis. *MHC Reconnaissance Survey Town Report for Haverhill, Massachusetts*. Boston: Massachusetts Historical District Commission, 1985.

garrisonhouse.org/ The Old Chelmsford Garrison House.

Giorgi, Valerie Dyer. *Bartholomew Heath of Haverhill, Massachusetts and Some of His Descendants*. Haverhill Public Library Special Collections, privately published, Santa Monica, CA, 1994.

Goodrich, Charles A. *A History of the United States*, web excerpt, originally published in 1857.

Hawthorne, Nathaniel. "The Duston Family," *The American Magazine of Useful and Entertaining Knowledge*, May 1836.

Heath, Lawrence "Larry" Alan and Beverly Ann. *Our Family Legacy: Heath—Hill—Gerlach—Mogch*, Haverhill Public Library Special Collections, privately published in Canada by Lawrence and Beverly Heath, Coquitlam, BC, 1992.

Herr, Michael. *Dispatches*. New York: Alfred A. Knopf, 1977.

Hogg, Ian V. *An Illustrated History of Firearms*. London: New Burlington Books, 1983.

Howe, Jos. S. and Mack, Ernest G. *Historical Sketch of the Town of Methuen From Its Settlement To The Year 1876*, by Jos. S. Howe, originally published by E. L. Houghton & Co., Methuen, Massachusetts, 1876. *Bridges From the Past*, by Ernest G. Mack, published in 1976. Special Combined Edition. Andover, Massachusetts: The Merrimack Valley Preservation Press, established by the Merrimack Valley Preservation Group, Inc., 2003.

Hubbard, William and Drake, Samuel G. *The History of the Indian Wars in New England.* Vol 1. Roxbury, MA: W. Elliott Woodward, 1865.

Johnson, Claudia Durst. *Daily Life in Colonial New England.* Westport, CT and London: Greenwood Press, 2002.

LaPlante, Eve. *Salem Witch Judge: the Life and Repentance of Samuel Sewall.* New York: HarperOne, 2007.

Lawson, Russell M. *Passaconaway's Realm: Captain John Evans and the Exploration of Mount Washington.* Hanover, NH: University Press of New England, 2004.

Little, William. *The History of Weare, New Hampshire 1735–1888.* Haverhill Public Library Special Collections, originally published by S. W. Huse & Co., Lowell, MA, 1888.

Mann, Helen R. *Gallant Warrior.* Grand Rapids, MI: Wm. B. Eerdsmans Publishing Company, 1955.

Mather, Cotton (1663–1728). *Magnalia Christi Americana: or The Ecclesiastical History of New England.* "Now Reproduced from the Edition of 1852 and Published in 1967 by Russell & Russell, A Division of Atheneum House, Inc." From: Volume 2, Article XXV, 634–36. matherproject.org/node/36.

Meader, J. W. *The Merrimack River; its Source and its Tributaries.* Boston: B. B. Russell, 1869.

Mirick, B. L. *History of Haverhill Massachusetts.* Haverhill Public Library Special Collections, A. W. Thayer, Haverhill, MA, 1832.

Montes-Bradley, Saul M. *The Bradleys of Essex County Revisited: A Genealogy of the Descendants of Daniell Broadley of Bingley, Yorkshire and Haverhill, Massachusetts From 1613 to 2004.* Haverhill Public Library Special Collections, Haverhill, MA, 2004.

Parkman, Francis. *Francis Parkman: France and England in North America*, Vol. II. New York: The Library of America, 1983.

Pendergast, John. *Life Along the Merrimack: Collected Histories of the Native Americans Who Lived on Its Banks.* Tynsborough, MA: Merrimac River Press, 1995.

Penhallow, Samuel, Esq. *The History of the Wars of New-England with the Eastern Indians, or a Narrative of their continued Perfidy and Cruelty.* Haverhill Public Library Special Collections, Haverhill, MA, originally published in a Boston Edition of 1726, and by Wm. Dodge, Cincinnati, OH, 1859.

Peters, Eleanor Bradley. *Bradley of Essex County Early Records: From 1643 to 1746.* Haverhill Public Library Special Collections, Haverhill, MA, originally published by Knickerbocker Press, New York, 1915.

Purvis, Thomas L., ed. *Colonial America to 1763.* Almanacs of American Life. New York: Facts on File, Inc., 1999.

Russell, Howard S. *Indian New England Before the Mayflower.* Hanover, NH and London: University Press of New England, 1980.

Salisbury, Neal, ed. *The Sovereignty and Goodness of God by Mary Rowlandson with Related Documents.* Boston: Bedford Books, 1997.

Sewall, Samuel. *The Diary of Samuel Sewall.* Collection of Massachusetts Historical Society, 1878.

Sprinkle, Jacqueline Lee. *The Captives of Abb's Valley: A Legend of Frontier Life. By a Son of Mary Moore*. Originally published by The Presbyterian Board of Publication and Sabbath-School Work, by A. W. Mitchell, MD, 1854. Reprinted by Sprinkle Publications, Harrisonburg, VA, 2002.

Thoreau, Henry David. "A Week on the Concord and the Merrimack." *Journal*, Vol. III, 1849.

Town of Merrimack, New Hampshire Master Plan Update, 2002.

Vital Records of Haverhill, Massachusetts. Haverhill Public Library Special Collections, Haverhill MA.

whiteoak.org/historical-library/fur-trade/the-beaver-fur-hat/.

Whitford, Kathryn. "Hannah Dustin: The Judgment of History." *Essex Historical Collections*, Haverhill Public Library Special Collections, Haverhill, MA, 1972.

Whittier, John Greenleaf. *The Legends of New England*, "A Mother's Revenge," 1821.

Wilbur, C. Keith. *The New England Indians*. Chester, CT: Globe Pequot Press, 1978.

Wilhelm, Robert. *Murder & Mayhem in Essex County*. Charleston, SC: History Press, 2011.

Wills, Chuck. *The Illustrated History of Weaponry: From Flint Axes to Automatic Weapons*. Irvington, NY: Hylas Publishing, 2006.

Wood, William. *New England's Prospect, A true, lively, and experimentall description of that part of America, commonly called New England*. Printed at London by Tho. Cotes for John Bellamie, 1634.

Index

About the Author

Jay Atkinson, called "the bard of New England toughness" by *Men's Health* magazine, is the author of eight books. *Caveman Politics* was a Barnes & Noble Discover Great New Writers Program selection and a finalist for the Discover Great New Writers Award; *Ice Time* was a *Publishers Weekly* Notable Book of the Year and a New England Bookseller's Association bestseller; and *Legends of Winter Hill* spent seven weeks on the *Boston Globe* hardcover best-seller list. He has written for the *New York Times, Boston Globe, Newsday, Portland Oregonian, Men's Health, Boston Sunday Herald,* and *Boston Globe* magazine, among other publications. Atkinson teaches writing at Boston University and has been nominated for the Pushcart Prize three times. He grew up hearing Hannah Duston's story in his hometown of Methuen, Massachusetts, which was part of Haverhill until 1724.

ALSO BY JAY ATKINSON

Legends of Winter Hill
Memoirs of a Rugby-Playing Man
City in Amber
Ice Time
Paradise Road
Caveman Politics
Tauvernier Street: Stories